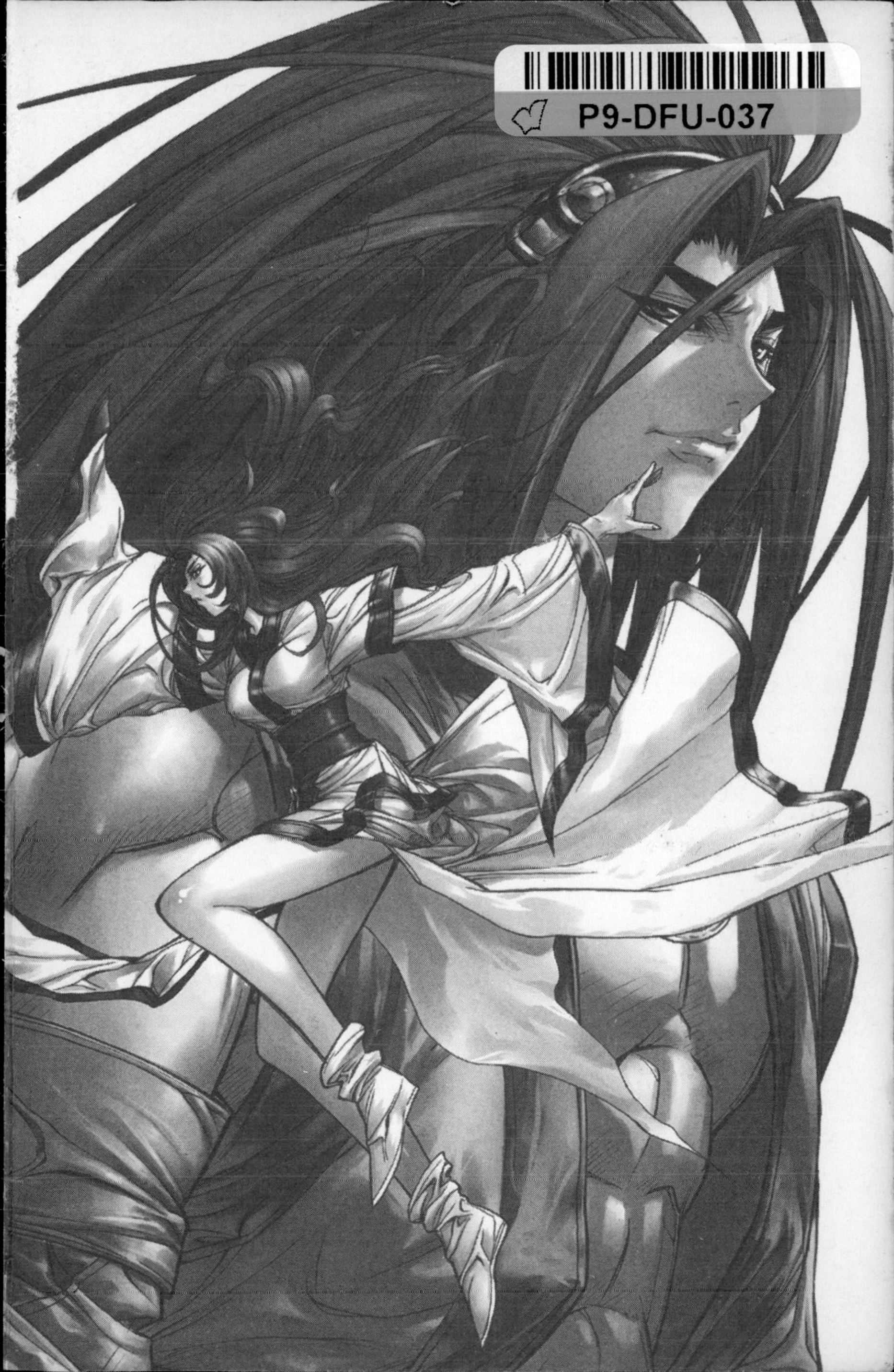

King of Hell Vol. 12
Written by Ra In-Soo
Illustrated by Kim Jae-Hwan

Translation - Lauren Na
English Adaptation - R.A. Jones
Copy Editor - Eric Althoff
Retouch and Lettering - Erika Terriquez
Cover Design - Seth Cable

Editor - Rob Tokar
Digital Imaging Manager - Chris Buford
Production Managers - Jennifer Miller and Mutsumi Miyazaki
Managing Editor - Lindsey Johnston
VP of Production - Ron Klamert
Publisher and E.I.C. - Mike Kiley
President and C.O.O. - John Parker
C.E.O. - Stuart Levy

A **TOKYOPOP** Manga

TOKYOPOP Inc.
5900 Wilshire Blvd. Suite 2000
Los Angeles, CA 90036

E-mail: info@TOKYOPOP.com
Come visit us online at www.TOKYOPOP.com

ISBN: 1-59816-060-5

First TOKYOPOP printing: February 2006
10 9 8 7 6 5 4 3 2 1
Printed in Canada

VOLUME 12

BY
RA IN-SOO
&
KIM JAE-HWAN

HAMBURG // LONDON // LOS ANGELES // TOKYO

KING OF HELL™

Who the Hell...?

MAJEH:

When he was alive, Majeh was an extremely powerful and much-feared warrior. In death, Majeh was recruited to be a collector of souls for the King of Hell. Recently, Majeh was returned to his human form in order to destroy the escaped evil spirits for the King of Hell. There are two catches, however: Majeh's full powers are restrained by a mystical seal and his physical form is that of a teenage boy.

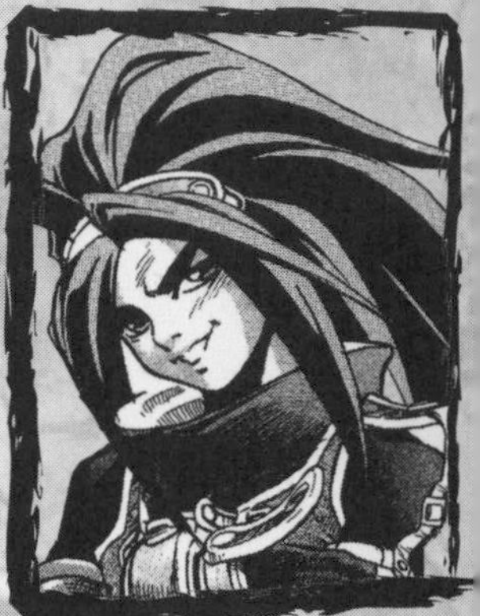

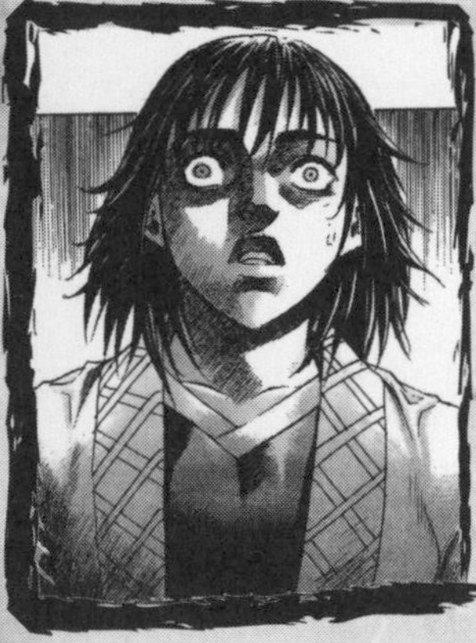

CHUNG POONG NAMGOONG:

A coward from a once-respected family, Chung Poong left home hoping to prove himself at the Martial Arts Tournament in Nakyang. Broke and desperate, Chung Poong tried to rob Majeh. In a very rare moment of pity, Majeh allowed Chung Poong to live...and to tag along with him to the tournament. Chung Poong was recently forced to fight--and kill--his older brother, who had been kidnapped and turned into a zombie.

DOHWA BAIK:

A vivacious vixen whose weapons of choice are poisoned needles. After repeatedly humiliating the hapless trio known as the Insane Hounds, she joined Majeh and Chung Poong on the way to the tournament.

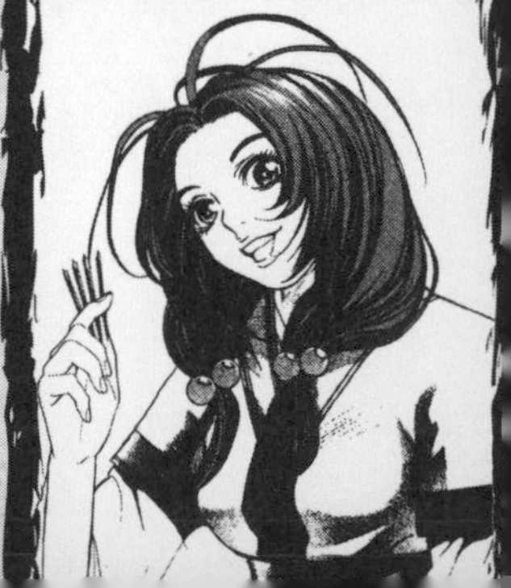

SAMHUK:

Originally sent by the King of Hell to spy on the unpredictable Majeh, Samhuk was quickly discovered and now--much to his dismay--acts as the warrior's ghostly manservant.

DOHAK:

A 15-year-old monk and a master at fighting with a rod, he was affiliated with the Sorim Temple in the Soong Mountains. After being kidnapped, Dohak was transformed into a fighting zombie of the Soo Ra Hyur Chun sect, making him a blood-craving killing machine who retained the fighting abilities he'd developed when he was alive. When Dohak was ordered to attack Majeh, Majeh had no choice but to slay the young monk. True to form, Dohak thanked Majeh with his dying breath. Somehow, though, he's back for more...

CRAZY DOG:

A 6-year-old, club-wielding hellion from a remote village, Crazy Dog lived up to his name right up to the moment of his death at the hands of a demon-possessed martial arts master. When the Dohak zombie was sent into battle, Mr. Secretary sent a mysteriously resurrected Crazy Dog to counter him.

MO YOUNG BAIK:

Self-described master of all the martial arts and host of the Nakyang Martial Arts Tournament. Though Mo Young has only a small understanding of Majeh's abilities, he has still placed his trust in Hell's cockiest envoy.

MR SECRETARY:

MoYoung's subordinate, he helped push Mo Young and the White Sects into war with the Black Sects.

What the Hell...?

Hell's worst inmates have escaped and fled to Earth. Seeking recently-deceased bodies to host their bitter souls, these malevolent master fighters are part of an evil scheme that could have dire consequences for both This World and the Next World. It is believed that the escaped fiends are hunting for bodies of martial arts experts, as only bodies trained in martial arts would be capable of properly employing their incredible skills.

To make matters even more difficult, the otherworldly energy emitted by the fugitives will dissipate within one month's time...after which, they will be indistinguishable from normal humans and undetectable to those from the Next World. The King of Hell has assigned Majeh to hunt down Hell's Most Wanted and return them to the Next World...but Majeh doesn't always do exactly what he's told.

Majeh was a master swordsman in life and, in death, he serves as an envoy for the King of Hell, escorting souls of the dead to the Next World. Majeh caught Samhuk--a servant for the King of Hell--spying on him and, after making the appropriate threats, now uses Samhuk as his own servant as well.

The King of Hell has reunited Majeh's spirit with his physical body, which was perfectly preserved for 300 years. Due to the influence of a Superhuman Strength Sealing Symbol (designed to keep the rebellious and powerful Majeh in check), Majeh's physical form has reverted to a teenaged state. Even with the seal in place, however, Majeh is still an extremely formidable warrior.

Along with the young, wannabe-warrior called Chung Poong Namgoong and a beautiful femme fatale named Dohwa Baik, Majeh made his way to the much-heralded Martial Arts Tournament at Nakyang--the most likely place for the warrior demons to make their appearance.

Though Majeh quickly seemed to forget his mission to capture Hell's Most Wanted, the escaped evil souls certainly had not forgotten him! While Majeh faced off against Crazy Dog, the tournament was suddenly interrupted. An elderly, one-armed martial arts master--whose body was inhabited by one of the fugitive demons--forced his way into the arena and effortlessly killed the contestant known as Crazy Dog, among others. Despite his best efforts, Majeh also seemed on the verge of total defeat...though, as his life-force dissipated, the Superhuman Strength Sealing spell that limits his abilities was broken!

Freed from restraint, Majeh rose and easily obliterated his opponent.

Though Majeh recovered very quickly from his battle injuries, he was still surprised to learn that, while he was out, his fellow contestants--including Chung Poong's older brother--were kidnapped.

Majeh searched for the missing martial artists and discovered a diabolical plot to transform the kidnapped fighters into zombies and start a war between the Black and White Sects. The architects of this evil plan appear to be the Sa Gok, a vicious, powerful group that almost brought down the entire martial arts world fifty years ago. Unfortunately, most of the sects believe the Sa Gok were utterly eradicated...which means they can only blame each other for their missing children.

After braving a mountain filled with mysteries and uncovering the masters behind the near-unstoppable zombies, Majeh and his companions discovered that the White and Black Sects were lining up for battle on a nearby plain. Without a moment's hesitation, Majeh decided to fight them all--one at a time. As quickly as fighters from each Sect would step up to face him, Hell's cockiest envoy would smack them down. The sheer spectacle was enough to turn a field full of warriors into slack-jawed spectators (and broken-jawed competitors.)

Realizing that the battle had been averted, Lord Gok sent his zombie warriors to destroy everyone on both sides. In the ensuing melee, Chung Poong was forced to fight and kill his older brother. Witnessing Chung Poong's pain, Majeh vowed to put a stop to the Sa Gok himself. Since the zombies are nearly unstoppable, Majeh reasoned that his best chance of success would be to find the one controlling them.

Majeh quickly located Dong Sa, who sent a resurrected Dohak zombie to join the battle against the White and Black Sects. In response to the Dohak attack, Mr. Secretary unleashed a resurrected Crazy Dog and sicced him on the young, dead monk. Though Dohak and Crazy Dog seemed evenly matched when they were alive, it's anyone's guess which reanimated corpse is more powerful!

While Majeh battled Dong Sa's guardian zombies, Majeh managed to convince the Insane Hounds to attack Dong Sa. Though the Hounds are bumbling fools, they were recently endowed with near invulnerability when they unknowingly bathed in a mystical pool. At this point, neither they nor Majeh nor Dong Sa really know their abilities or their limits... but they're all about to find out.

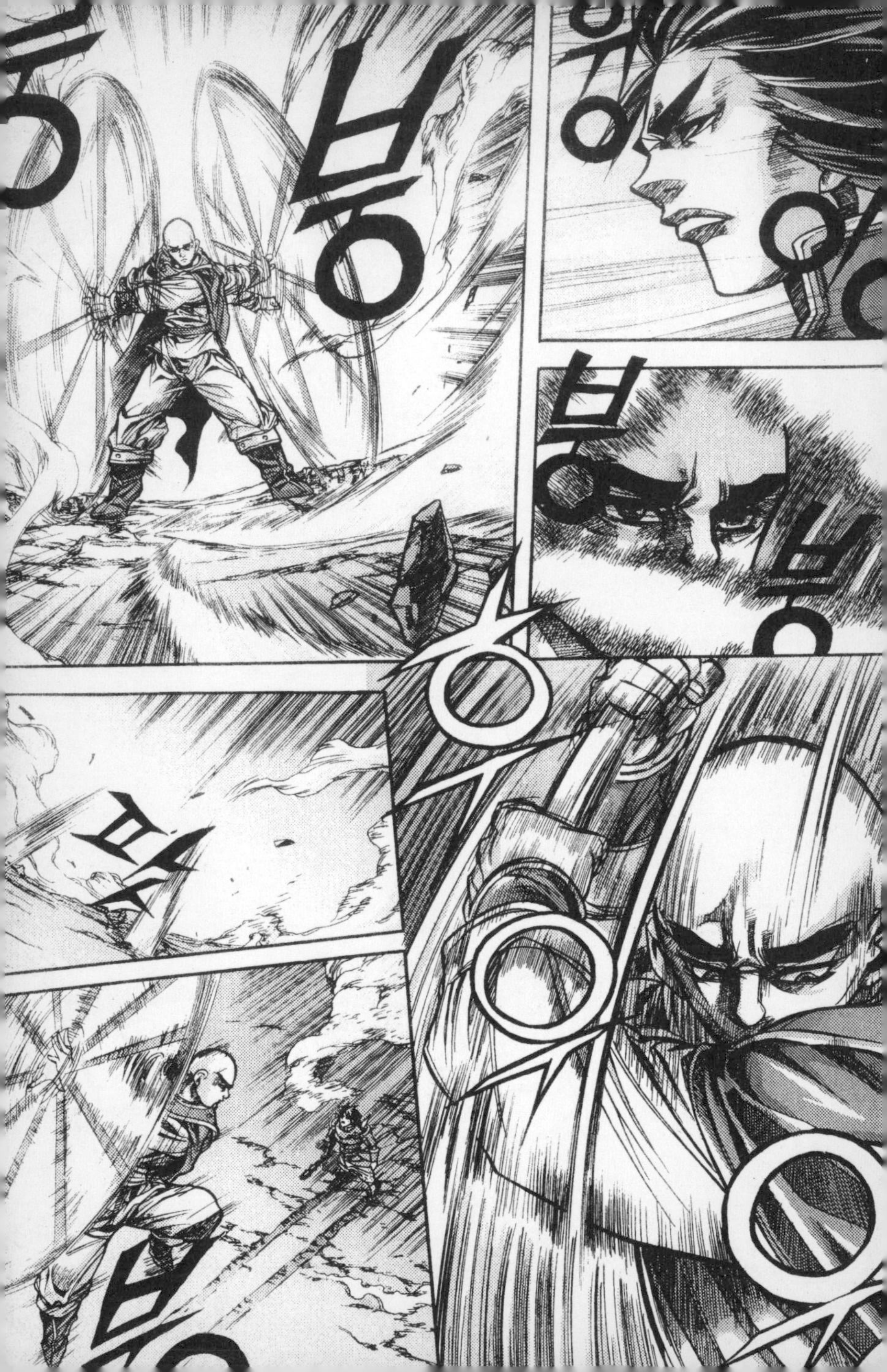

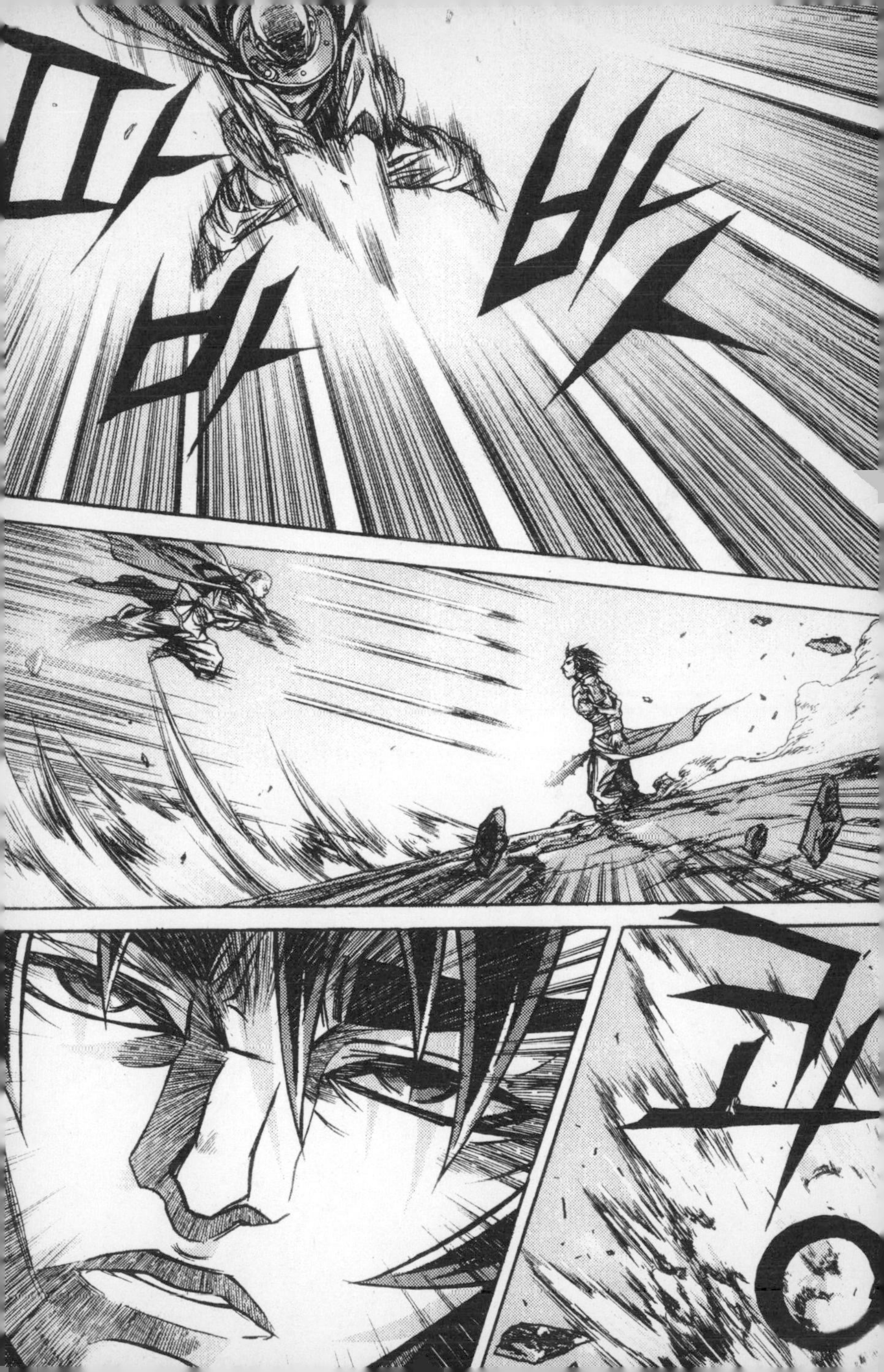
파바바
쾅

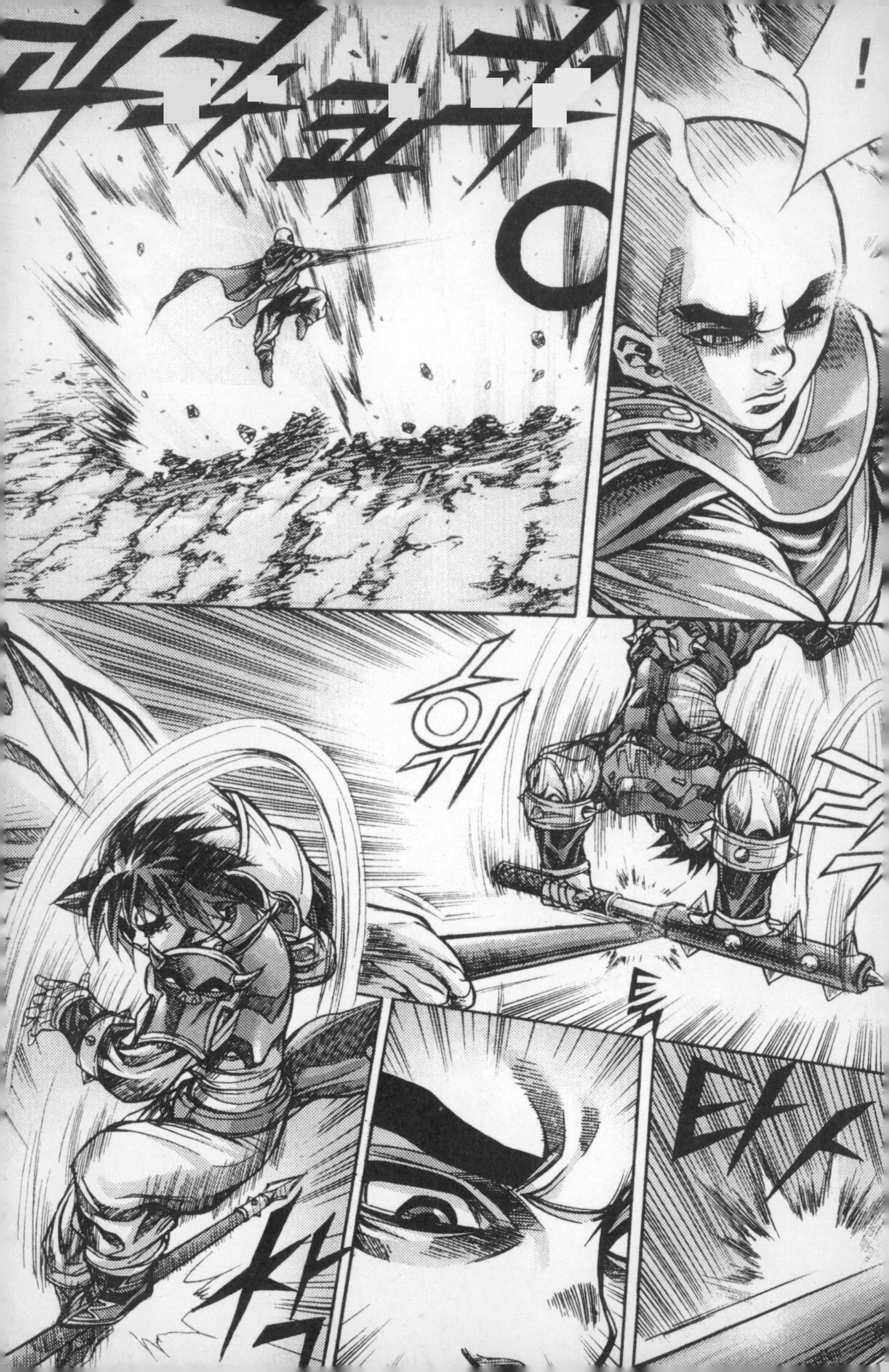
!

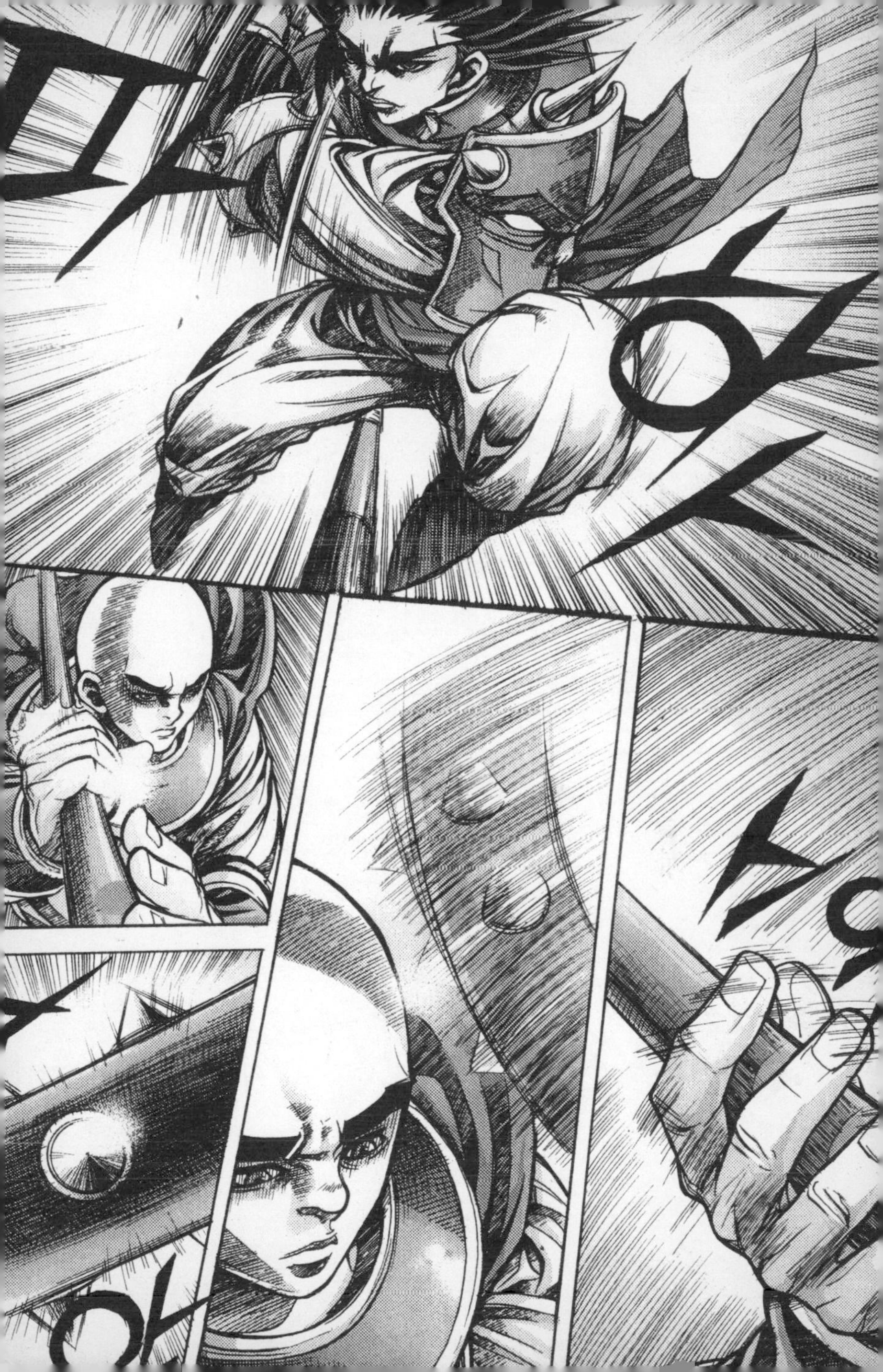

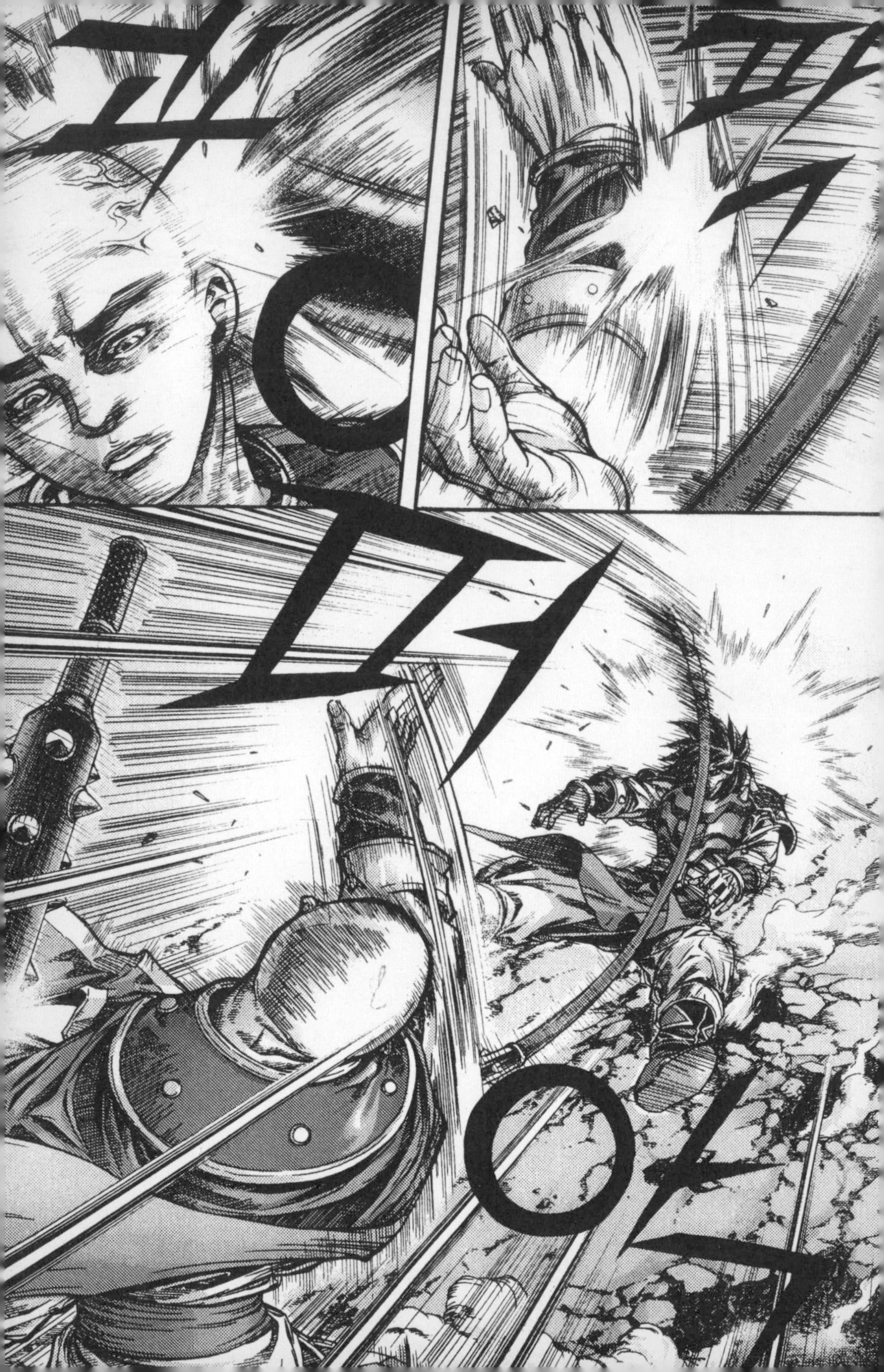

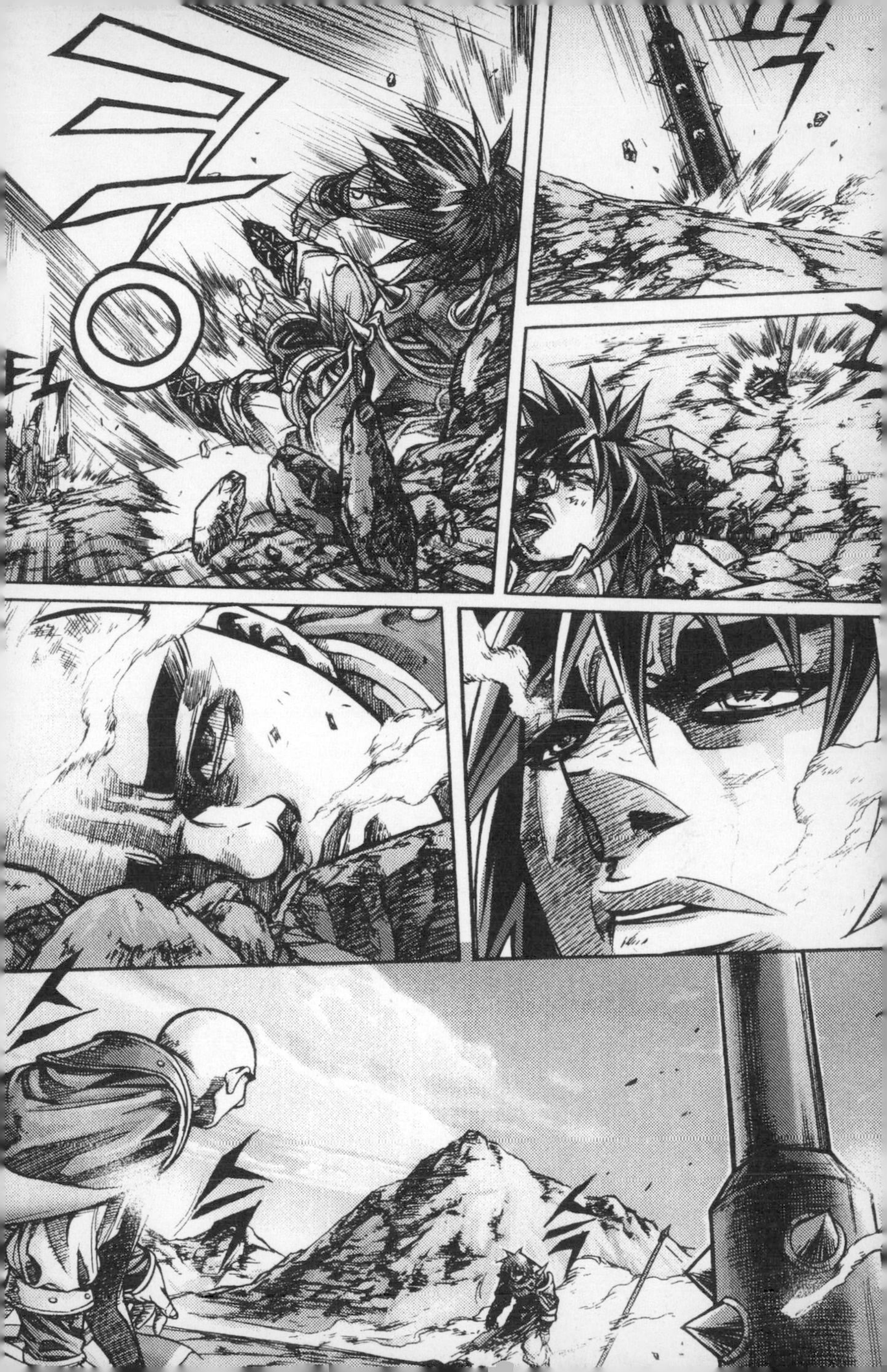

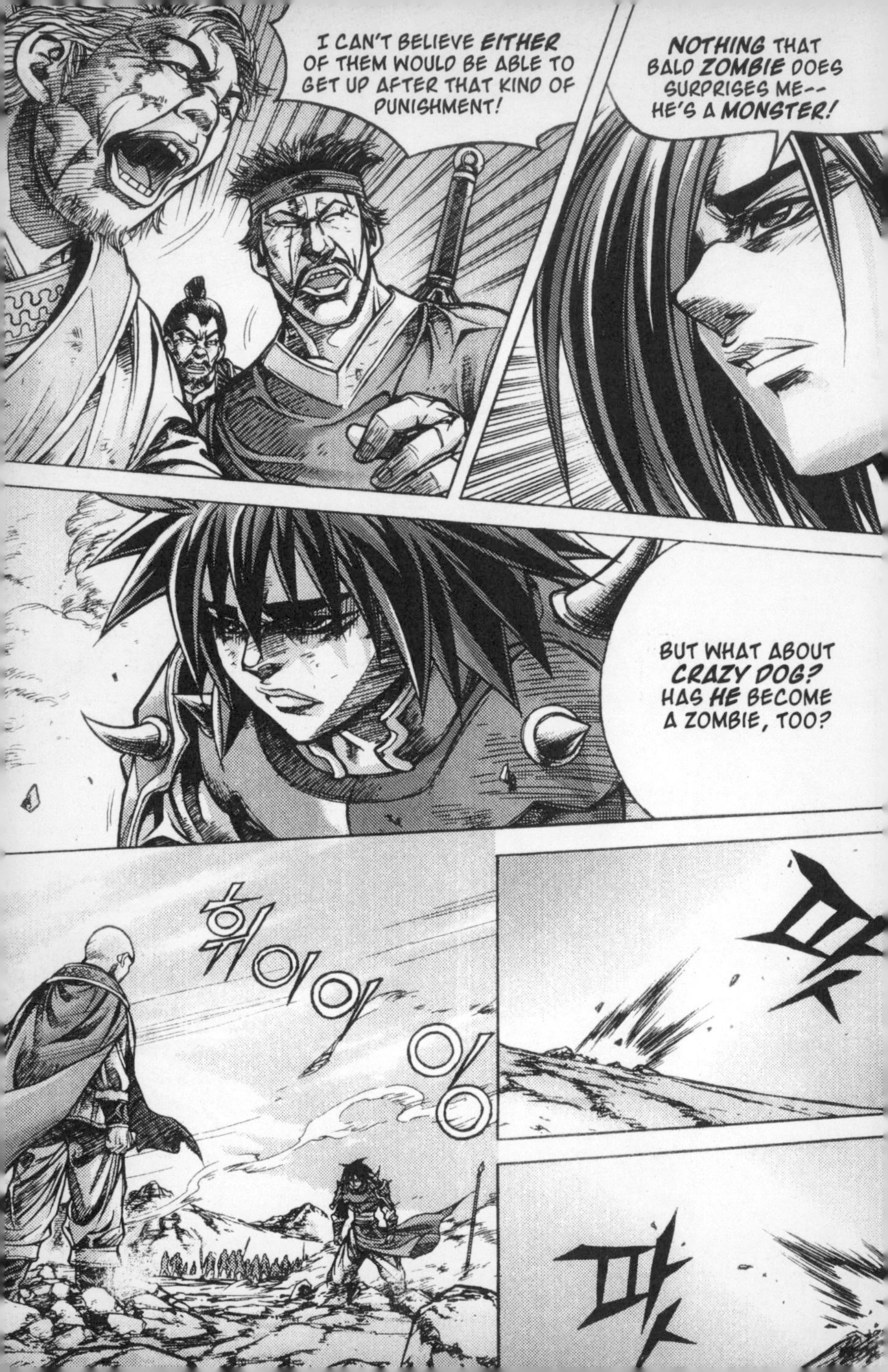
I CAN'T BELIEVE EITHER OF THEM WOULD BE ABLE TO GET UP AFTER THAT KIND OF PUNISHMENT!
NOTHING THAT BALD ZOMBIE DOES SURPRISES ME-- HE'S A MONSTER!
BUT WHAT ABOUT CRAZY DOG? HAS HE BECOME A ZOMBIE, TOO?
팟
팟

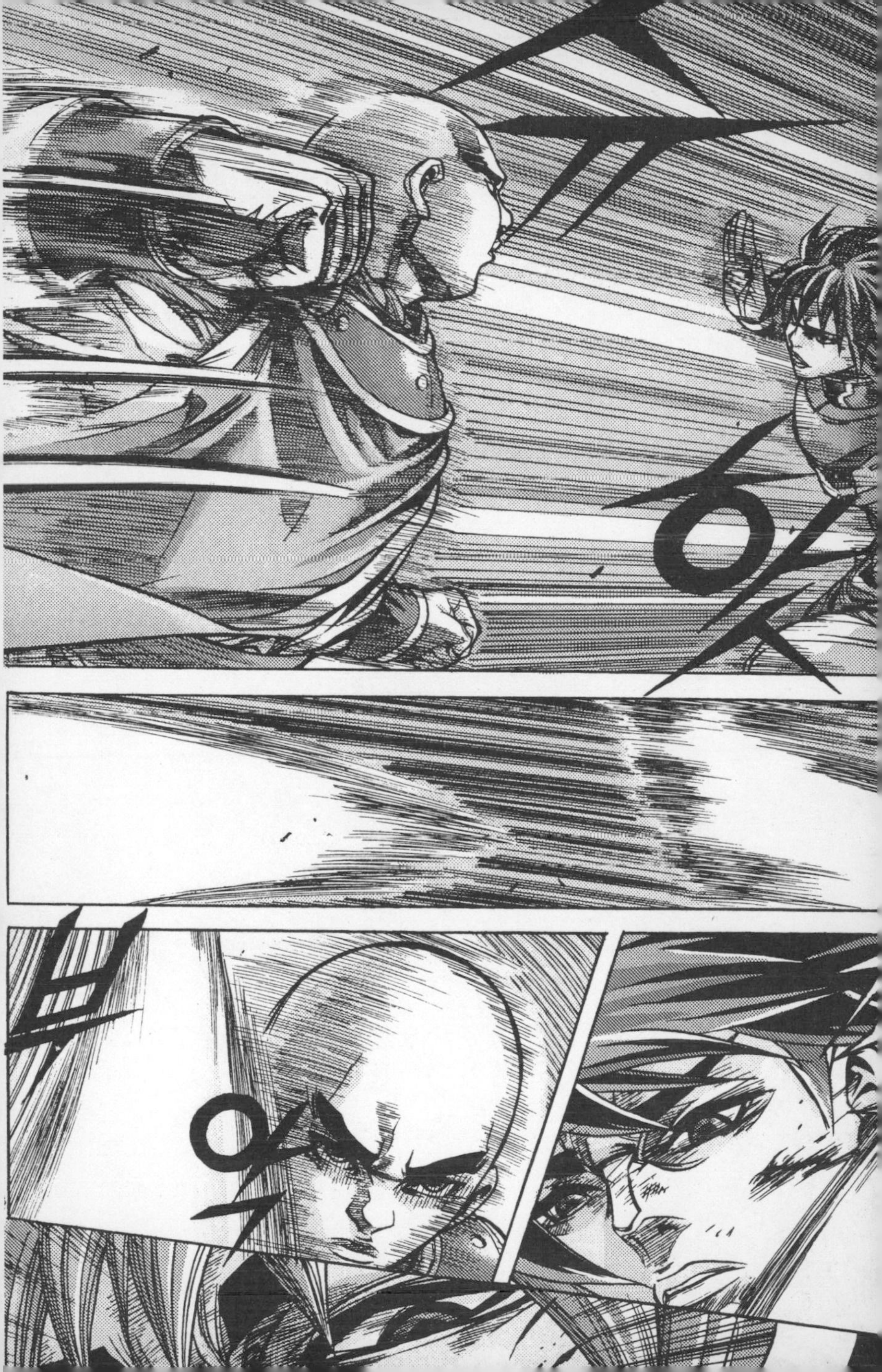

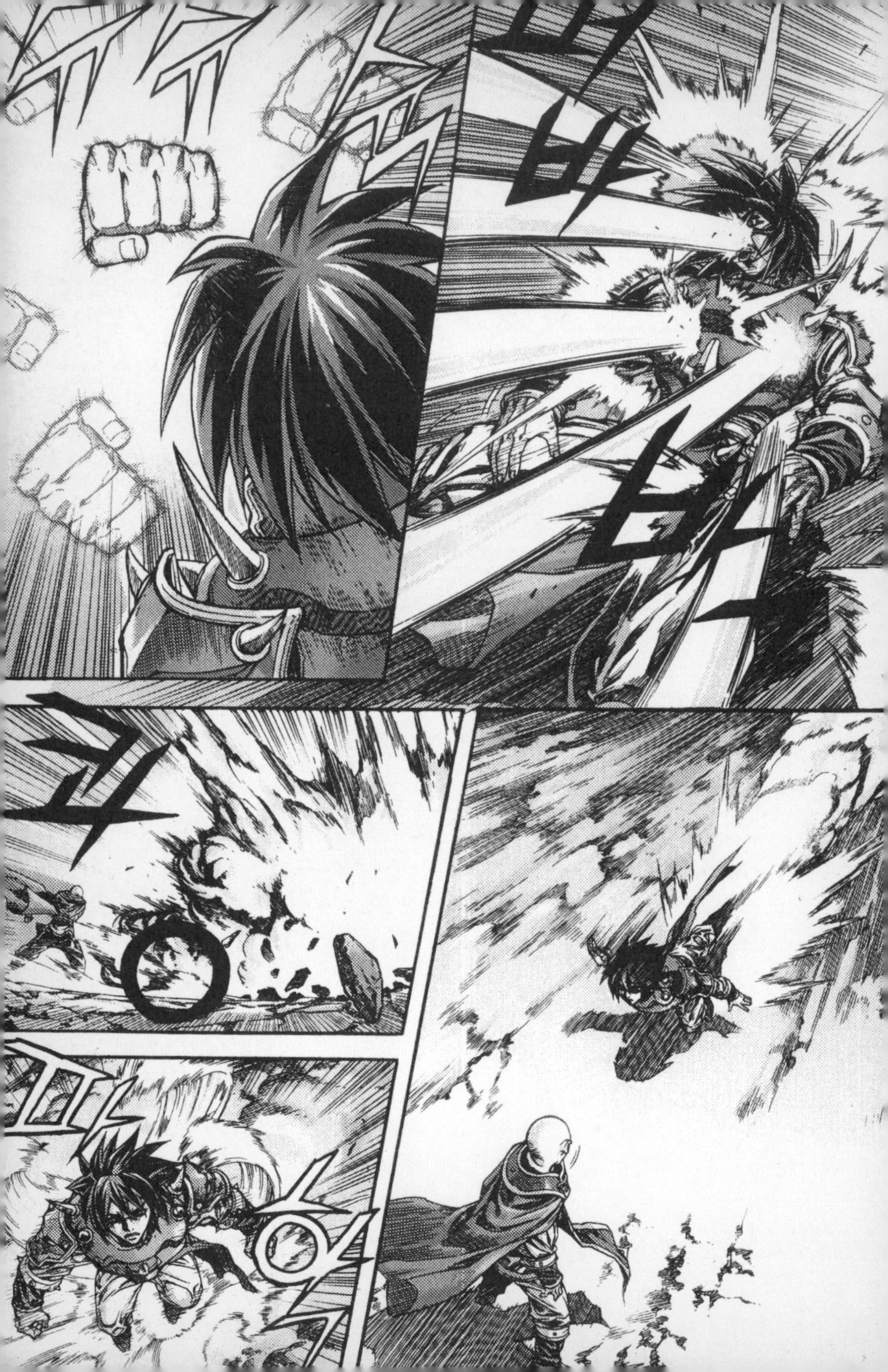

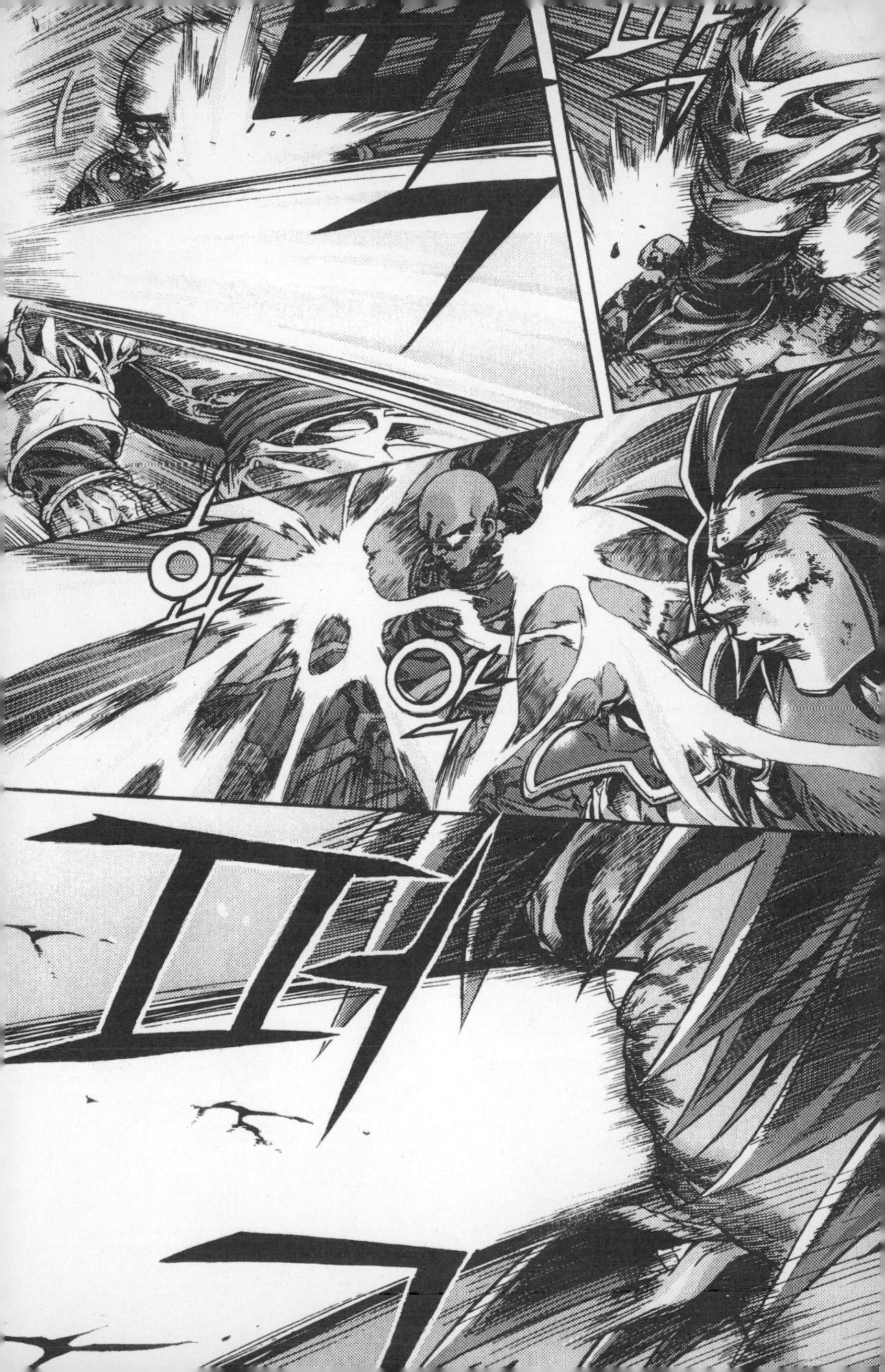

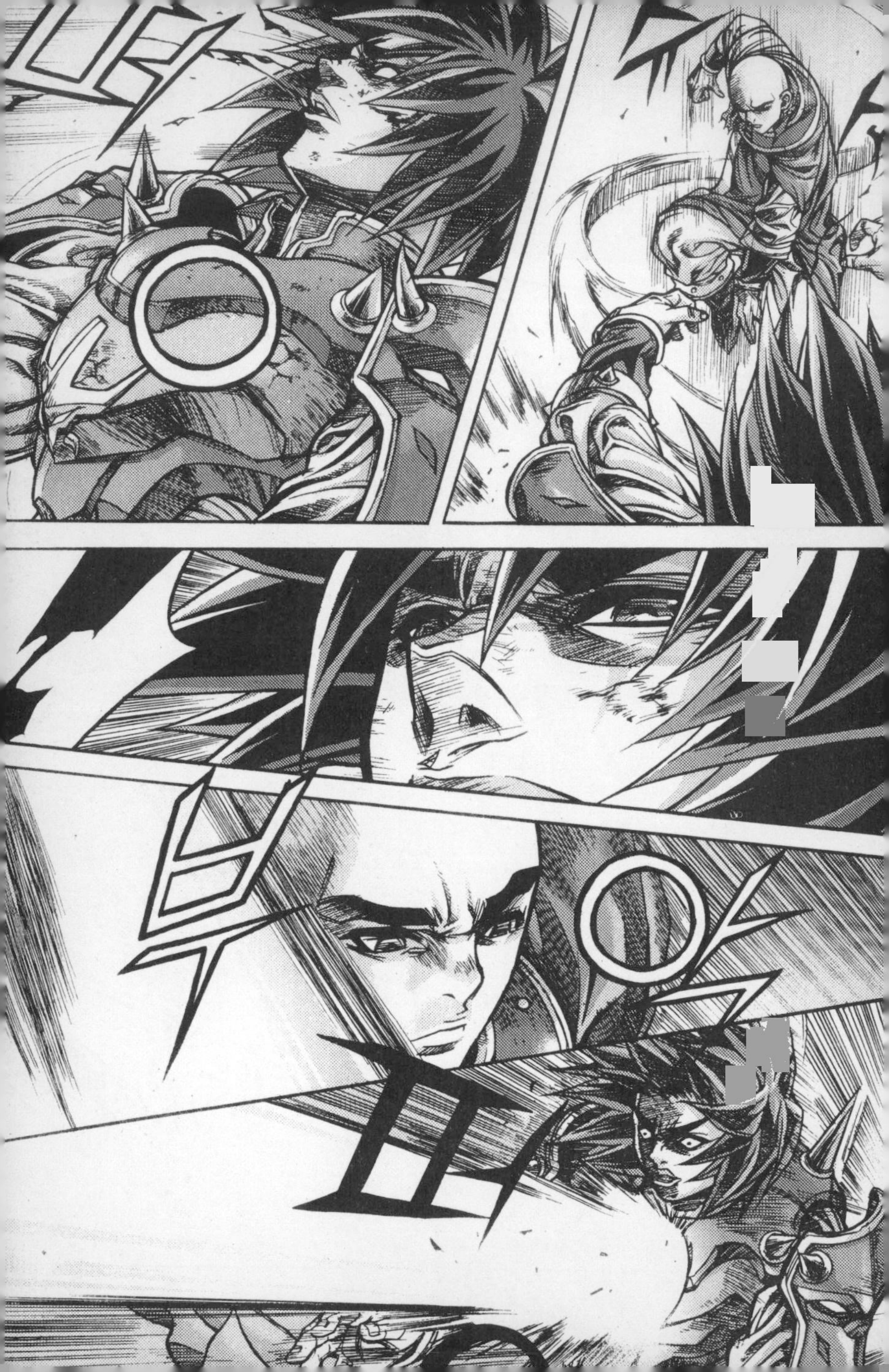

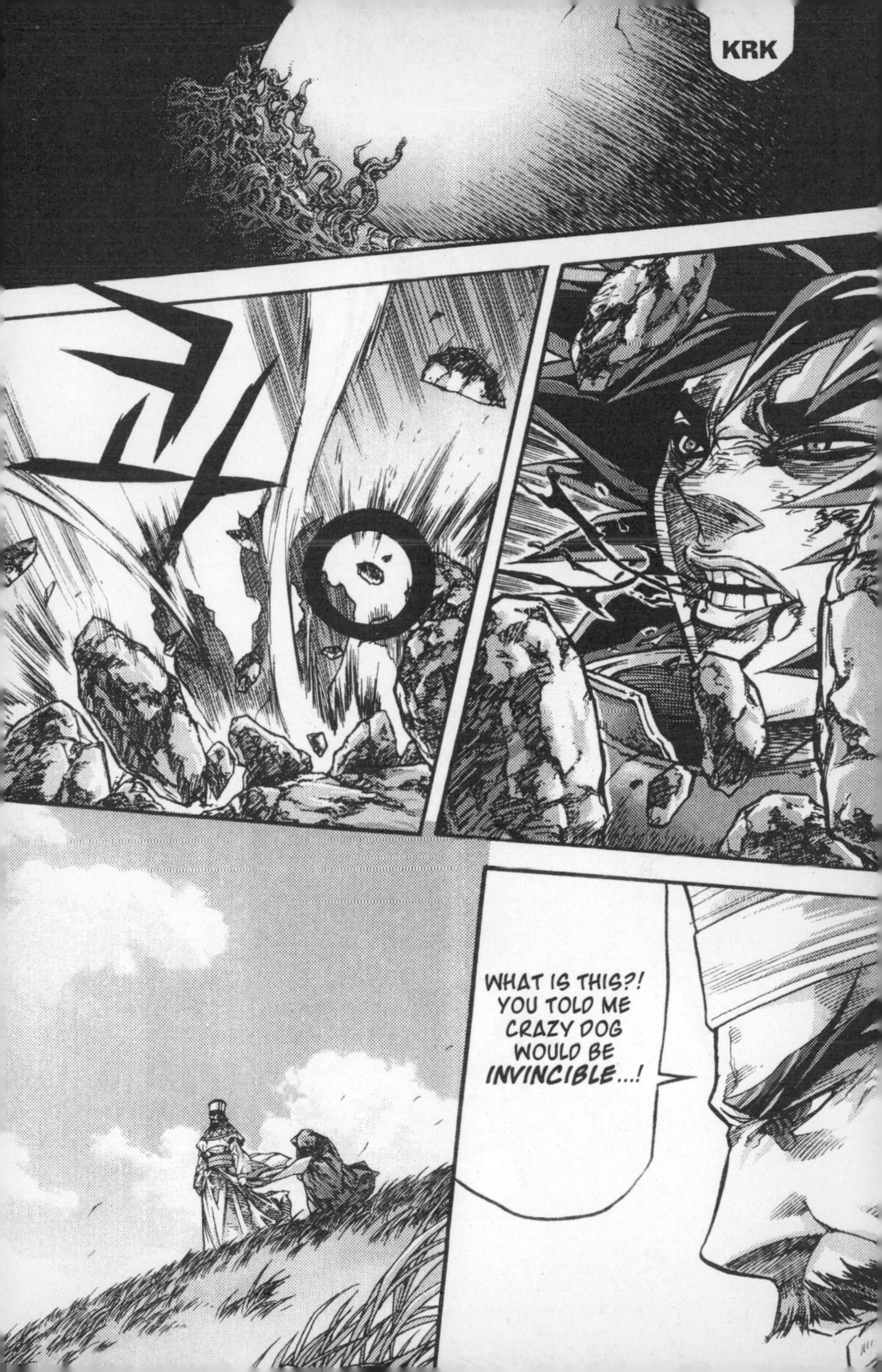
KRK
WHAT IS THIS?! YOU TOLD ME CRAZY DOG WOULD BE INVINCIBLE...!

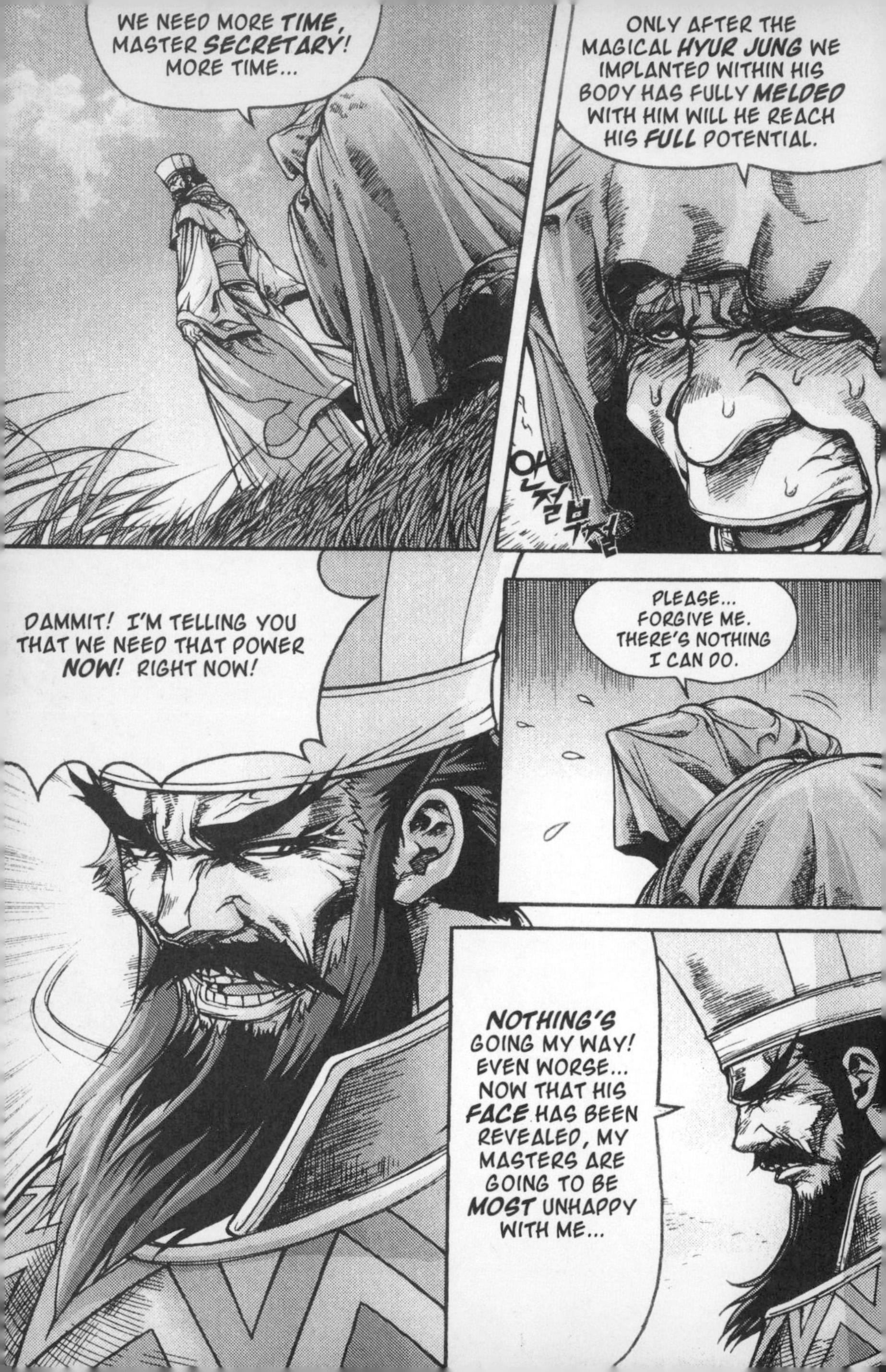
WE NEED MORE TIME, MASTER SECRETARY! MORE TIME...
ONLY AFTER THE MAGICAL HYUR JUNG WE IMPLANTED WITHIN HIS BODY HAS FULLY MELDED WITH HIM WILL HE REACH HIS FULL POTENTIAL.
안절부절
DAMMIT! I'M TELLING YOU THAT WE NEED THAT POWER NOW! RIGHT NOW!
PLEASE... FORGIVE ME. THERE'S NOTHING I CAN DO.
NOTHING'S GOING MY WAY! EVEN WORSE... NOW THAT HIS FACE HAS BEEN REVEALED, MY MASTERS ARE GOING TO BE MOST UNHAPPY WITH ME...

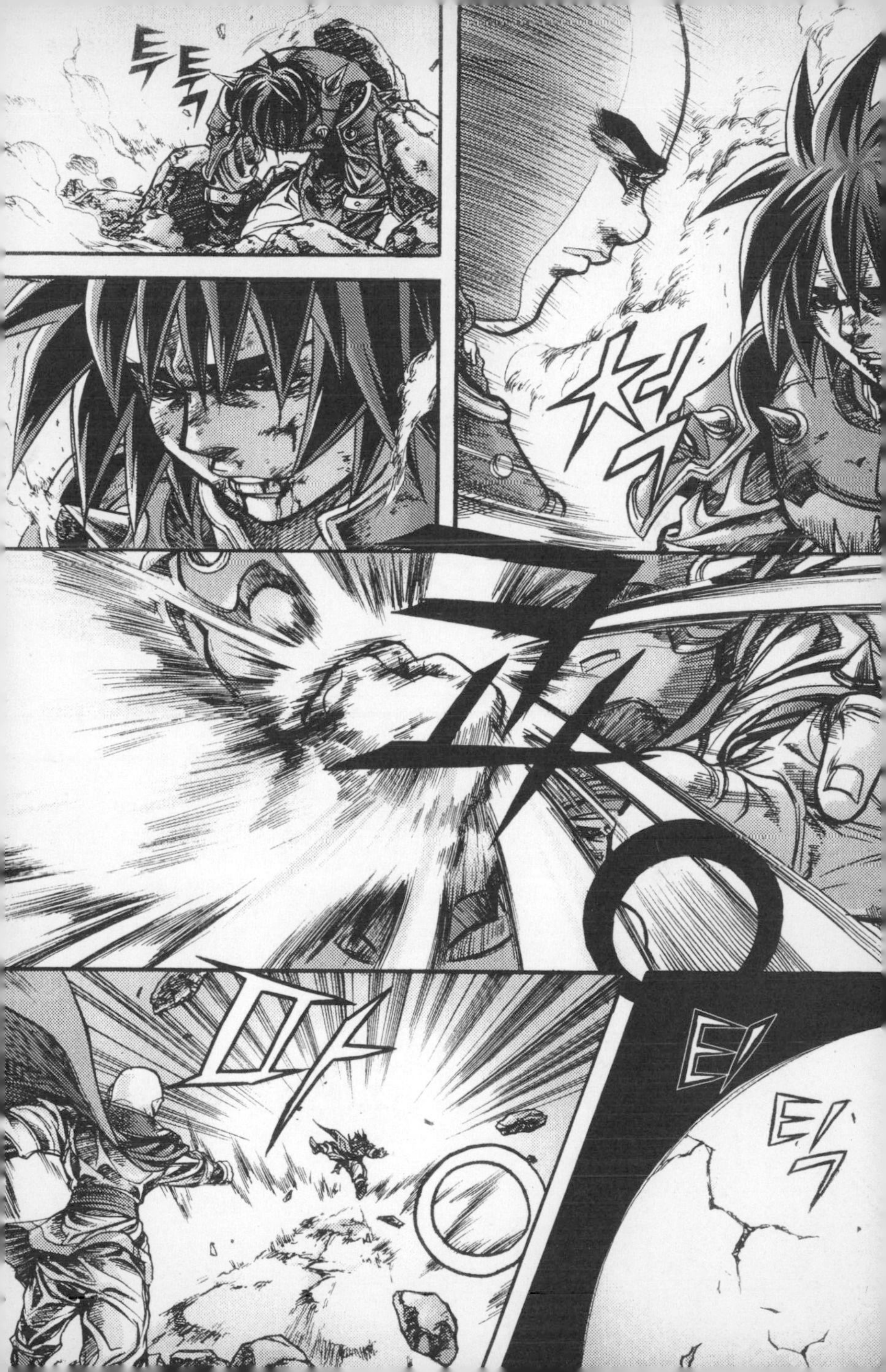
투툭
척
콰
파
티
티틱

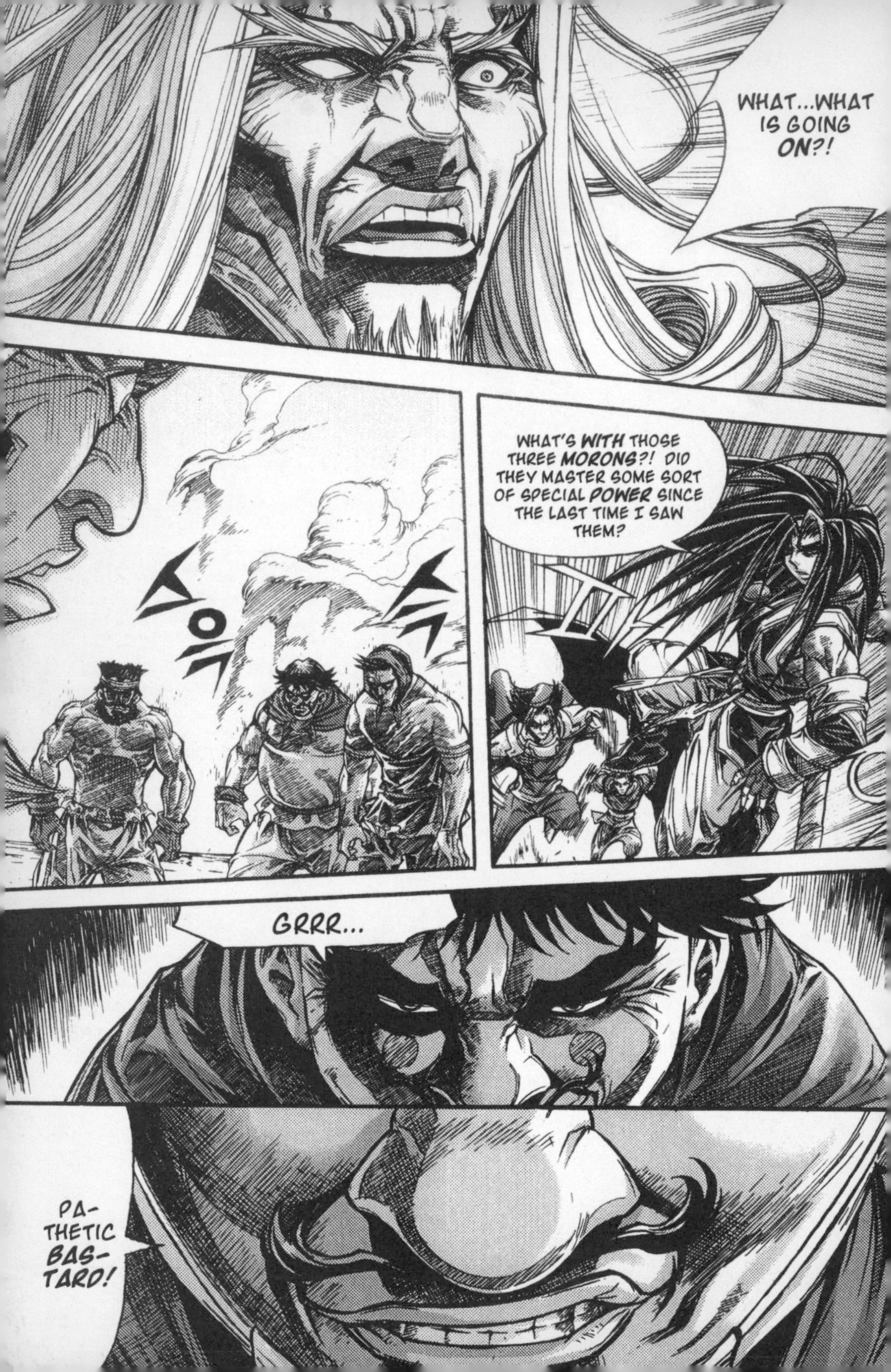
WHAT...WHAT IS GOING ON?!
WHAT'S WITH THOSE THREE MORONS?! DID THEY MASTER SOME SORT OF SPECIAL POWER SINCE THE LAST TIME I SAW THEM?
GRRR...
PA-THETIC BAS-TARD!

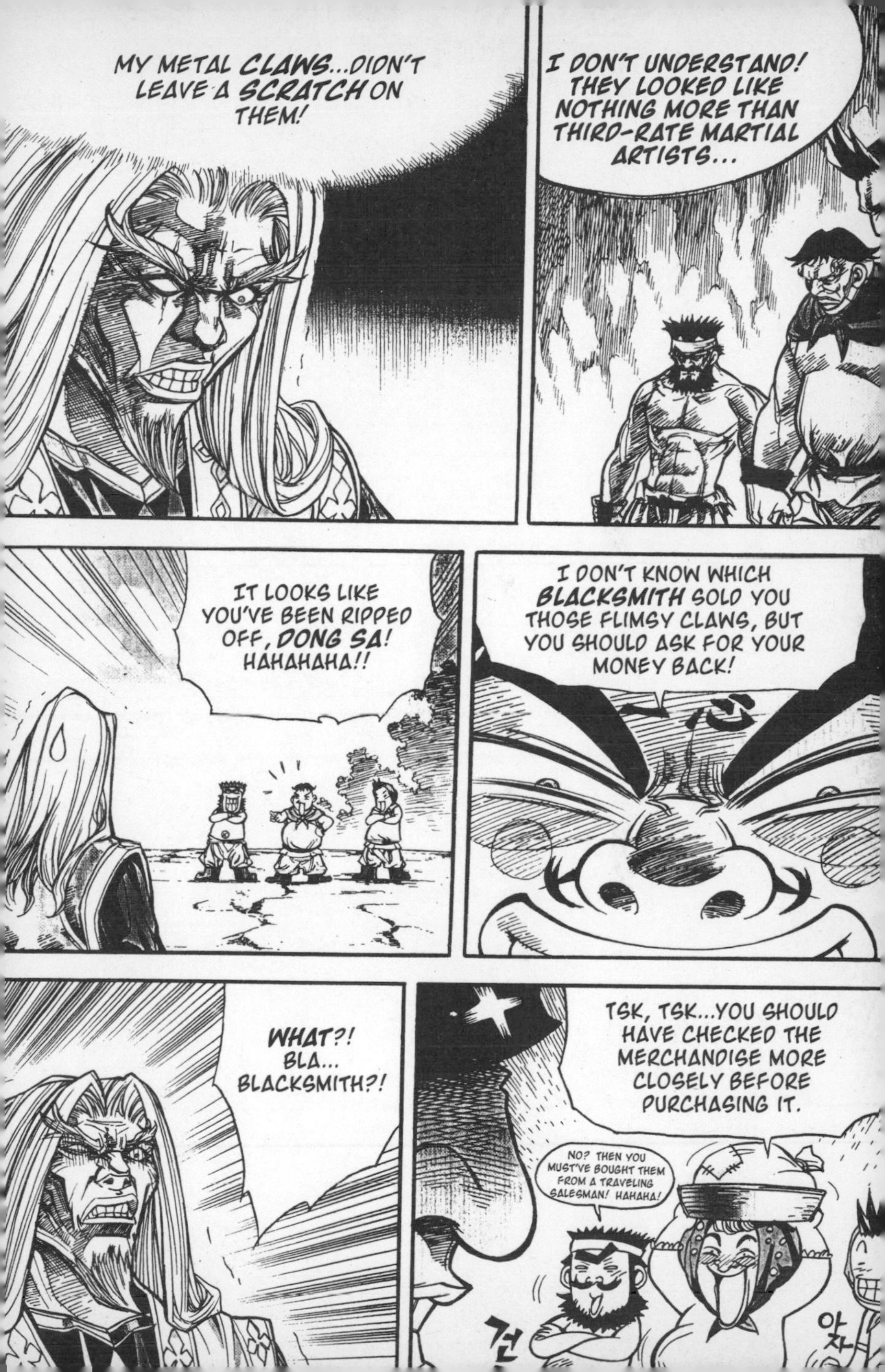
MY METAL CLAWS...DIDN'T LEAVE A SCRATCH ON THEM!
I DON'T UNDERSTAND! THEY LOOKED LIKE NOTHING MORE THAN THIRD-RATE MARTIAL ARTISTS...
IT LOOKS LIKE YOU'VE BEEN RIPPED OFF, DONG SA! HAHAHAHA!!
I DON'T KNOW WHICH BLACKSMITH SOLD YOU THOSE FLIMSY CLAWS, BUT YOU SHOULD ASK FOR YOUR MONEY BACK!
WHAT?! BLA... BLACKSMITH?!
TSK, TSK...YOU SHOULD HAVE CHECKED THE MERCHANDISE MORE CLOSELY BEFORE PURCHASING IT.
NO? THEN YOU MUST'VE BOUGHT THEM FROM A TRAVELING SALESMAN! HAHAHA!
건
아자

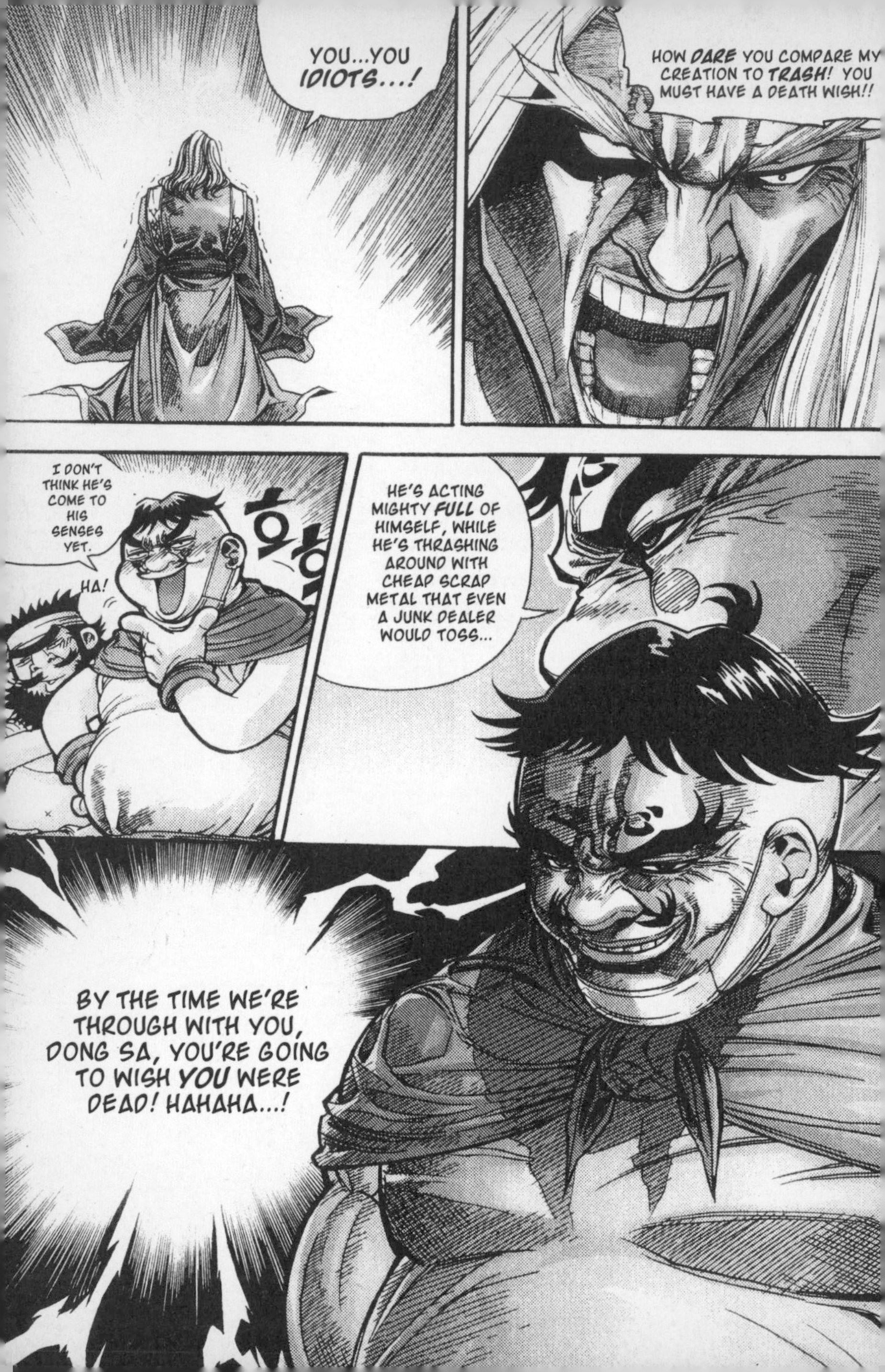
YOU...YOU IDIOTS...!
HOW DARE YOU COMPARE MY CREATION TO TRASH! YOU MUST HAVE A DEATH WISH!!
I DON'T THINK HE'S COME TO HIS SENSES YET.
HA!
호호
HE'S ACTING MIGHTY FULL OF HIMSELF, WHILE HE'S THRASHING AROUND WITH CHEAP SCRAP METAL THAT EVEN A JUNK DEALER WOULD TOSS...
BY THE TIME WE'RE THROUGH WITH YOU, DONG SA, YOU'RE GOING TO WISH YOU WERE DEAD! HAHAHA...!

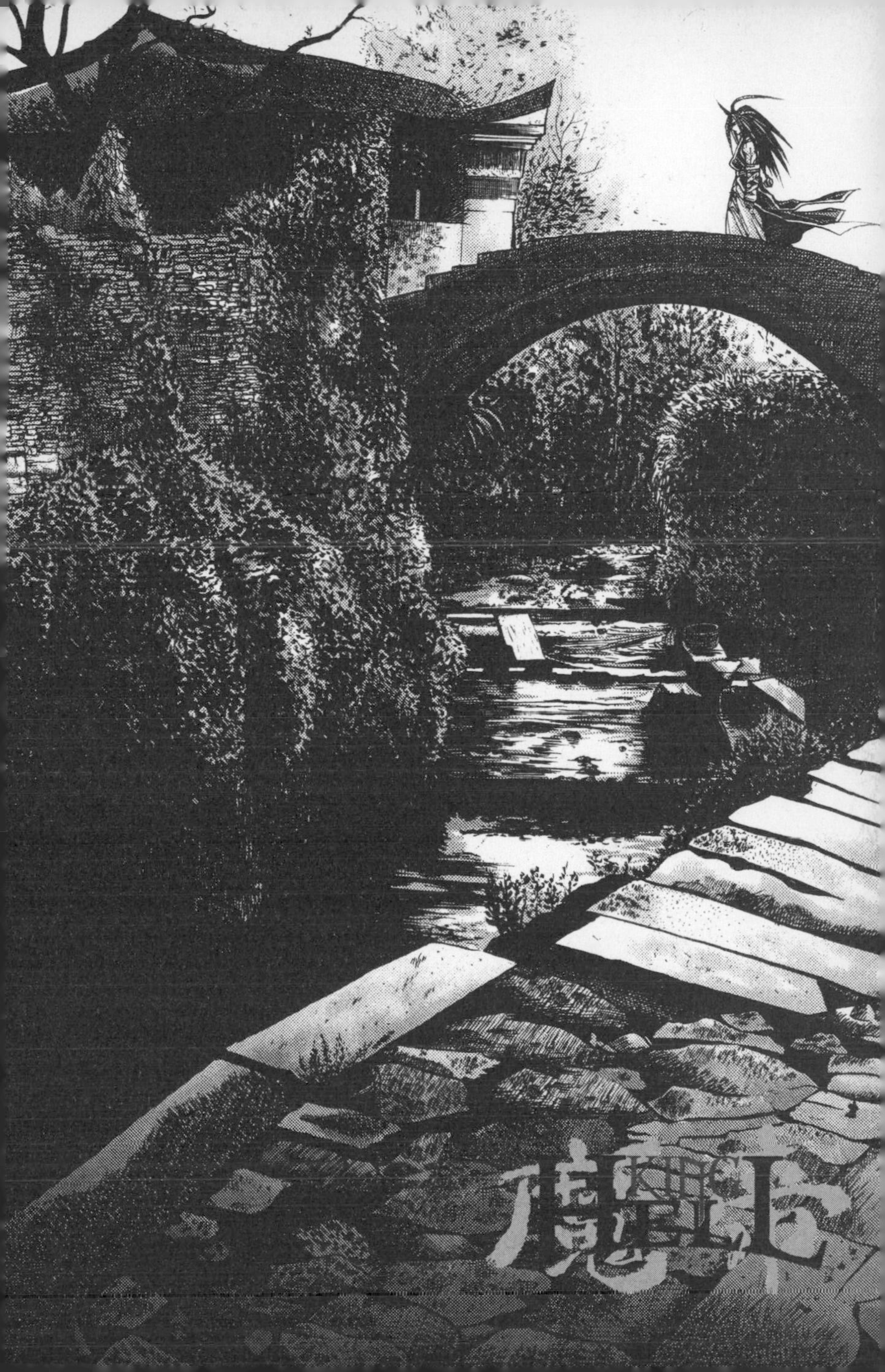
魔

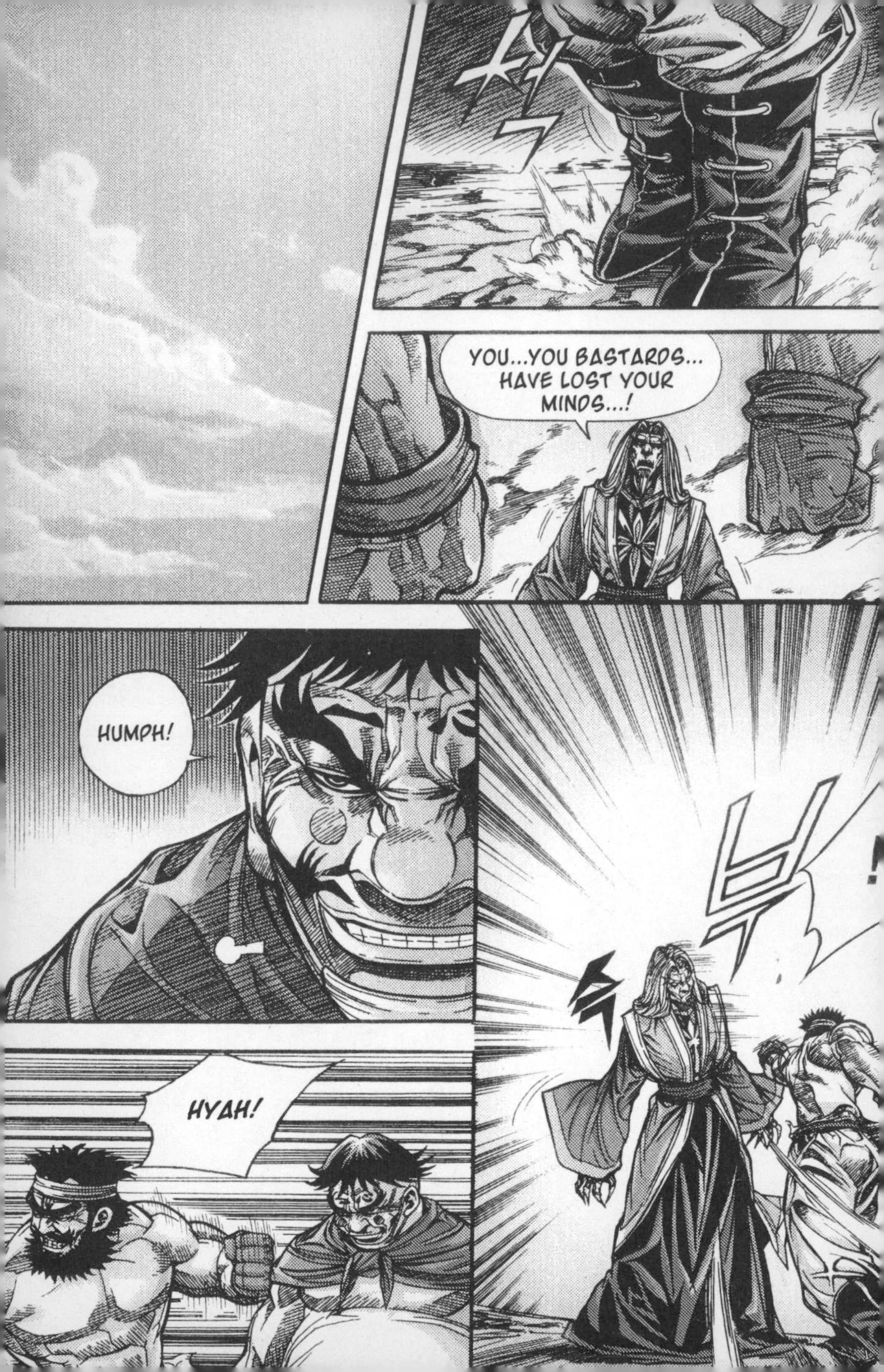
YOU...YOU BASTARDS... HAVE LOST YOUR MINDS...!
HUMPH!
HYAH!

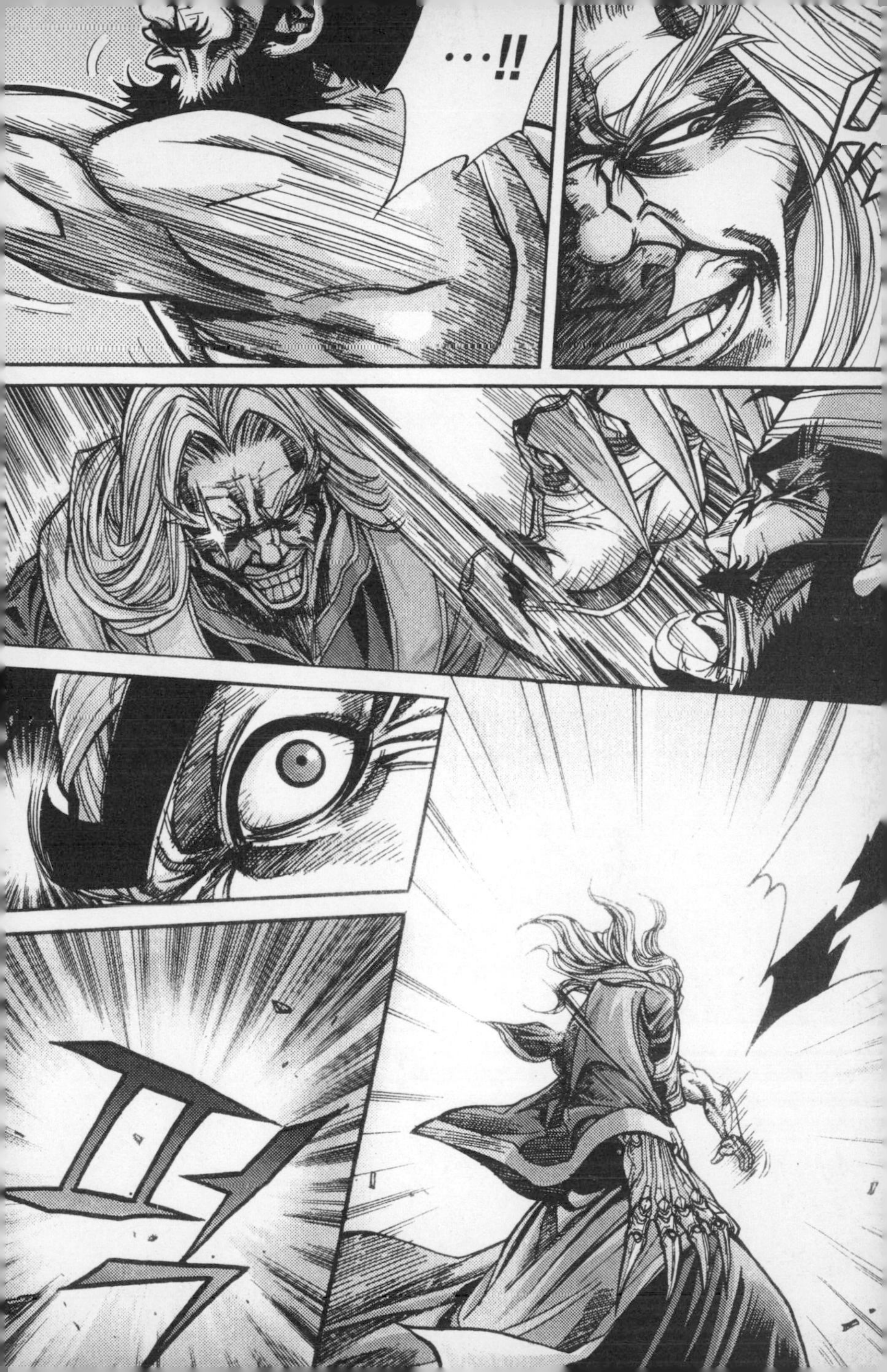
...!!

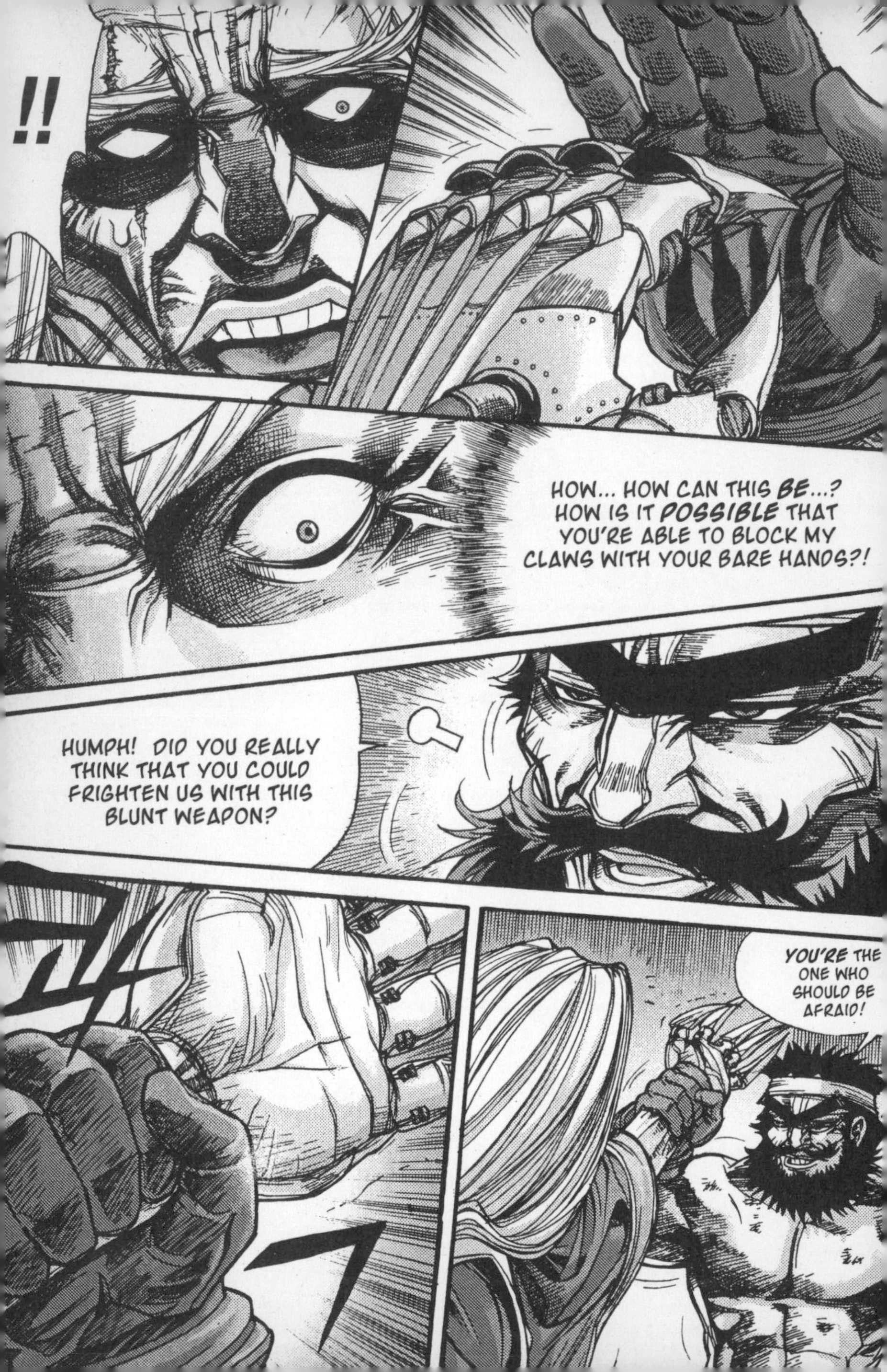
!!
HOW... HOW CAN THIS BE...? HOW IS IT POSSIBLE THAT YOU'RE ABLE TO BLOCK MY CLAWS WITH YOUR BARE HANDS?!
HUMPH! DID YOU REALLY THINK THAT YOU COULD FRIGHTEN US WITH THIS BLUNT WEAPON?
YOU'RE THE ONE WHO SHOULD BE AFRAID!

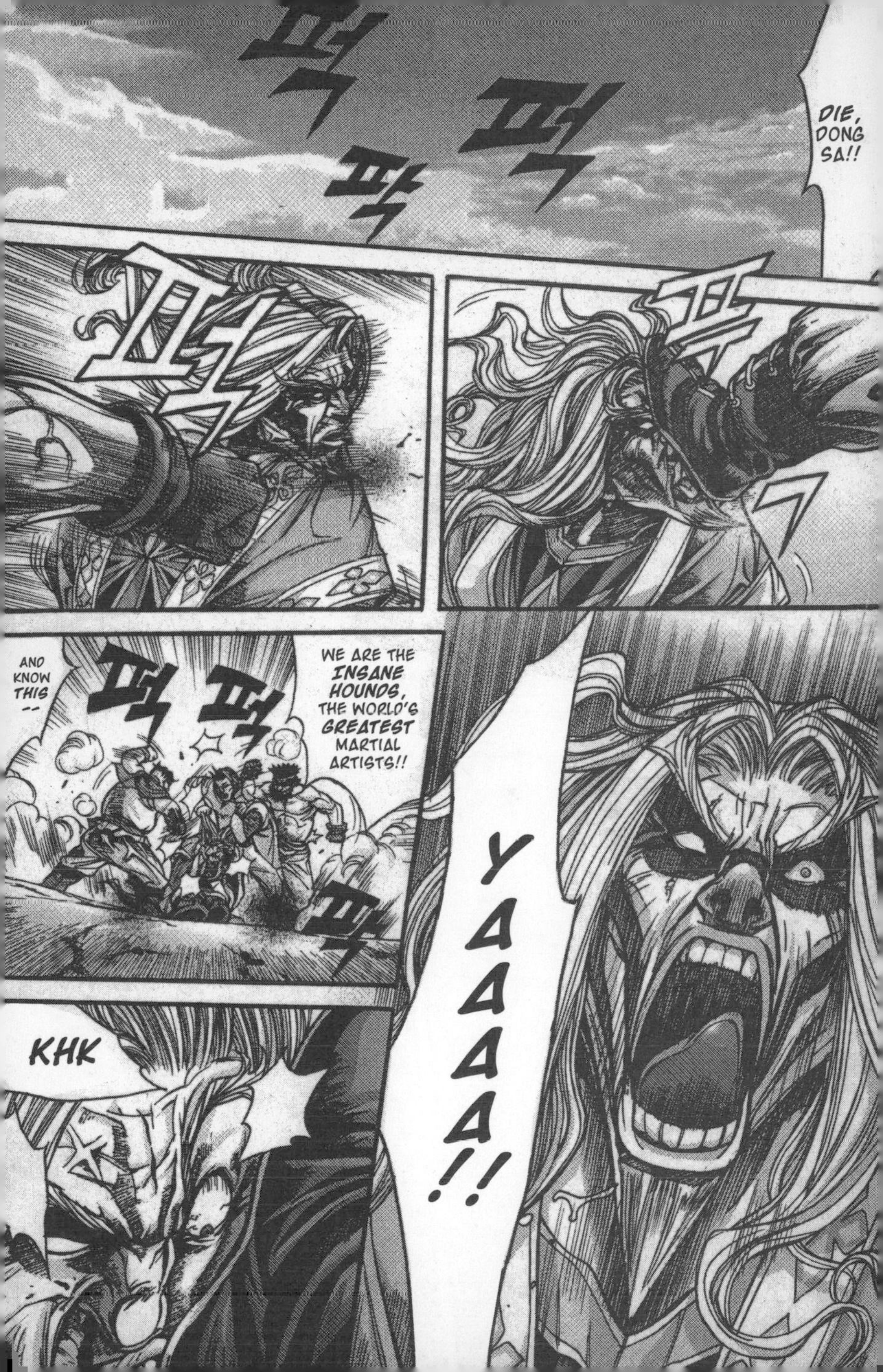

퍽
퍽
퍽
DIE, DONG SA!!
퍽
퍽
AND KNOW THIS --
퍽 퍽
WE ARE THE INSANE HOUNDS, THE WORLD'S GREATEST MARTIAL ARTISTS!!
퍽
KHK
YAAAAA!!

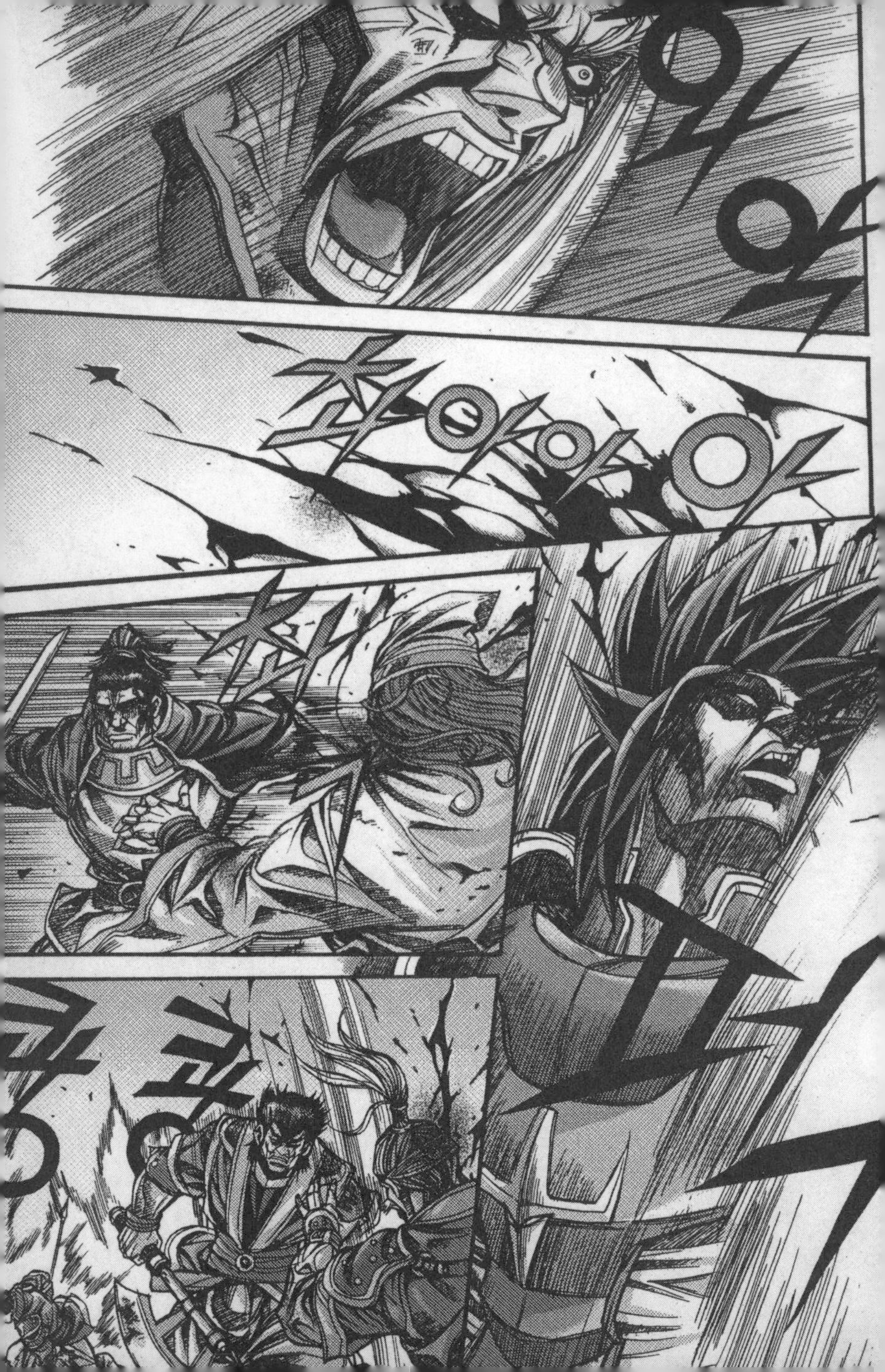
아악
좌아아아
쿵 쿵

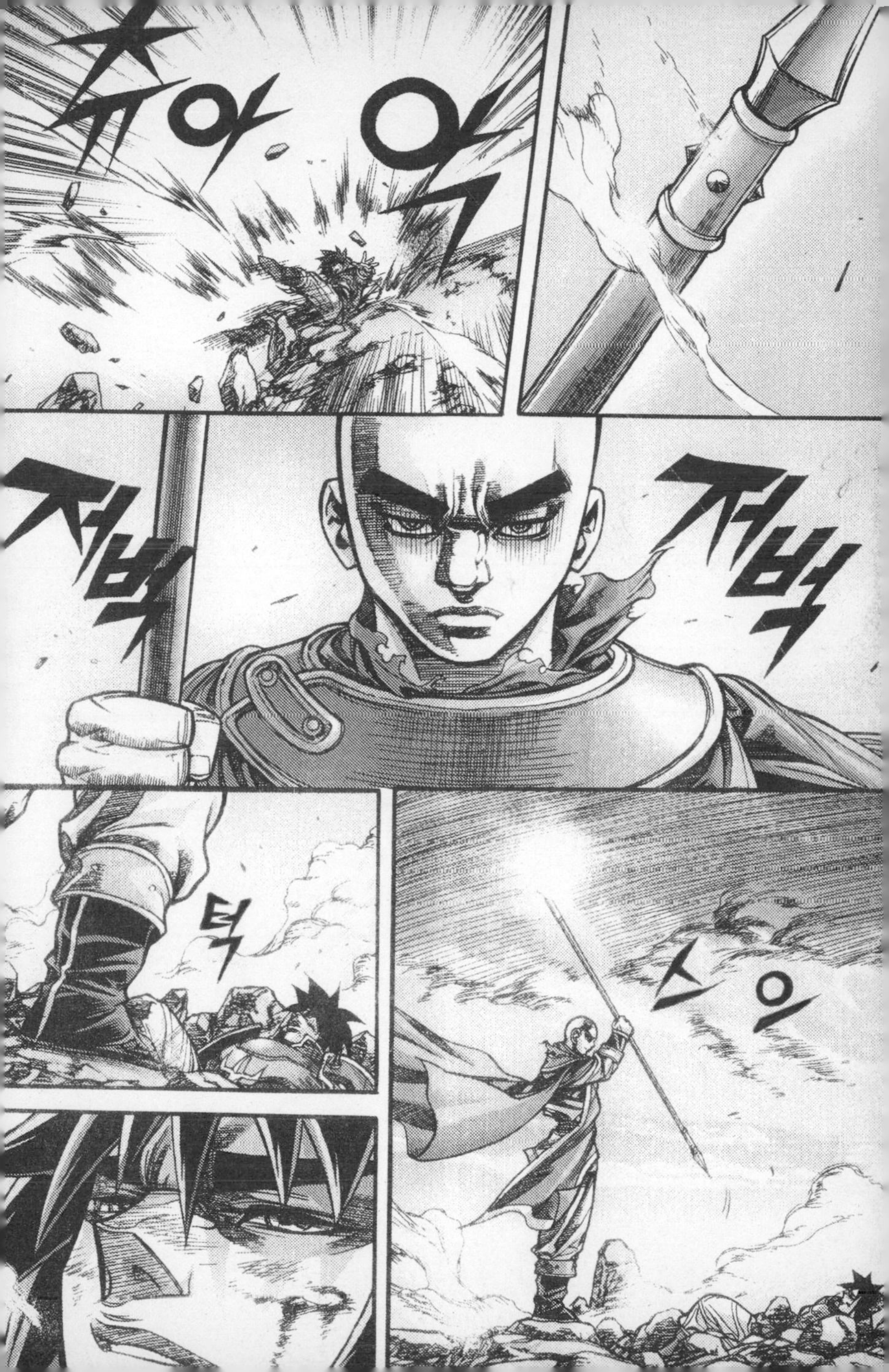

차아앙
저벅
저벅
턱
스으

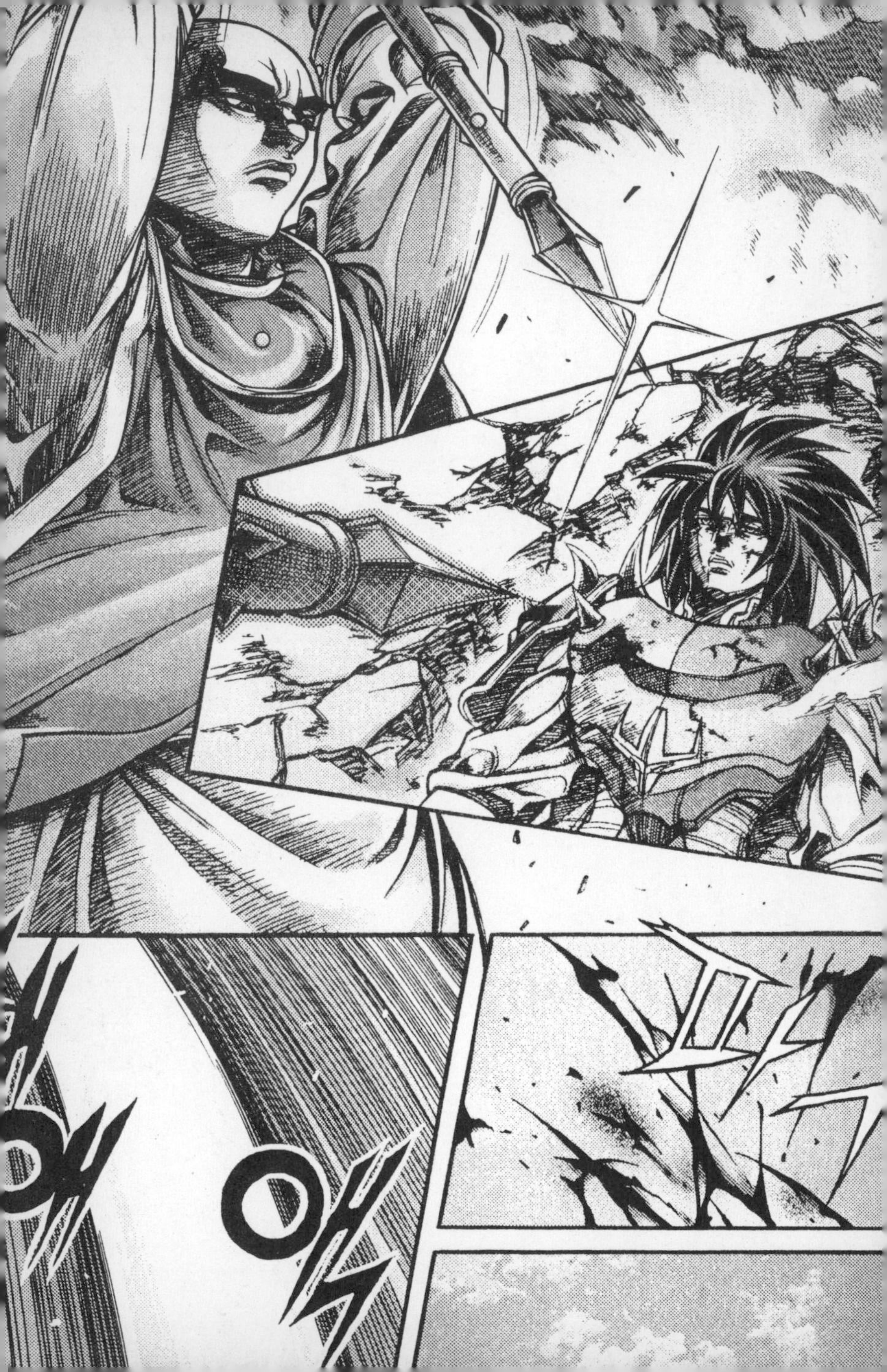

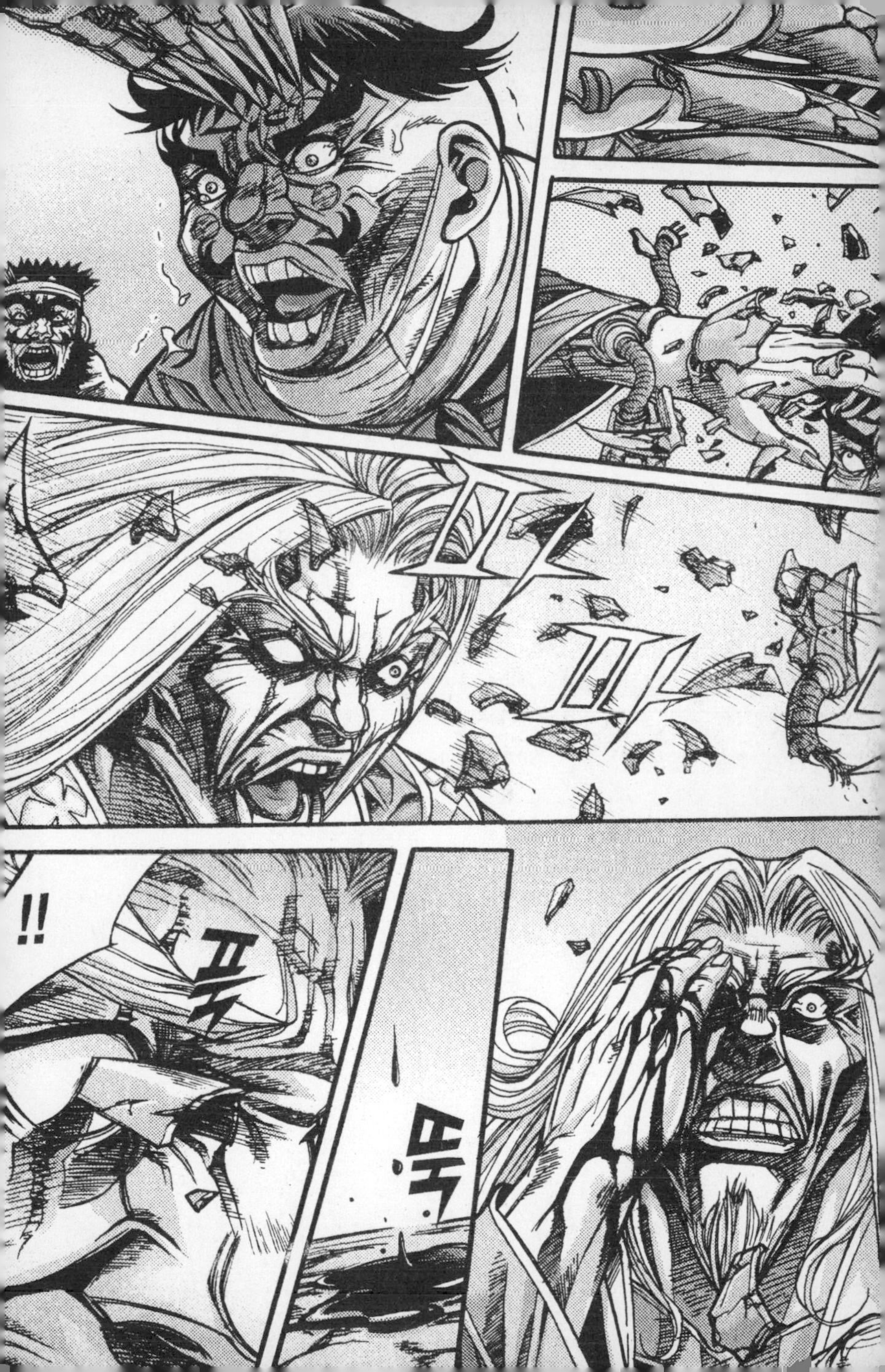
!!

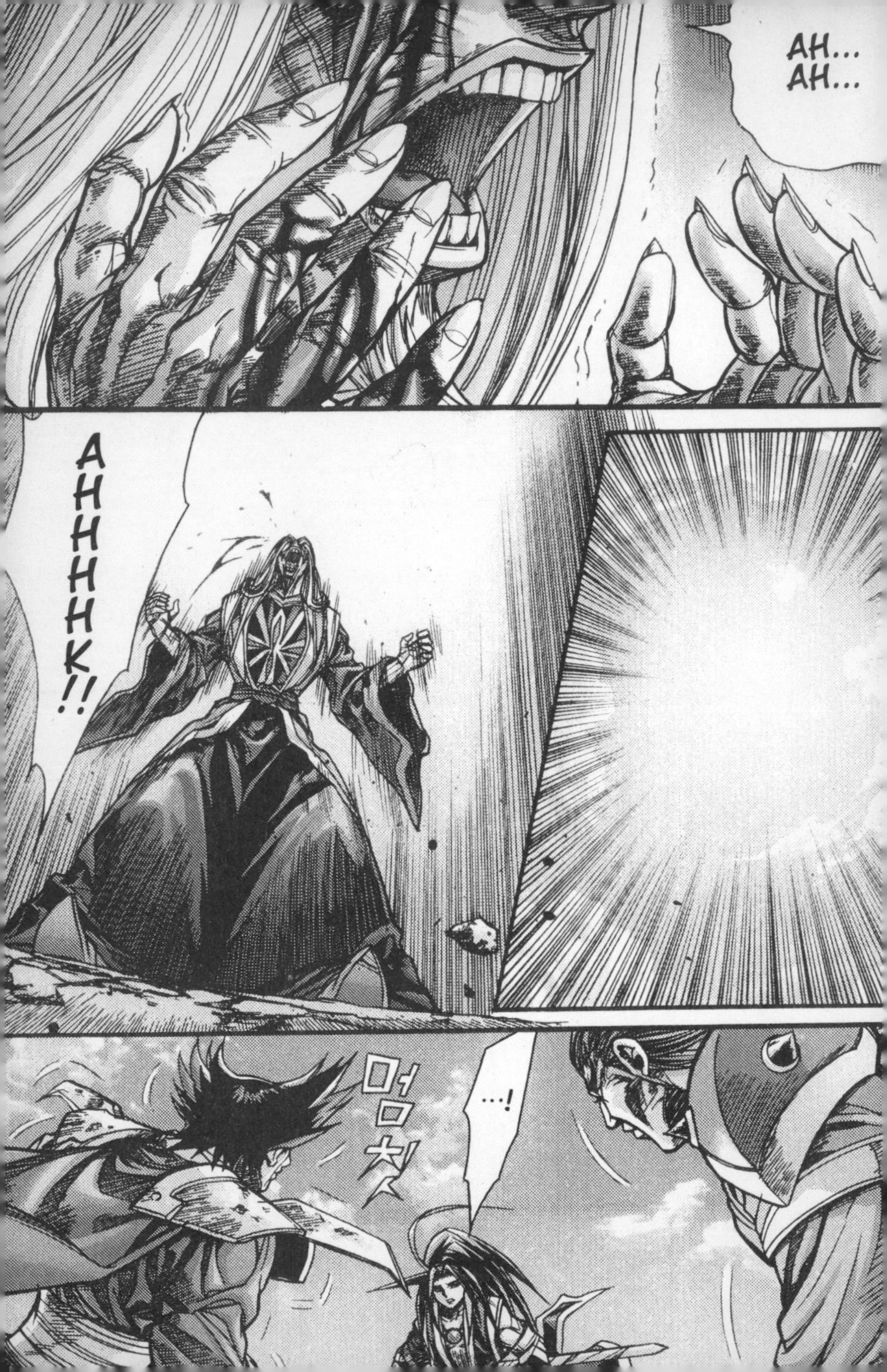
AH...
AH...
AHHHHHK!!
멈칫
...!

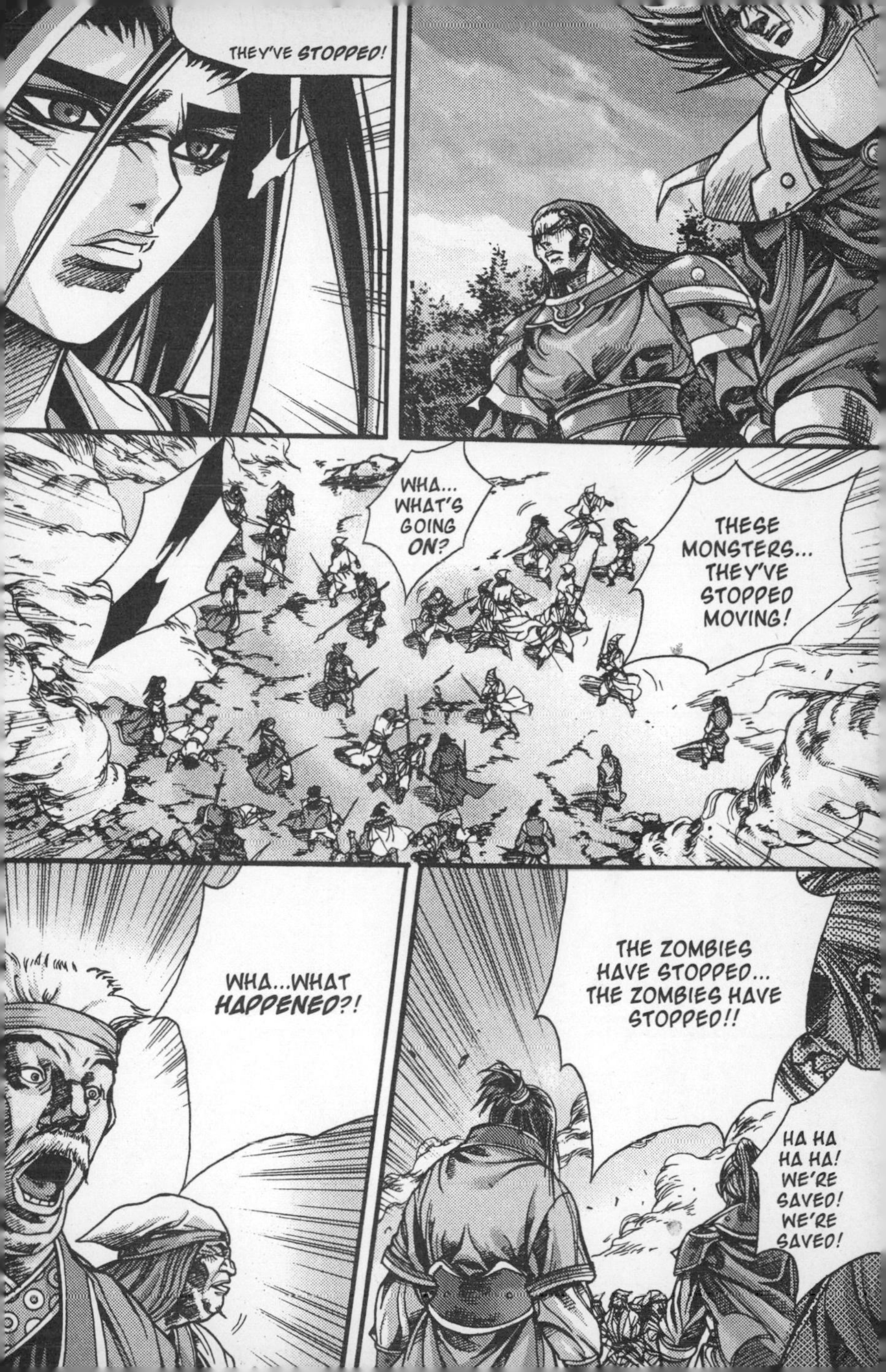
THEY'VE STOPPED!
WHA... WHAT'S GOING ON?
THESE MONSTERS... THEY'VE STOPPED MOVING!
WHA...WHAT HAPPENED?!
THE ZOMBIES HAVE STOPPED... THE ZOMBIES HAVE STOPPED!!
HA HA HA HA! WE'RE SAVED! WE'RE SAVED!

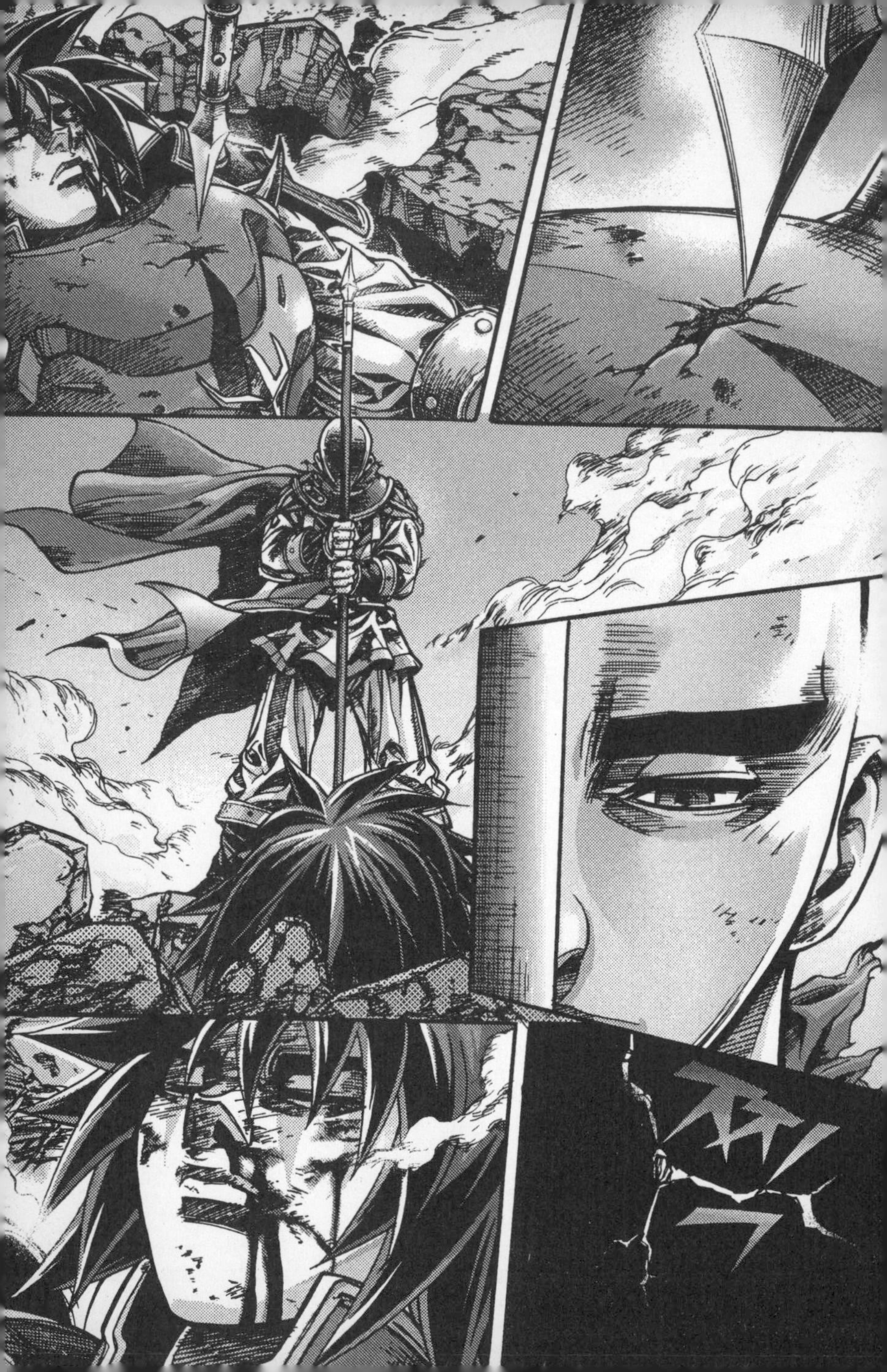

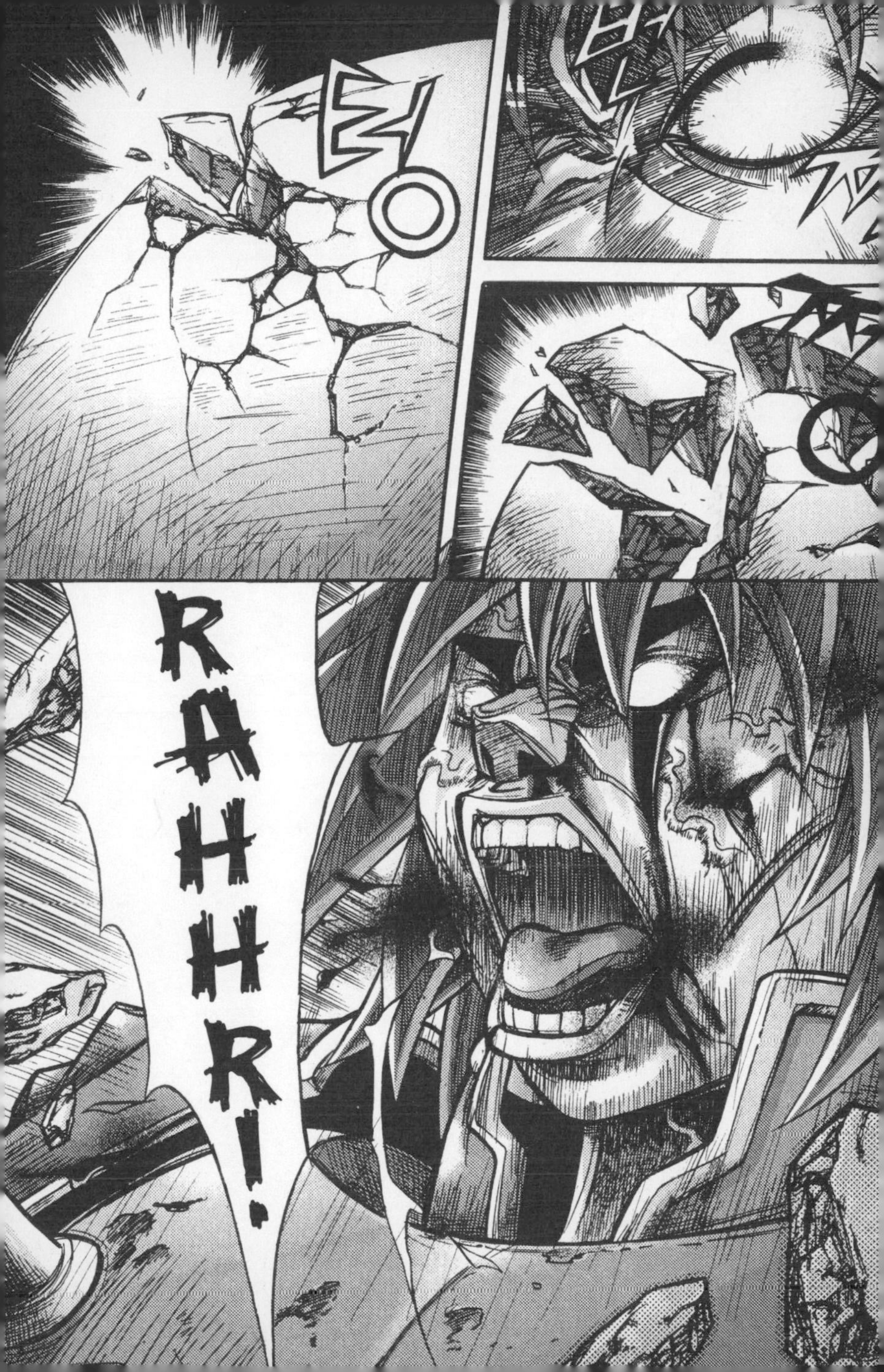
RAHHR!

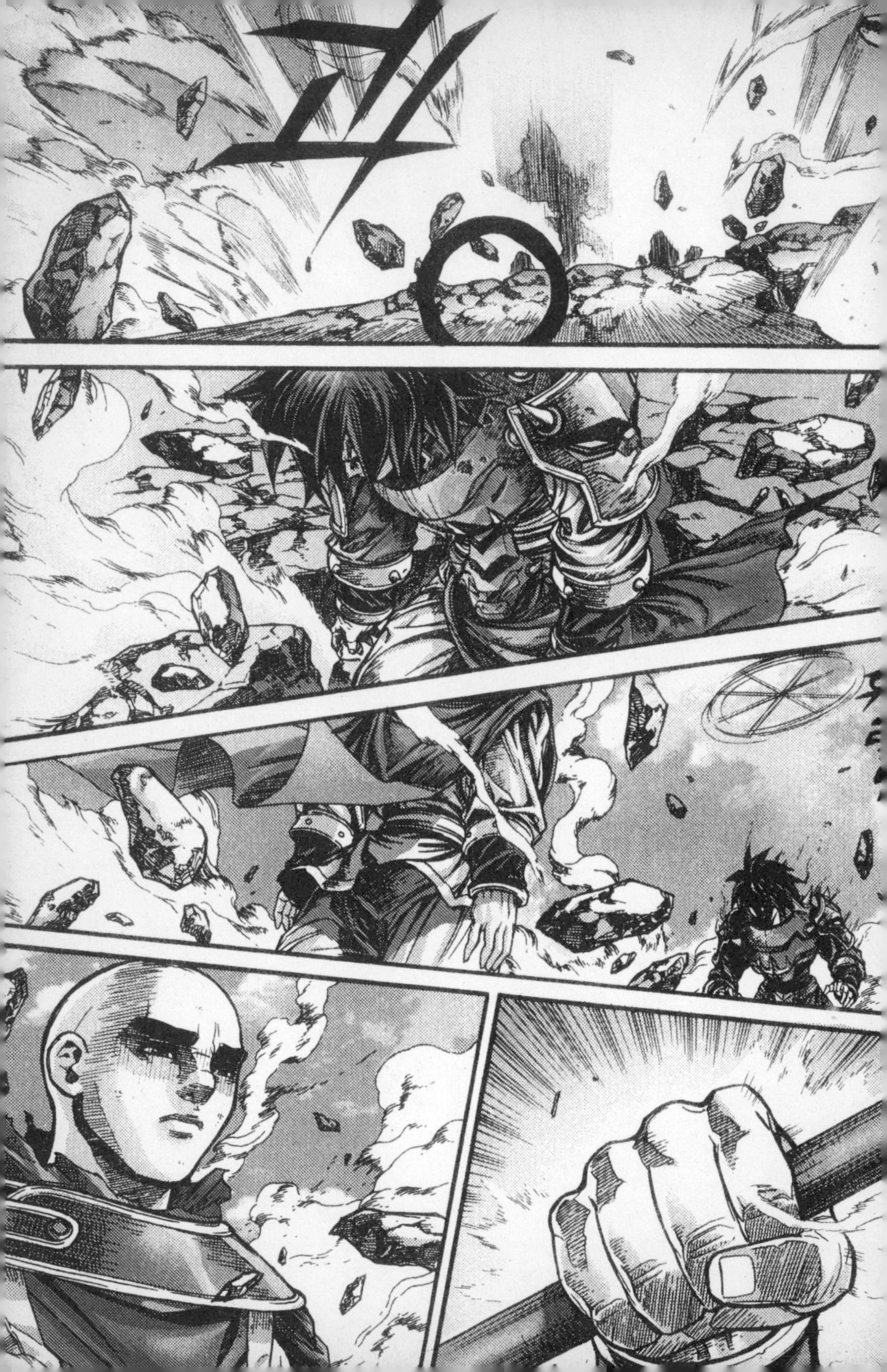

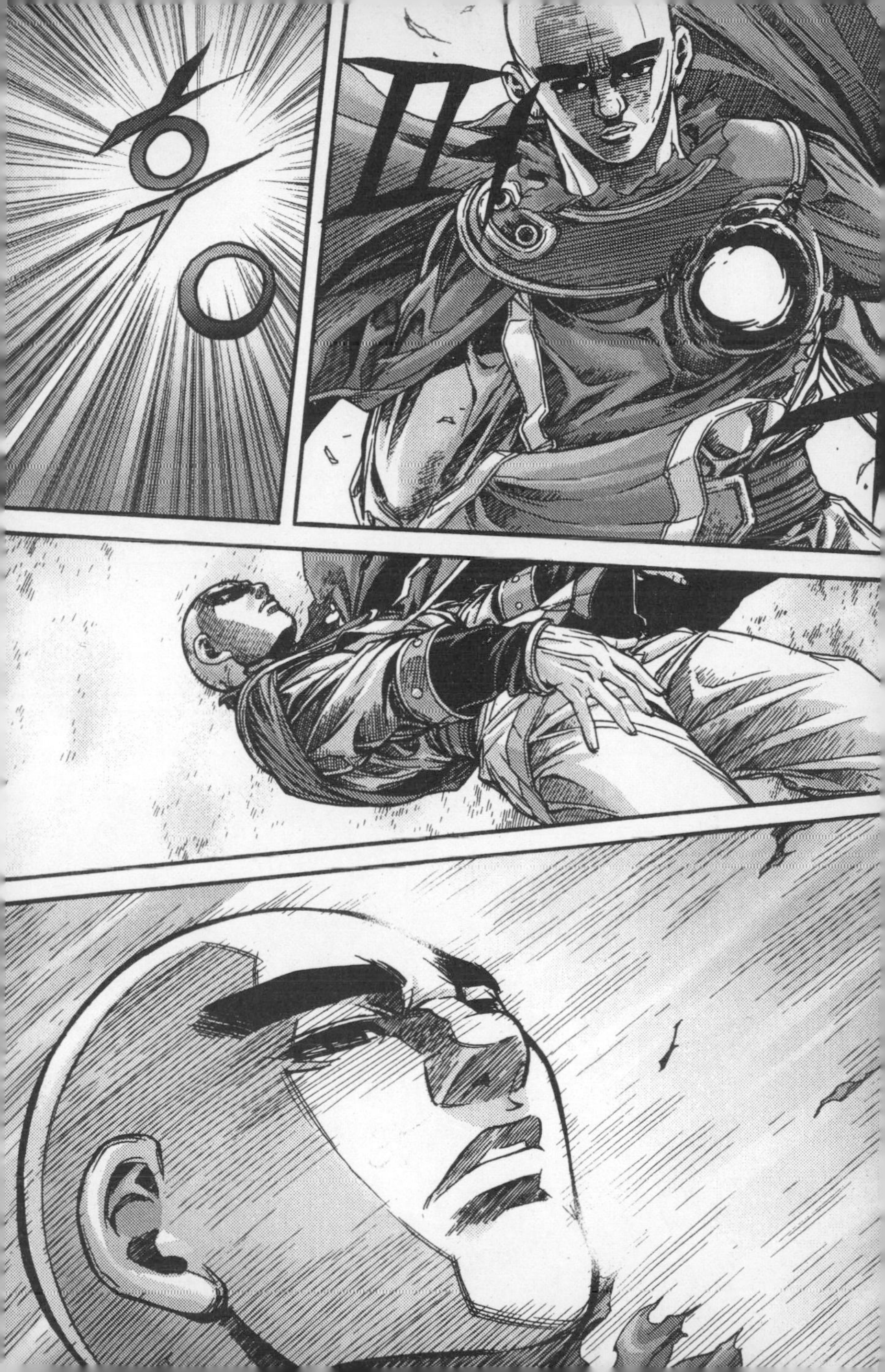

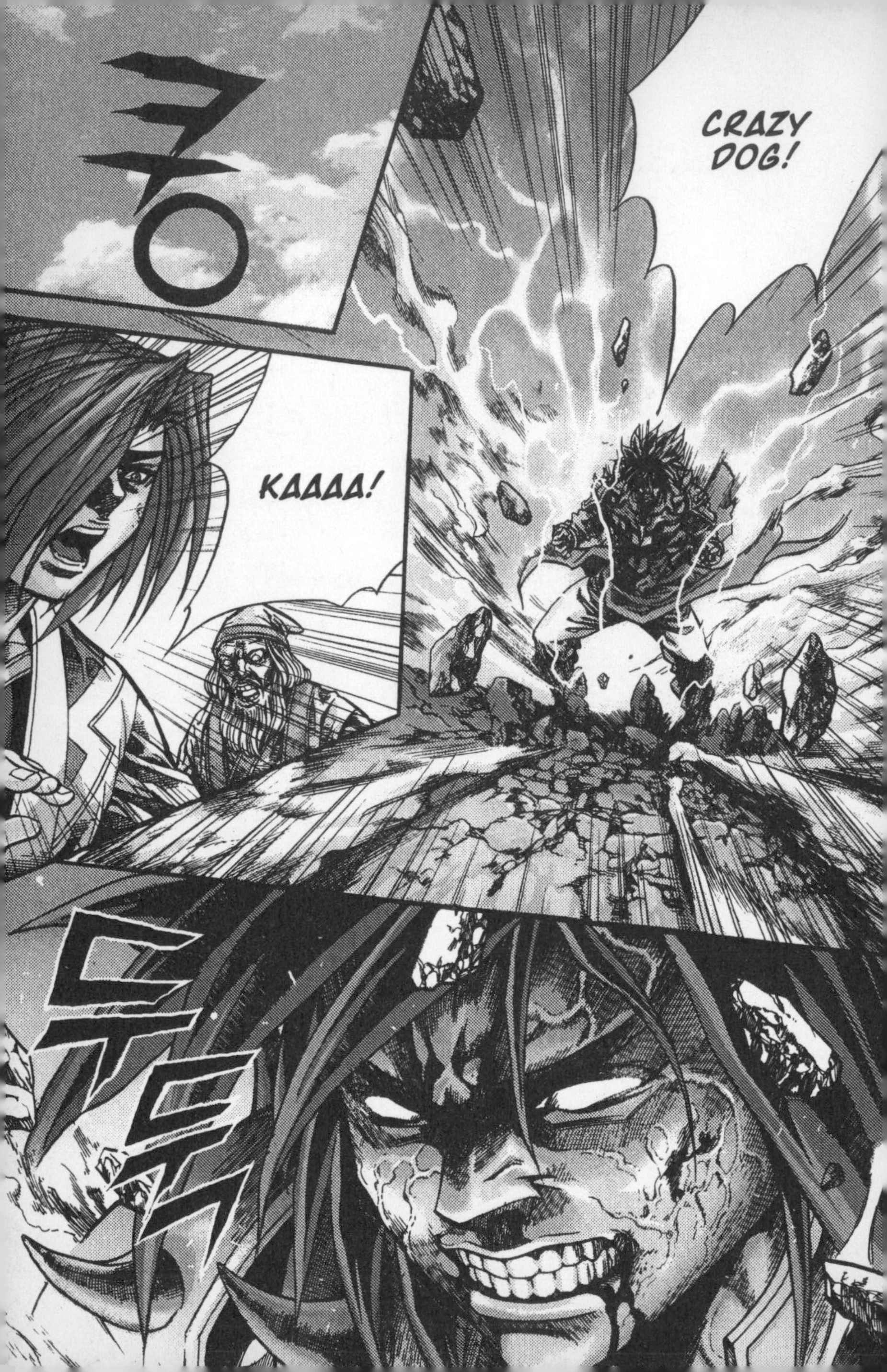
CRAZY DOG!
KAAAA!

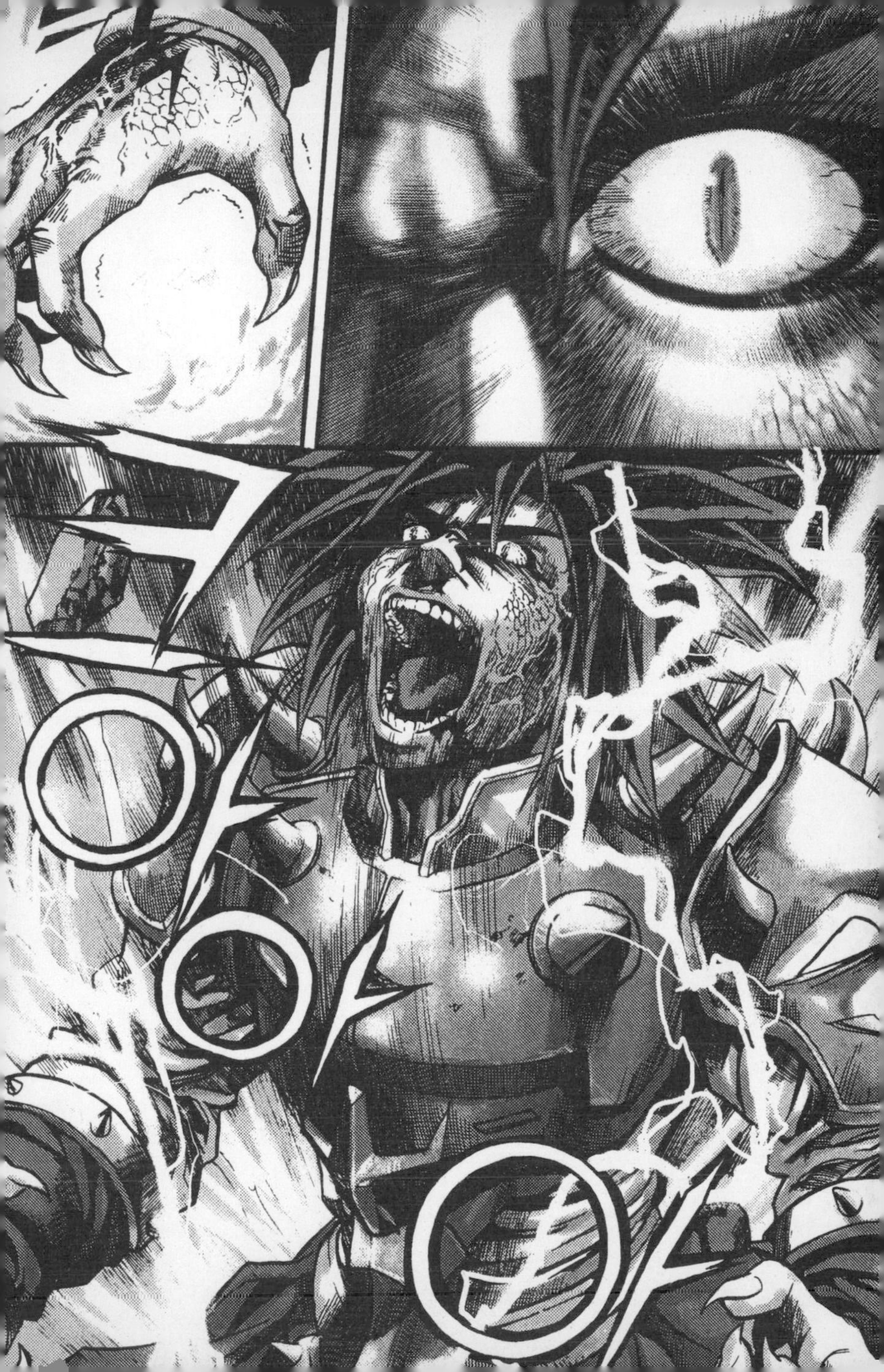

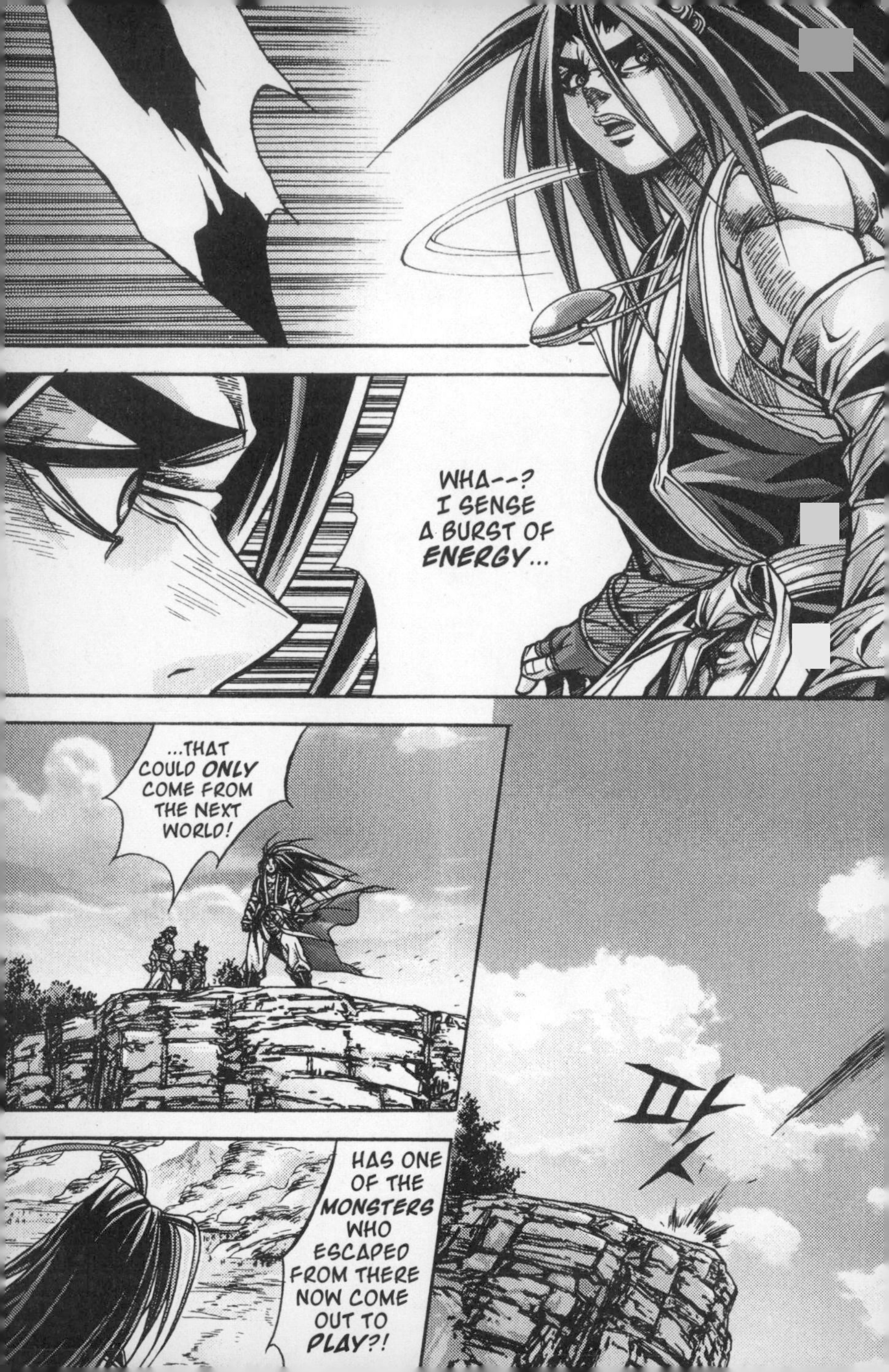
WHA--? I SENSE A BURST OF ENERGY...
...THAT COULD ONLY COME FROM THE NEXT WORLD!
HAS ONE OF THE MONSTERS WHO ESCAPED FROM THERE NOW COME OUT TO PLAY?!

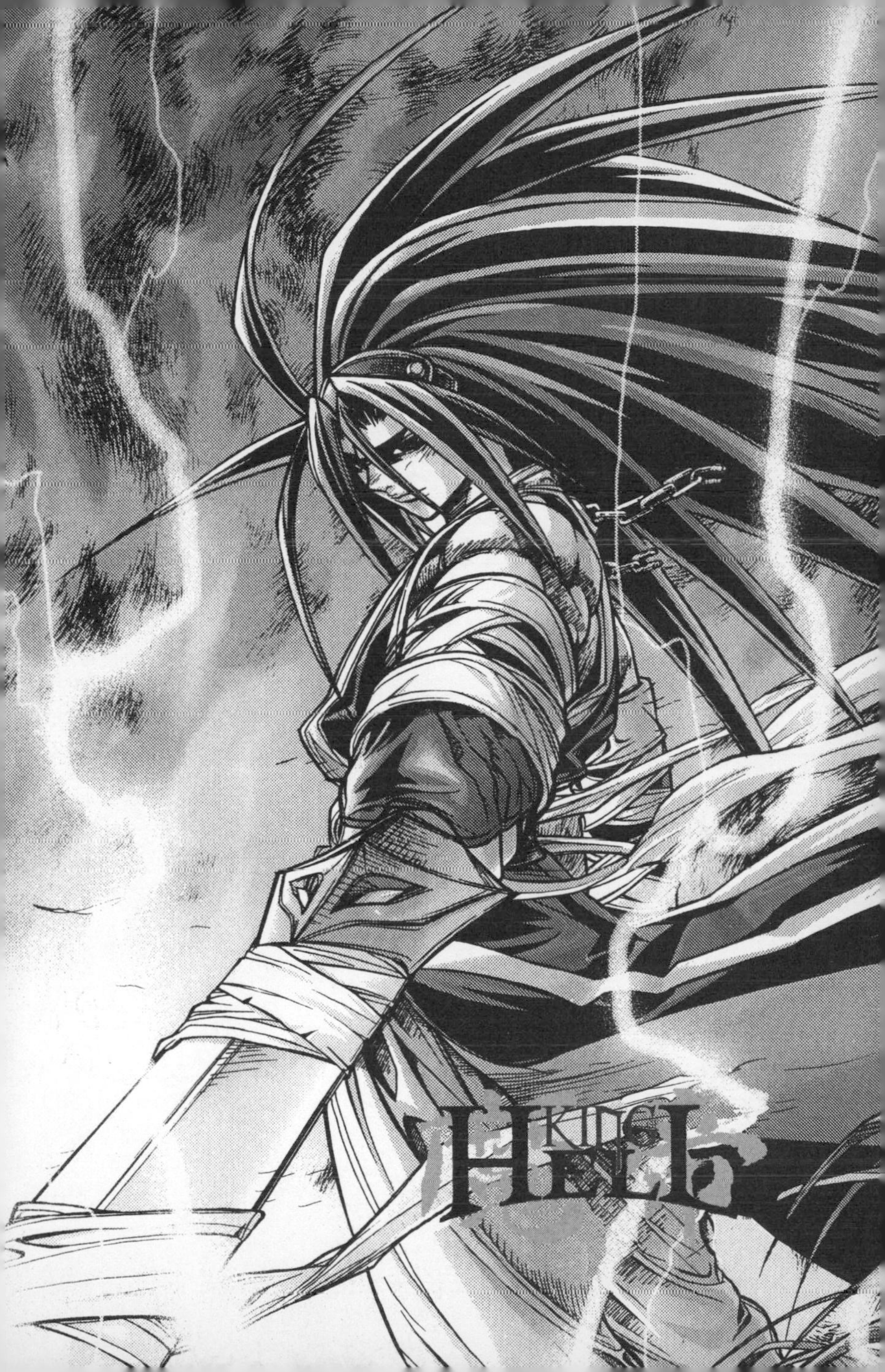
KING
HELL

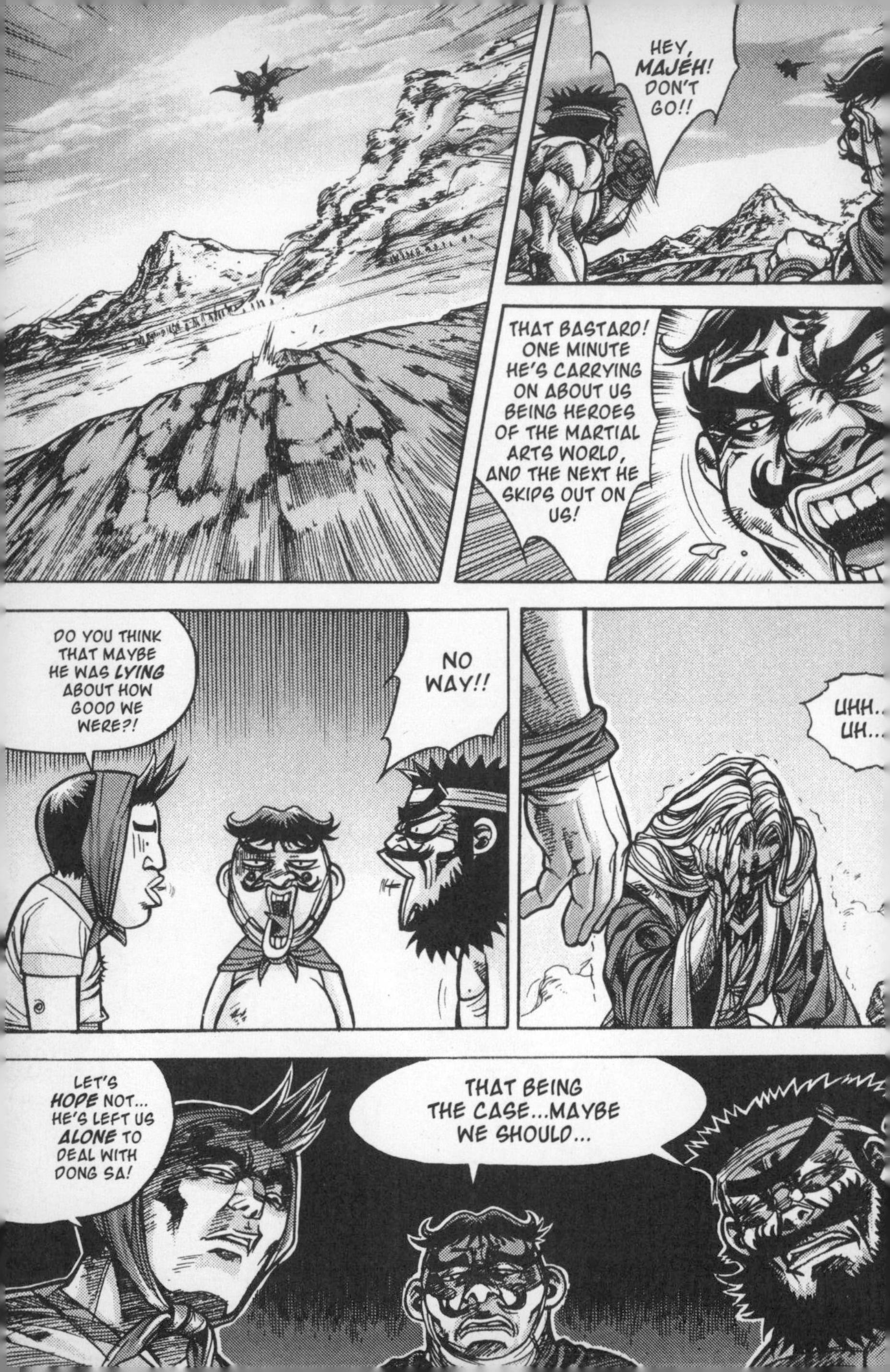
HEY, MAJEH! DON'T GO!!
THAT BASTARD! ONE MINUTE HE'S CARRYING ON ABOUT US BEING HEROES OF THE MARTIAL ARTS WORLD, AND THE NEXT HE SKIPS OUT ON US!
DO YOU THINK THAT MAYBE HE WAS LYING ABOUT HOW GOOD WE WERE?!
NO WAY!!
UHH... UH...
LET'S HOPE NOT... HE'S LEFT US ALONE TO DEAL WITH DONG SA!
THAT BEING THE CASE...MAYBE WE SHOULD...

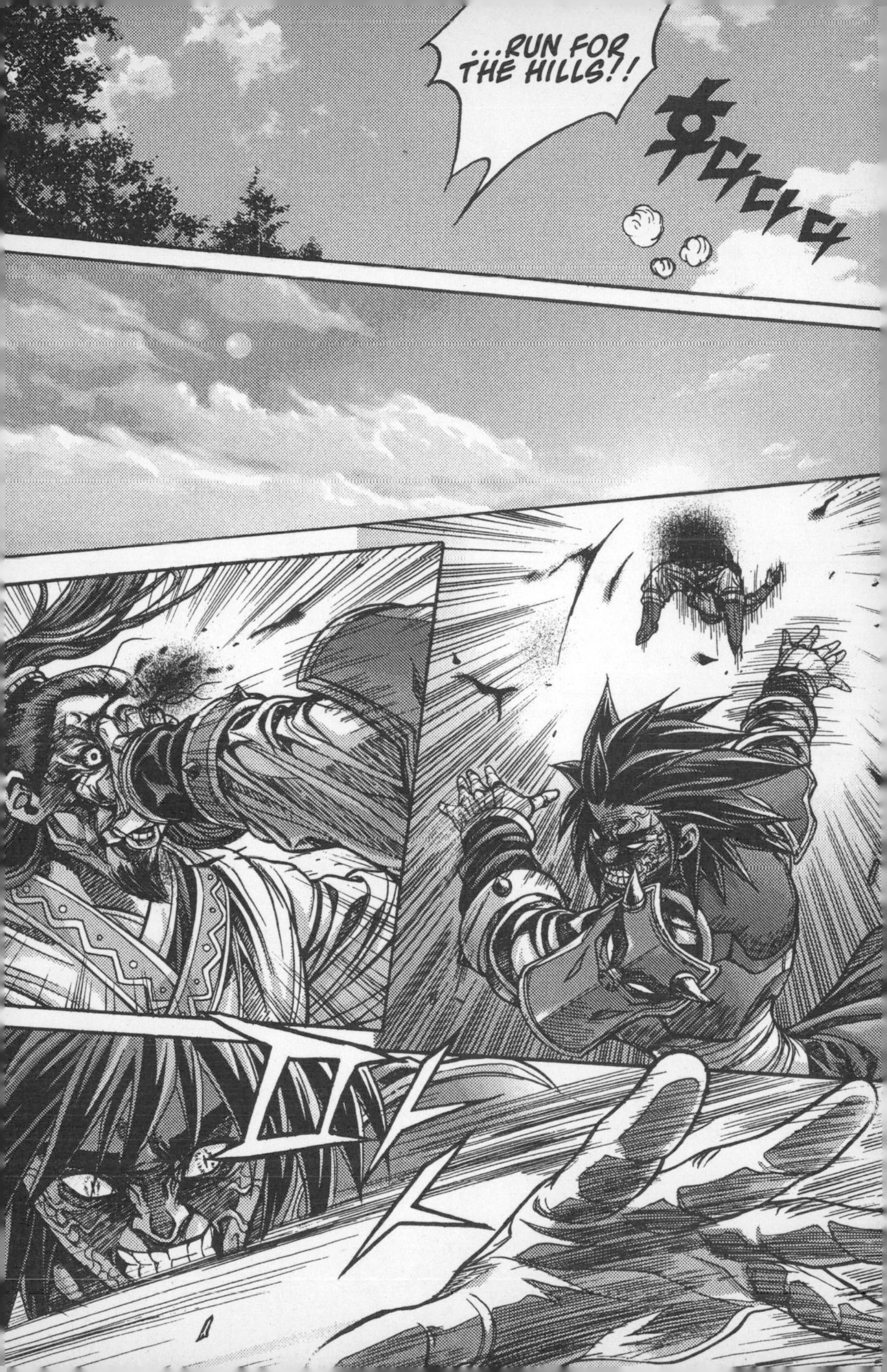
...RUN FOR THE HILLS?!

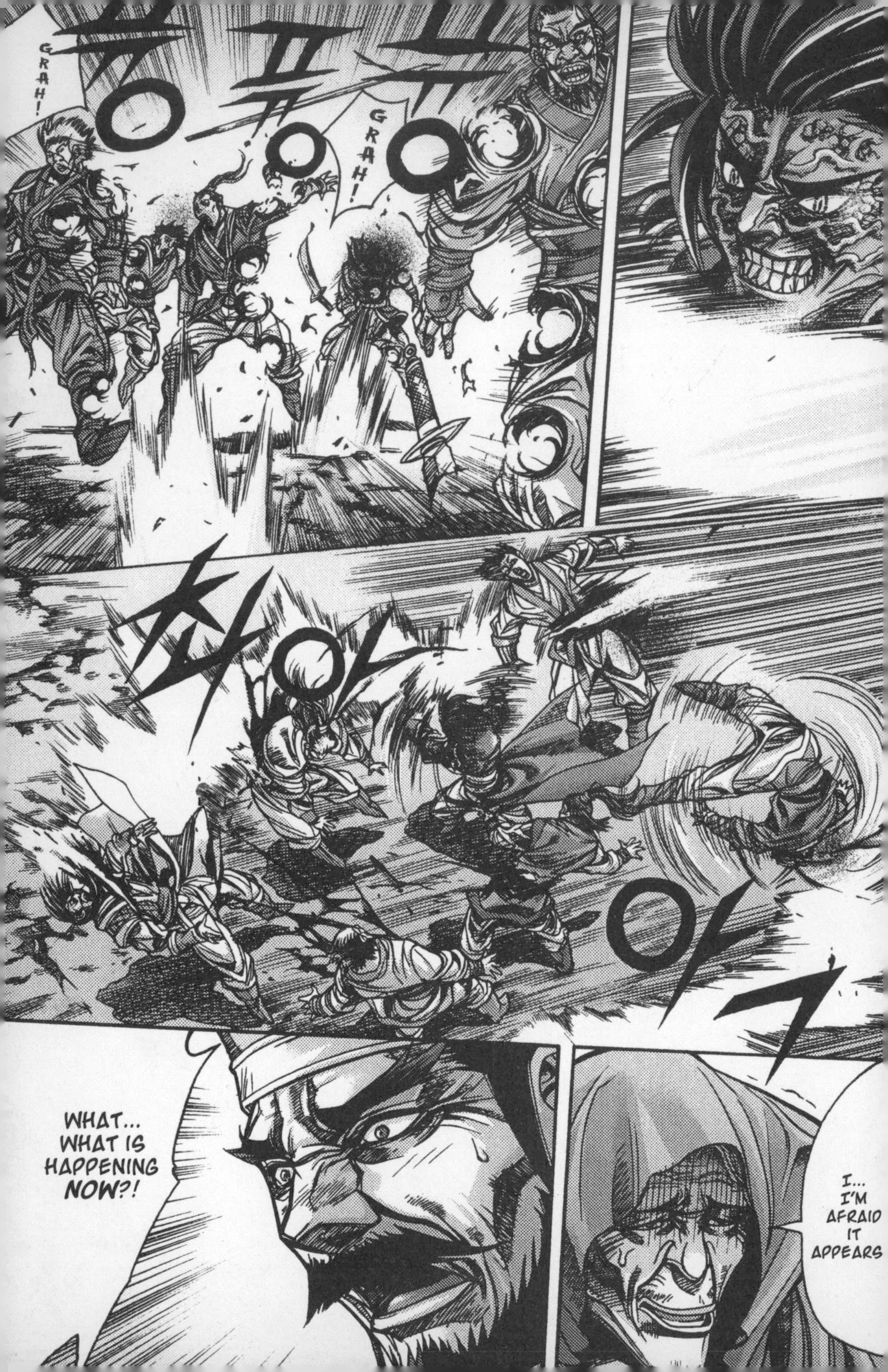
GRAH!
GRAH!
WHAT... WHAT IS HAPPENING NOW?!
I... I'M AFRAID IT APPEARS

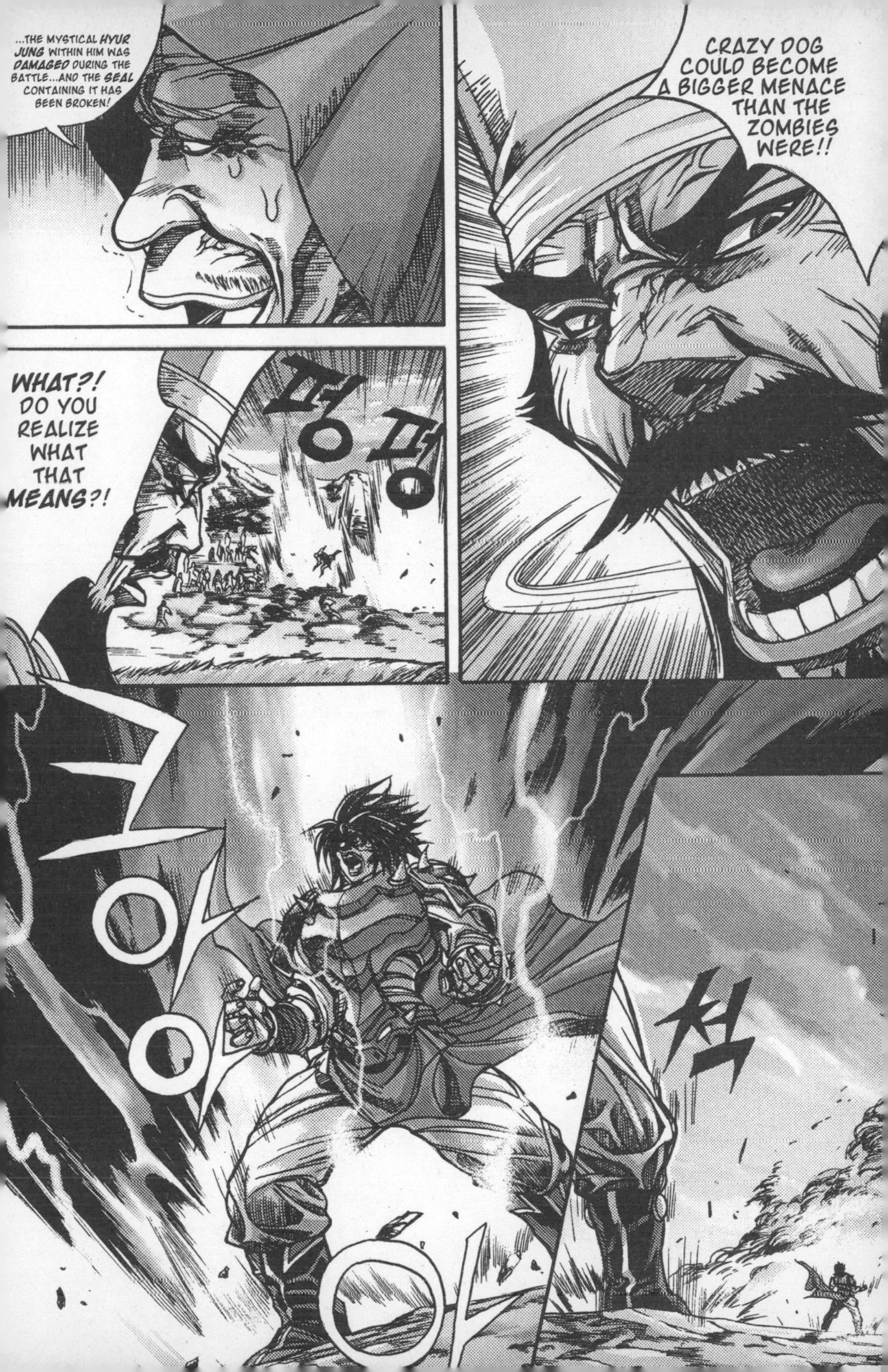

...THE MYSTICAL HYUR JUNG WITHIN HIM WAS DAMAGED DURING THE BATTLE...AND THE SEAL CONTAINING IT HAS BEEN BROKEN!
WHAT?! DO YOU REALIZE WHAT THAT MEANS?!
CRAZY DOG COULD BECOME A BIGGER MENACE THAN THE ZOMBIES WERE!!

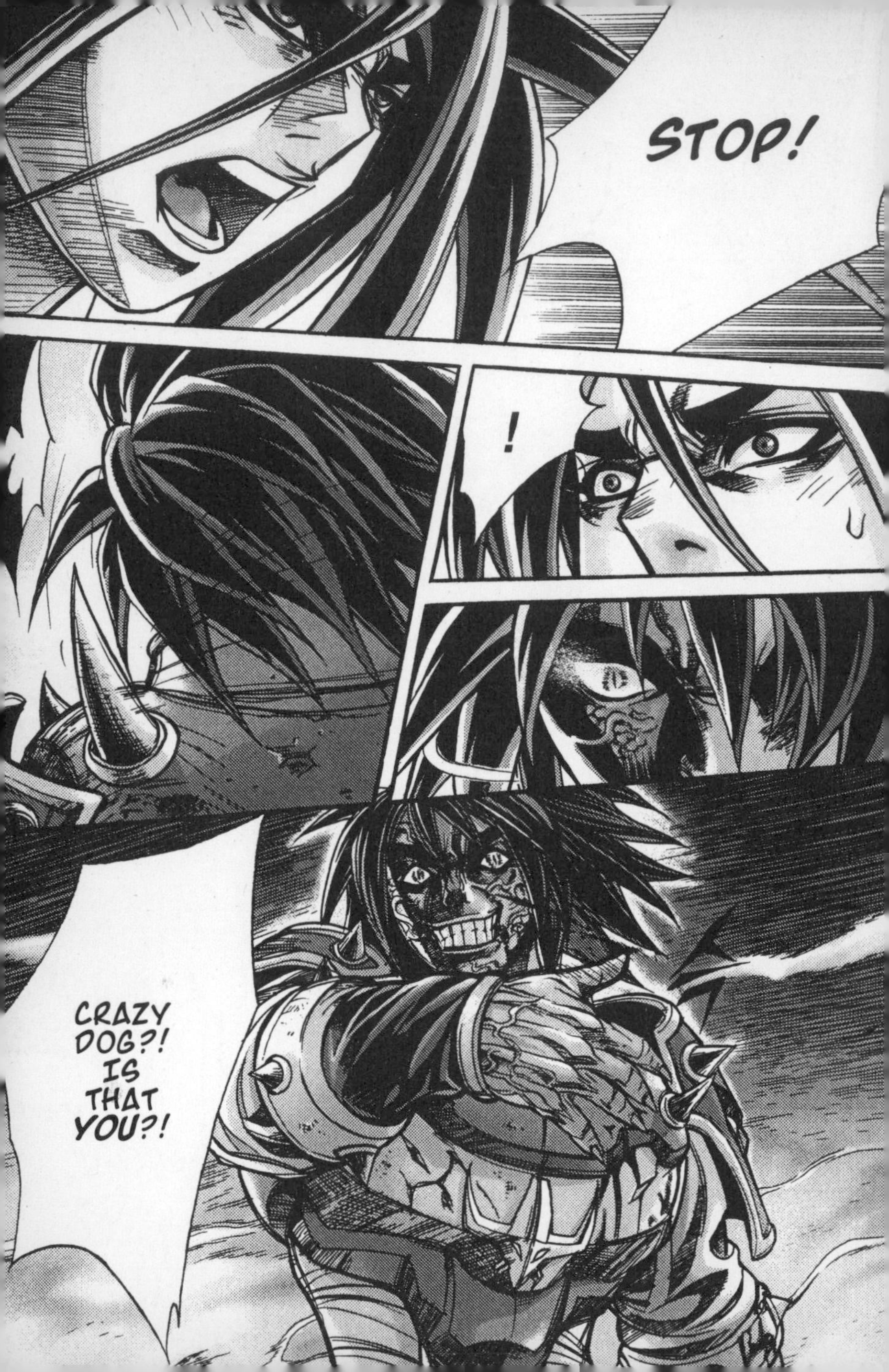
STOP!
!
CRAZY DOG?! IS THAT YOU?!

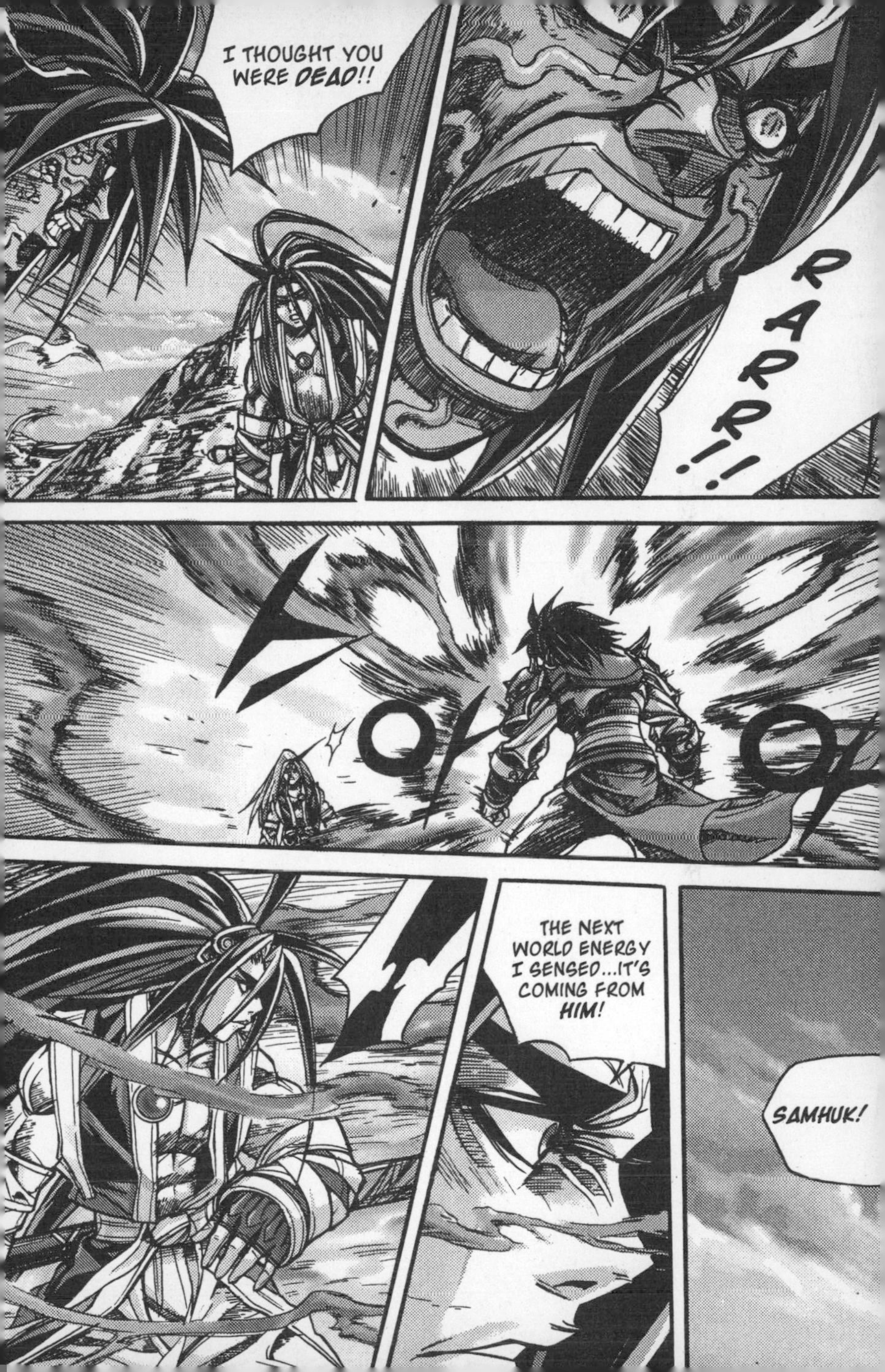
I THOUGHT YOU WERE DEAD!!
RARRR!!!
THE NEXT WORLD ENERGY I SENSED...IT'S COMING FROM HIM!
SAMHUK!

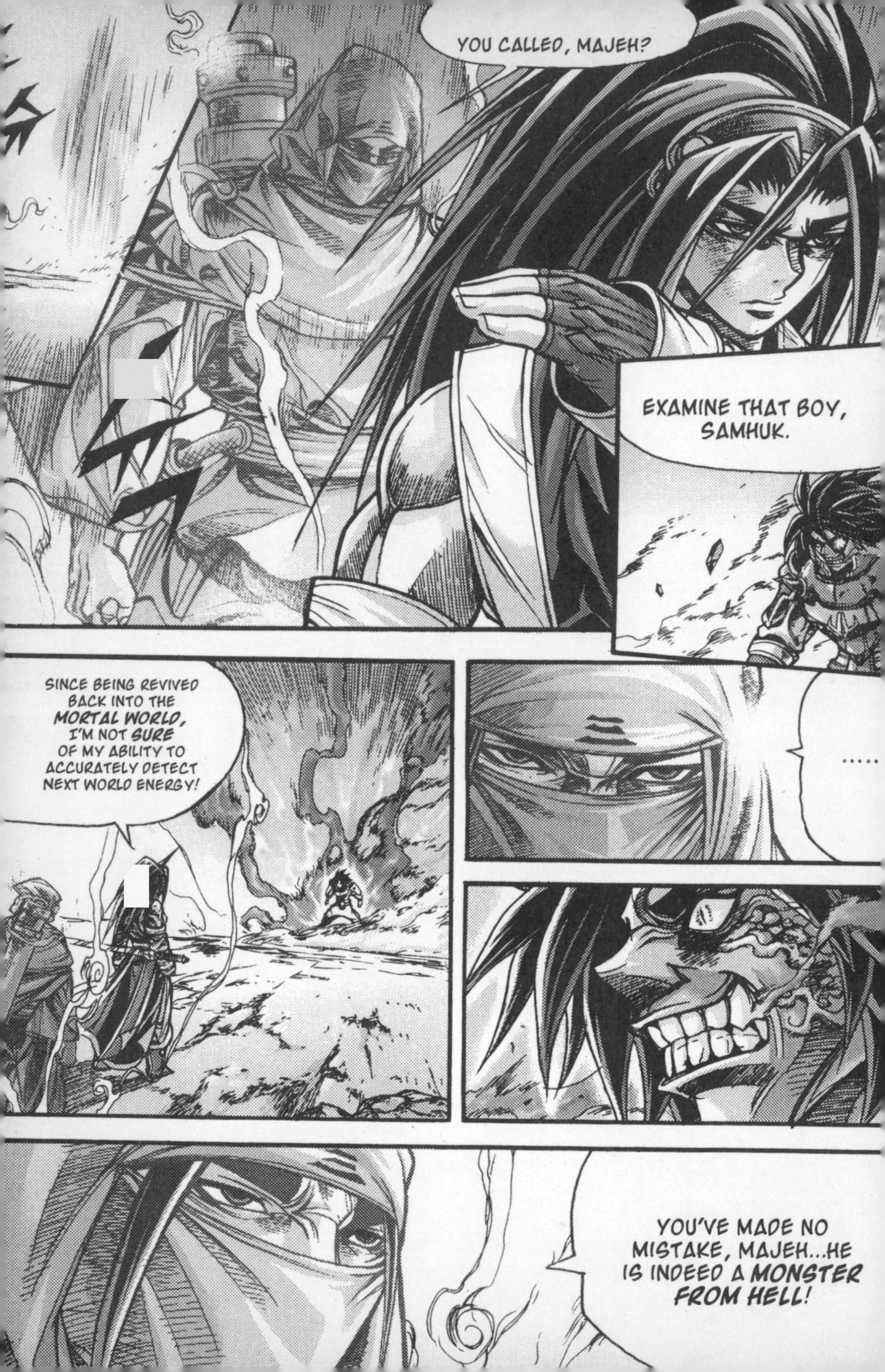
YOU CALLED, MAJEH?
EXAMINE THAT BOY, SAMHUK.
SINCE BEING REVIVED BACK INTO THE MORTAL WORLD, I'M NOT SURE OF MY ABILITY TO ACCURATELY DETECT NEXT WORLD ENERGY!
.....
YOU'VE MADE NO MISTAKE, MAJEH...HE IS INDEED A MONSTER FROM HELL!

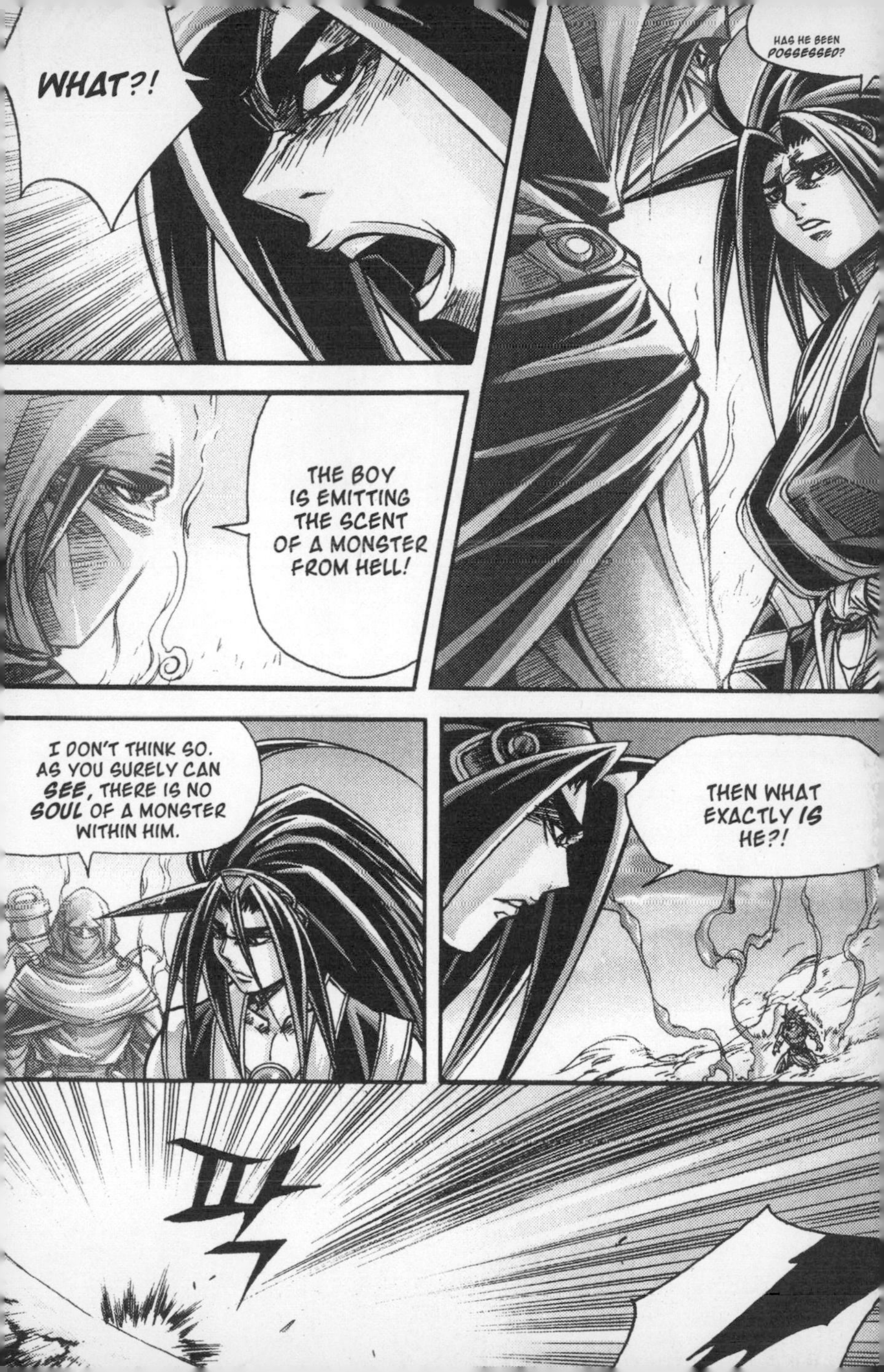
WHAT?!
THE BOY IS EMITTING THE SCENT OF A MONSTER FROM HELL!
HAS HE BEEN POSSESSED?
I DON'T THINK SO. AS YOU SURELY CAN SEE, THERE IS NO SOUL OF A MONSTER WITHIN HIM.
THEN WHAT EXACTLY IS HE?!

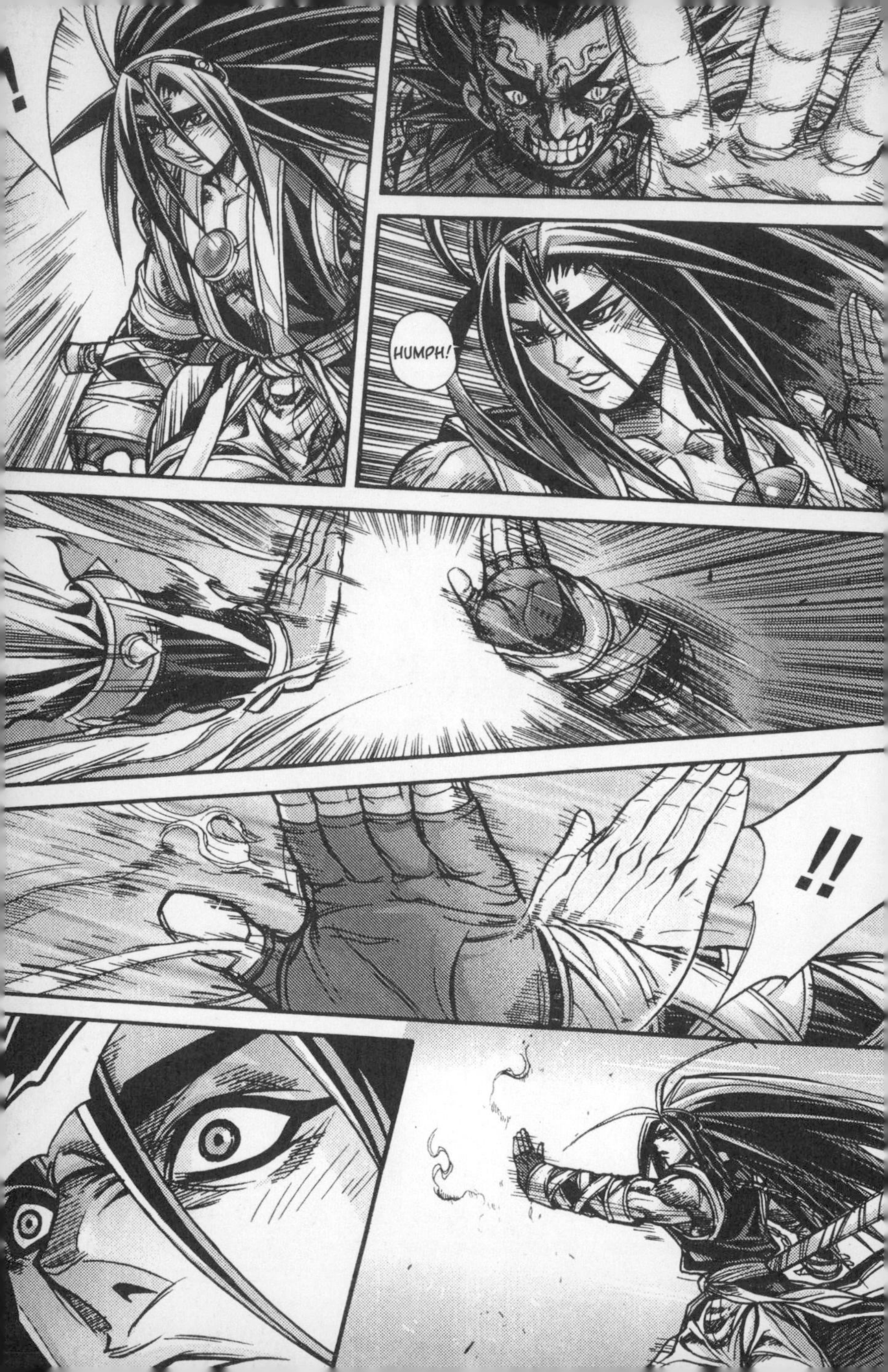
!
HUMPH!
!!

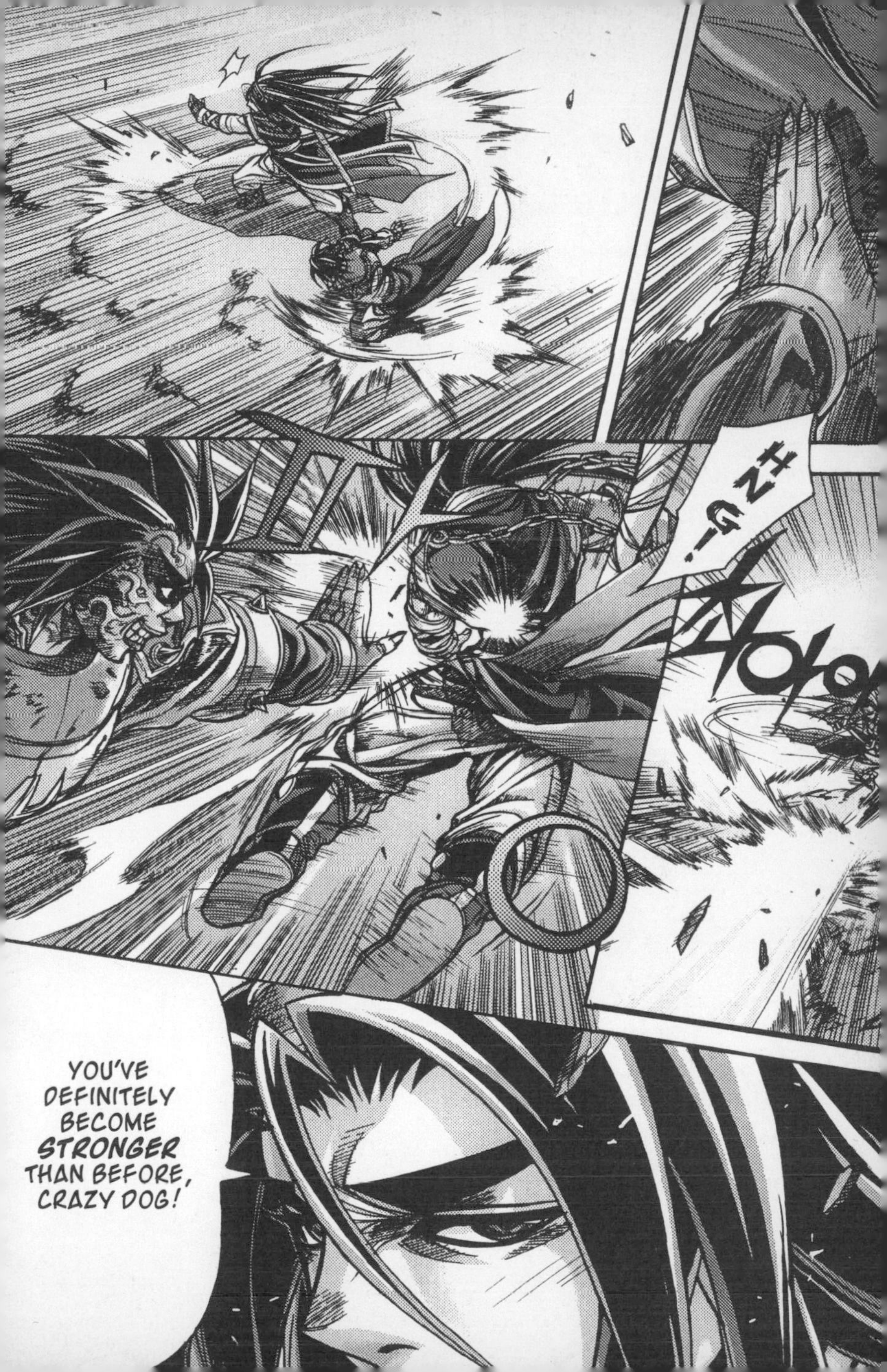
HNG!
YOU'VE DEFINITELY BECOME **STRONGER** THAN BEFORE, CRAZY DOG!

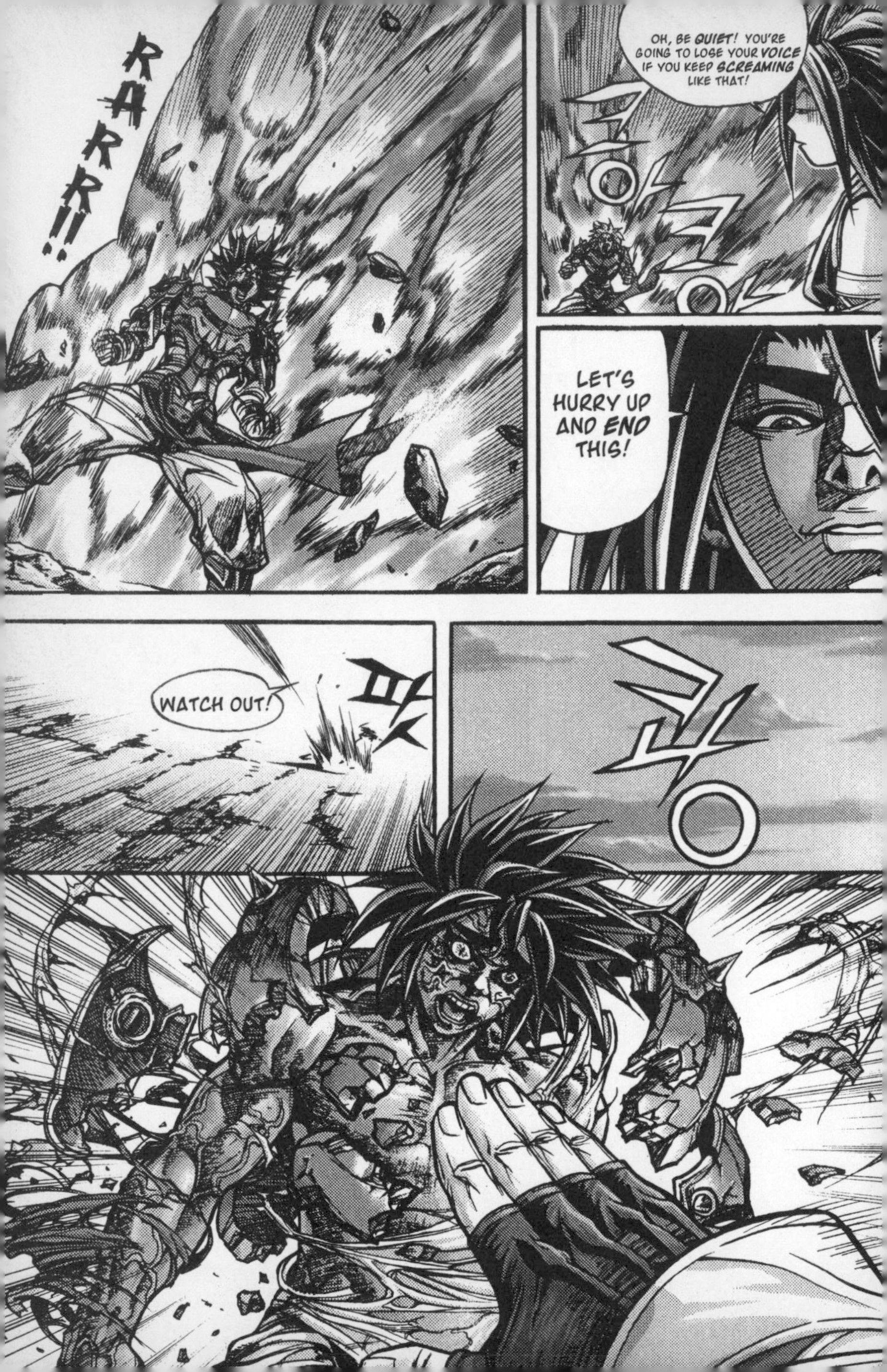
RARRR!!
OH, BE QUIET! YOU'RE GOING TO LOSE YOUR VOICE IF YOU KEEP SCREAMING LIKE THAT!
LET'S HURRY UP AND END THIS!
WATCH OUT!

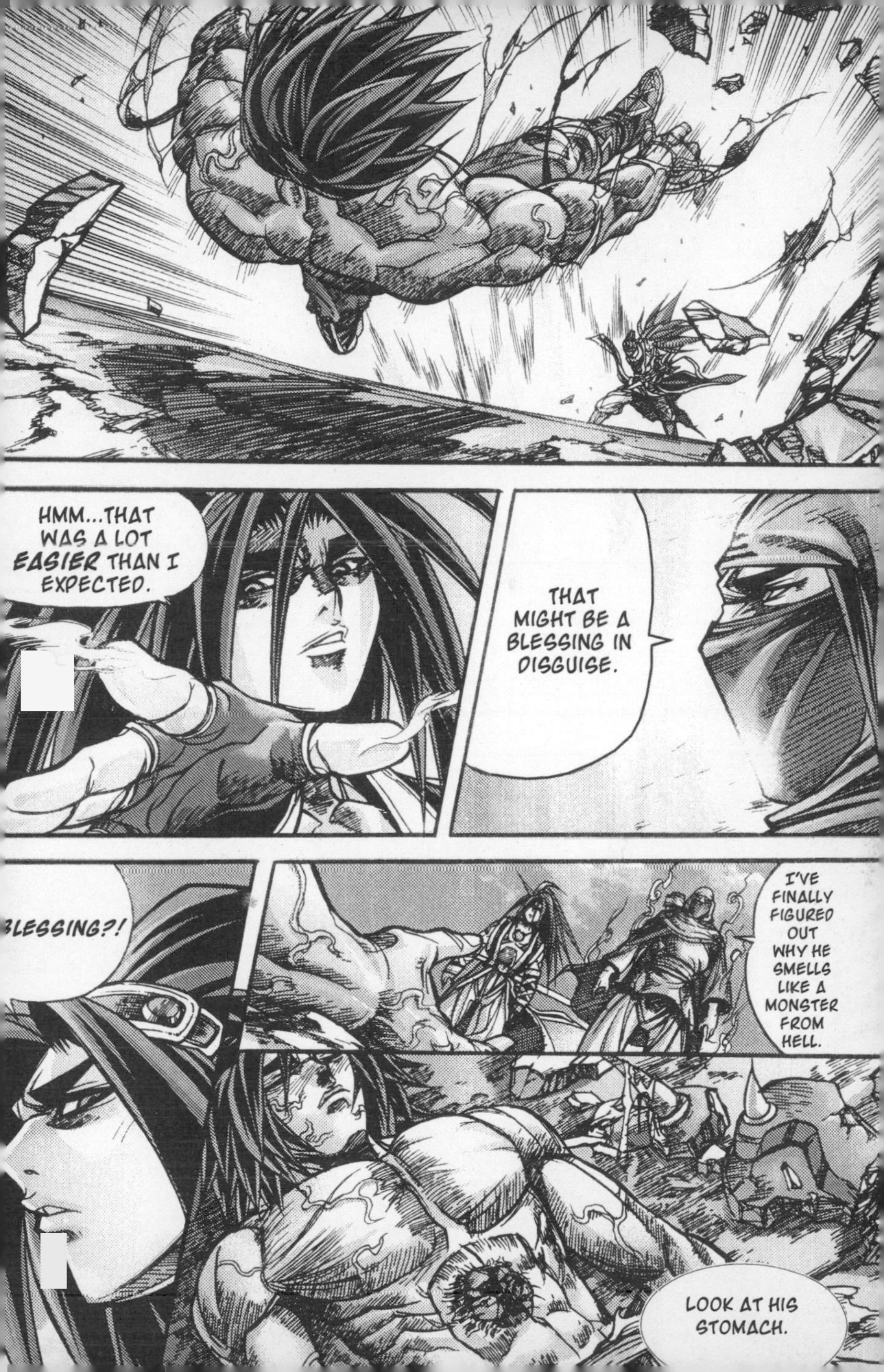
HMM...THAT WAS A LOT EASIER THAN I EXPECTED.
THAT MIGHT BE A BLESSING IN DISGUISE.
BLESSING?!
I'VE FINALLY FIGURED OUT WHY HE SMELLS LIKE A MONSTER FROM HELL.
LOOK AT HIS STOMACH.

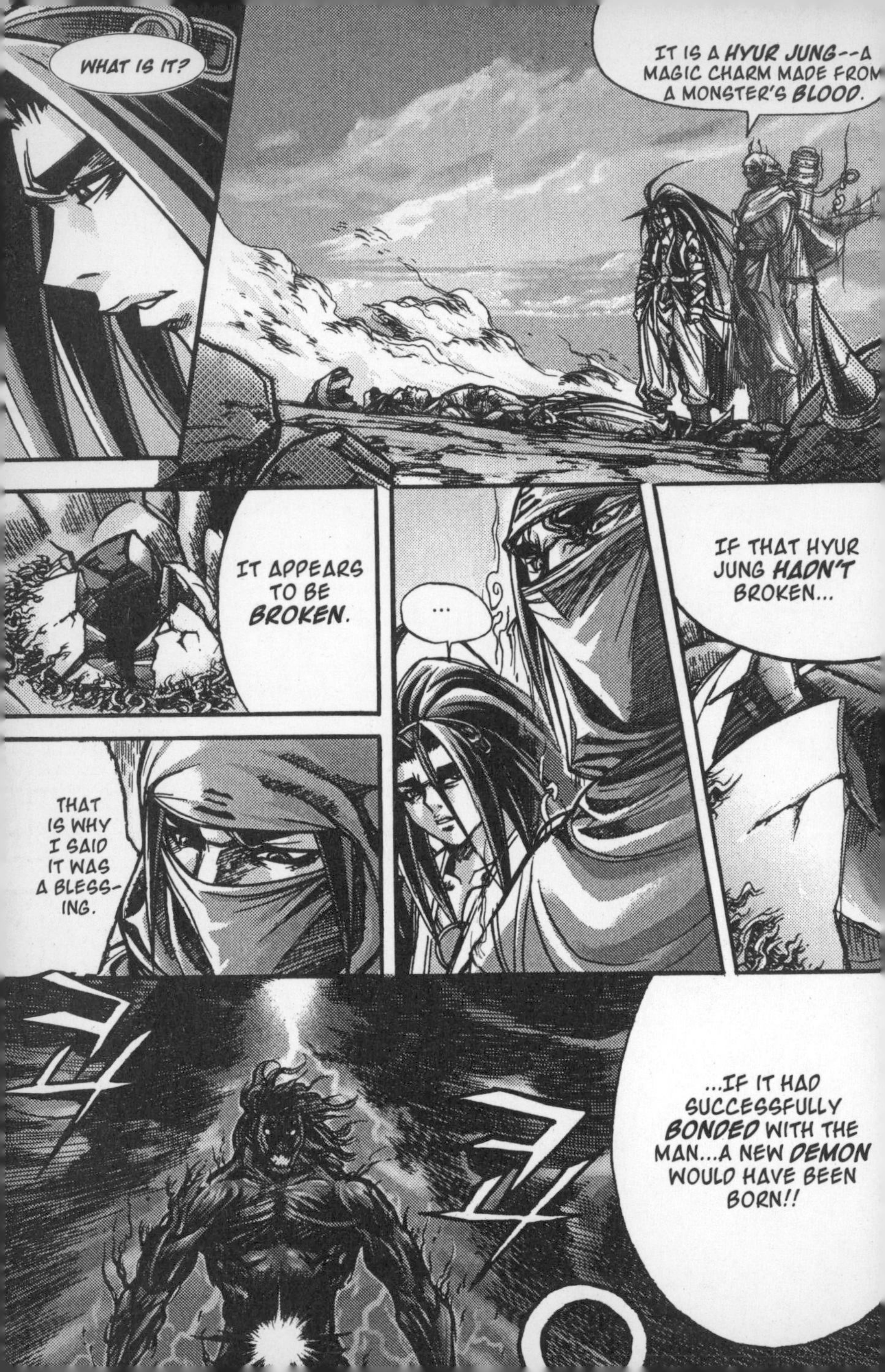
WHAT IS IT?
IT IS A HYUR JUNG--A MAGIC CHARM MADE FROM A MONSTER'S BLOOD.
IT APPEARS TO BE BROKEN.
...
IF THAT HYUR JUNG HADN'T BROKEN...
THAT IS WHY I SAID IT WAS A BLESS-ING.
...IF IT HAD SUCCESSFULLY BONDED WITH THE MAN...A NEW DEMON WOULD HAVE BEEN BORN!!

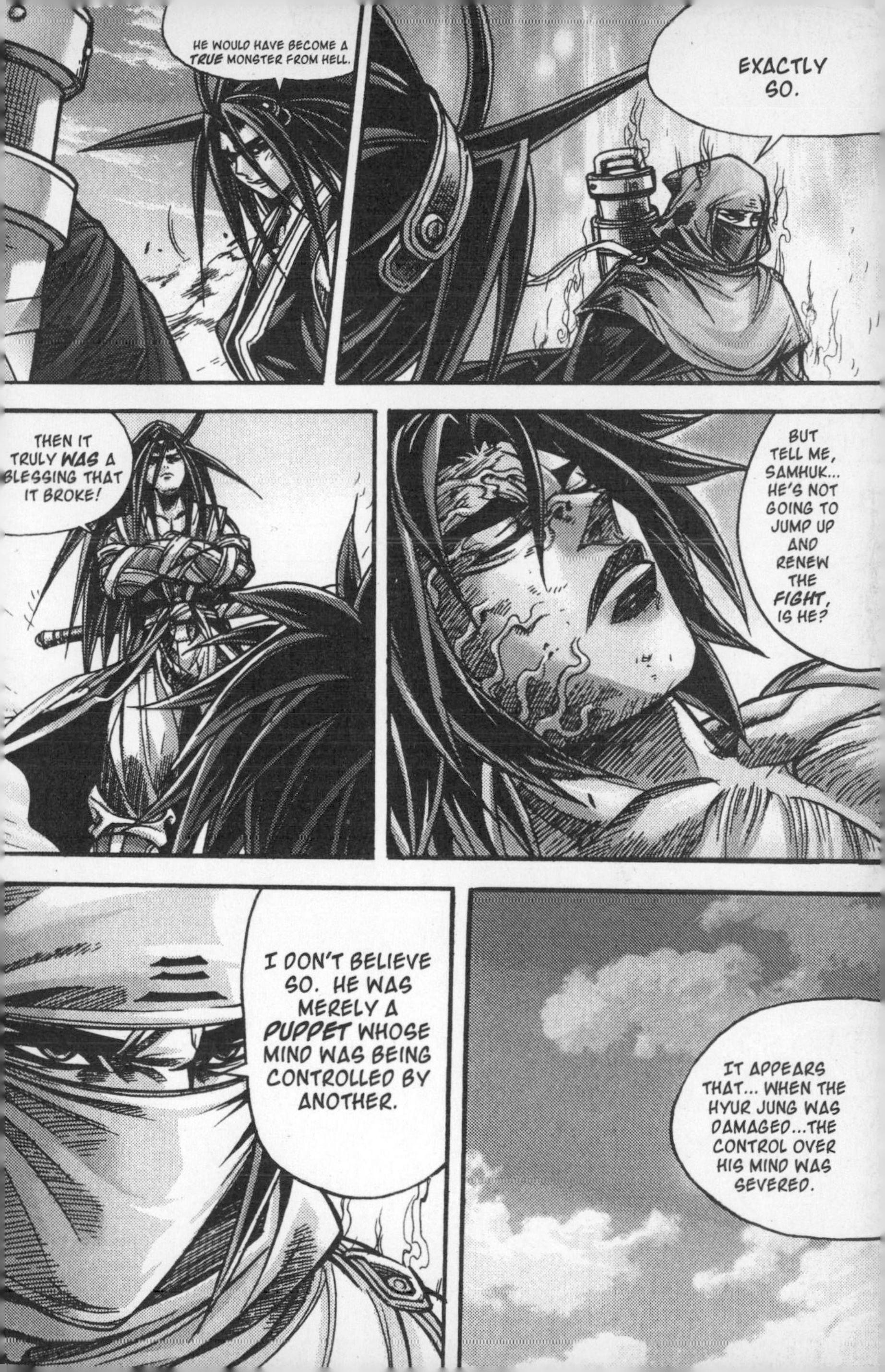
HE WOULD HAVE BECOME A TRUE MONSTER FROM HELL.
EXACTLY SO.
THEN IT TRULY WAS A BLESSING THAT IT BROKE!
BUT TELL ME, SAMHUK... HE'S NOT GOING TO JUMP UP AND RENEW THE FIGHT, IS HE?
I DON'T BELIEVE SO. HE WAS MERELY A PUPPET WHOSE MIND WAS BEING CONTROLLED BY ANOTHER.
IT APPEARS THAT... WHEN THE HYUR JUNG WAS DAMAGED...THE CONTROL OVER HIS MIND WAS SEVERED.

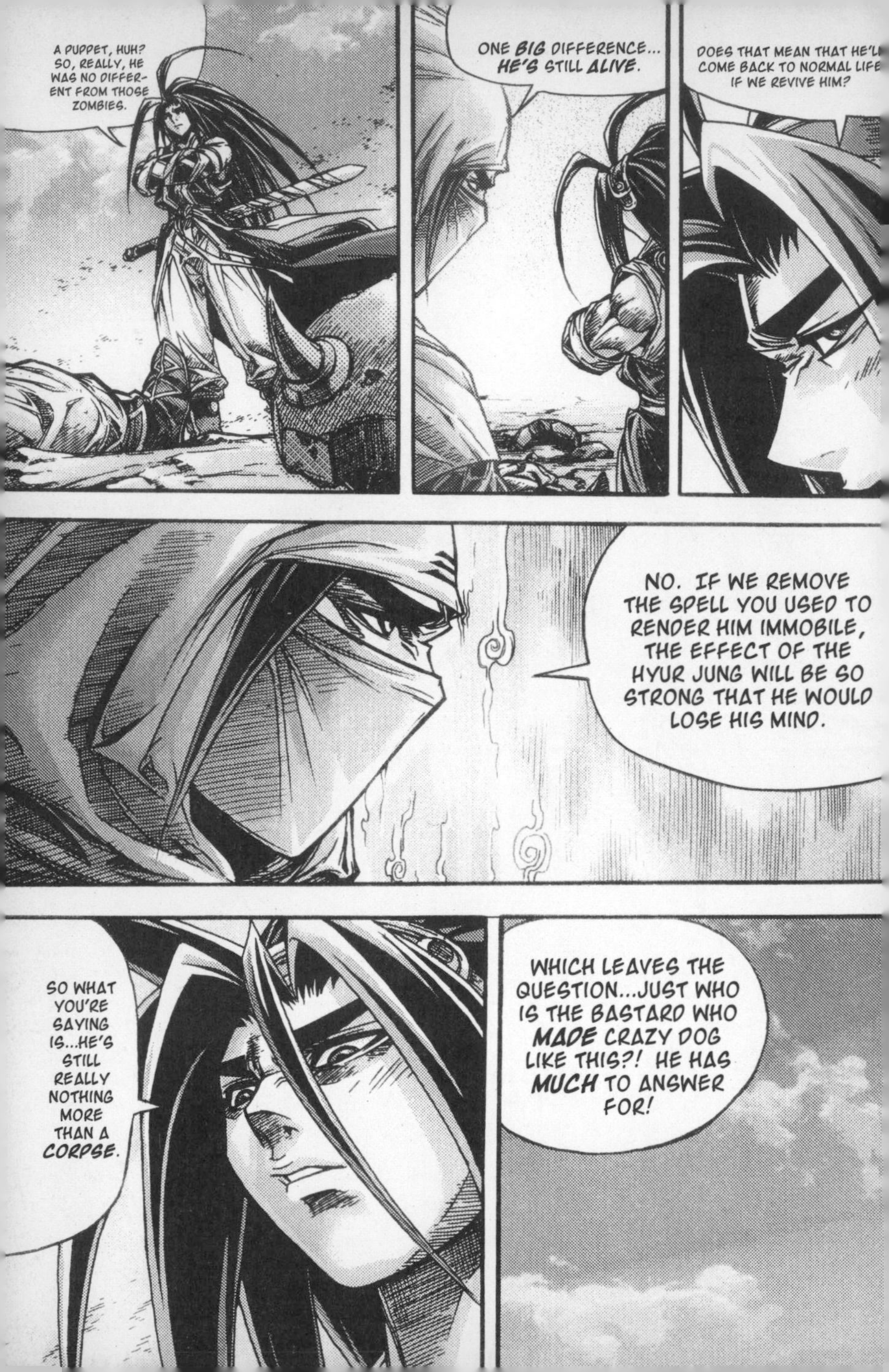
A PUPPET, HUH? SO, REALLY, HE WAS NO DIFFERENT FROM THOSE ZOMBIES.
ONE BIG DIFFERENCE... HE'S STILL ALIVE.
DOES THAT MEAN THAT HE'LL COME BACK TO NORMAL LIFE IF WE REVIVE HIM?
NO. IF WE REMOVE THE SPELL YOU USED TO RENDER HIM IMMOBILE, THE EFFECT OF THE HYUR JUNG WILL BE SO STRONG THAT HE WOULD LOSE HIS MIND.
SO WHAT YOU'RE SAYING IS...HE'S STILL REALLY NOTHING MORE THAN A CORPSE.
WHICH LEAVES THE QUESTION...JUST WHO IS THE BASTARD WHO MADE CRAZY DOG LIKE THIS?! HE HAS MUCH TO ANSWER FOR!

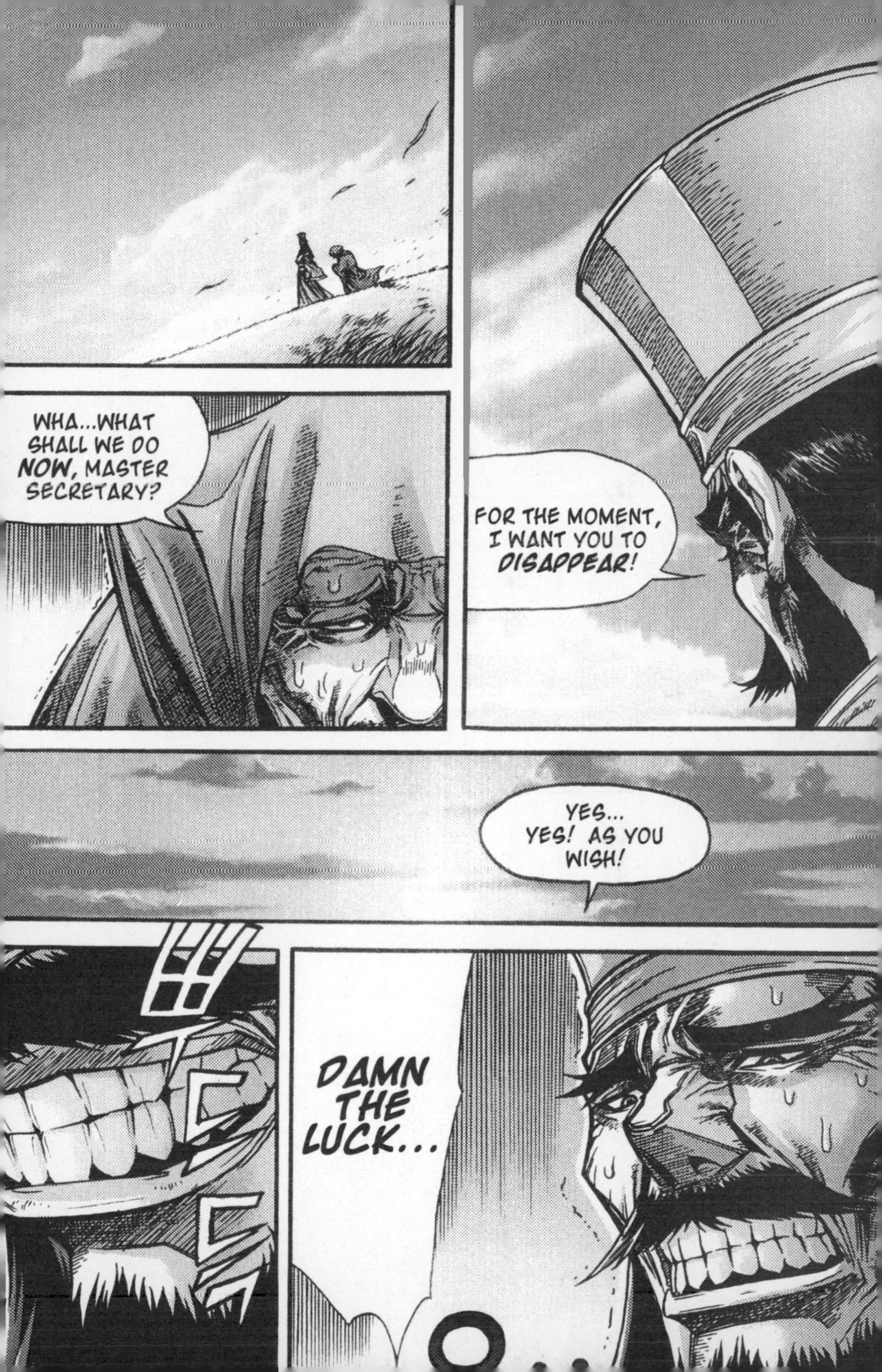
WHA...WHAT SHALL WE DO NOW, MASTER SECRETARY?
FOR THE MOMENT, I WANT YOU TO DISAPPEAR!
YES... YES! AS YOU WISH!
DAMN THE LUCK...

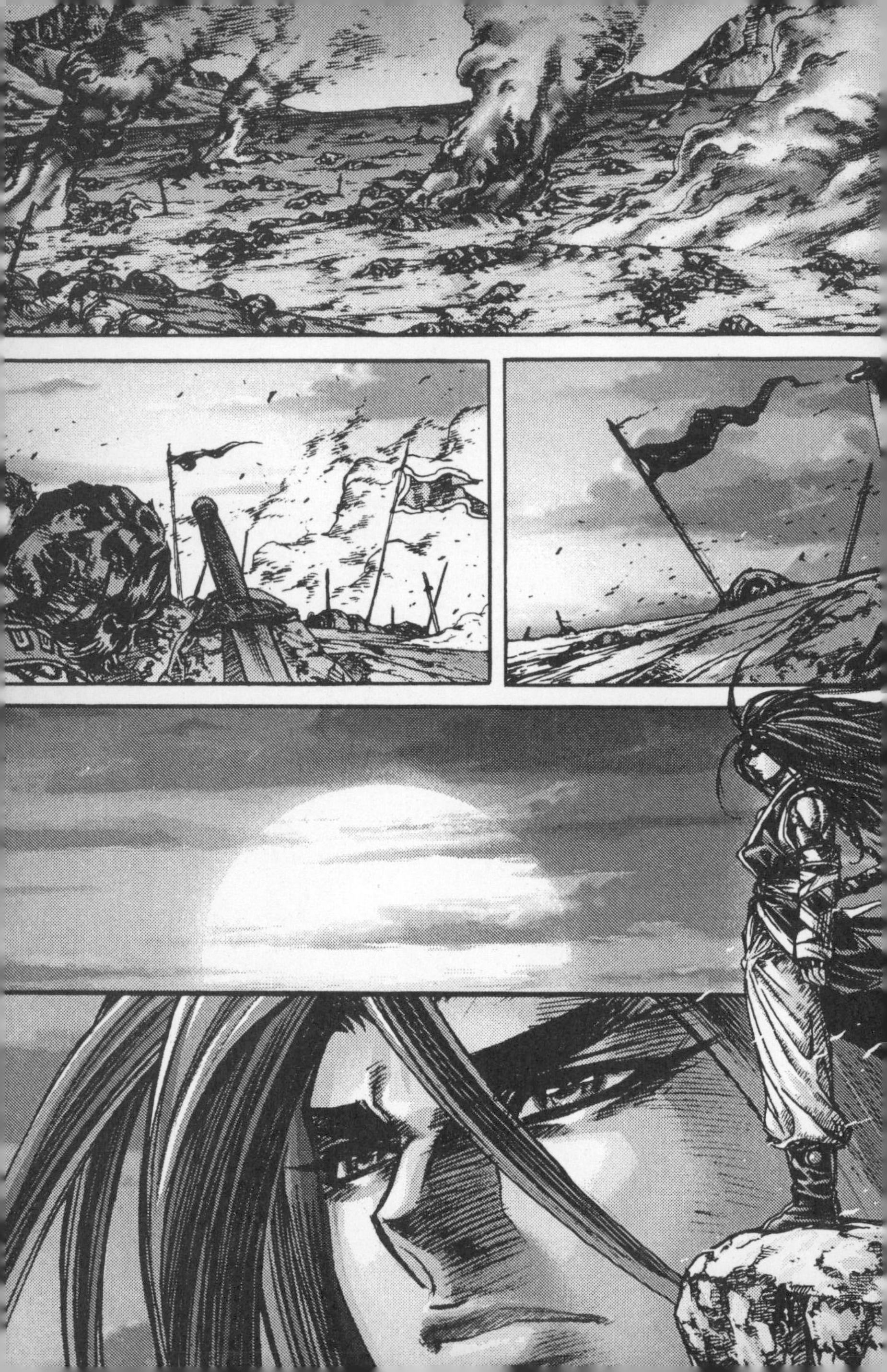

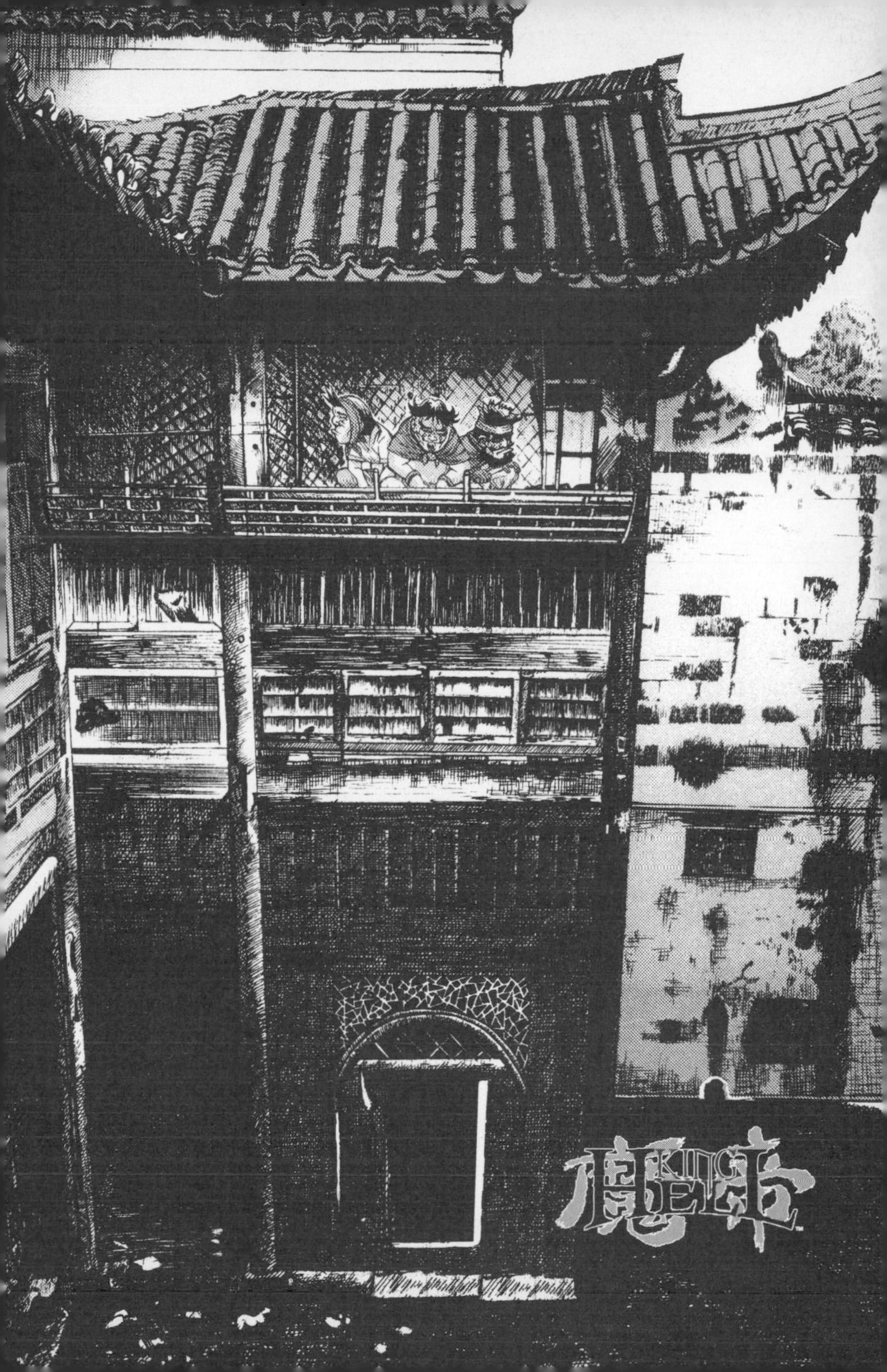

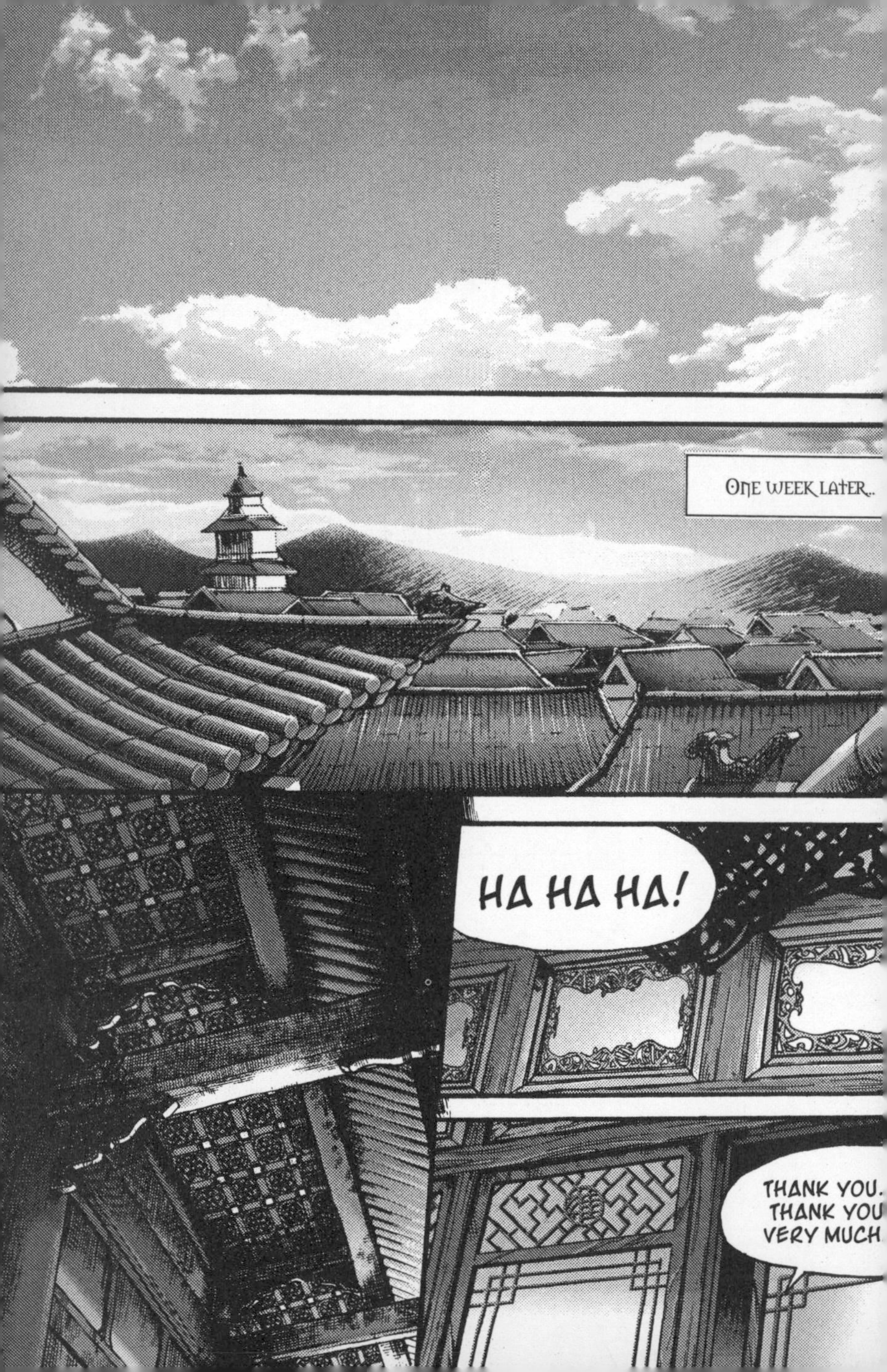
One week later..
HA HA HA!
THANK YOU. THANK YOU VERY MUCH.

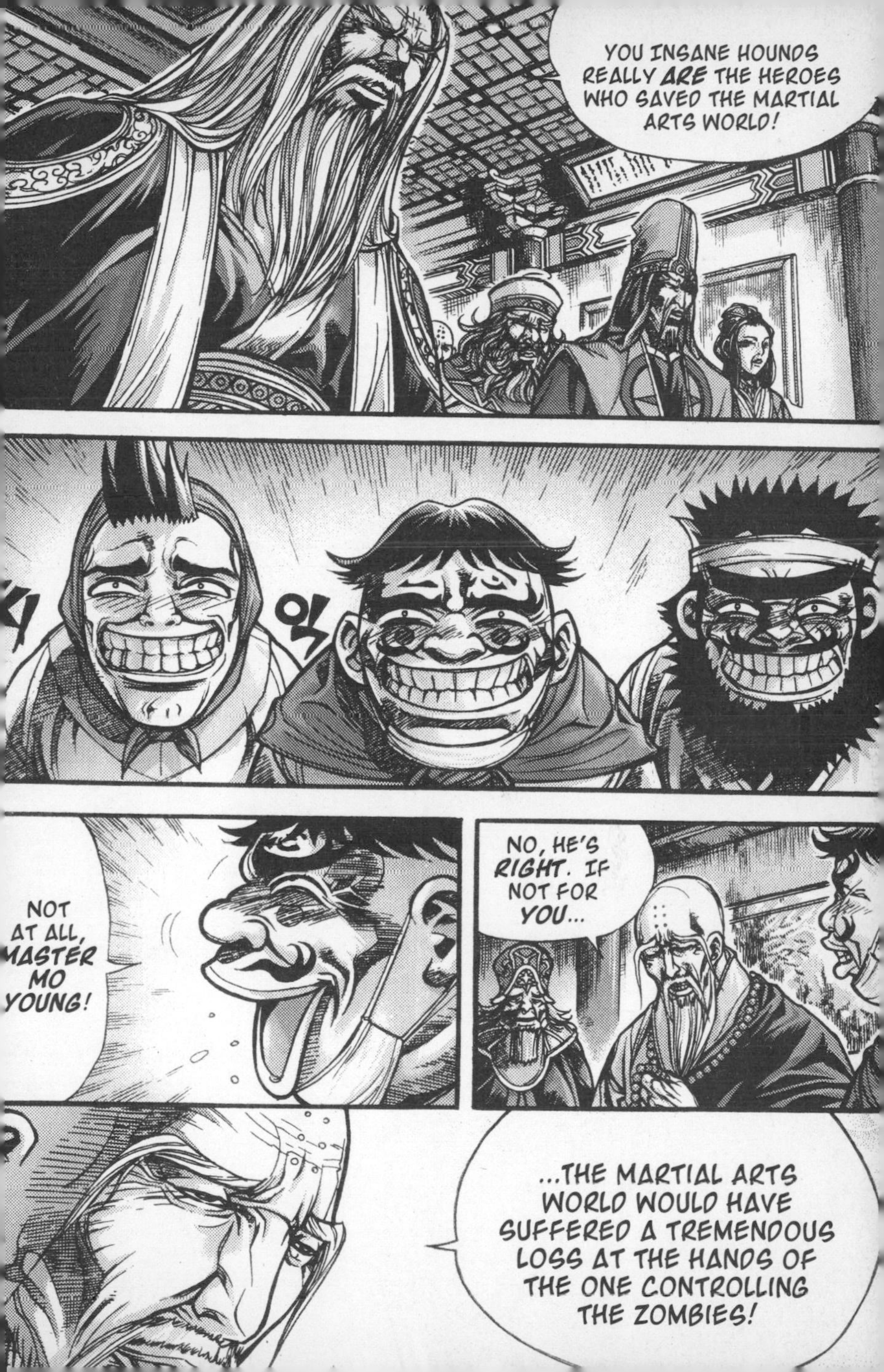
YOU INSANE HOUNDS REALLY *ARE* THE HEROES WHO SAVED THE MARTIAL ARTS WORLD!
NOT AT ALL, MASTER MO YOUNG!
NO, HE'S *RIGHT*. IF NOT FOR *YOU*...
...THE MARTIAL ARTS WORLD WOULD HAVE SUFFERED A TREMENDOUS LOSS AT THE HANDS OF THE ONE CONTROLLING THE ZOMBIES!

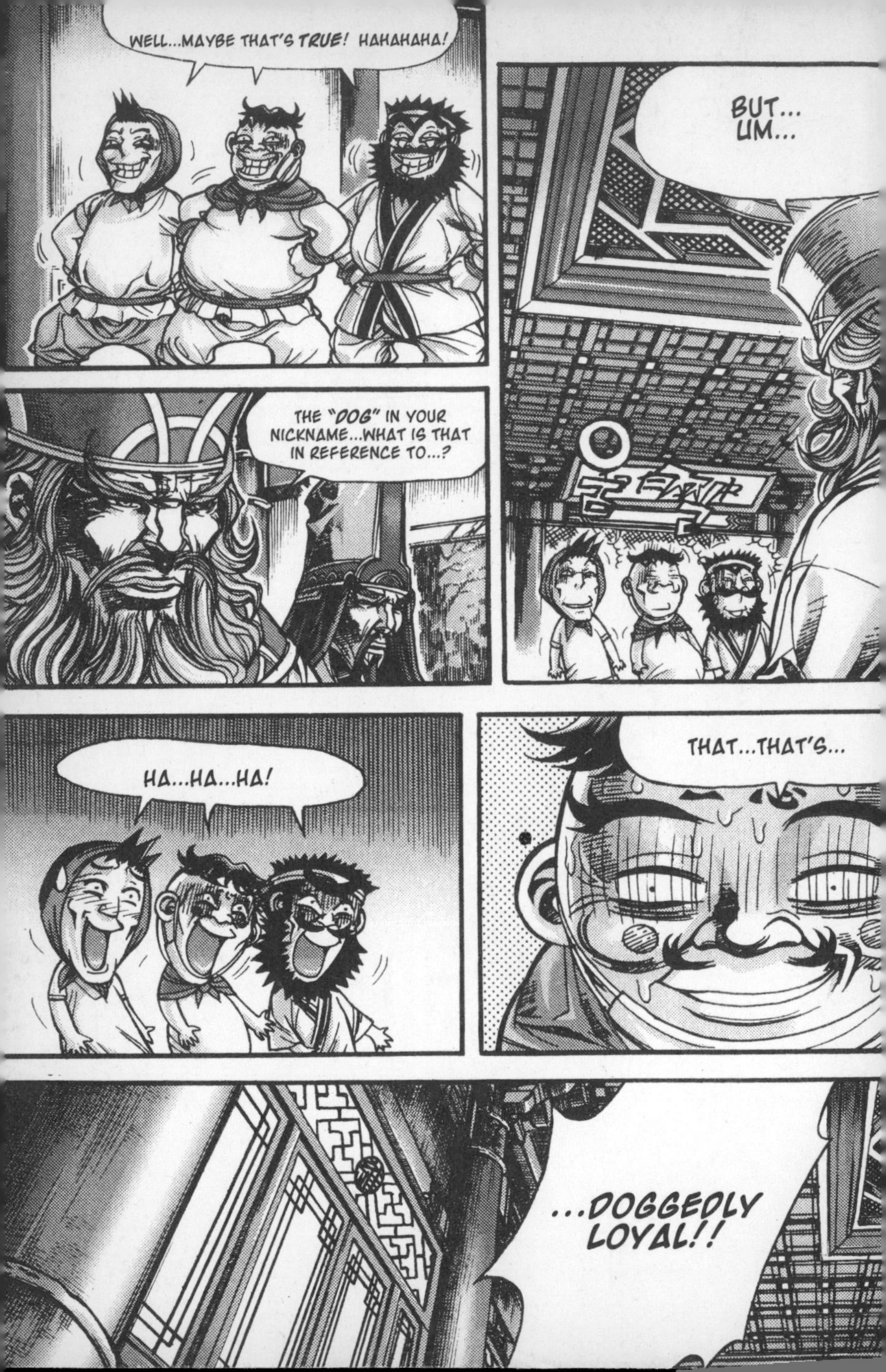
WELL...MAYBE THAT'S TRUE! HAHAHAHA!
BUT... UM...
THE "DOG" IN YOUR NICKNAME...WHAT IS THAT IN REFERENCE TO...?
HA...HA...HA!
THAT...THAT'S...
...DOGGEDLY LOYAL!!

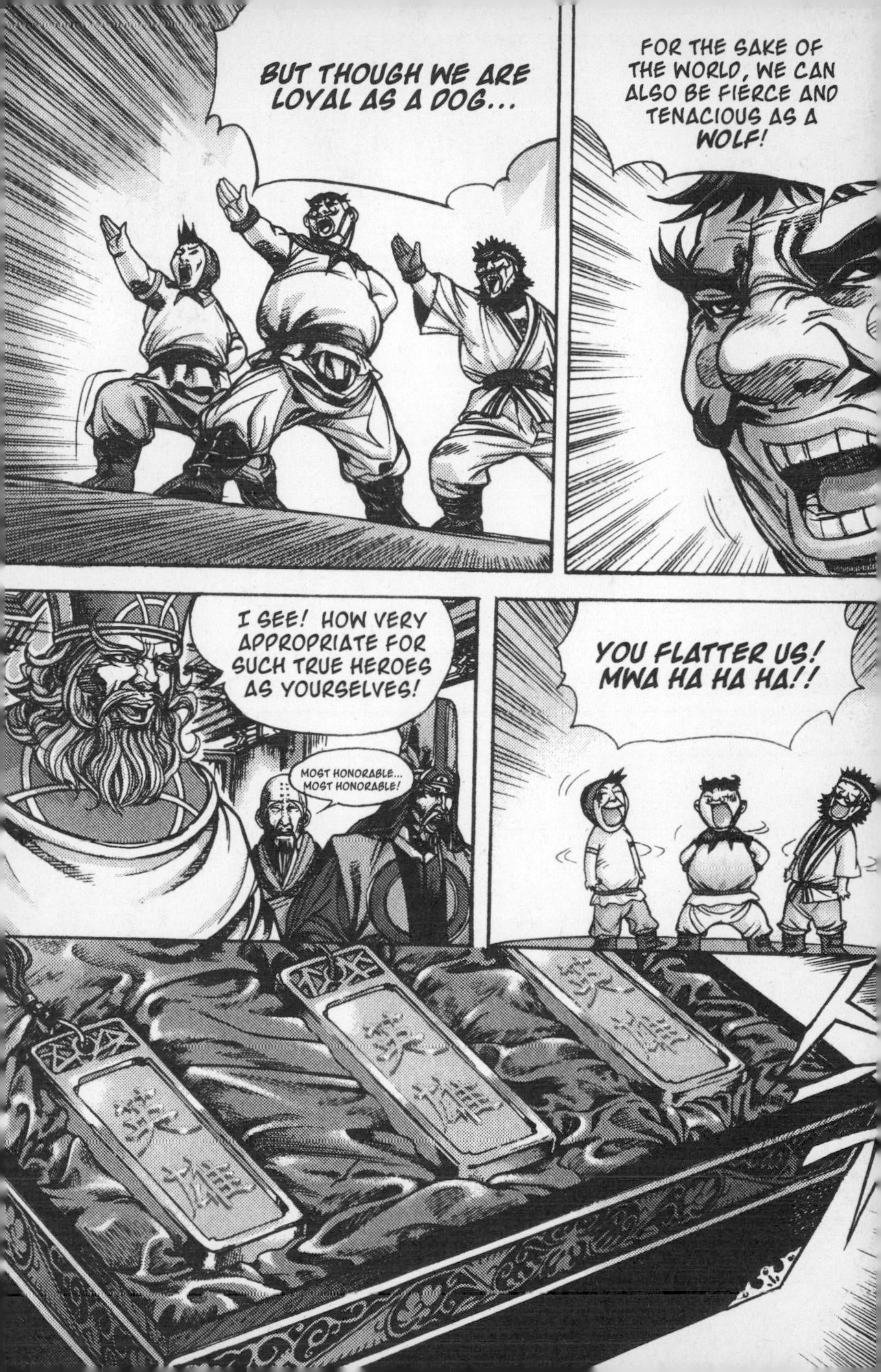
BUT THOUGH WE ARE LOYAL AS A DOG...
FOR THE SAKE OF THE WORLD, WE CAN ALSO BE FIERCE AND TENACIOUS AS A WOLF!
I SEE! HOW VERY APPROPRIATE FOR SUCH TRUE HEROES AS YOURSELVES!
MOST HONORABLE... MOST HONORABLE!
YOU FLATTER US! MWA HA HA HA!!

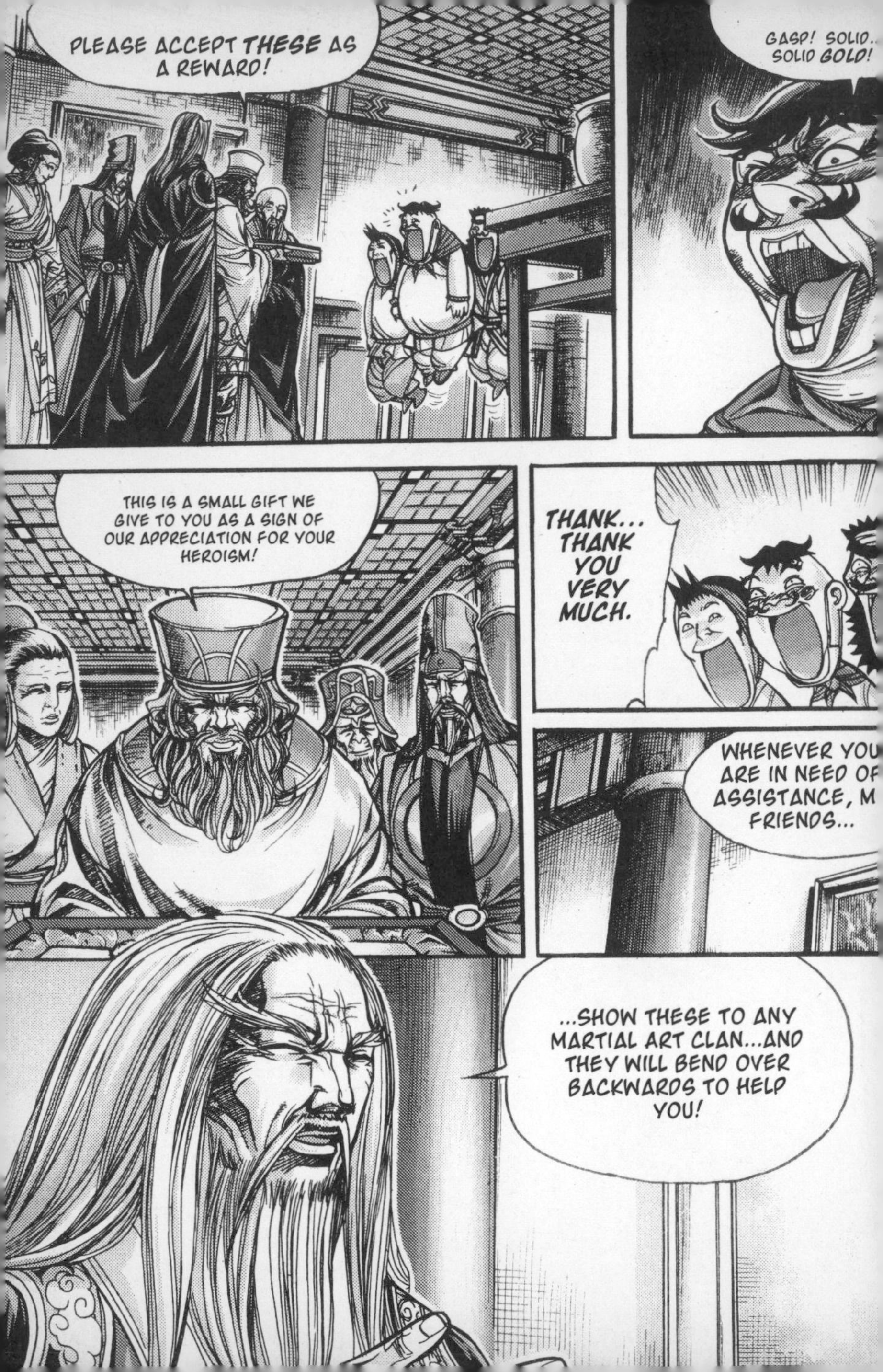
PLEASE ACCEPT THESE AS A REWARD!
GASP! SOLID... SOLID GOLD!
THIS IS A SMALL GIFT WE GIVE TO YOU AS A SIGN OF OUR APPRECIATION FOR YOUR HEROISM!
THANK... THANK YOU VERY MUCH.
WHENEVER YOU ARE IN NEED OF ASSISTANCE, M FRIENDS...
...SHOW THESE TO ANY MARTIAL ART CLAN...AND THEY WILL BEND OVER BACKWARDS TO HELP YOU!

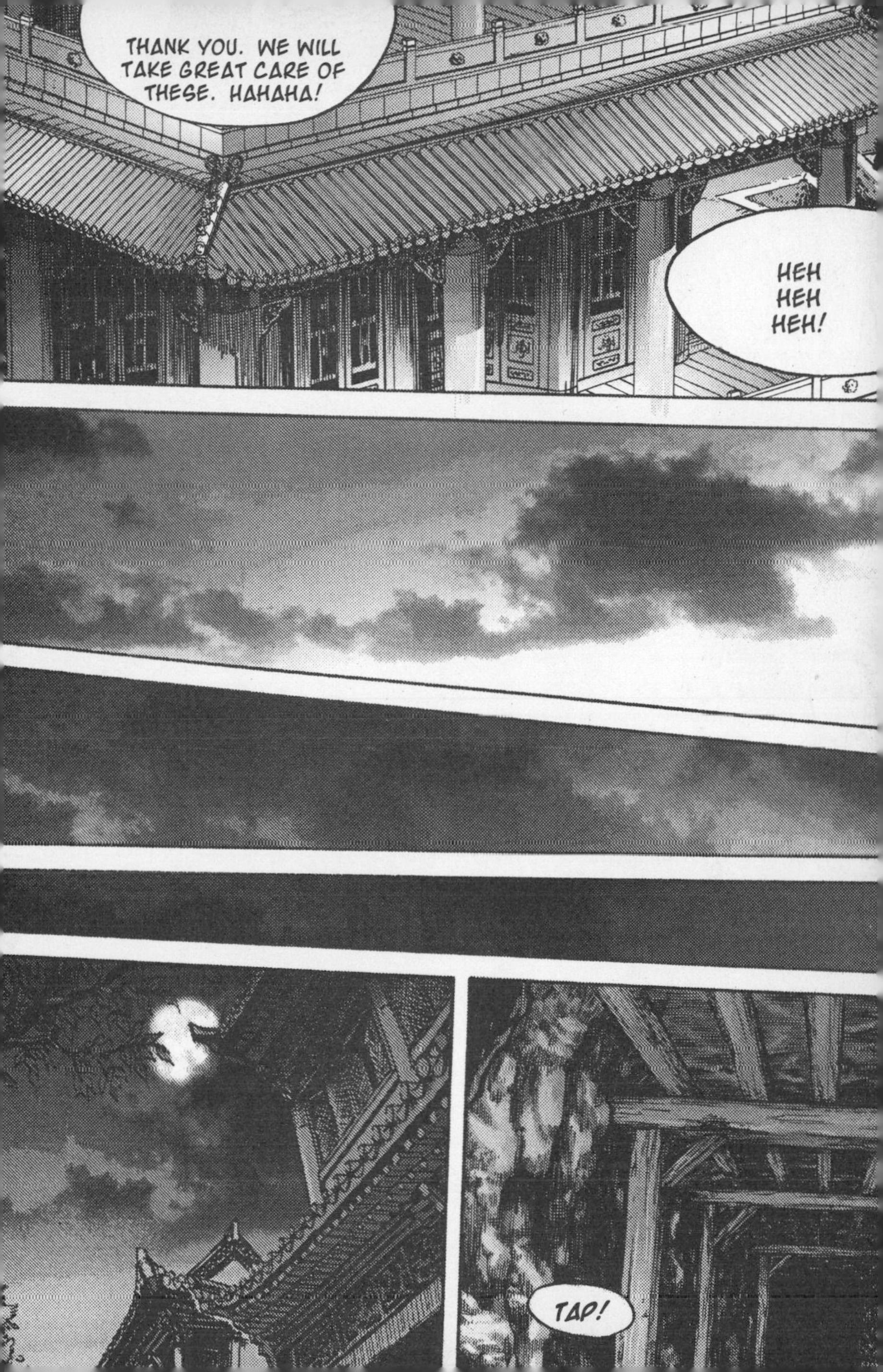
THANK YOU. WE WILL TAKE GREAT CARE OF THESE. HAHAHA!
HEH HEH HEH!
TAP!

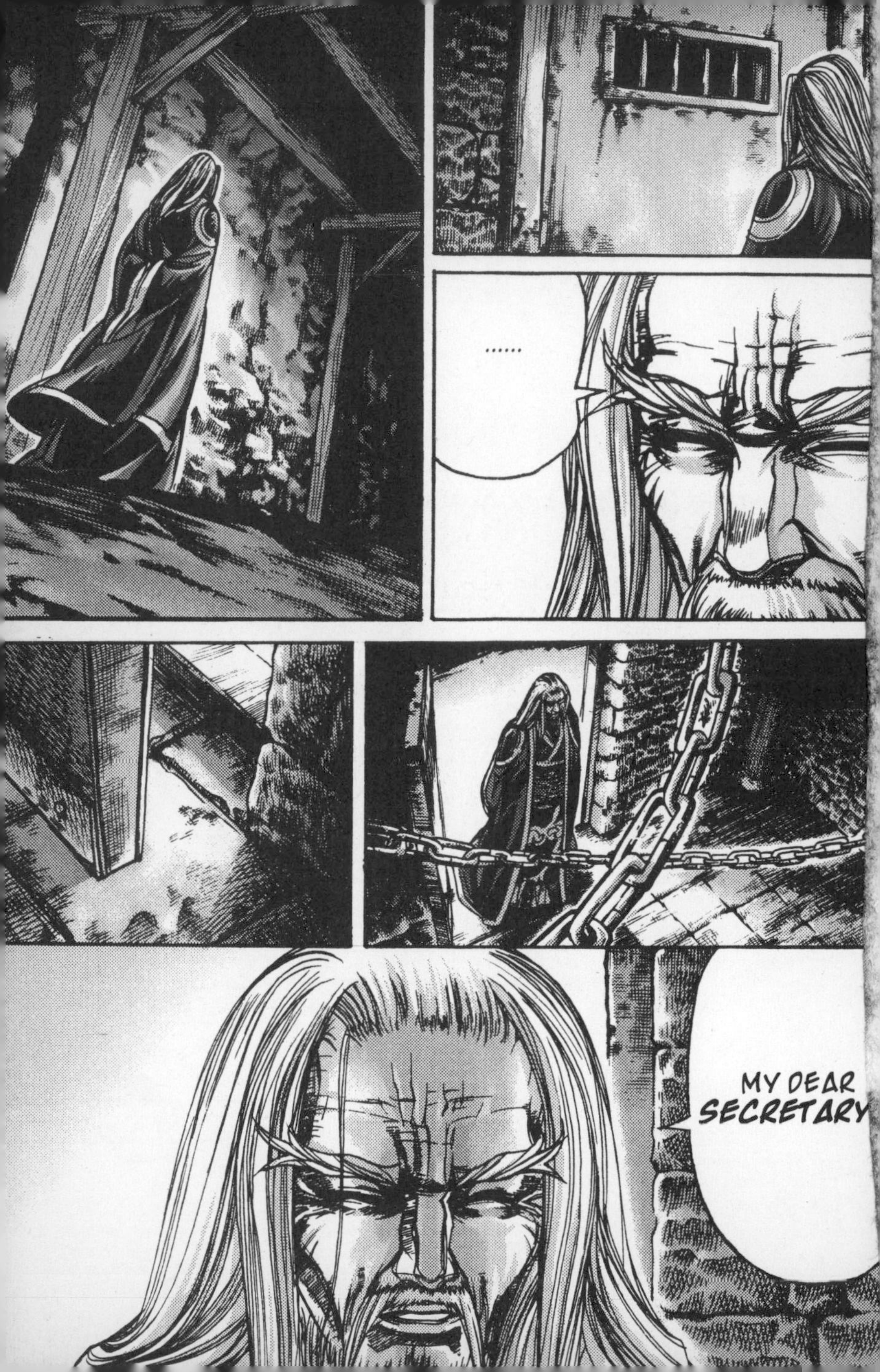

......
MY DEAR SECRETARY

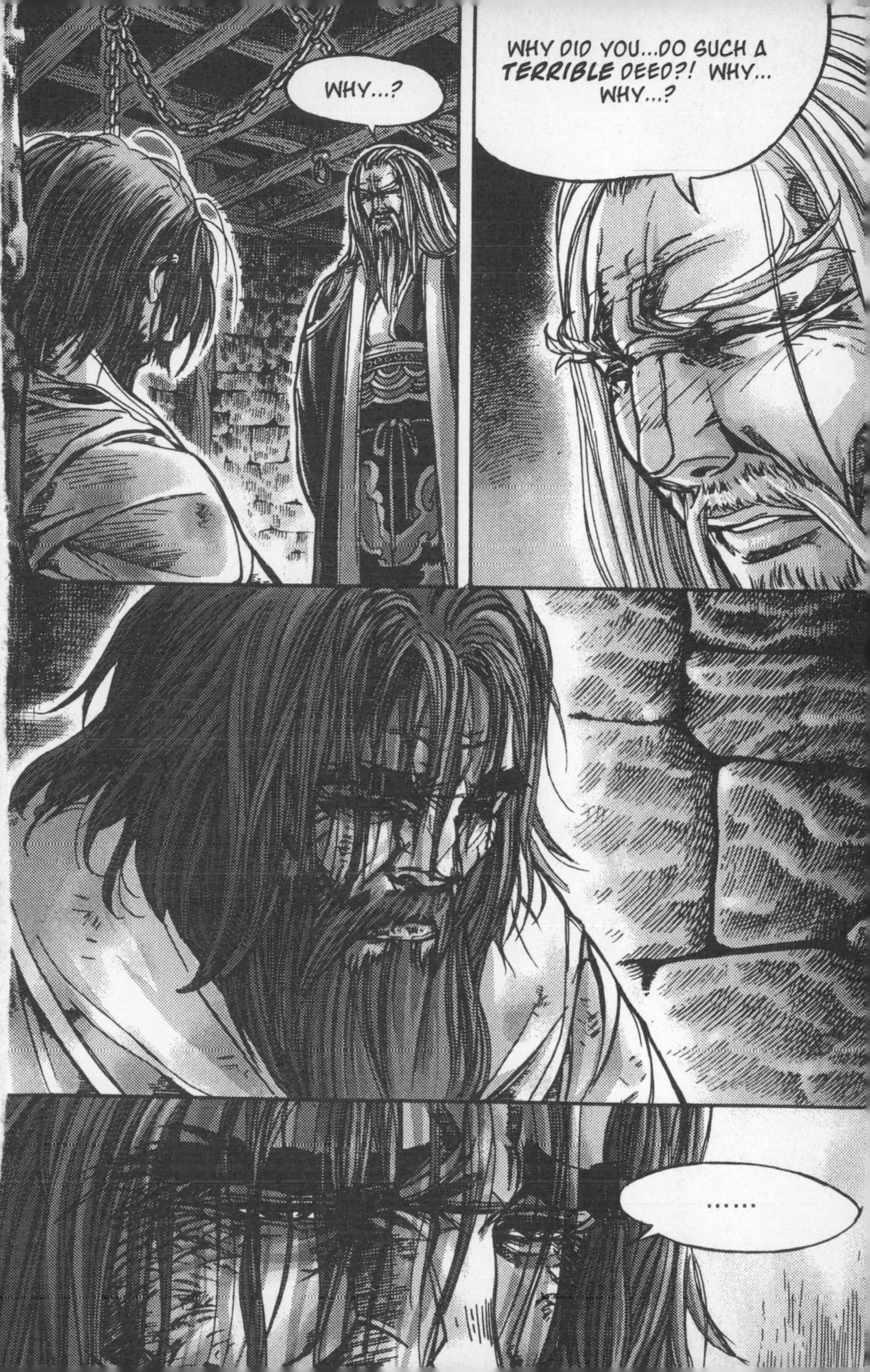
WHY...?
WHY DID YOU...DO SUCH A TERRIBLE DEED?! WHY... WHY...?
......

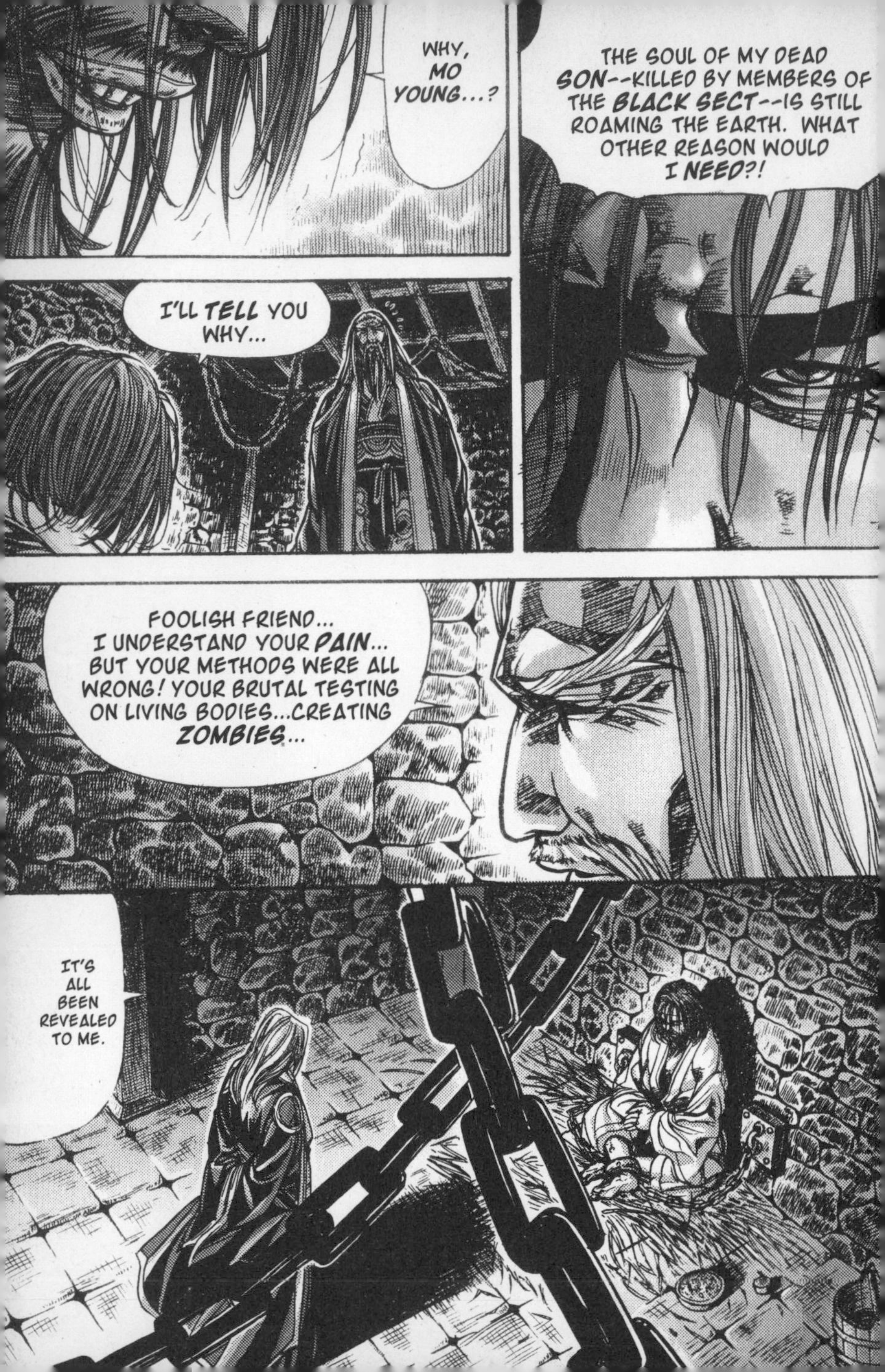
WHY, MO YOUNG...?
THE SOUL OF MY DEAD SON--KILLED BY MEMBERS OF THE BLACK SECT--IS STILL ROAMING THE EARTH. WHAT OTHER REASON WOULD I NEED?!
I'LL TELL YOU WHY...
FOOLISH FRIEND... I UNDERSTAND YOUR PAIN... BUT YOUR METHODS WERE ALL WRONG! YOUR BRUTAL TESTING ON LIVING BODIES...CREATING ZOMBIES...
IT'S ALL BEEN REVEALED TO ME.

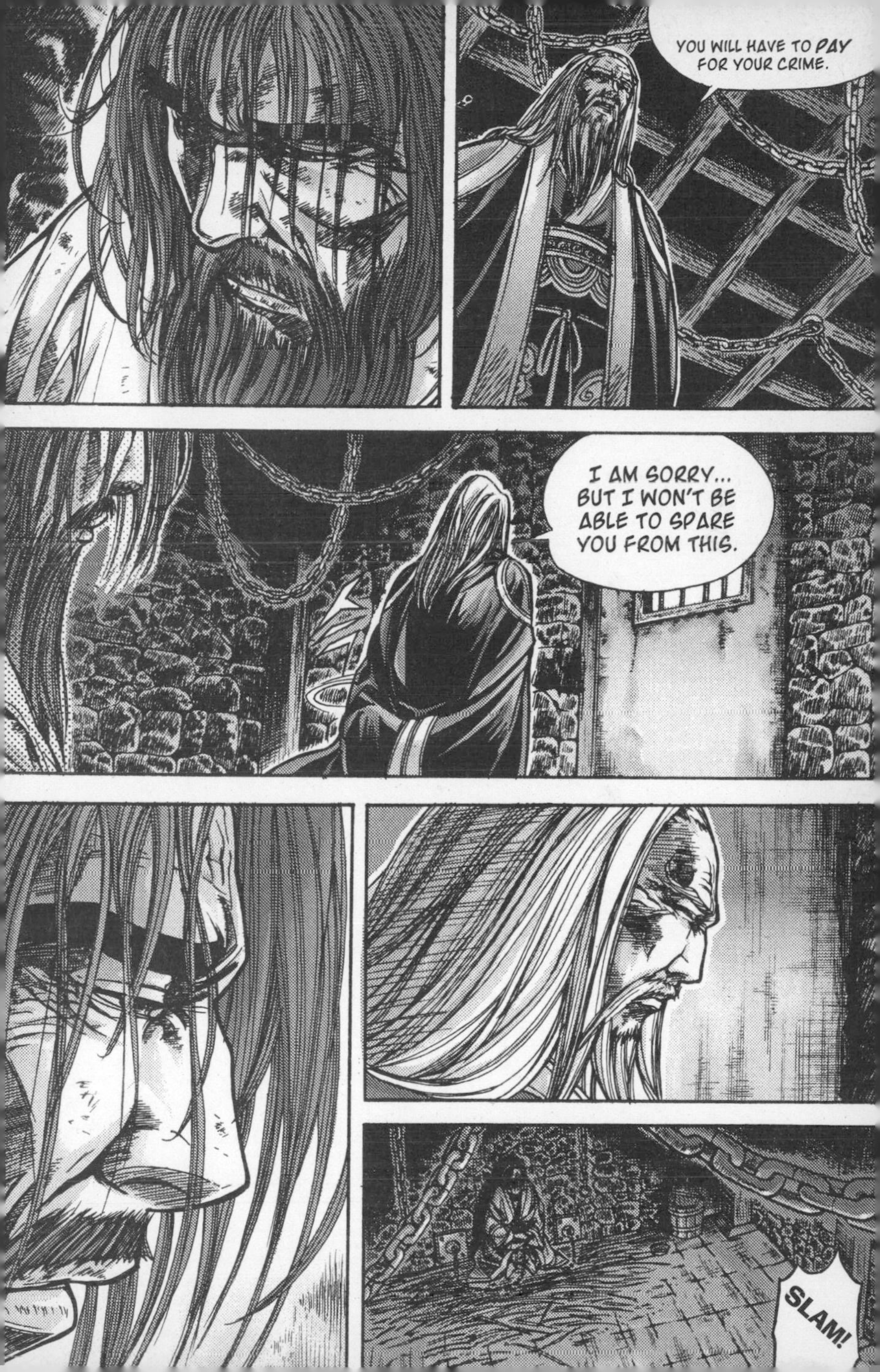
YOU WILL HAVE TO PAY FOR YOUR CRIME.
I AM SORRY... BUT I WON'T BE ABLE TO SPARE YOU FROM THIS.
SLAM!

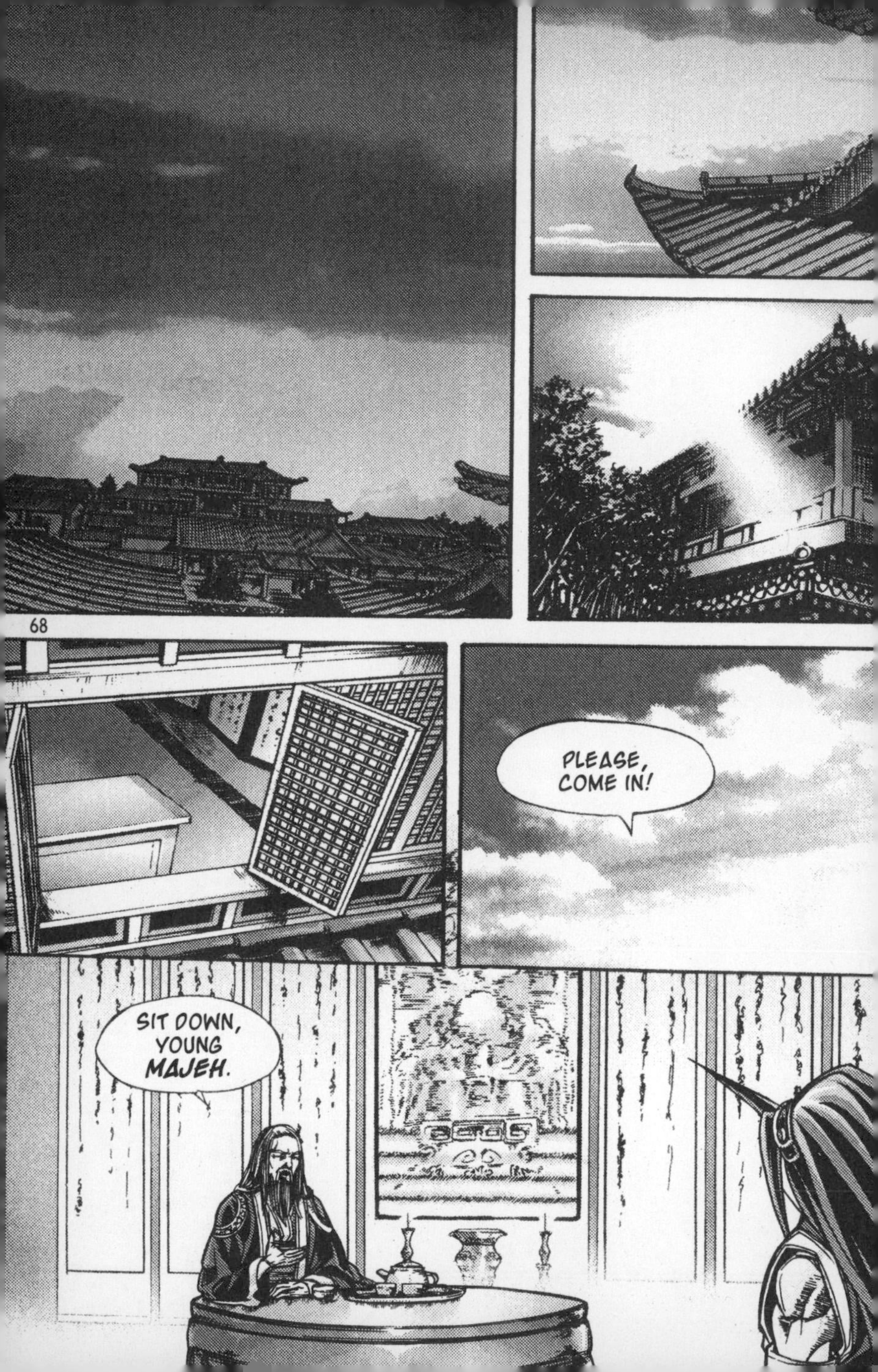
PLEASE, COME IN!
SIT DOWN, YOUNG MAJEH.

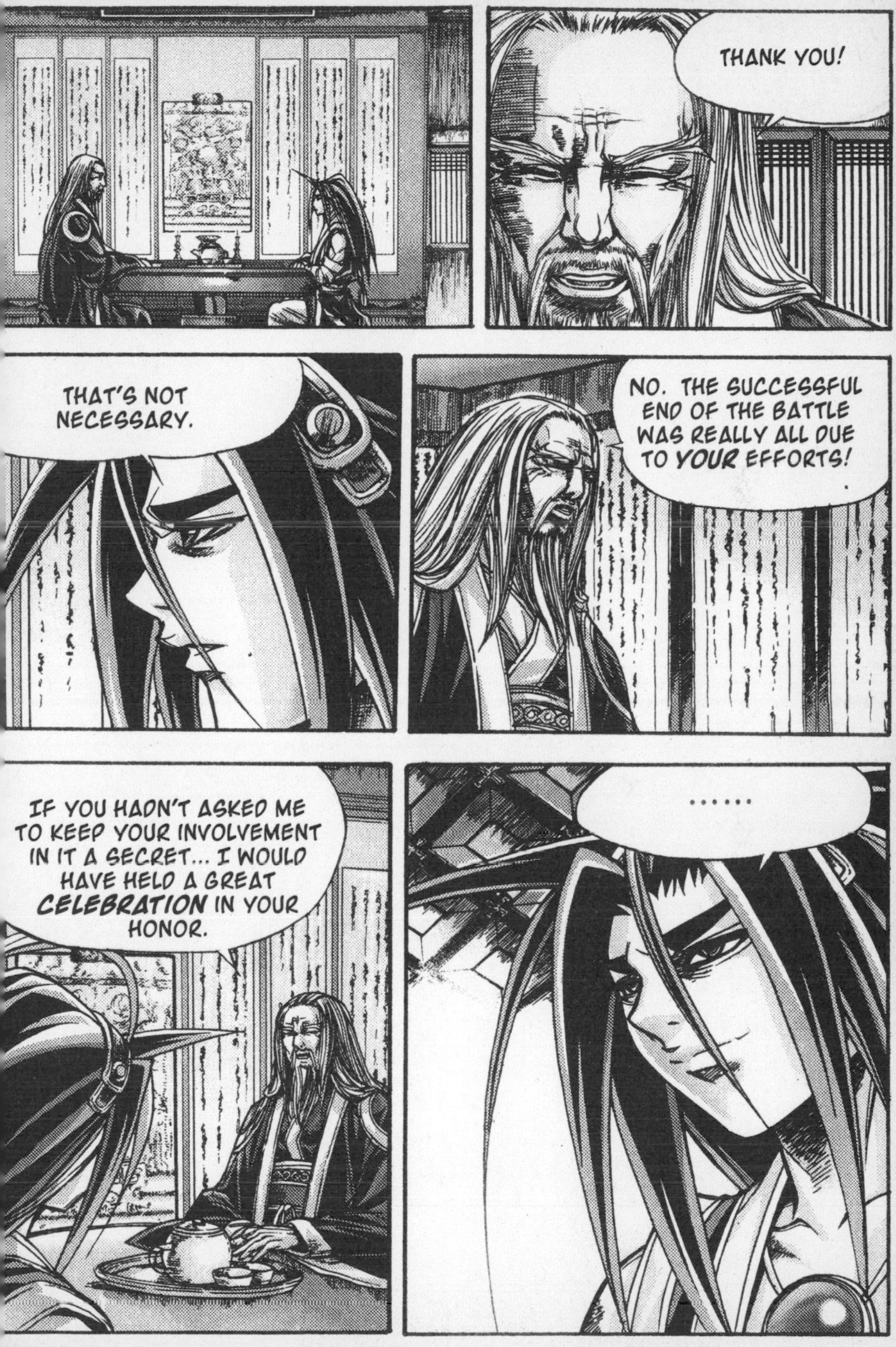
THANK YOU!
THAT'S NOT NECESSARY.
NO. THE SUCCESSFUL END OF THE BATTLE WAS REALLY ALL DUE TO YOUR EFFORTS!
IF YOU HADN'T ASKED ME TO KEEP YOUR INVOLVEMENT IN IT A SECRET... I WOULD HAVE HELD A GREAT CELEBRATION IN YOUR HONOR.
......

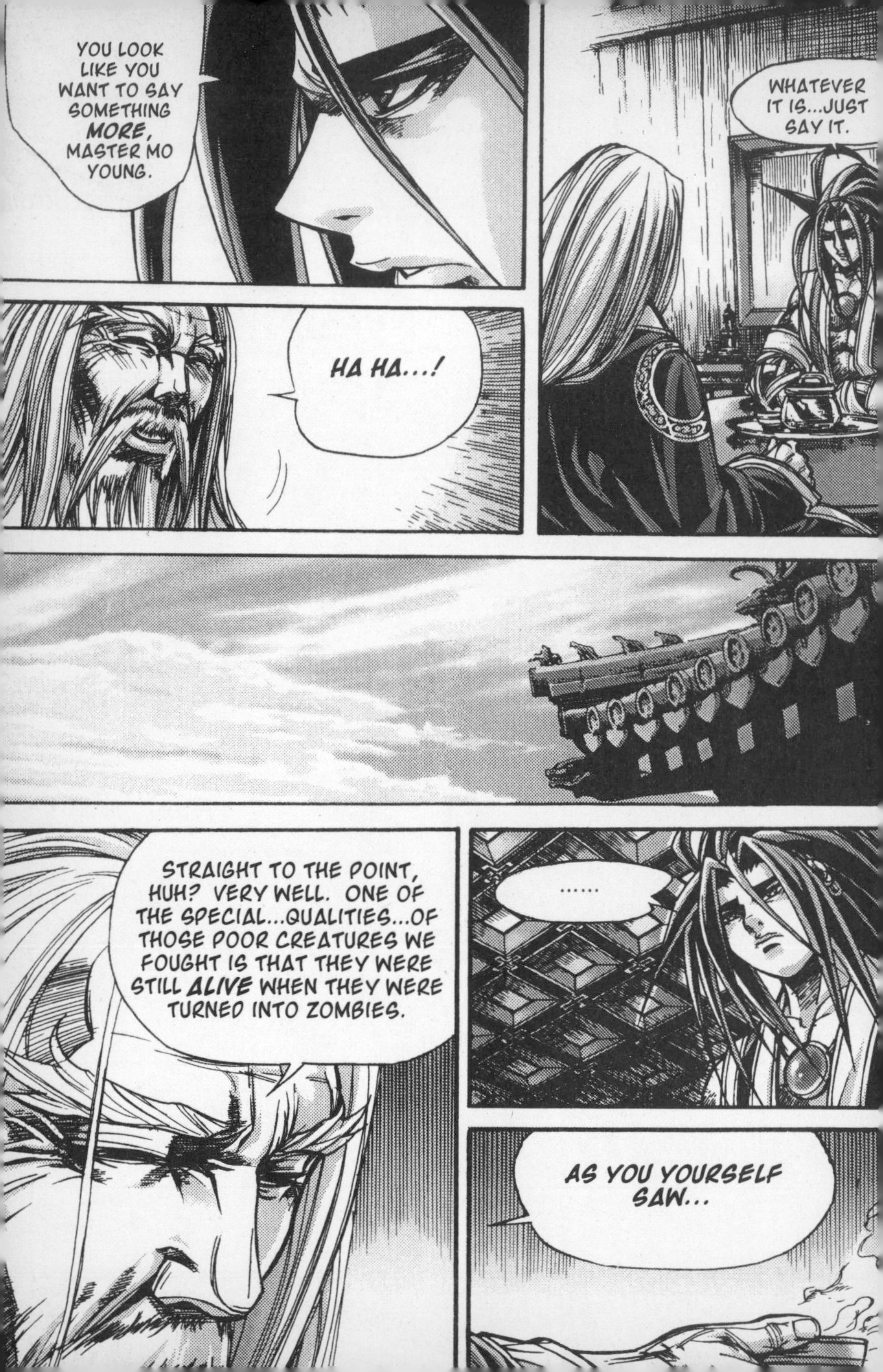
YOU LOOK LIKE YOU WANT TO SAY SOMETHING MORE, MASTER MO YOUNG.
HA HA...!
WHATEVER IT IS...JUST SAY IT.
STRAIGHT TO THE POINT, HUH? VERY WELL. ONE OF THE SPECIAL...QUALITIES...OF THOSE POOR CREATURES WE FOUGHT IS THAT THEY WERE STILL ALIVE WHEN THEY WERE TURNED INTO ZOMBIES.
......
AS YOU YOURSELF SAW...

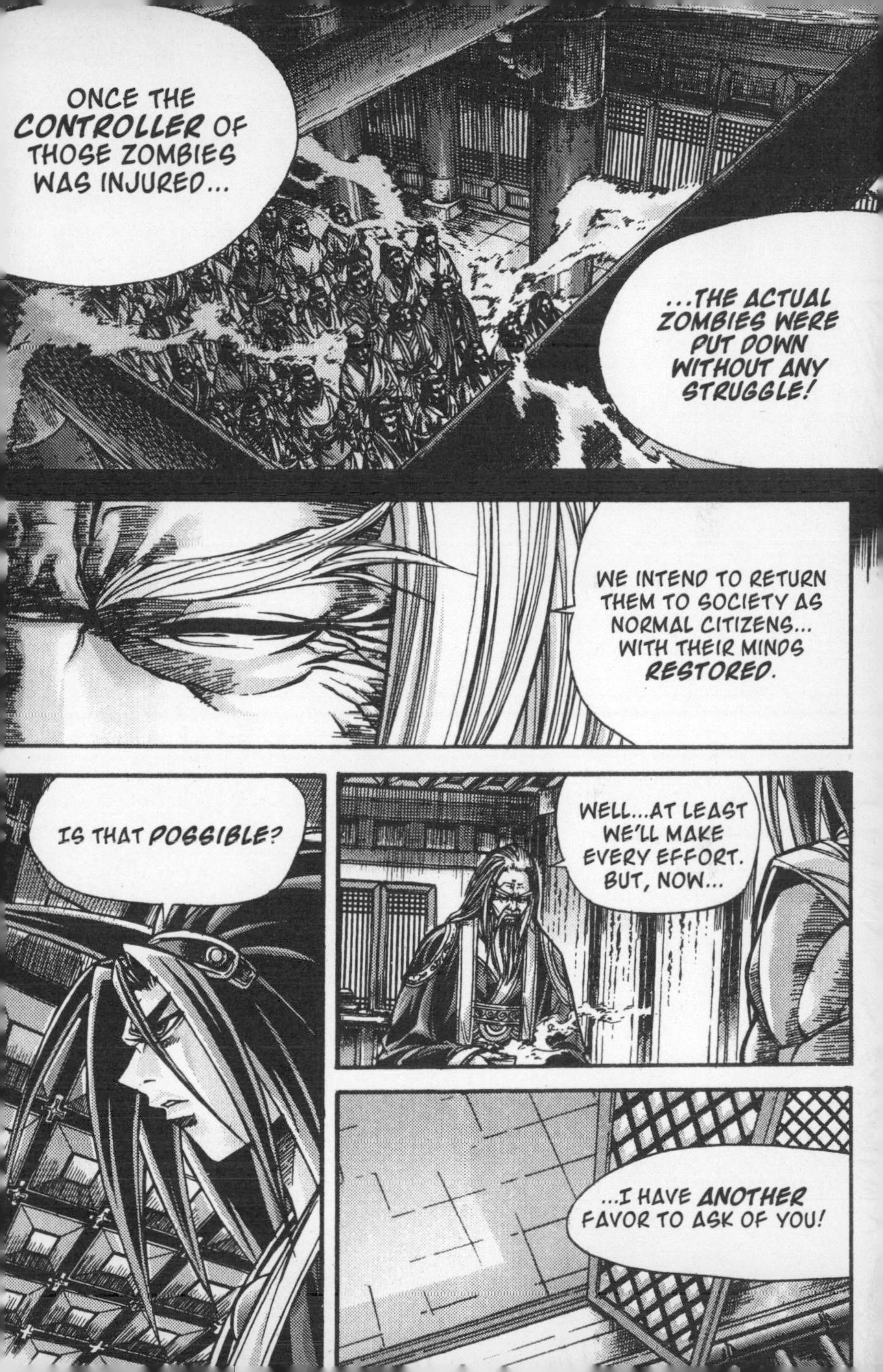
ONCE THE CONTROLLER OF THOSE ZOMBIES WAS INJURED...
...THE ACTUAL ZOMBIES WERE PUT DOWN WITHOUT ANY STRUGGLE!
WE INTEND TO RETURN THEM TO SOCIETY AS NORMAL CITIZENS... WITH THEIR MINDS RESTORED.
IS THAT POSSIBLE?
WELL...AT LEAST WE'LL MAKE EVERY EFFORT. BUT, NOW...
...I HAVE ANOTHER FAVOR TO ASK OF YOU!

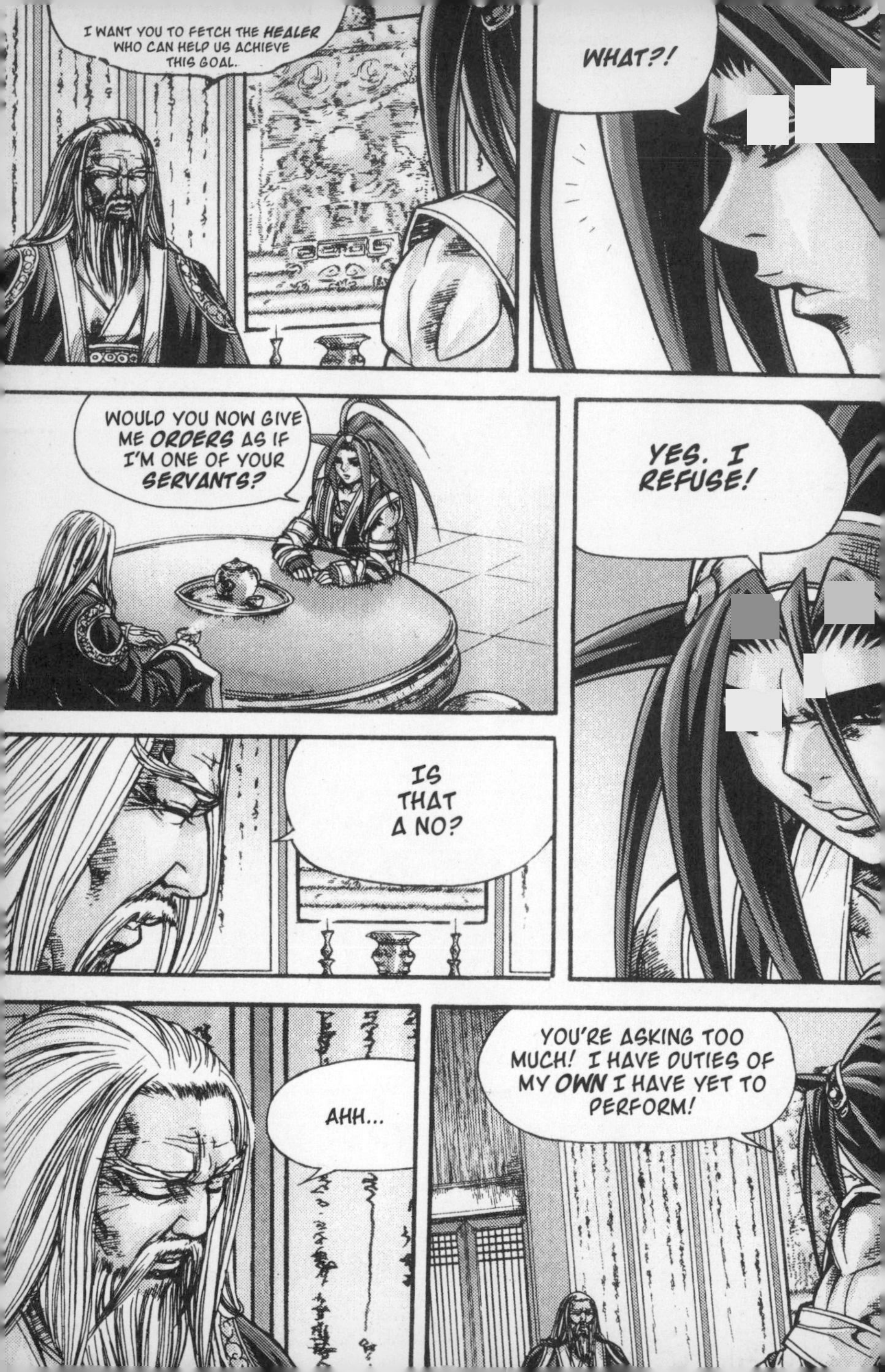
I WANT YOU TO FETCH THE HEALER WHO CAN HELP US ACHIEVE THIS GOAL.
WHAT?!
WOULD YOU NOW GIVE ME ORDERS AS IF I'M ONE OF YOUR SERVANTS?
IS THAT A NO?
YES. I REFUSE!
AHH...
YOU'RE ASKING TOO MUCH! I HAVE DUTIES OF MY OWN I HAVE YET TO PERFORM!

I UNDERSTAND. BUT YOU NEEDN'T ACTUALLY BRING HIM BACK HERE YOURSELF. COULD YOU AT LEAST RELAY THE MESSAGE TO HIM AS YOU'RE PASSING BY HIS DWELLING PLACE?

IF IT'S ON MY WAY... I'LL THINK ABOUT IT!

THANK YOU, MAJEH.

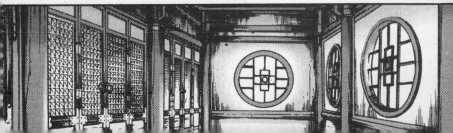

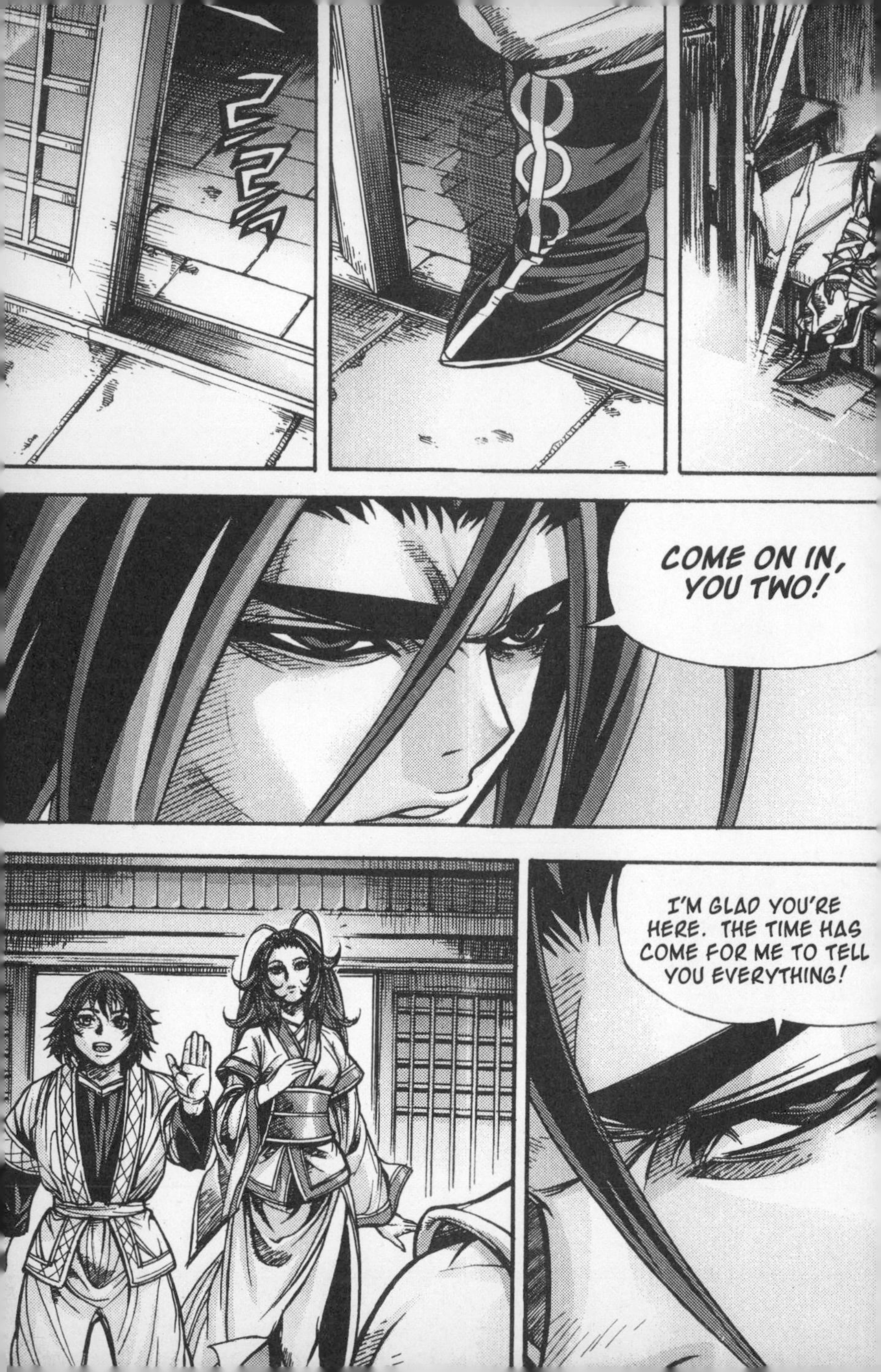
COME ON IN, YOU TWO!
I'M GLAD YOU'RE HERE. THE TIME HAS COME FOR ME TO TELL YOU EVERYTHING!

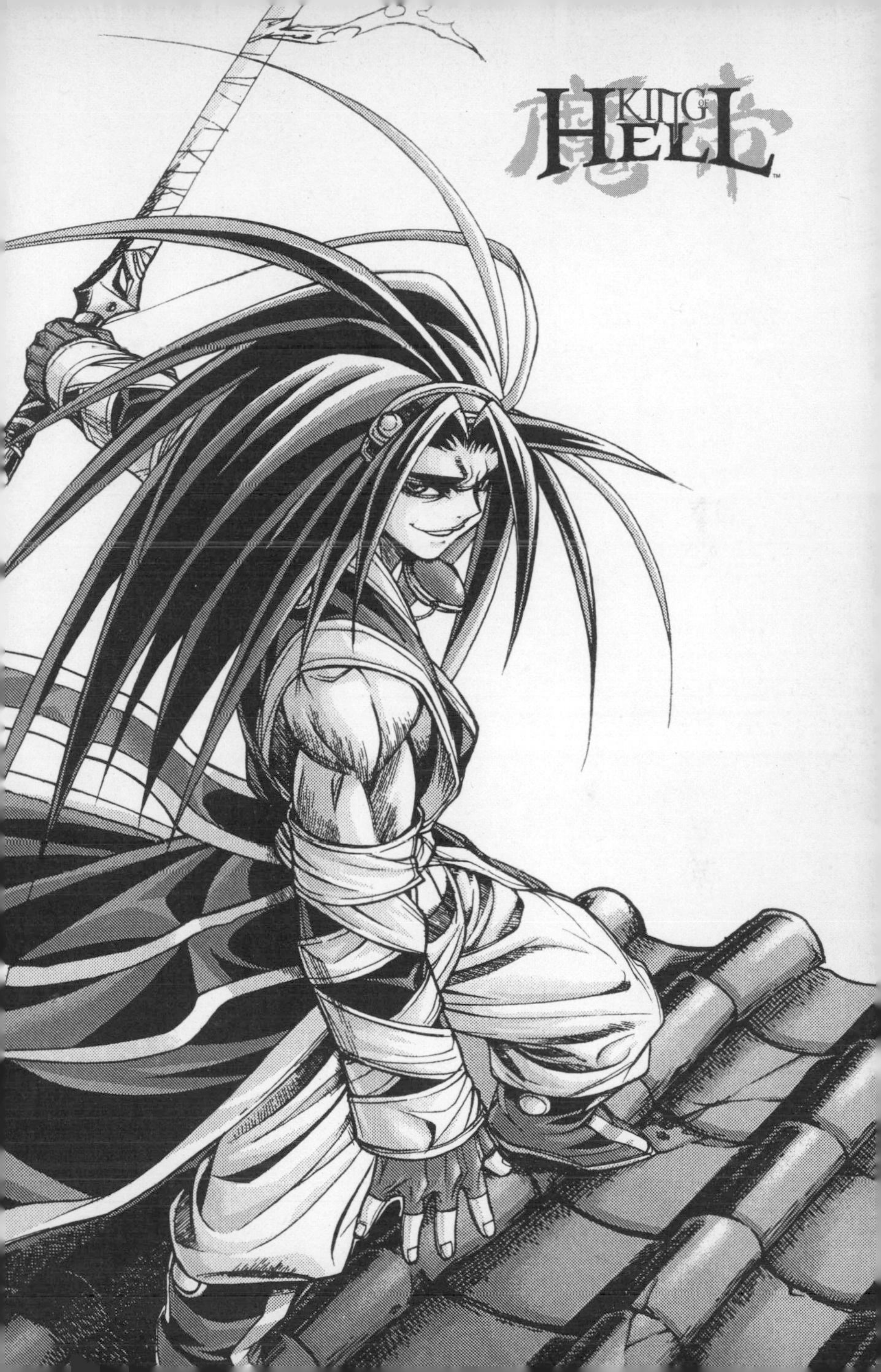
KING OF HELL

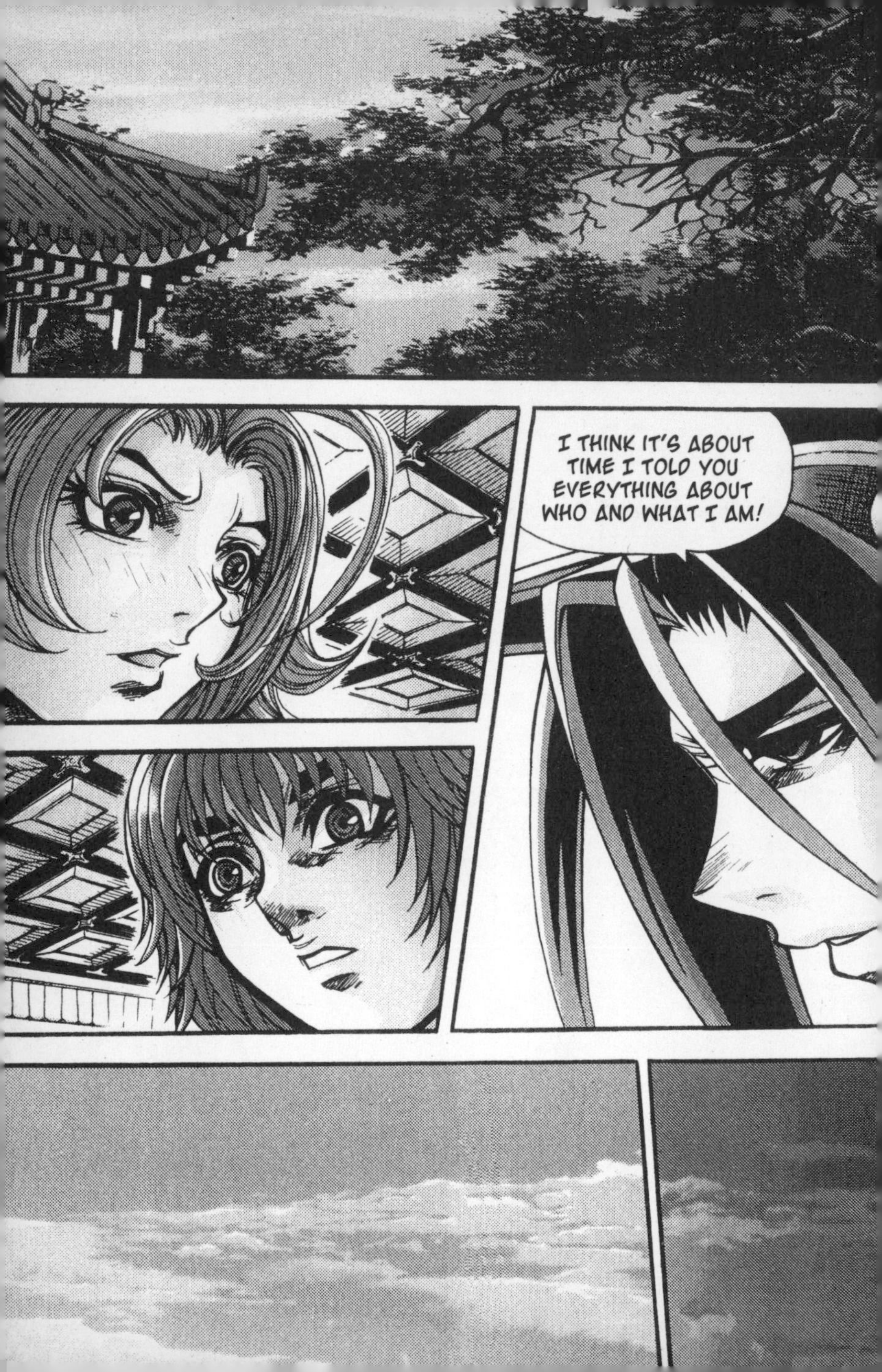
I THINK IT'S ABOUT TIME I TOLD YOU EVERYTHING ABOUT WHO AND WHAT I AM!

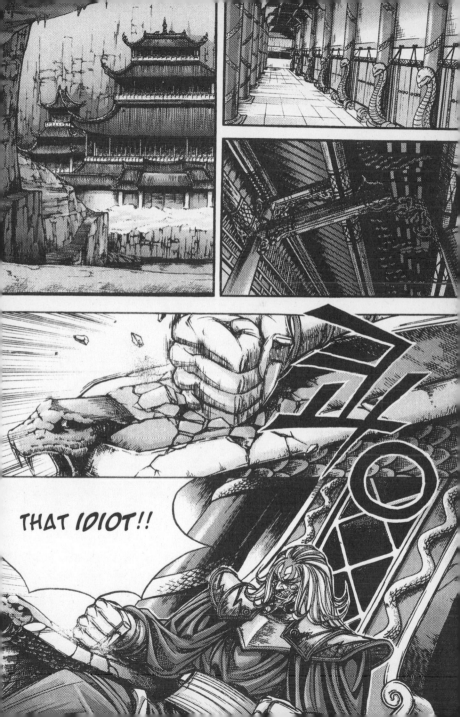

THAT *IDIOT!!*

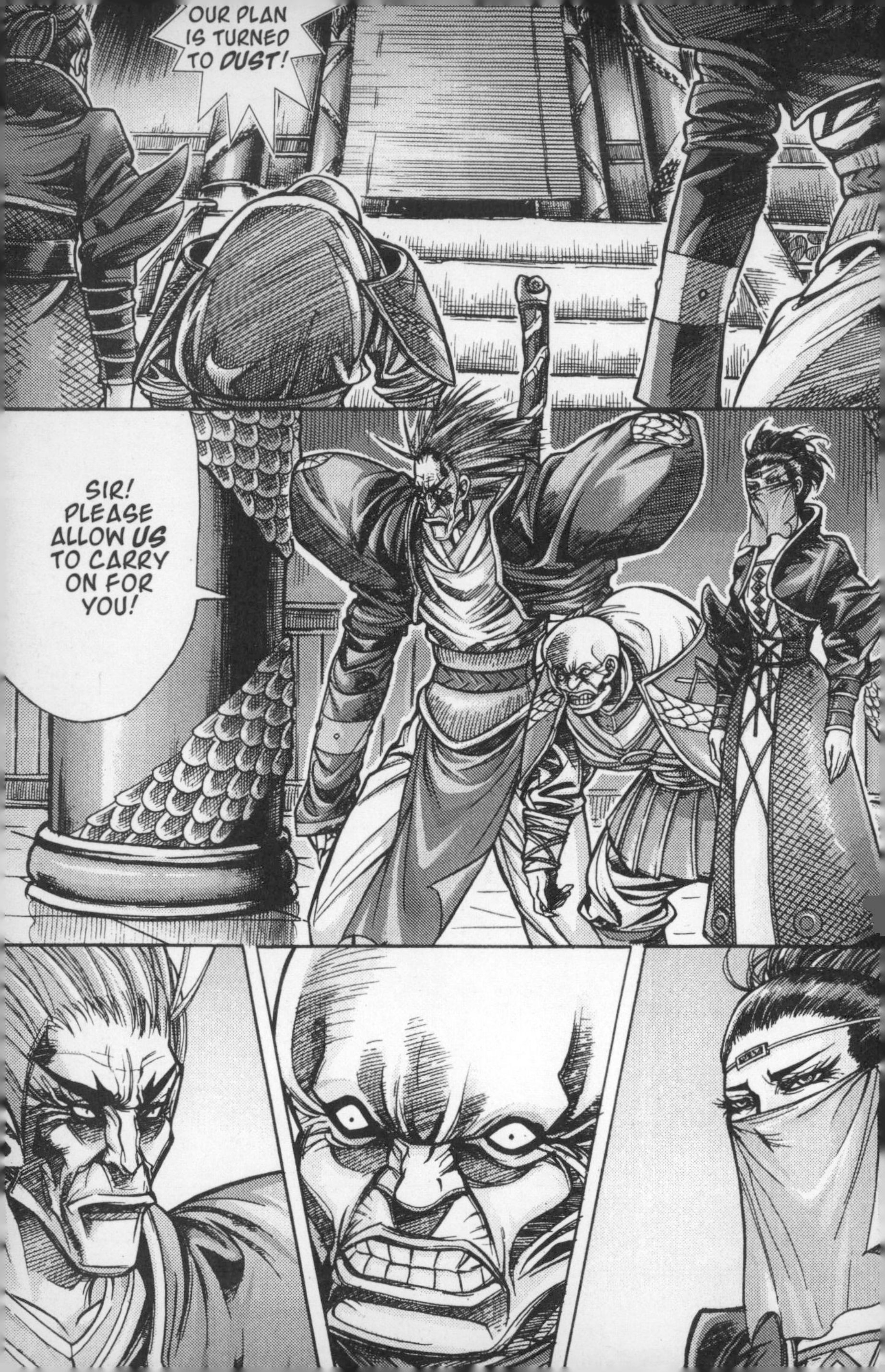
OUR PLAN IS TURNED TO DUST!
SIR! PLEASE ALLOW US TO CARRY ON FOR YOU!

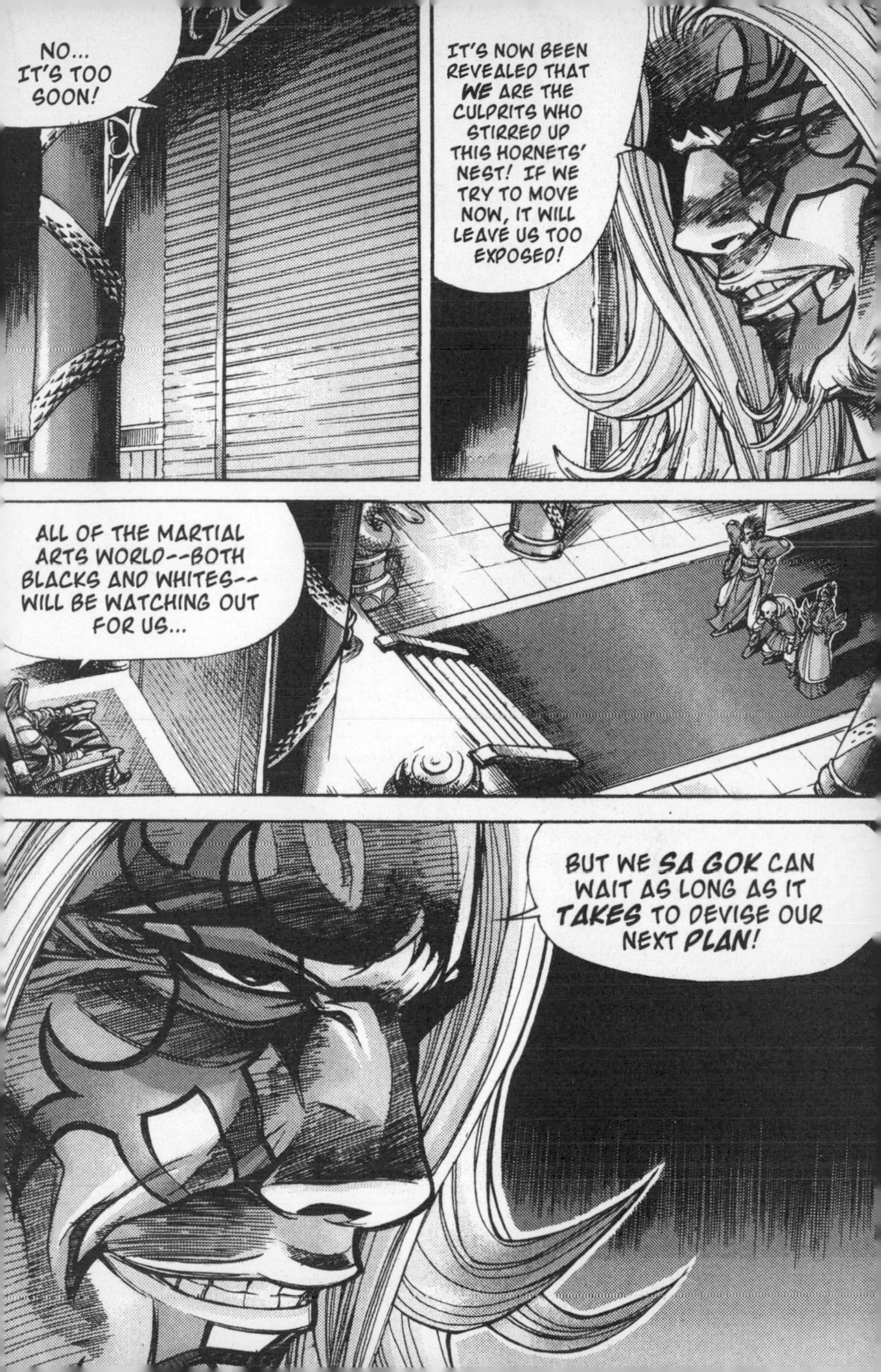
NO... IT'S TOO SOON!
IT'S NOW BEEN REVEALED THAT WE ARE THE CULPRITS WHO STIRRED UP THIS HORNETS' NEST! IF WE TRY TO MOVE NOW, IT WILL LEAVE US TOO EXPOSED!
ALL OF THE MARTIAL ARTS WORLD--BOTH BLACKS AND WHITES--WILL BE WATCHING OUT FOR US...
BUT WE SA GOK CAN WAIT AS LONG AS IT TAKES TO DEVISE OUR NEXT PLAN!

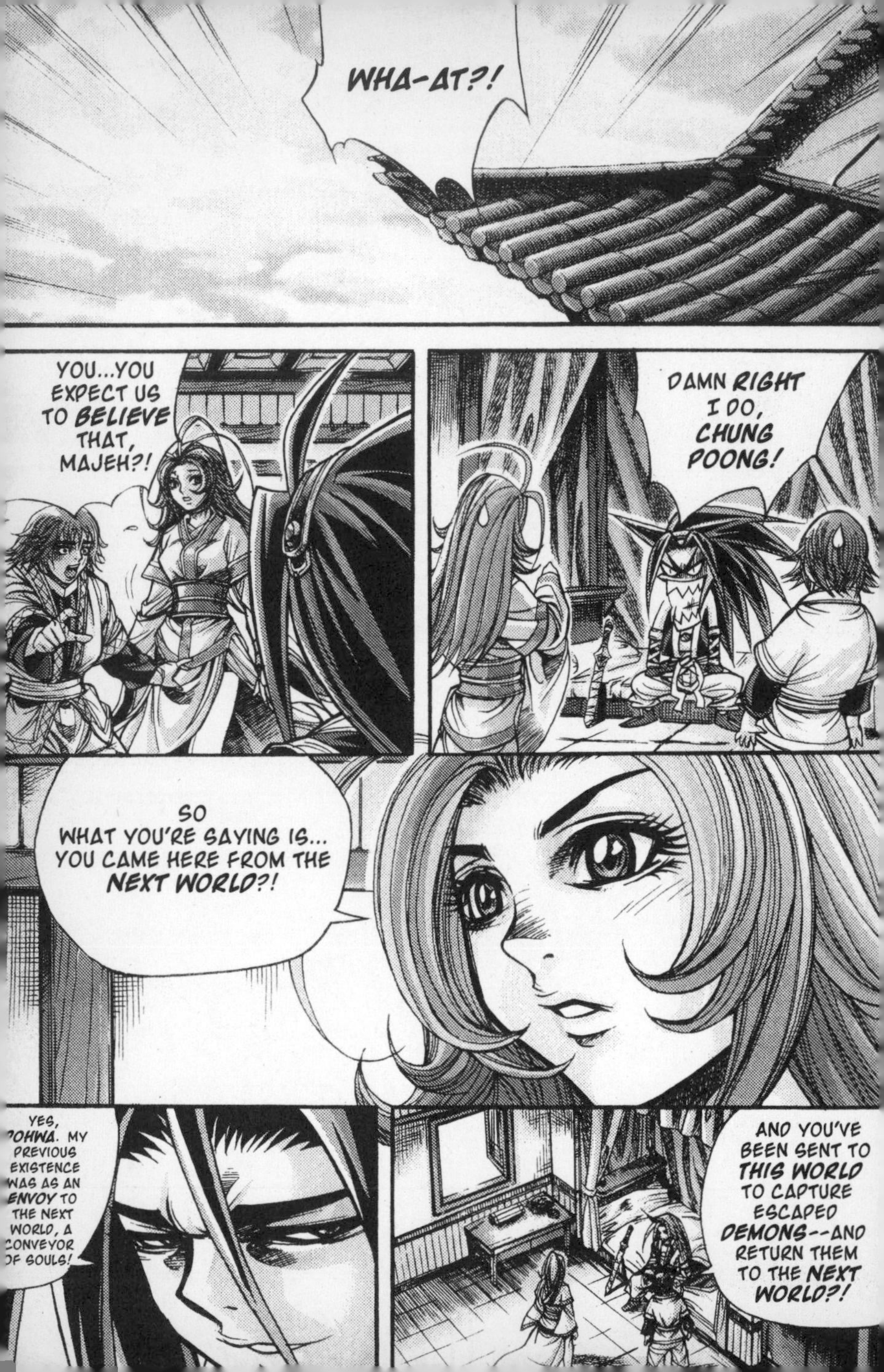
WHA-AT?!
YOU...YOU EXPECT US TO BELIEVE THAT, MAJEH?!
DAMN RIGHT I DO, CHUNG POONG!
SO WHAT YOU'RE SAYING IS... YOU CAME HERE FROM THE NEXT WORLD?!
YES, DOHWA. MY PREVIOUS EXISTENCE WAS AS AN ENVOY TO THE NEXT WORLD, A CONVEYOR OF SOULS!
AND YOU'VE BEEN SENT TO THIS WORLD TO CAPTURE ESCAPED DEMONS--AND RETURN THEM TO THE NEXT WORLD?!

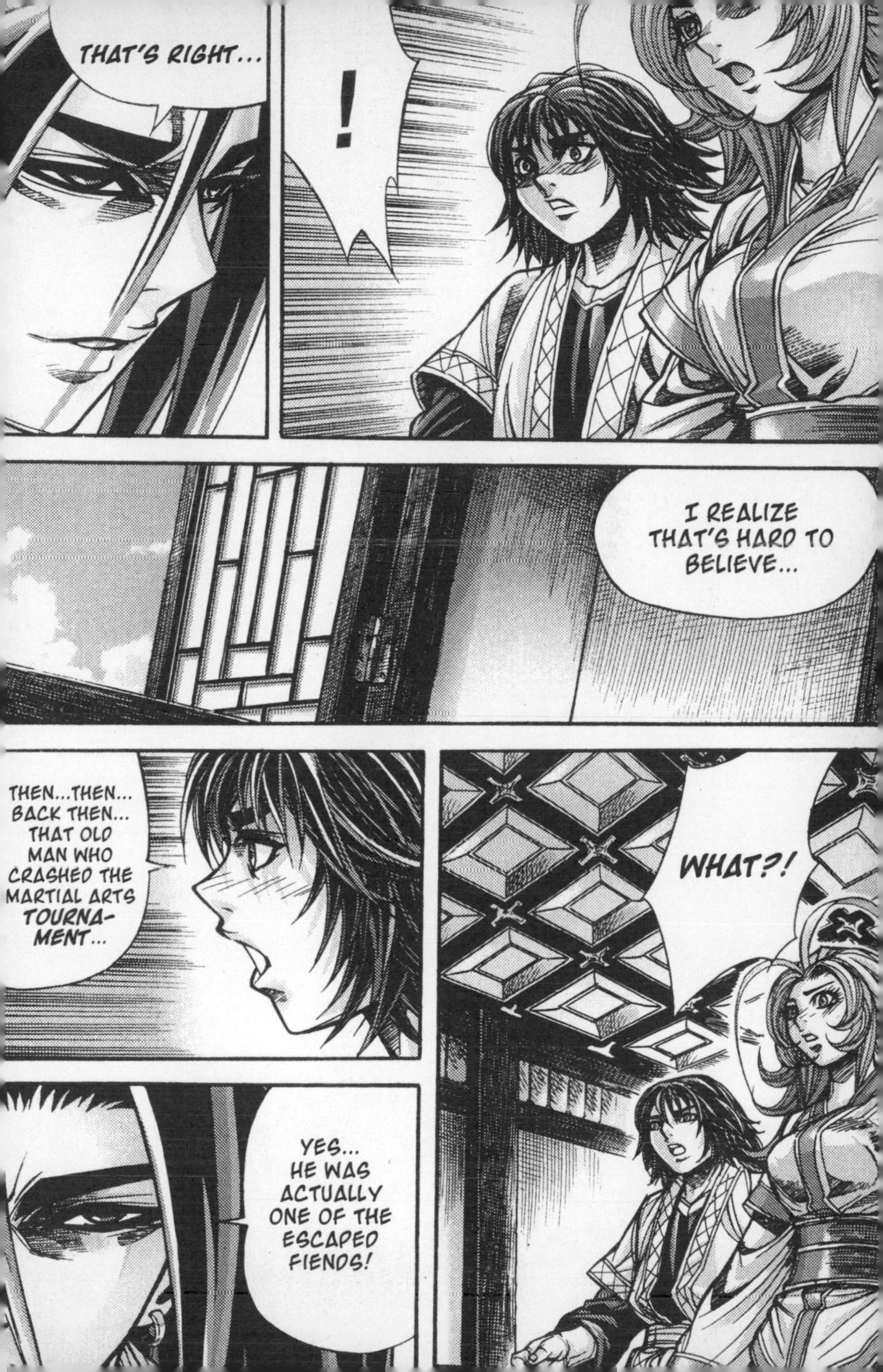
THAT'S RIGHT...
!
I REALIZE THAT'S HARD TO BELIEVE...
THEN...THEN... BACK THEN... THAT OLD MAN WHO CRASHED THE MARTIAL ARTS TOURNA-MENT...
YES... HE WAS ACTUALLY ONE OF THE ESCAPED FIENDS!
WHAT?!

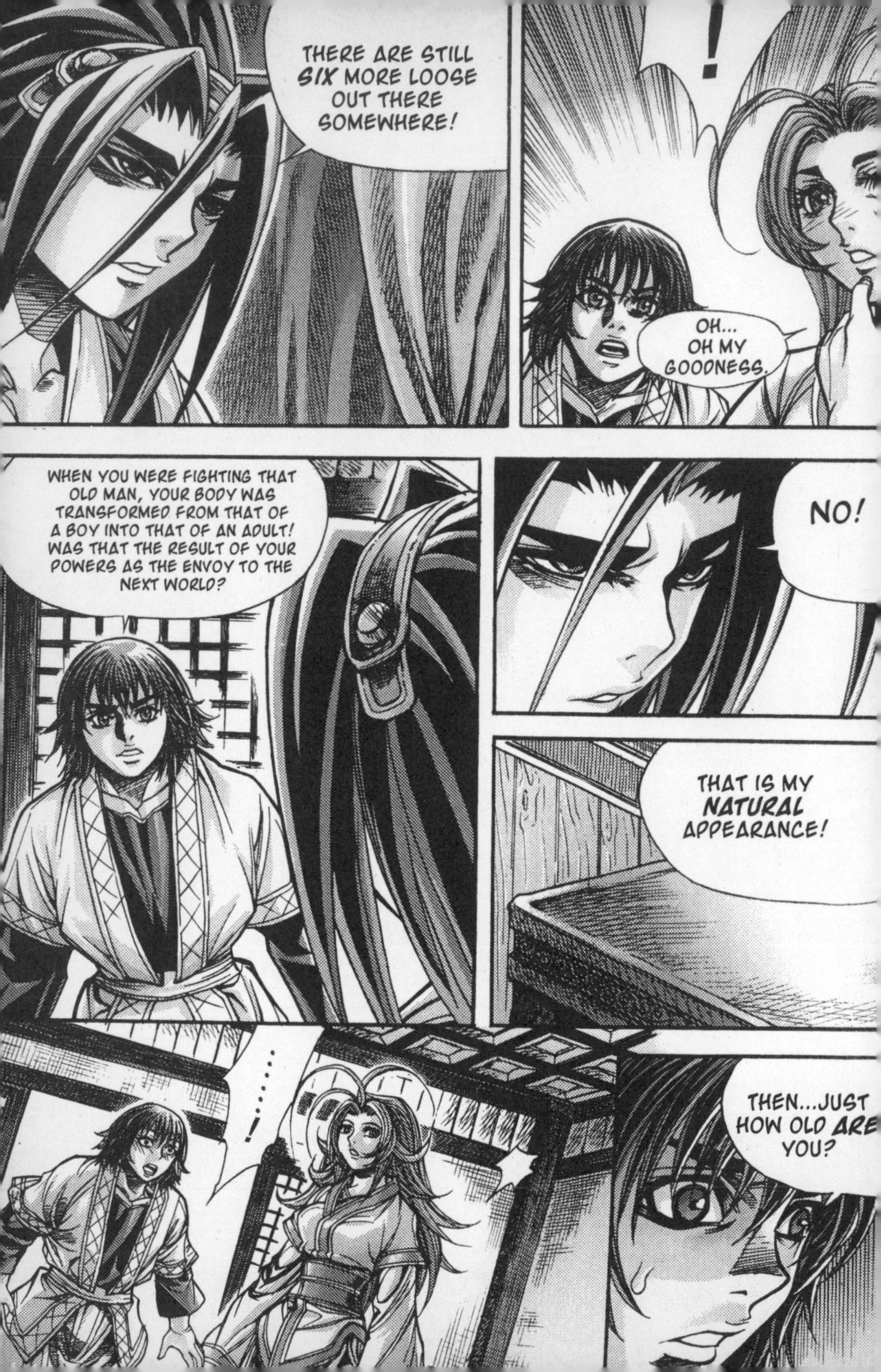
THERE ARE STILL SIX MORE LOOSE OUT THERE SOMEWHERE!
!
OH... OH MY GOODNESS.
WHEN YOU WERE FIGHTING THAT OLD MAN, YOUR BODY WAS TRANSFORMED FROM THAT OF A BOY INTO THAT OF AN ADULT! WAS THAT THE RESULT OF YOUR POWERS AS THE ENVOY TO THE NEXT WORLD?
NO!
THAT IS MY NATURAL APPEARANCE!
.....!
THEN...JUST HOW OLD ARE YOU?

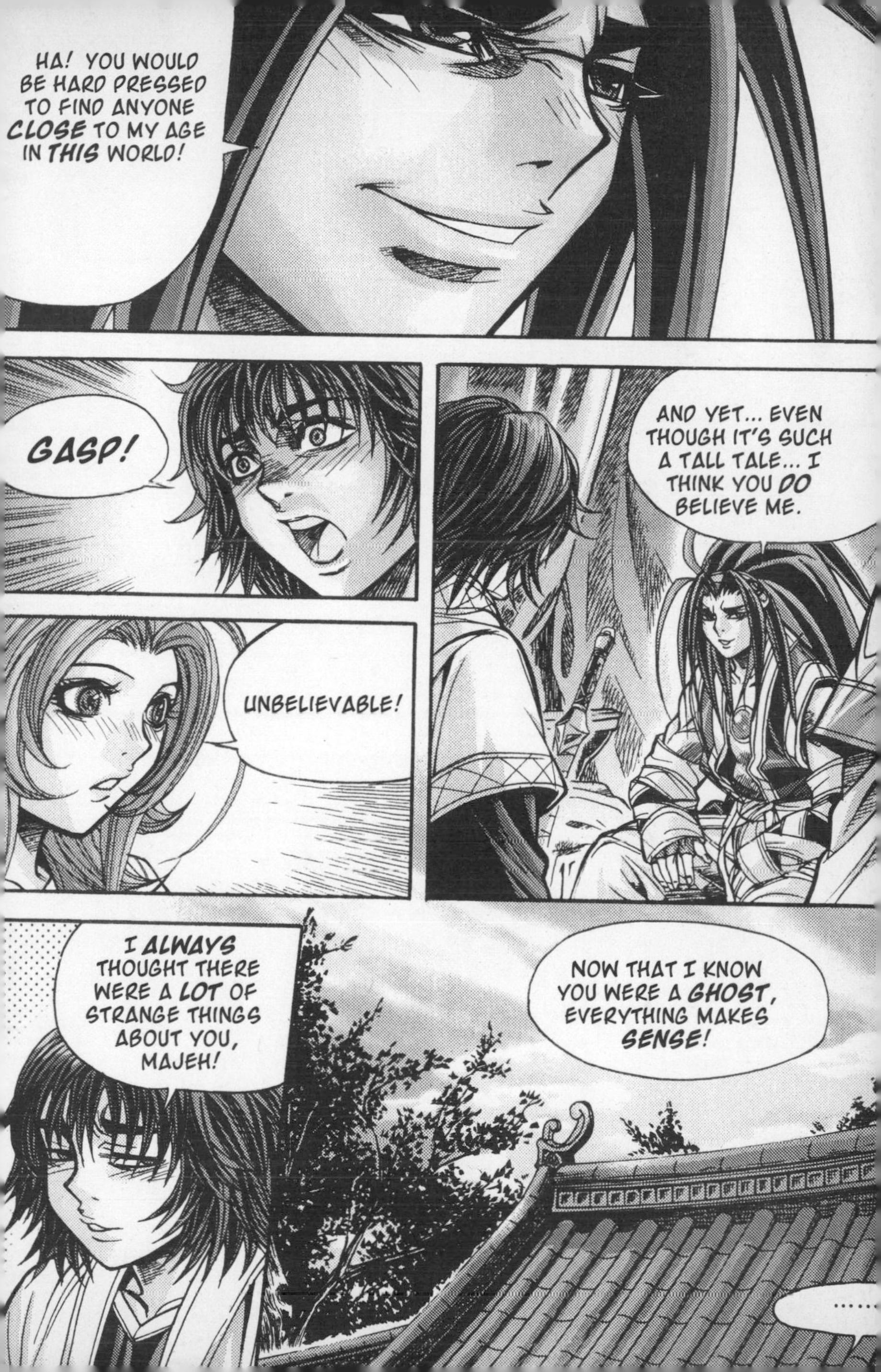
HA! YOU WOULD BE HARD PRESSED TO FIND ANYONE CLOSE TO MY AGE IN THIS WORLD!
GASP!
UNBELIEVABLE!
AND YET... EVEN THOUGH IT'S SUCH A TALL TALE... I THINK YOU DO BELIEVE ME.
I ALWAYS THOUGHT THERE WERE A LOT OF STRANGE THINGS ABOUT YOU, MAJEH!
NOW THAT I KNOW YOU WERE A GHOST, EVERYTHING MAKES SENSE!
......

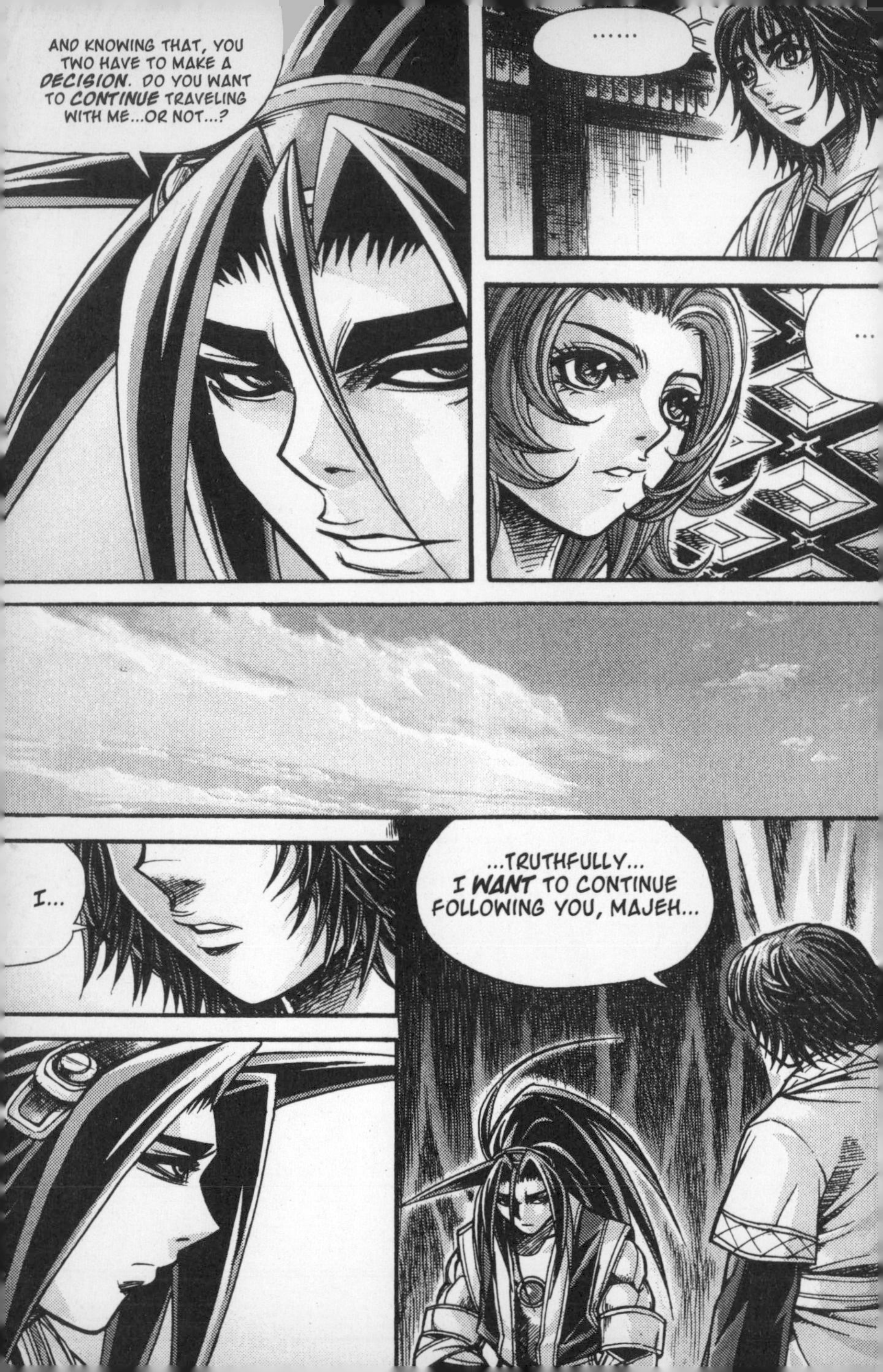
AND KNOWING THAT, YOU TWO HAVE TO MAKE A DECISION. DO YOU WANT TO CONTINUE TRAVELING WITH ME...OR NOT...?
......
...
I...
...TRUTHFULLY... I WANT TO CONTINUE FOLLOWING YOU, MAJEH...

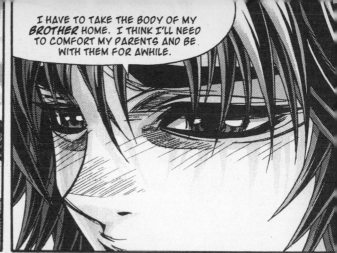

I HAVE TO TAKE THE BODY OF MY *BROTHER* HOME. I THINK I'LL NEED TO COMFORT MY PARENTS AND BE WITH THEM FOR AWHILE.

...BUT I CAN'T!

YOUR BROTHER... YES. I'M SURE HE'S GONE TO A BETTER PLACE!

THANK YOU, *MAJEH*...

AS A FORMER ENVOY TO THE NEXT WORLD, I KNOW SUCH THINGS.

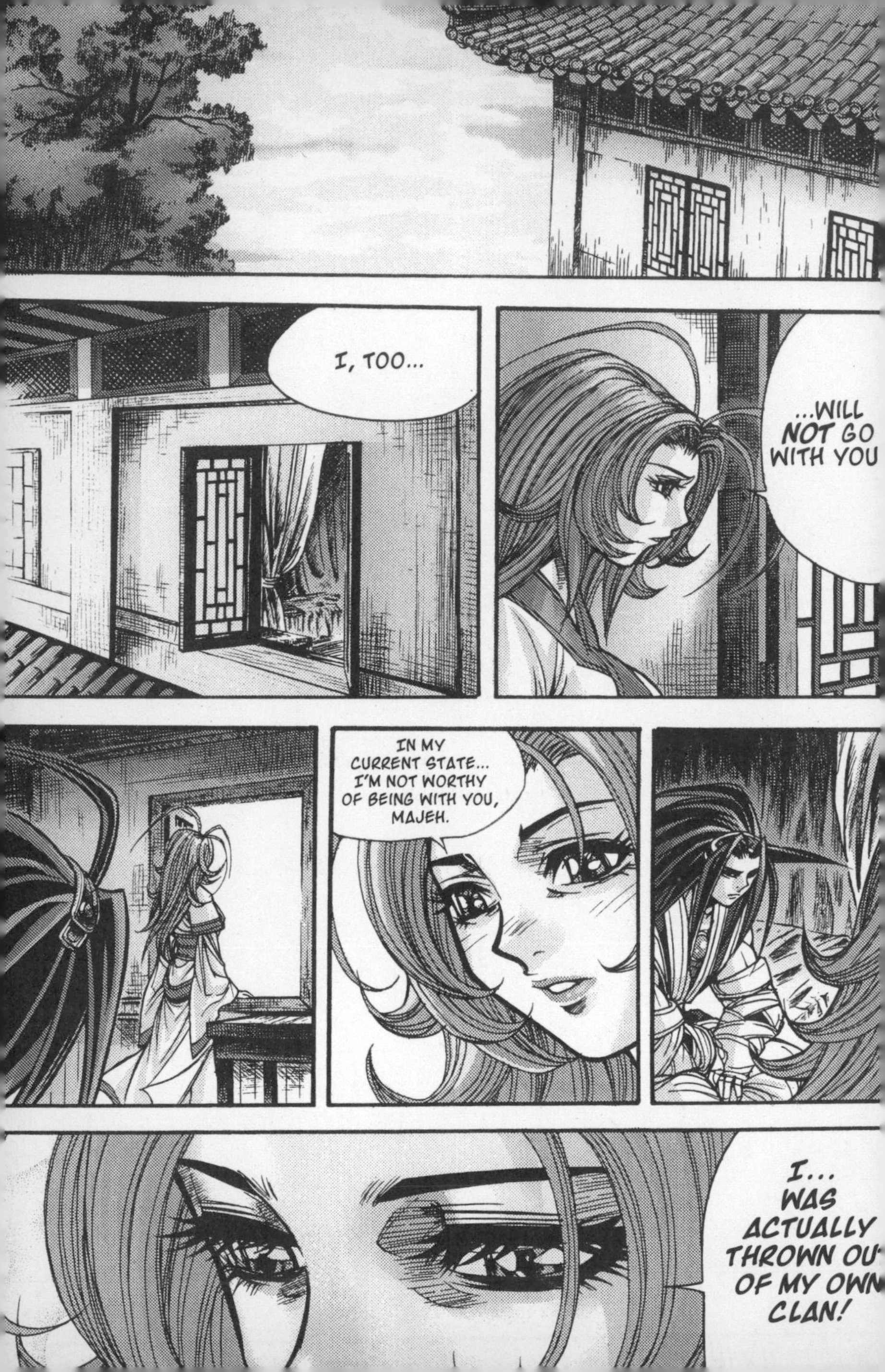
I, TOO...
...WILL NOT GO WITH YOU
IN MY CURRENT STATE... I'M NOT WORTHY OF BEING WITH YOU, MAJEH.
I... WAS ACTUALLY THROWN OU OF MY OWN CLAN!

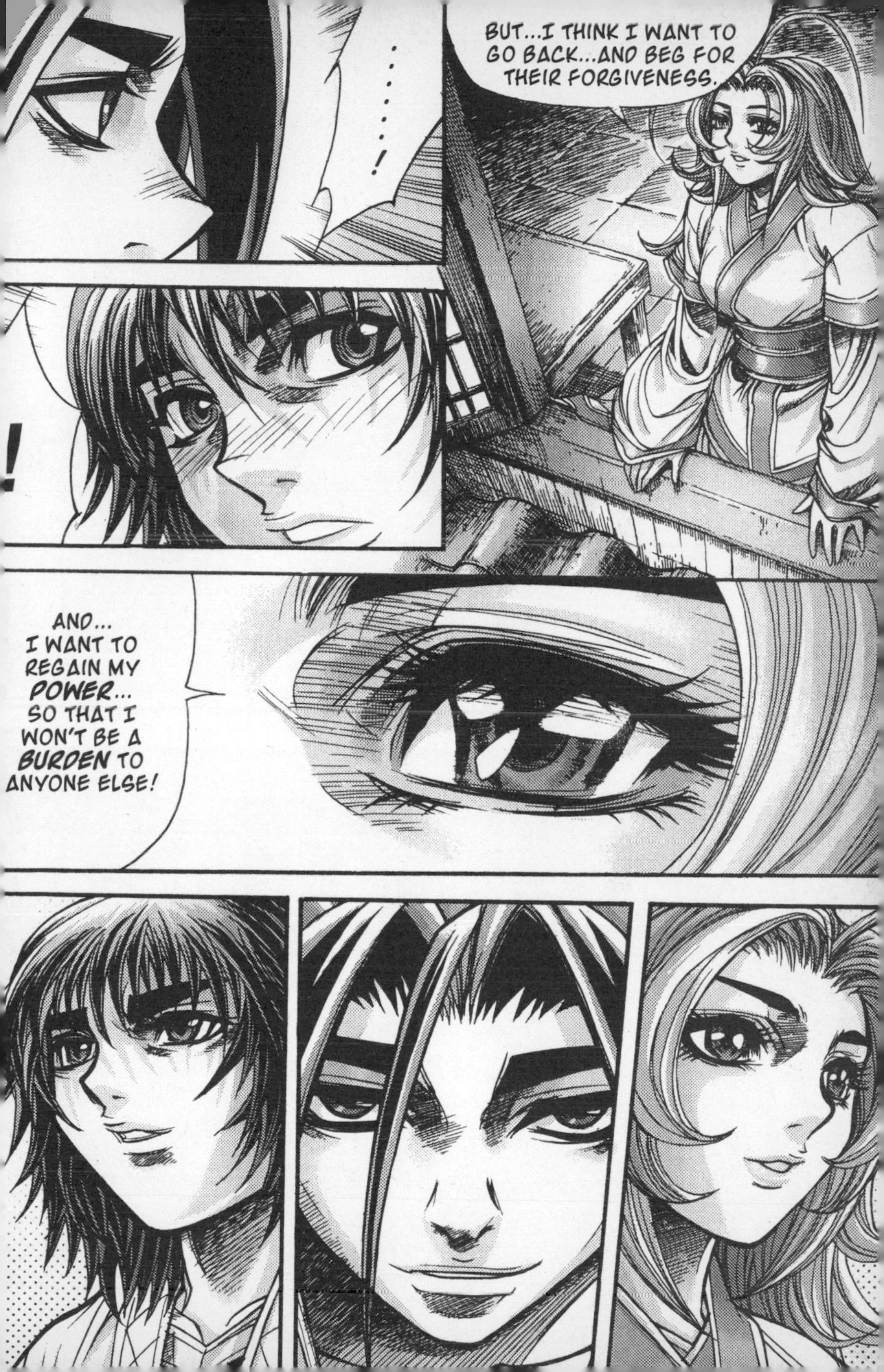

......!
BUT...I THINK I WANT TO GO BACK...AND BEG FOR THEIR FORGIVENESS.
!
AND... I WANT TO REGAIN MY POWER... SO THAT I WON'T BE A BURDEN TO ANYONE ELSE!

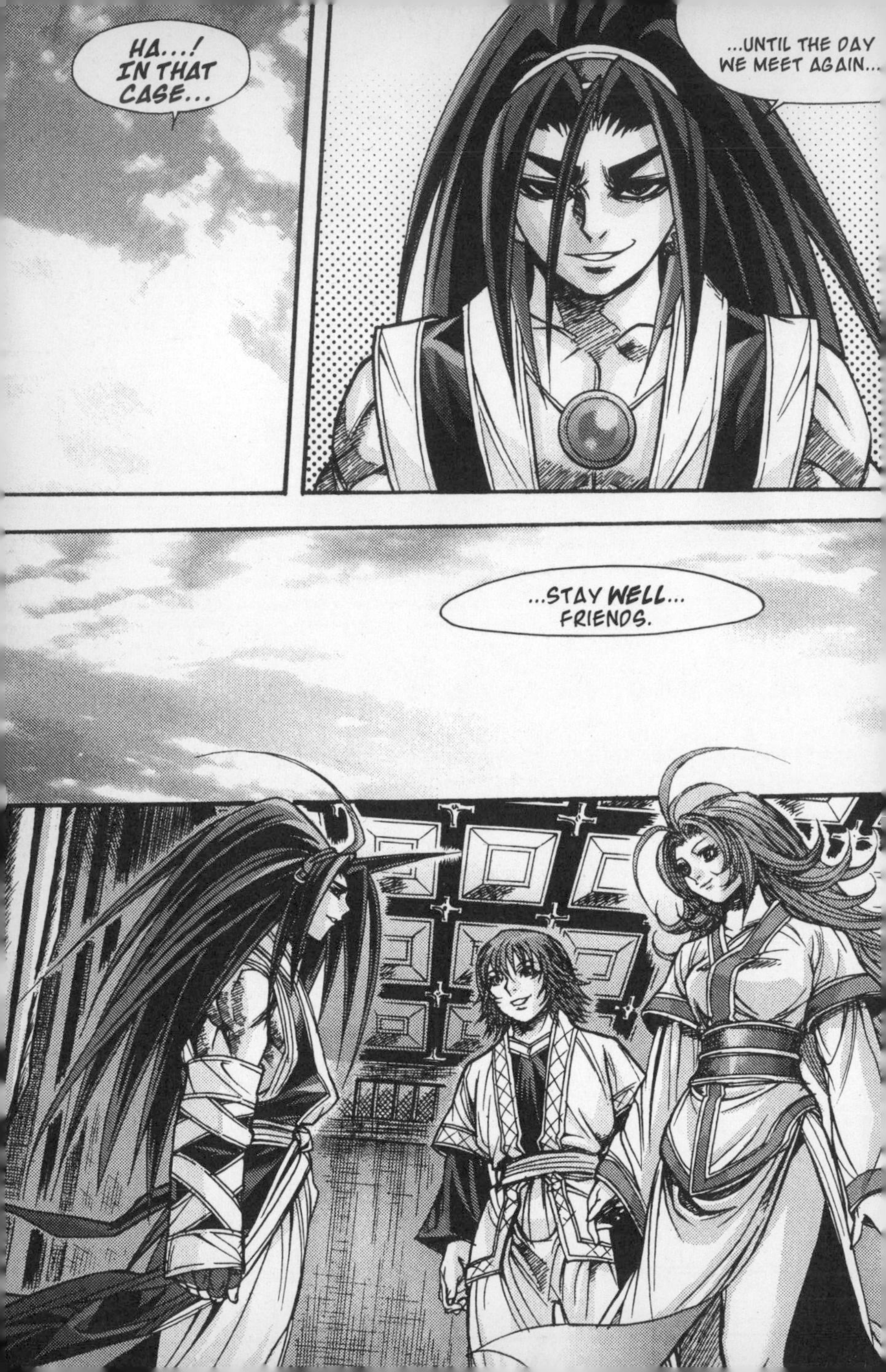
HA...! IN THAT CASE...
...UNTIL THE DAY WE MEET AGAIN...
...STAY WELL... FRIENDS.

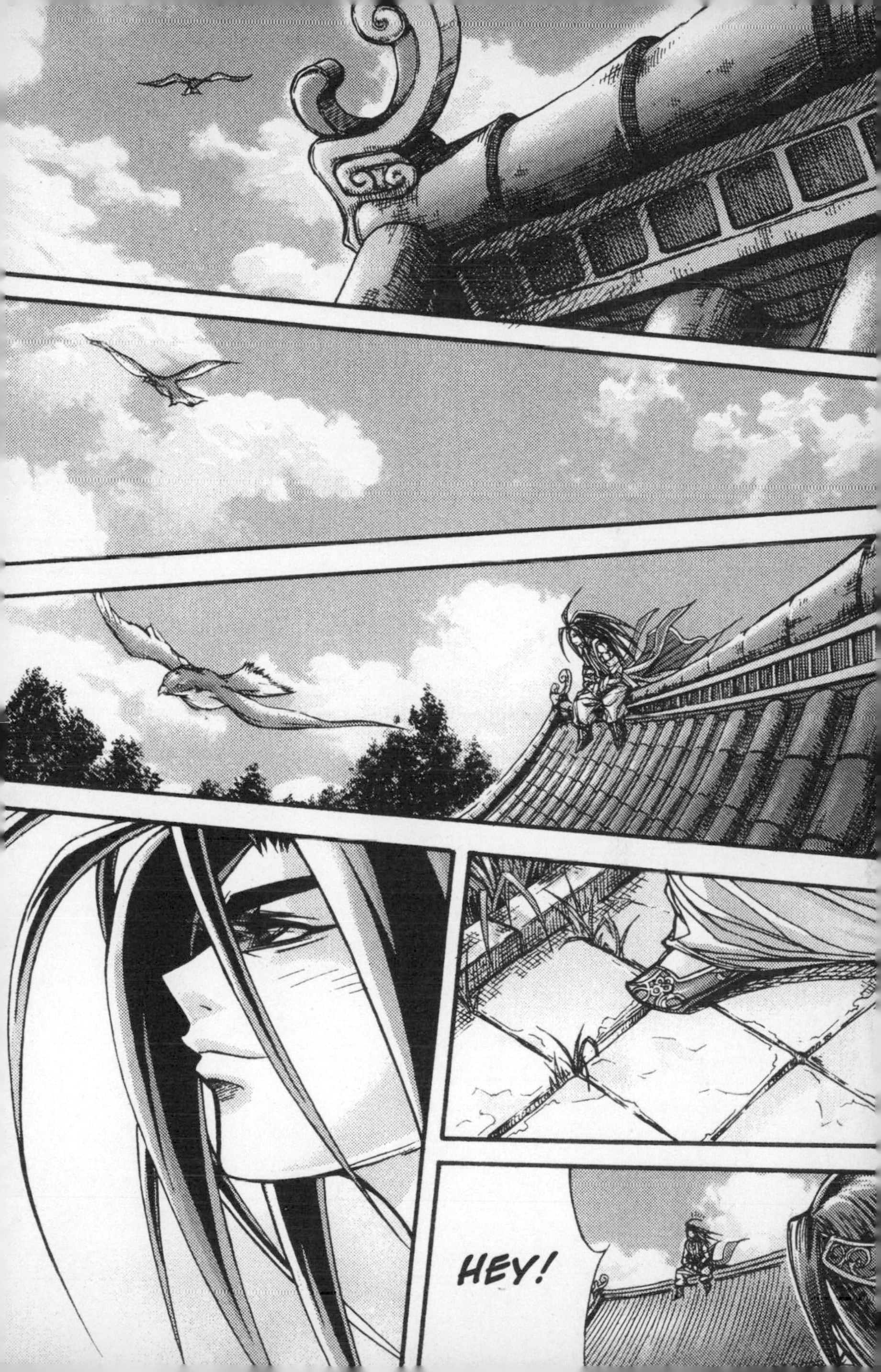
HEY!

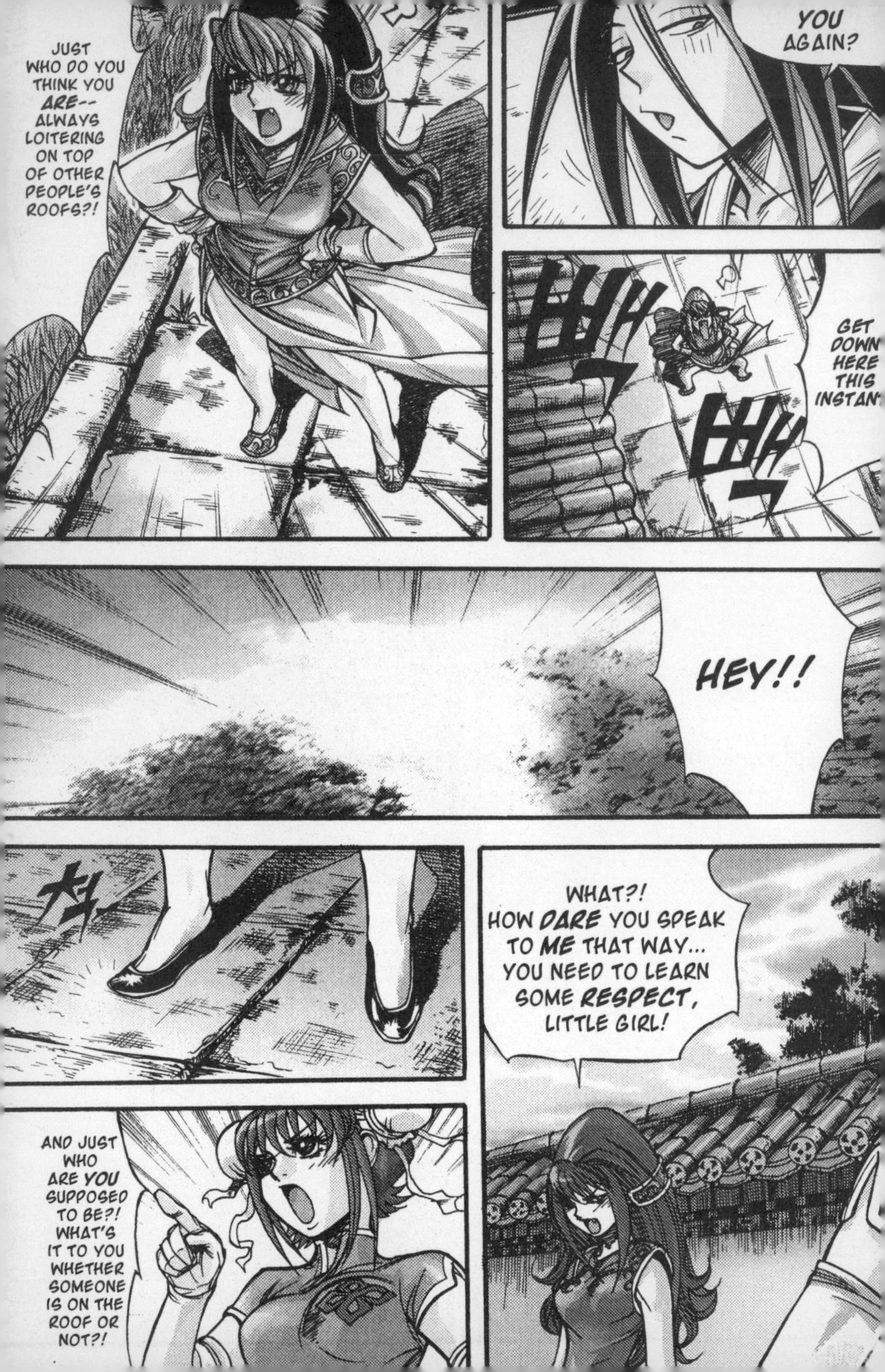
JUST WHO DO YOU THINK YOU ARE-- ALWAYS LOITERING ON TOP OF OTHER PEOPLE'S ROOFS?!
YOU AGAIN?
GET DOWN HERE THIS INSTAN
HEY!!
AND JUST WHO ARE YOU SUPPOSED TO BE?! WHAT'S IT TO YOU WHETHER SOMEONE IS ON THE ROOF OR NOT?!
WHAT?! HOW DARE YOU SPEAK TO ME THAT WAY... YOU NEED TO LEARN SOME RESPECT, LITTLE GIRL!

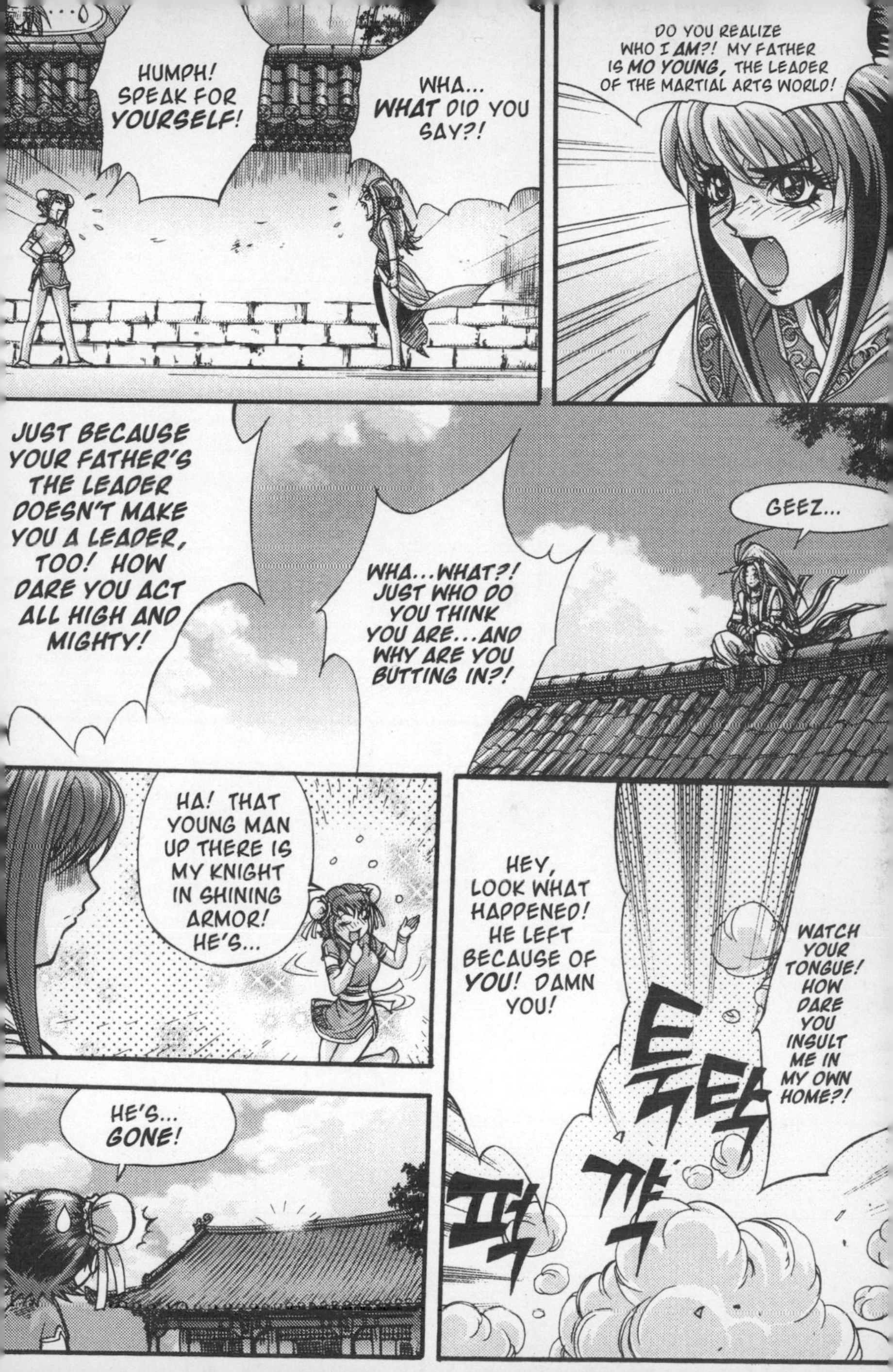
HUMPH! SPEAK FOR YOURSELF!
WHA... WHAT DID YOU SAY?!
DO YOU REALIZE WHO I AM?! MY FATHER IS MO YOUNG, THE LEADER OF THE MARTIAL ARTS WORLD!
JUST BECAUSE YOUR FATHER'S THE LEADER DOESN'T MAKE YOU A LEADER, TOO! HOW DARE YOU ACT ALL HIGH AND MIGHTY!
WHA...WHAT?! JUST WHO DO YOU THINK YOU ARE...AND WHY ARE YOU BUTTING IN?!
GEEZ...
HA! THAT YOUNG MAN UP THERE IS MY KNIGHT IN SHINING ARMOR! HE'S...
HE'S... GONE!
HEY, LOOK WHAT HAPPENED! HE LEFT BECAUSE OF YOU! DAMN YOU!
WATCH YOUR TONGUE! HOW DARE YOU INSULT ME IN MY OWN HOME?!

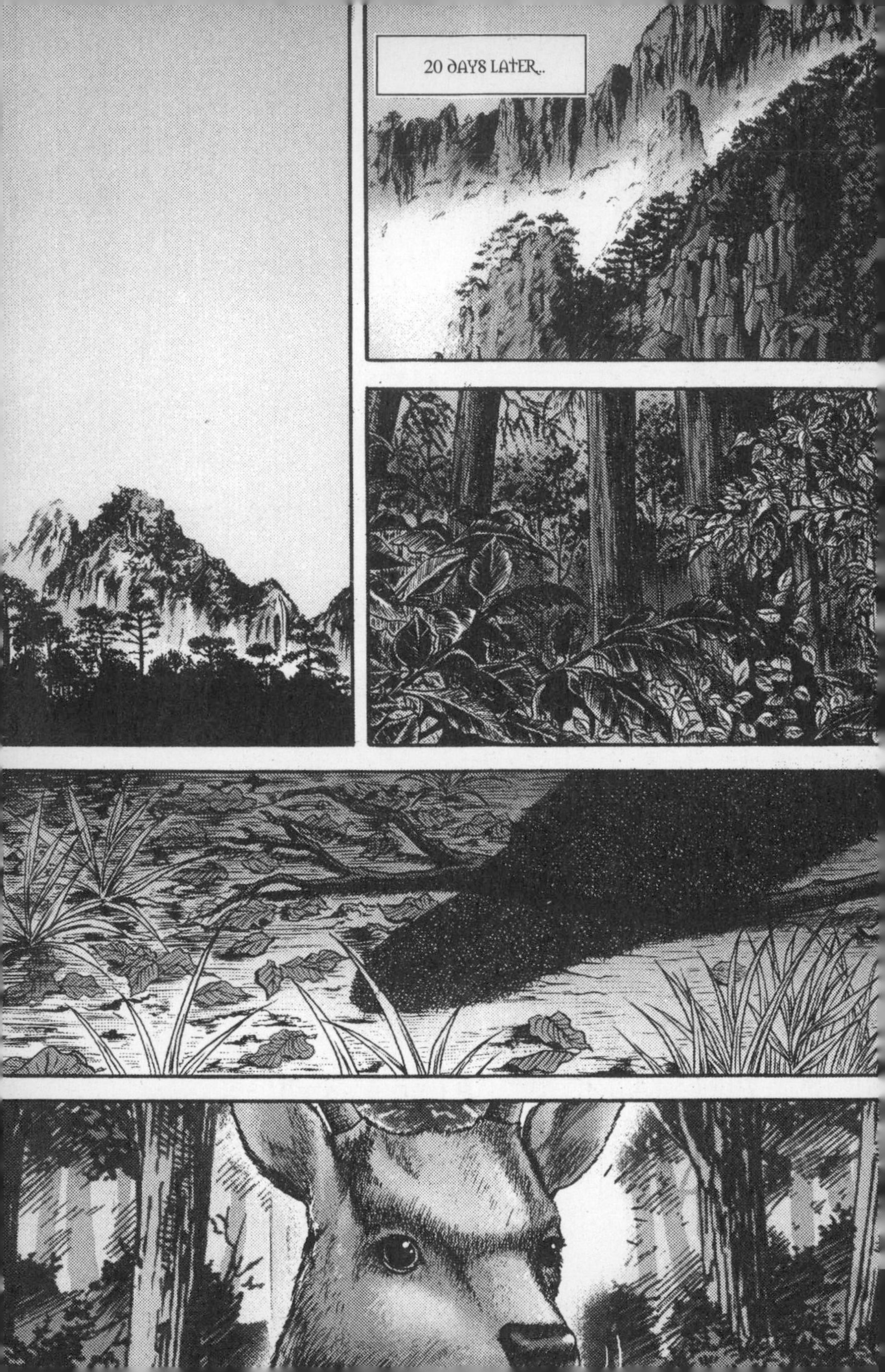
20 DAYS LATER...

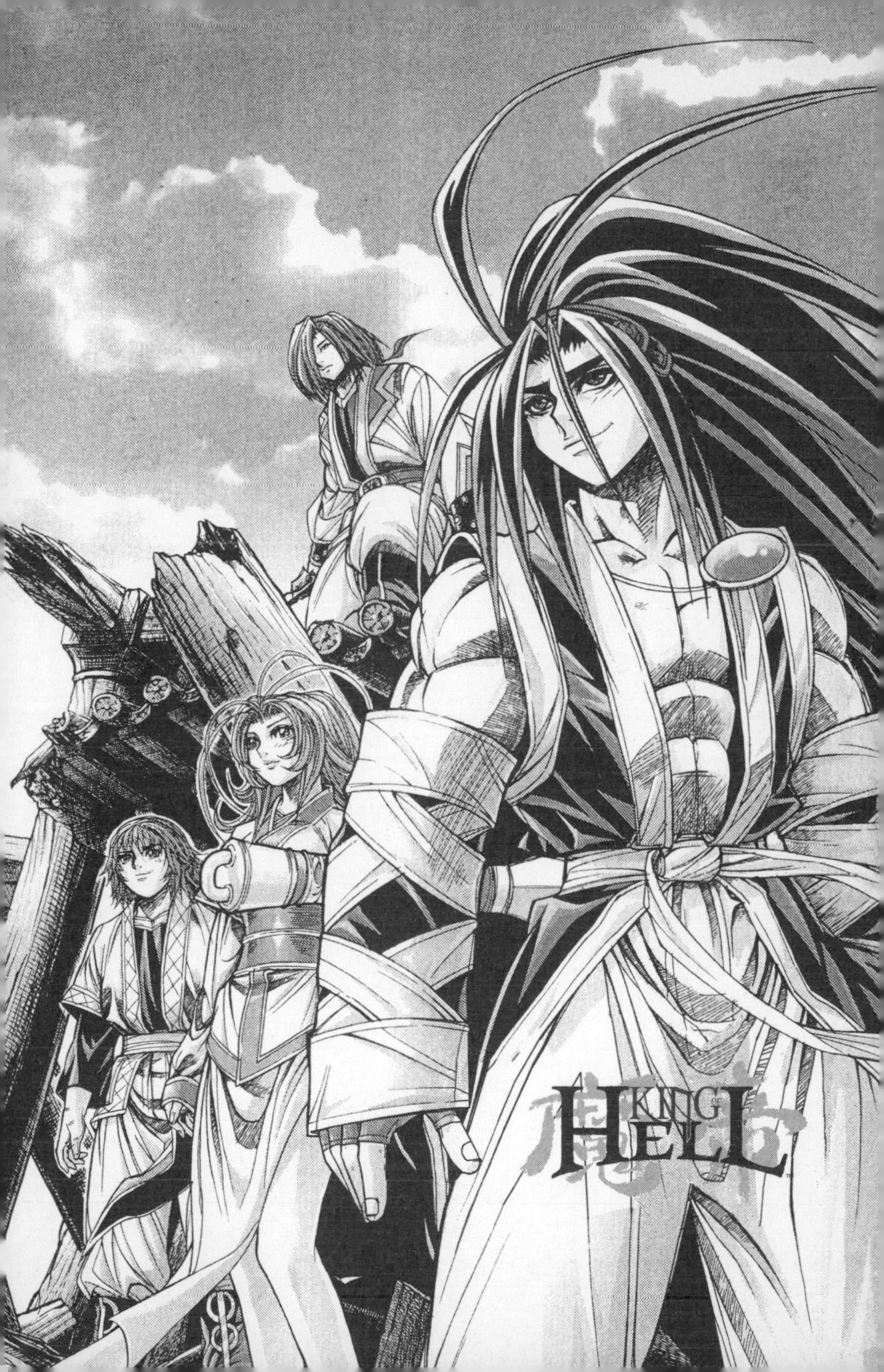
KING
HELL

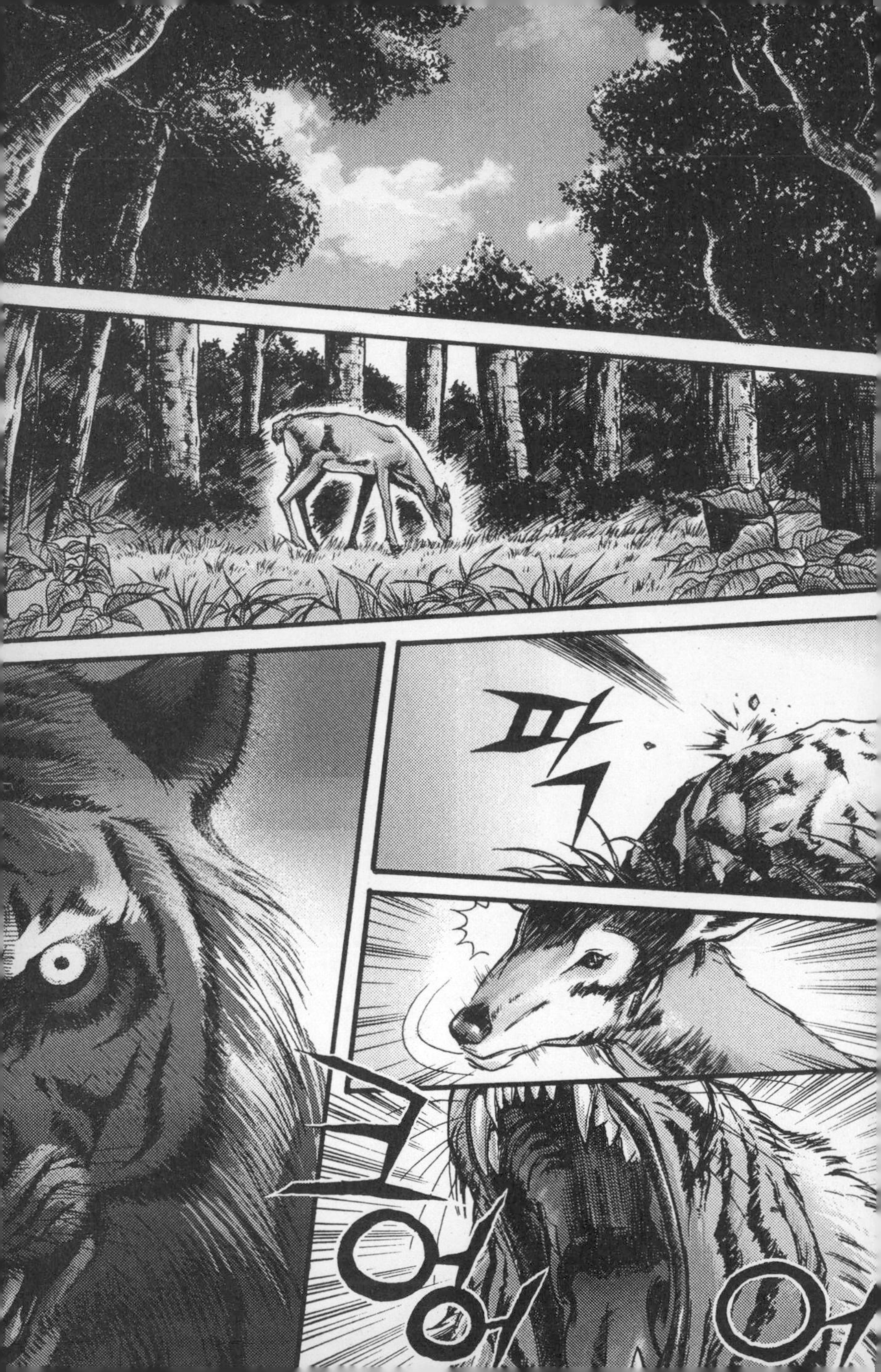
팟
크아아아

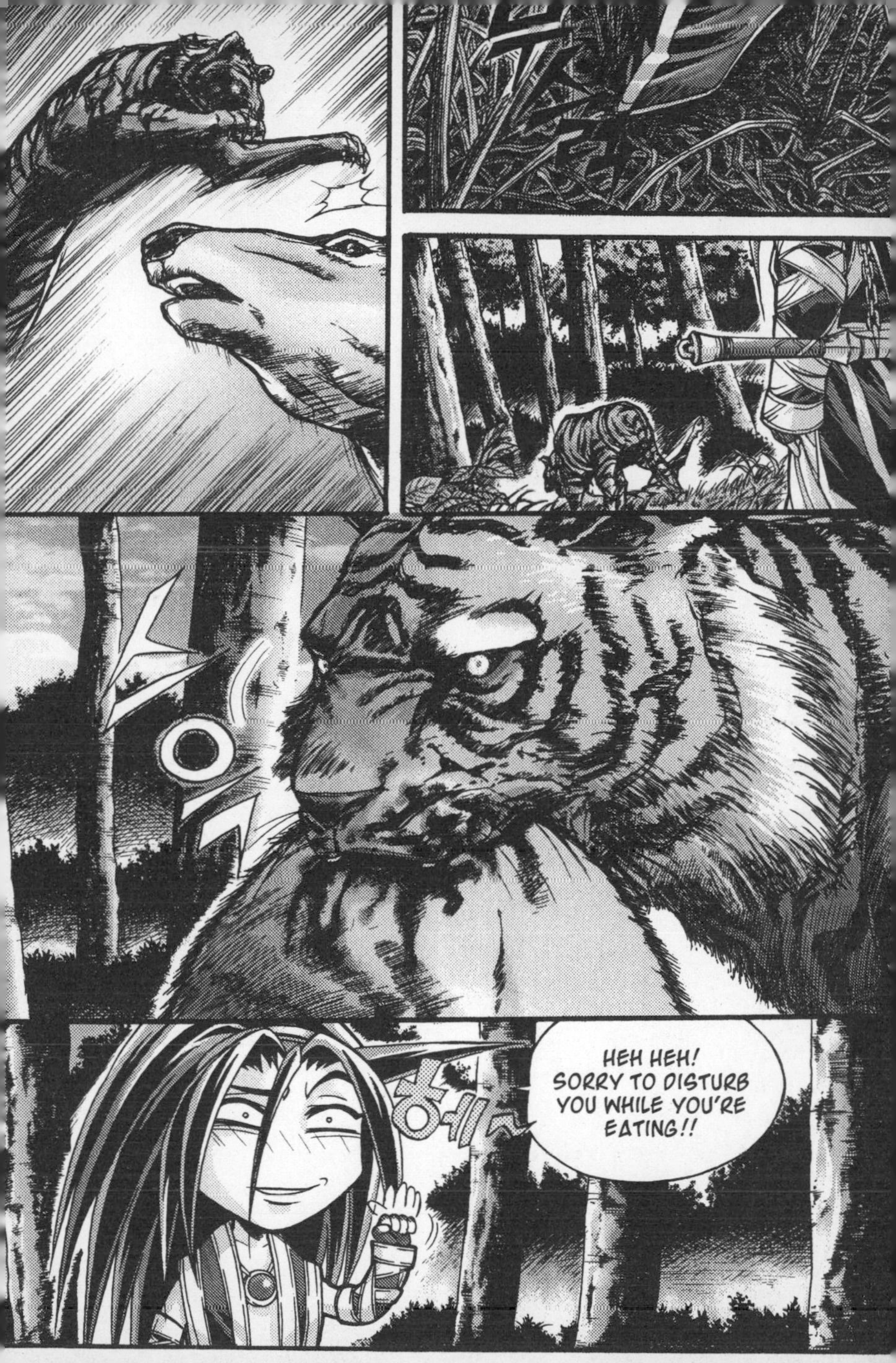
HEH HEH! SORRY TO DISTURB YOU WHILE YOU'RE EATING!!

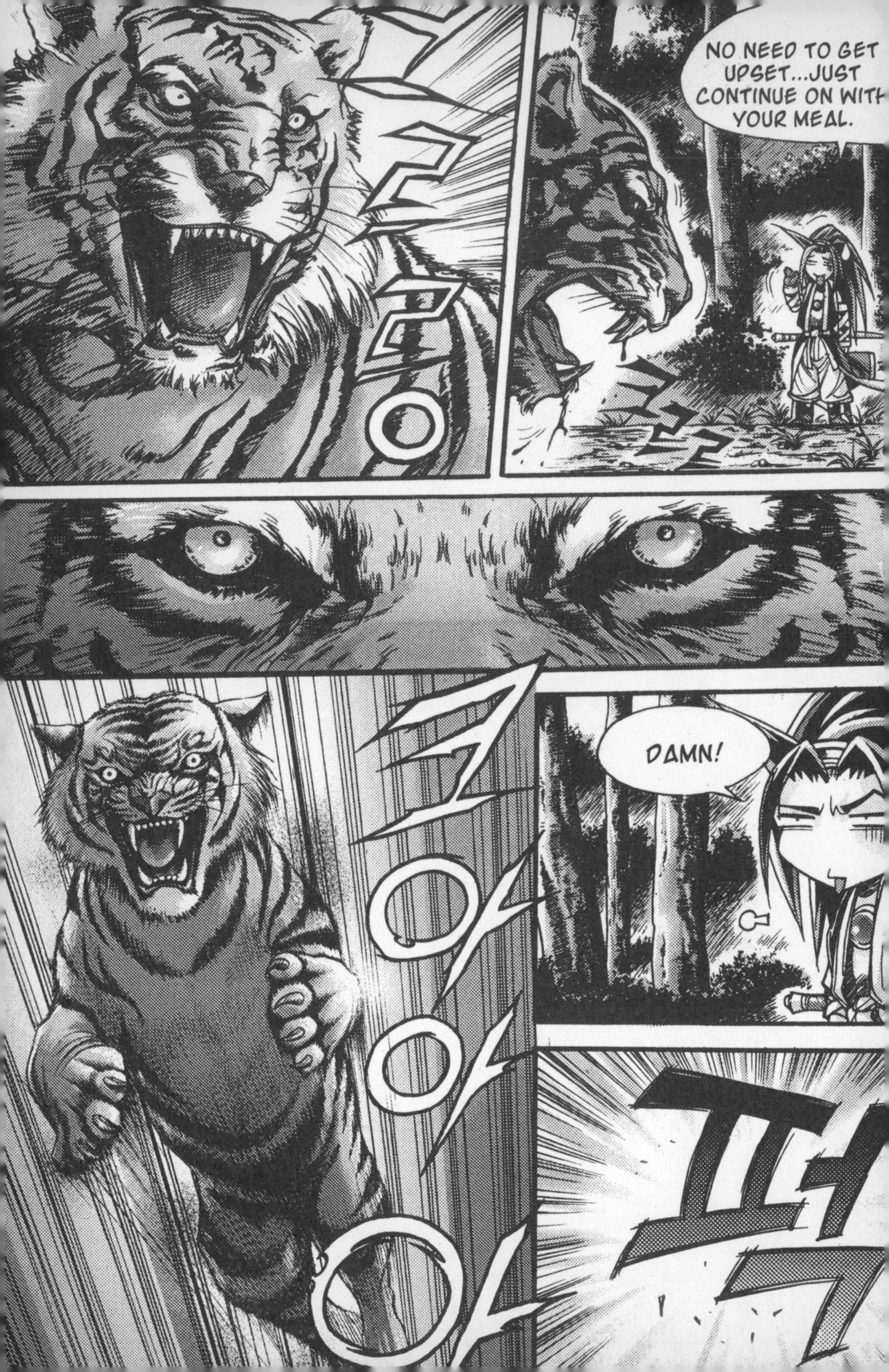
NO NEED TO GET UPSET...JUST CONTINUE ON WITH YOUR MEAL.
DAMN!

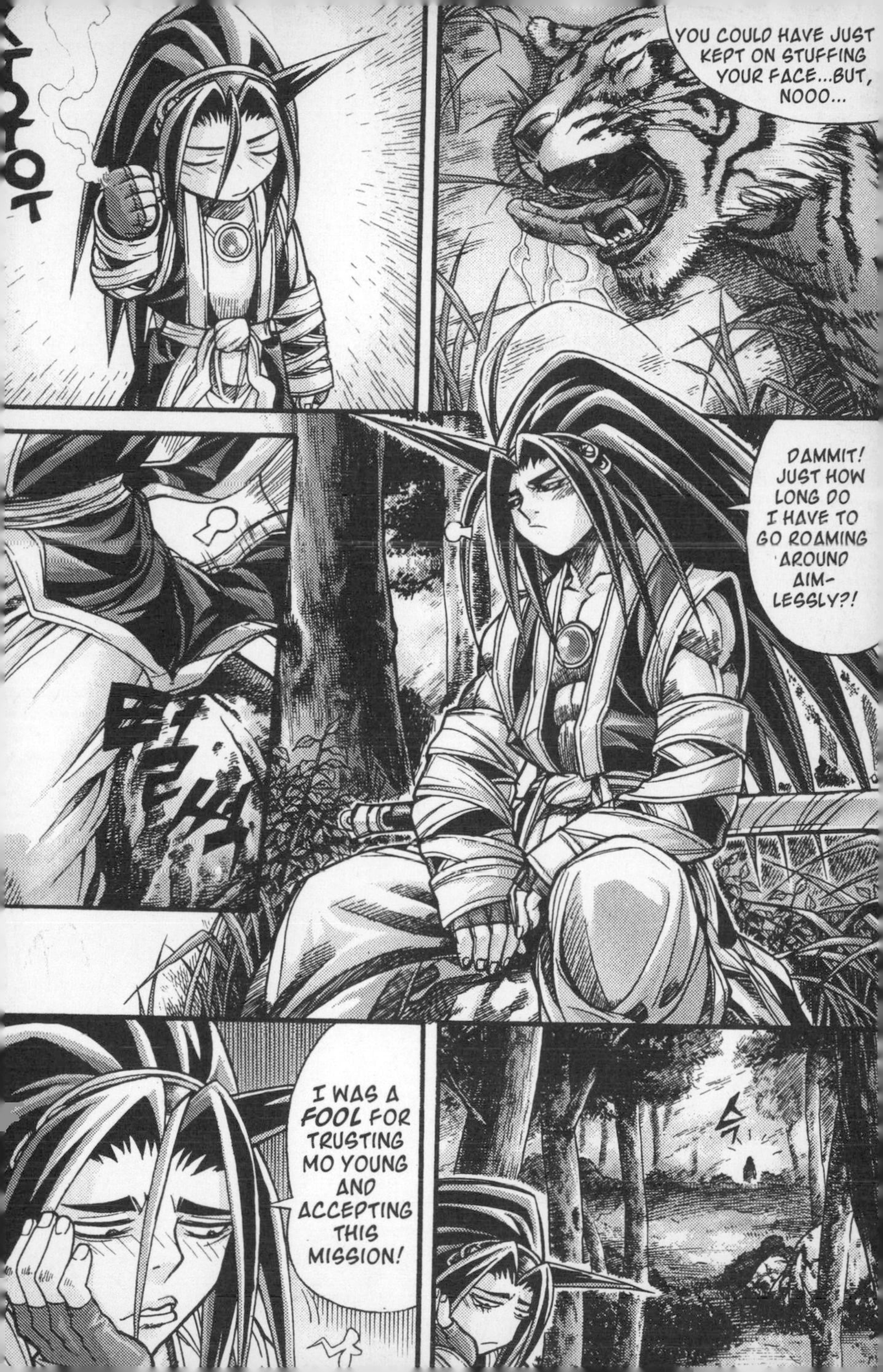
YOU COULD HAVE JUST KEPT ON STUFFING YOUR FACE...BUT, NOOO...
DAMMIT! JUST HOW LONG DO I HAVE TO GO ROAMING AROUND AIM-LESSLY?!
I WAS A *FOOL* FOR TRUSTING MO YOUNG AND ACCEPTING THIS MISSION!

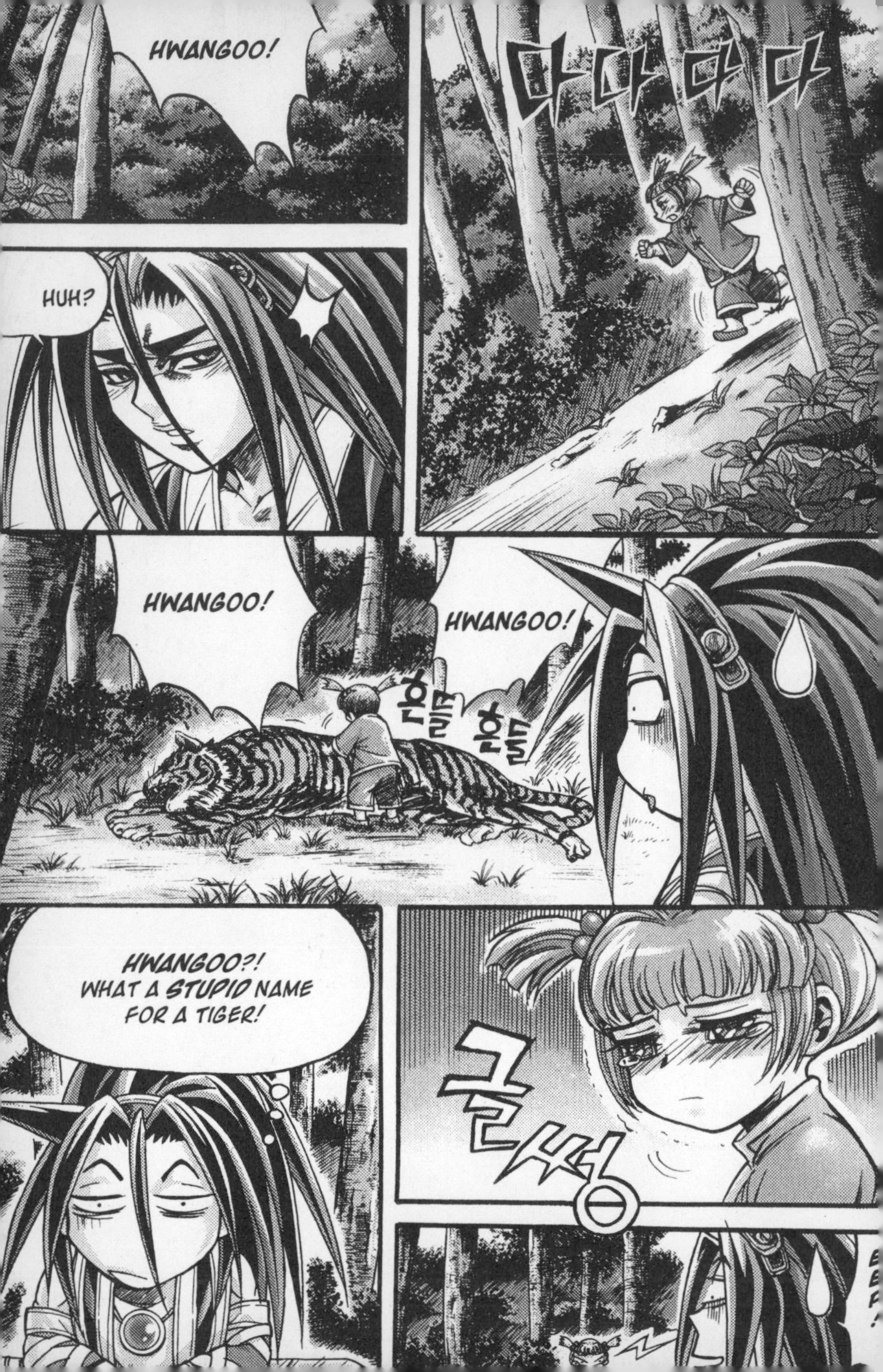
HWANGOO!
HUH?
다다다다
HWANGOO!
HWANGOO!
흔들 흔들
HWANGOO?! WHAT A STUPID NAME FOR A TIGER!
글썽

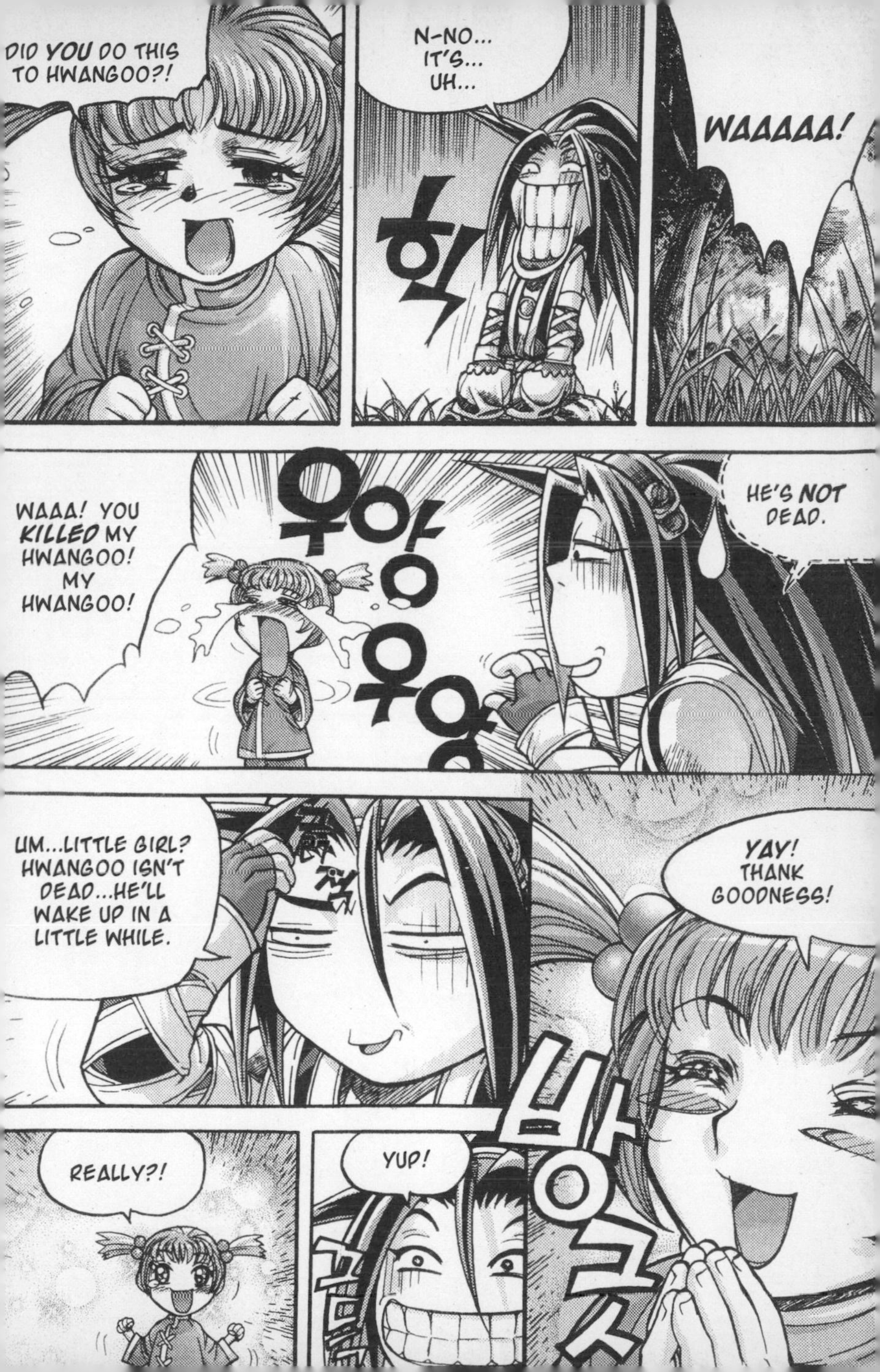
DID YOU DO THIS TO HWANGOO?!
N-NO... IT'S... UH...
헉
WAAAAA!
WAAA! YOU KILLED MY HWANGOO! MY HWANGOO!
HE'S NOT DEAD.
UM...LITTLE GIRL? HWANGOO ISN'T DEAD...HE'LL WAKE UP IN A LITTLE WHILE.
YAY! THANK GOODNESS!
REALLY?!
YUP!

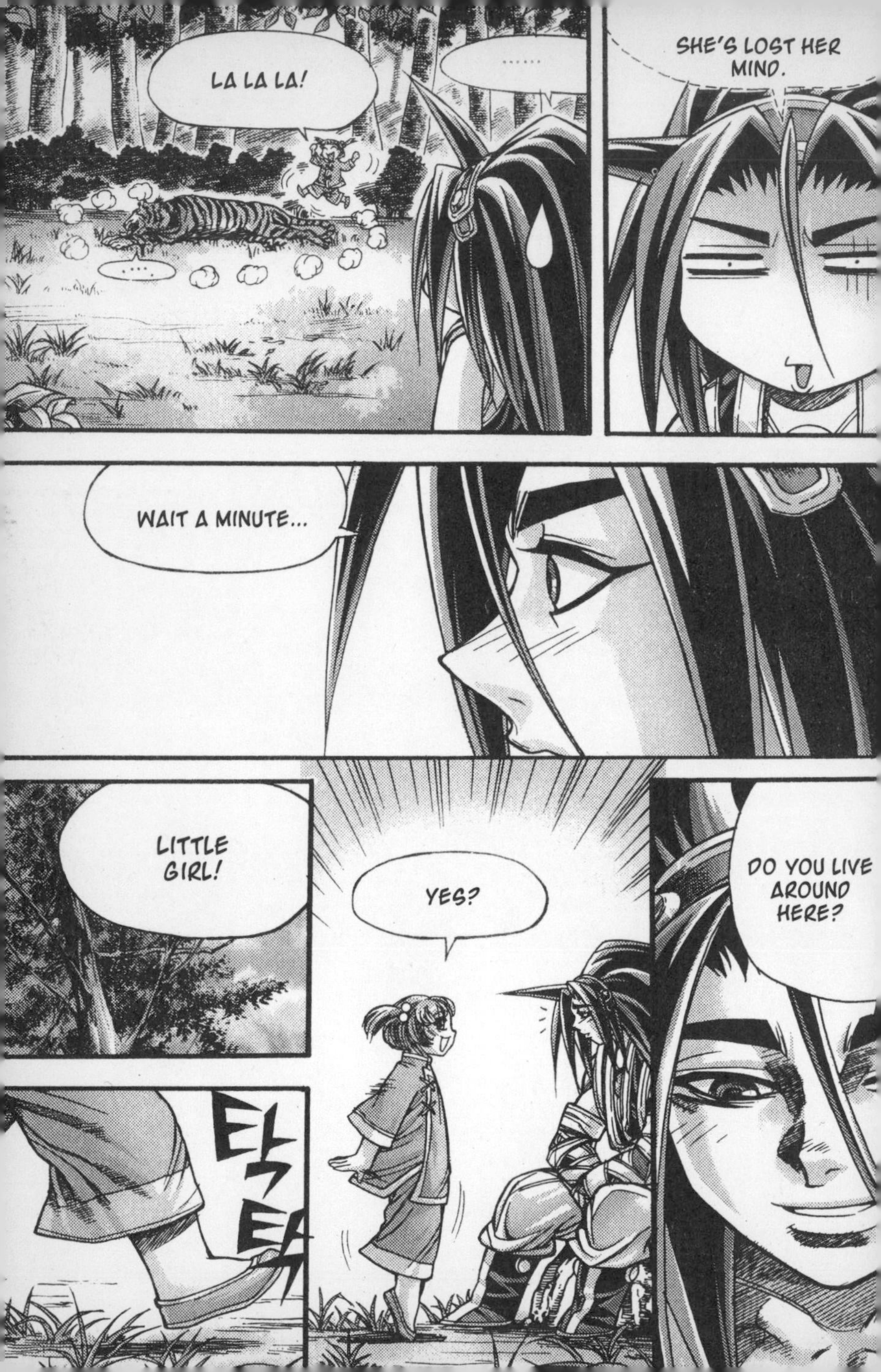
LA LA LA!
......
....
SHE'S LOST HER MIND.
WAIT A MINUTE...
LITTLE GIRL!
YES?
DO YOU LIVE AROUND HERE?

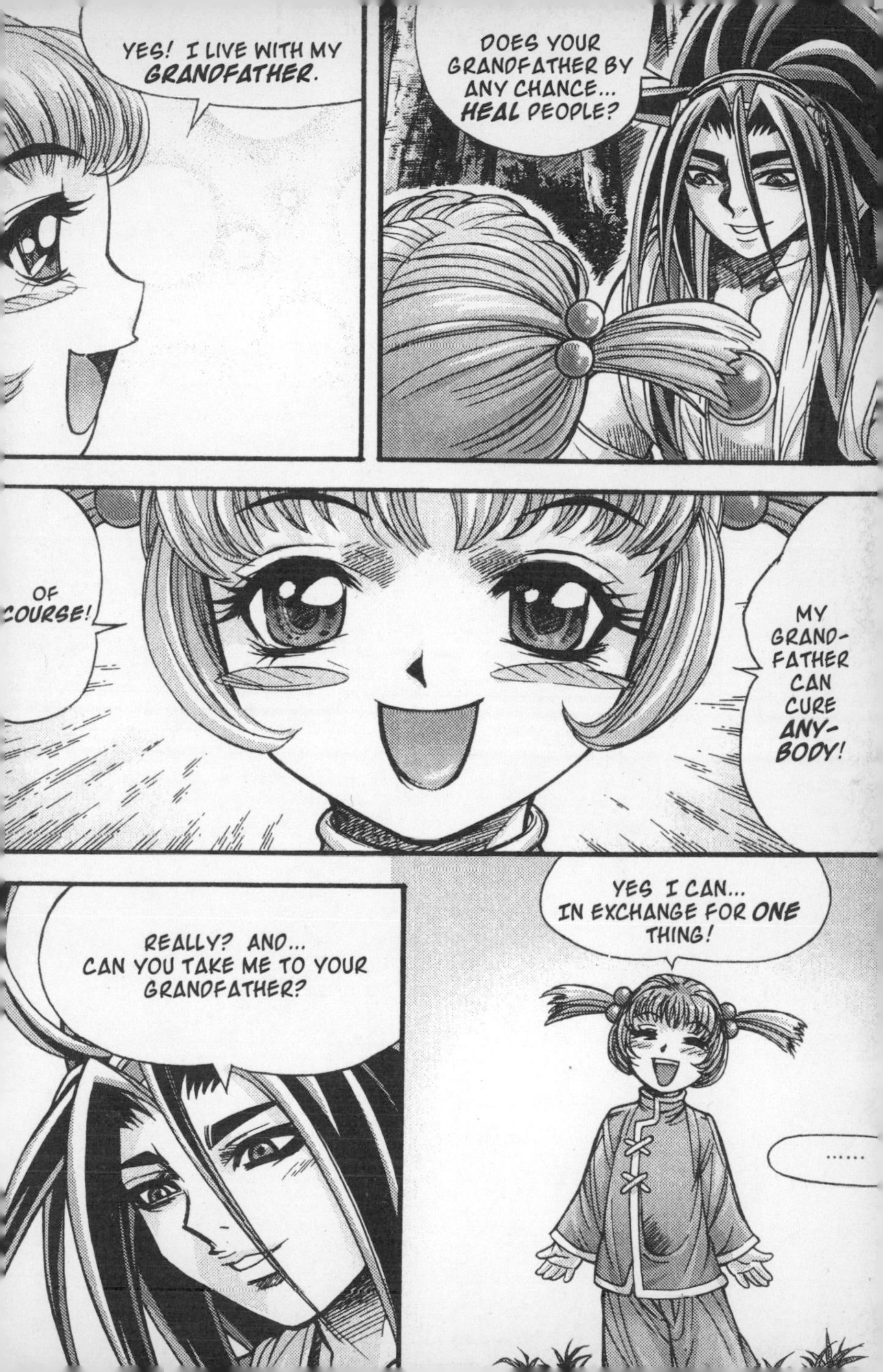
YES! I LIVE WITH MY GRANDFATHER.
DOES YOUR GRANDFATHER BY ANY CHANCE... HEAL PEOPLE?
OF COURSE!
MY GRANDFATHER CAN CURE ANYBODY!
REALLY? AND... CAN YOU TAKE ME TO YOUR GRANDFATHER?
YES I CAN... IN EXCHANGE FOR ONE THING!
......

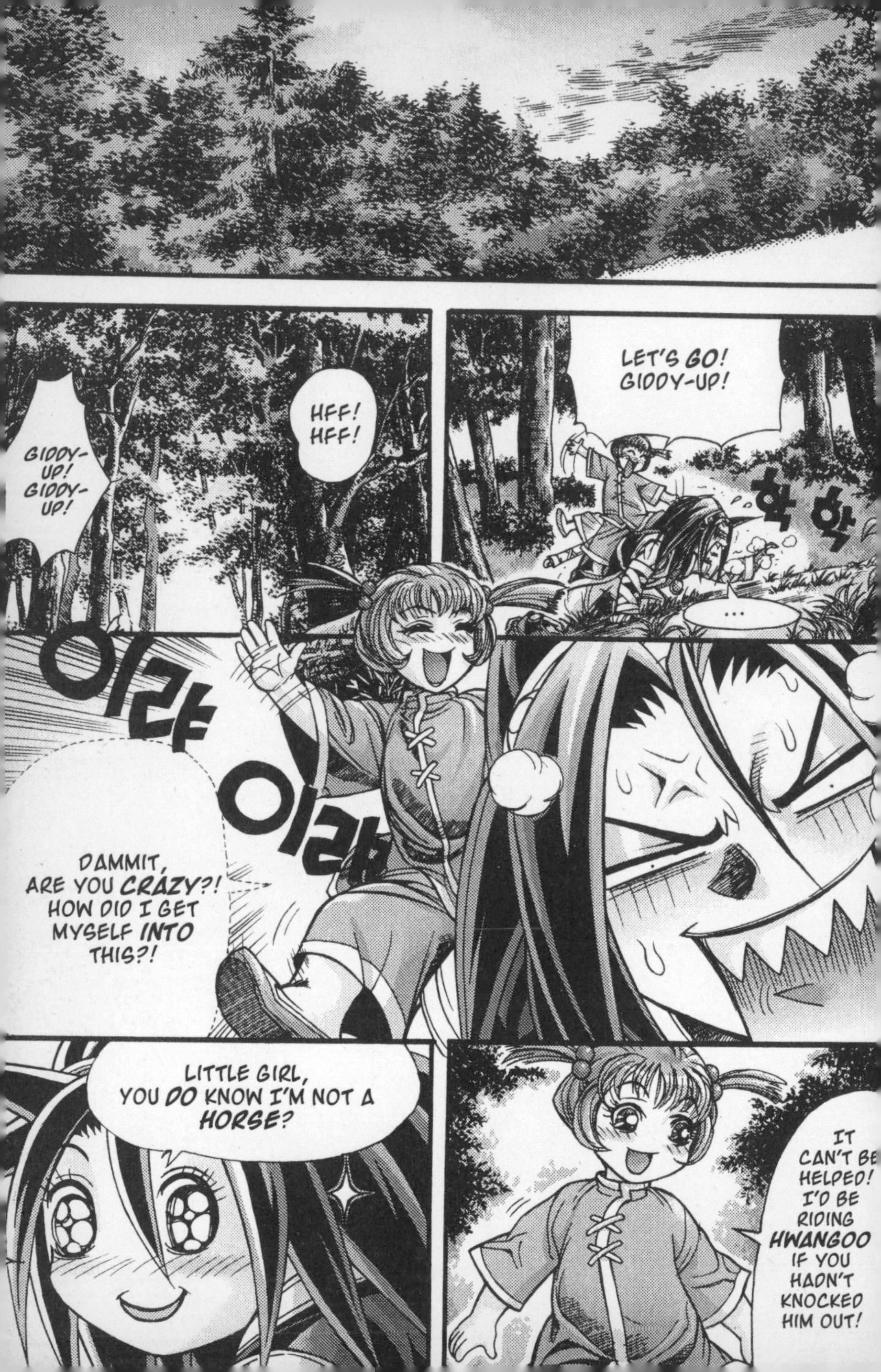
GIDDY-UP! GIDDY-UP!
HFF! HFF!
LET'S GO! GIDDY-UP!
헉 헉
...
이랴 이랴
DAMMIT, ARE YOU CRAZY?! HOW DID I GET MYSELF INTO THIS?!
LITTLE GIRL, YOU DO KNOW I'M NOT A HORSE?
IT CAN'T BE HELPED! I'D BE RIDING HWANGOO IF YOU HADN'T KNOCKED HIM OUT!

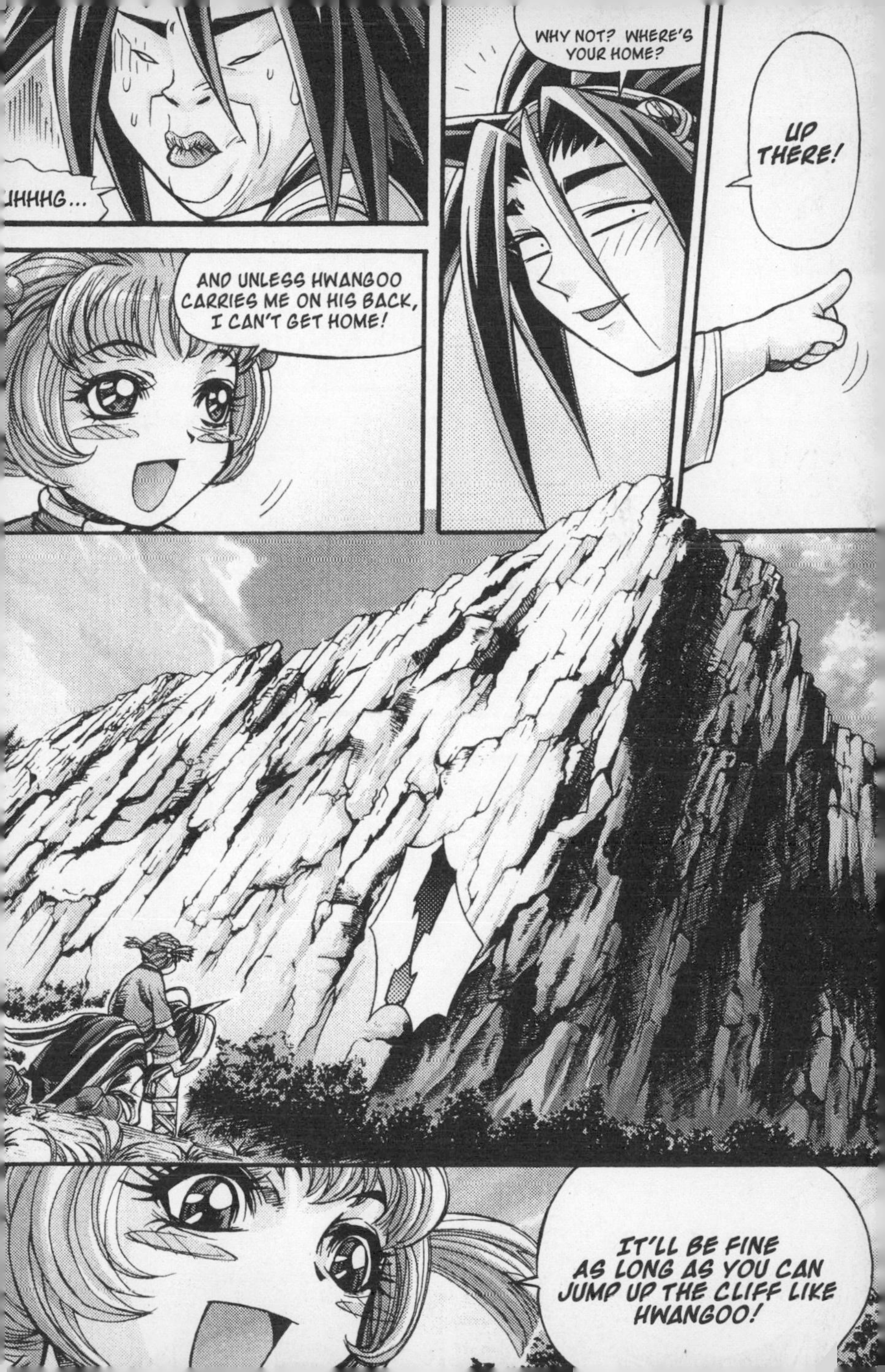
UHHHG...
WHY NOT? WHERE'S YOUR HOME?
UP THERE!
AND UNLESS HWANGOO CARRIES ME ON HIS BACK, I CAN'T GET HOME!
IT'LL BE FINE AS LONG AS YOU CAN JUMP UP THE CLIFF LIKE HWANGOO!

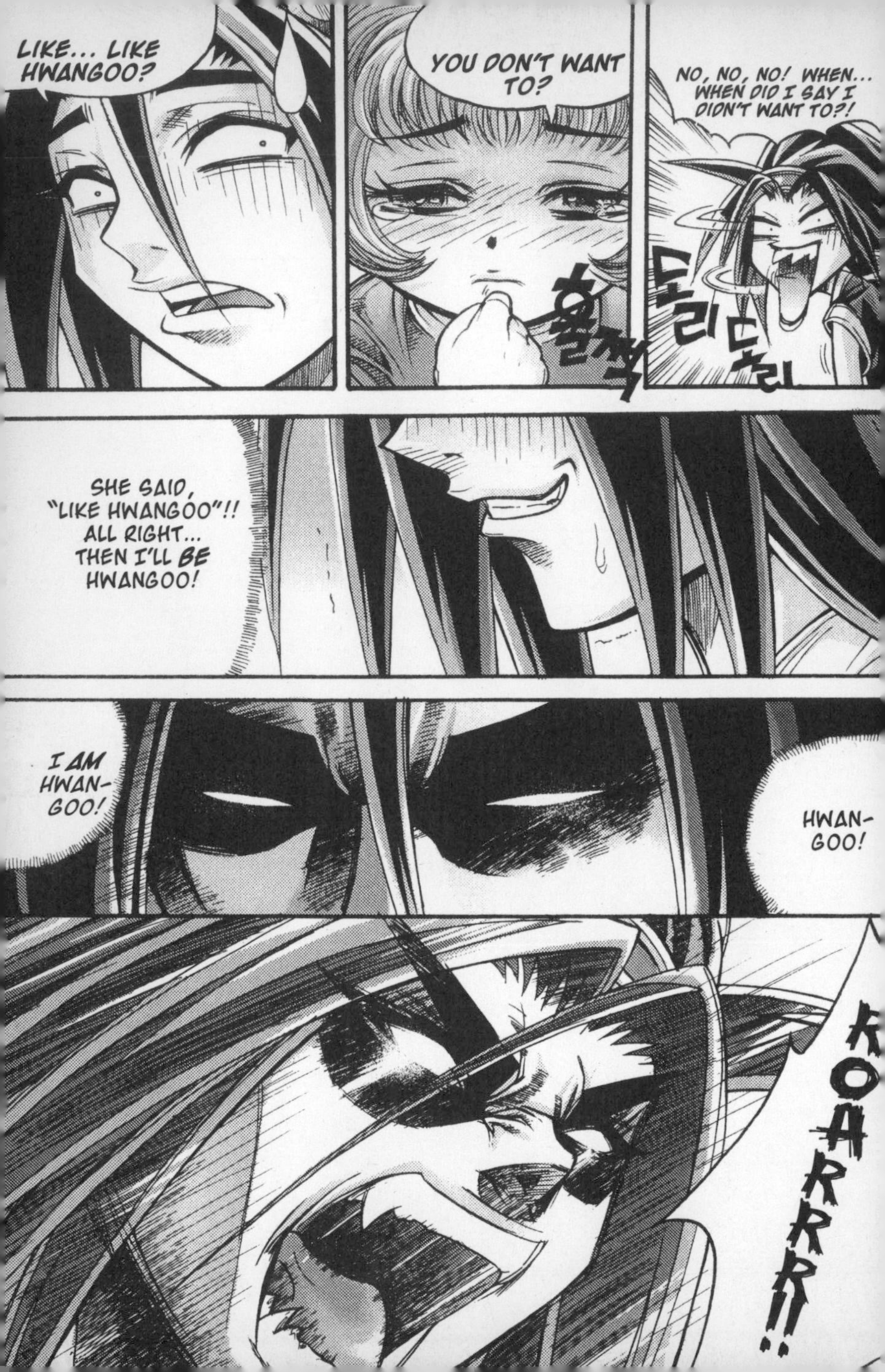
LIKE... LIKE HWANGOO?
YOU DON'T WANT TO?
훌쩍
NO, NO, NO! WHEN... WHEN DID I SAY I DIDN'T WANT TO?!
도리도리
SHE SAID, "LIKE HWANGOO"!! ALL RIGHT... THEN I'LL *BE* HWANGOO!
I AM HWAN-GOO!
HWAN-GOO!
KOARRRR!!

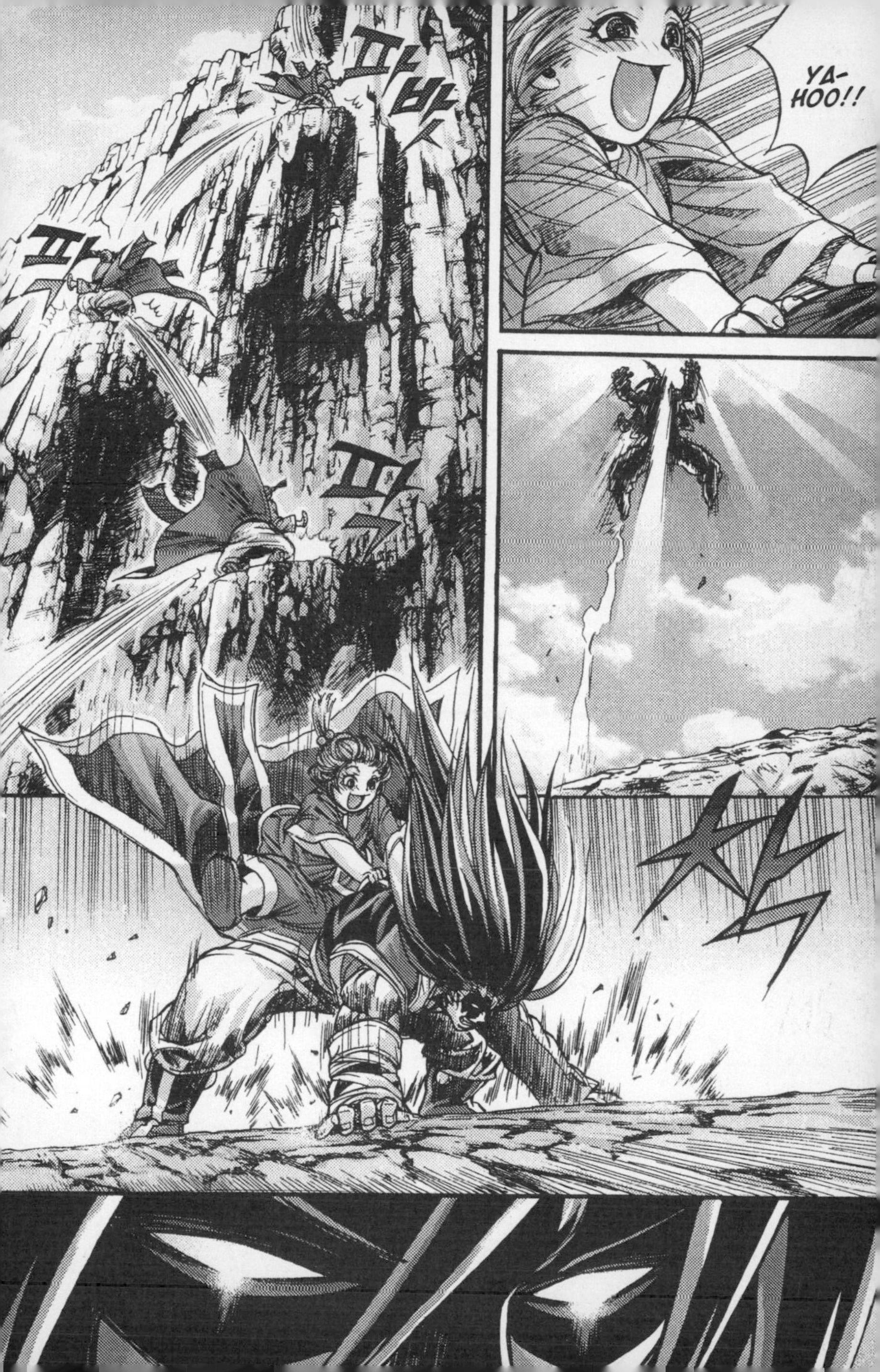
YA-HOO!!

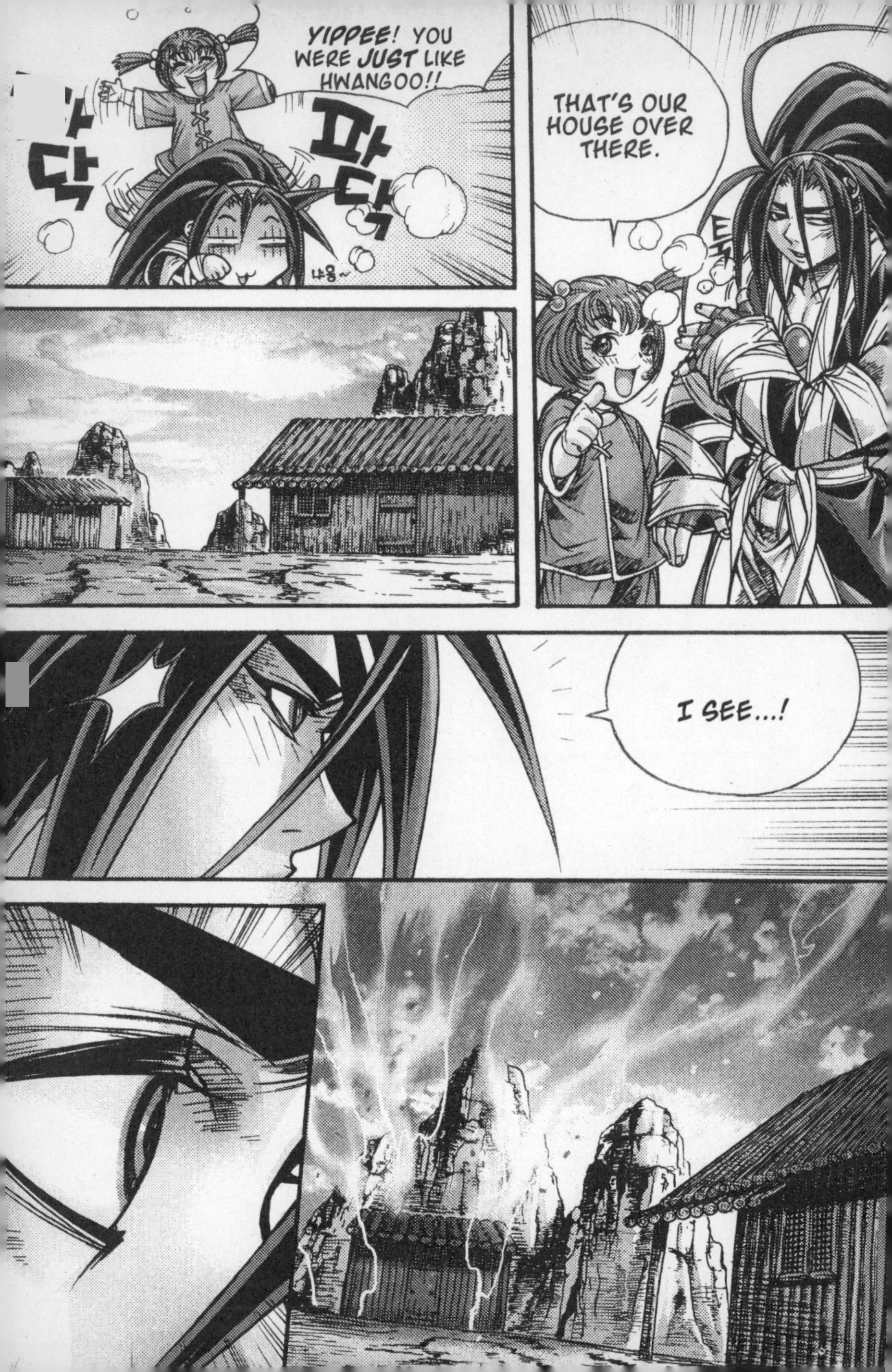
YIPPEE! YOU WERE JUST LIKE HWANGOO!!
파닥
THAT'S OUR HOUSE OVER THERE.
I SEE...!

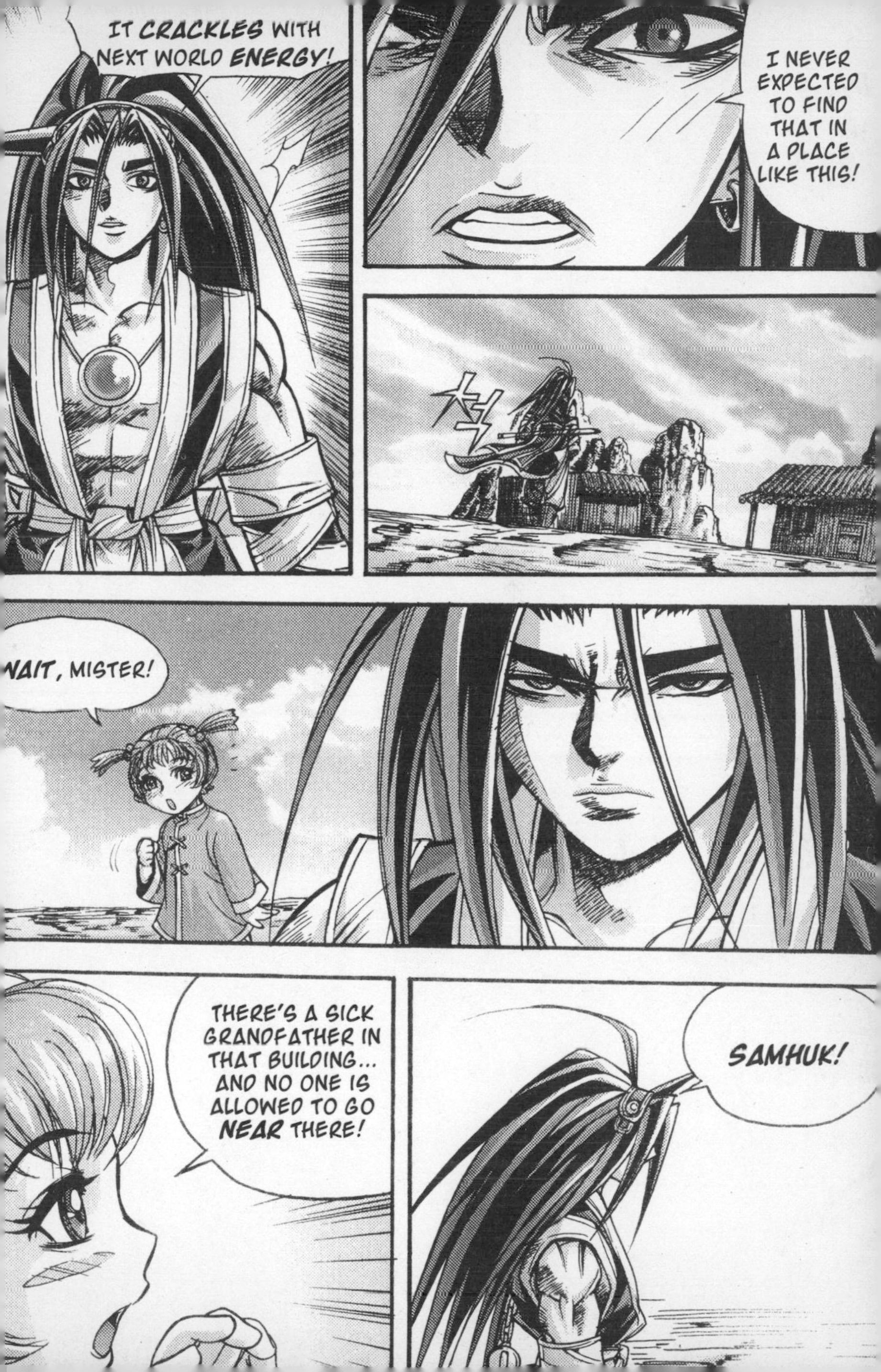
IT CRACKLES WITH NEXT WORLD ENERGY!
I NEVER EXPECTED TO FIND THAT IN A PLACE LIKE THIS!
NAIT, MISTER!
THERE'S A SICK GRANDFATHER IN THAT BUILDING... AND NO ONE IS ALLOWED TO GO NEAR THERE!
SAMHUK!

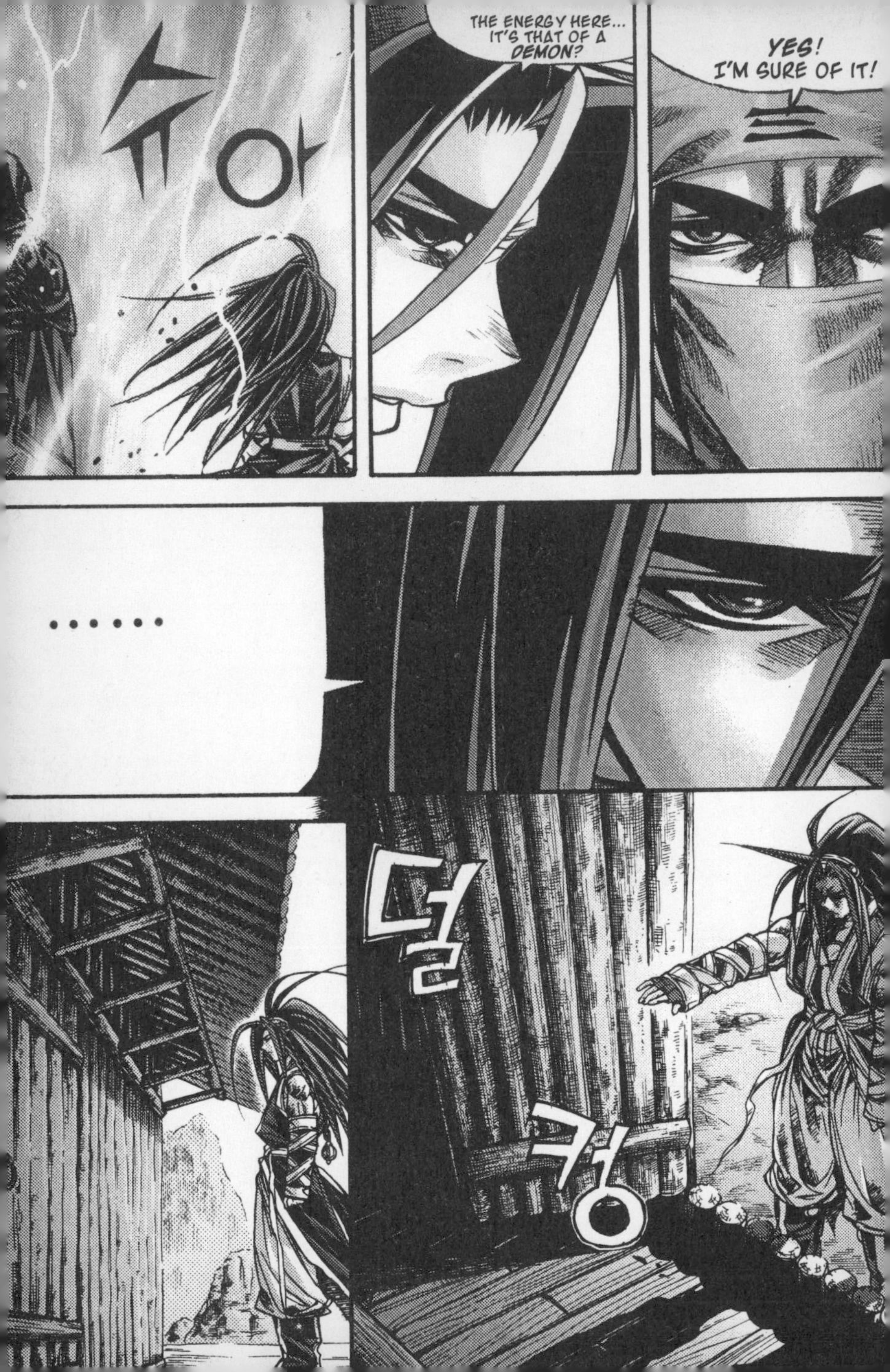
THE ENERGY HERE... IT'S THAT OF A *DEMON*?
YES! I'M SURE OF IT!
......
덜컹

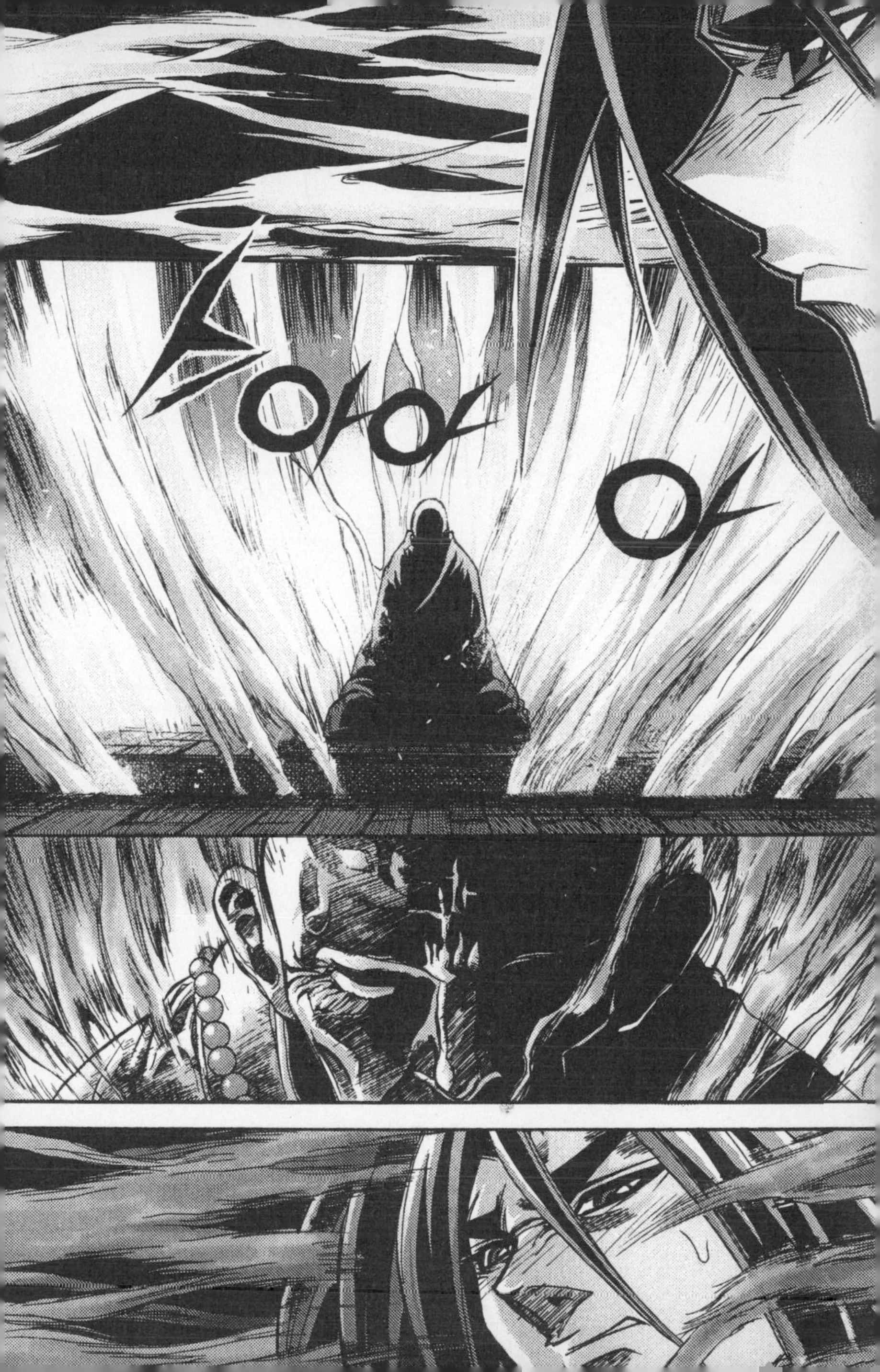

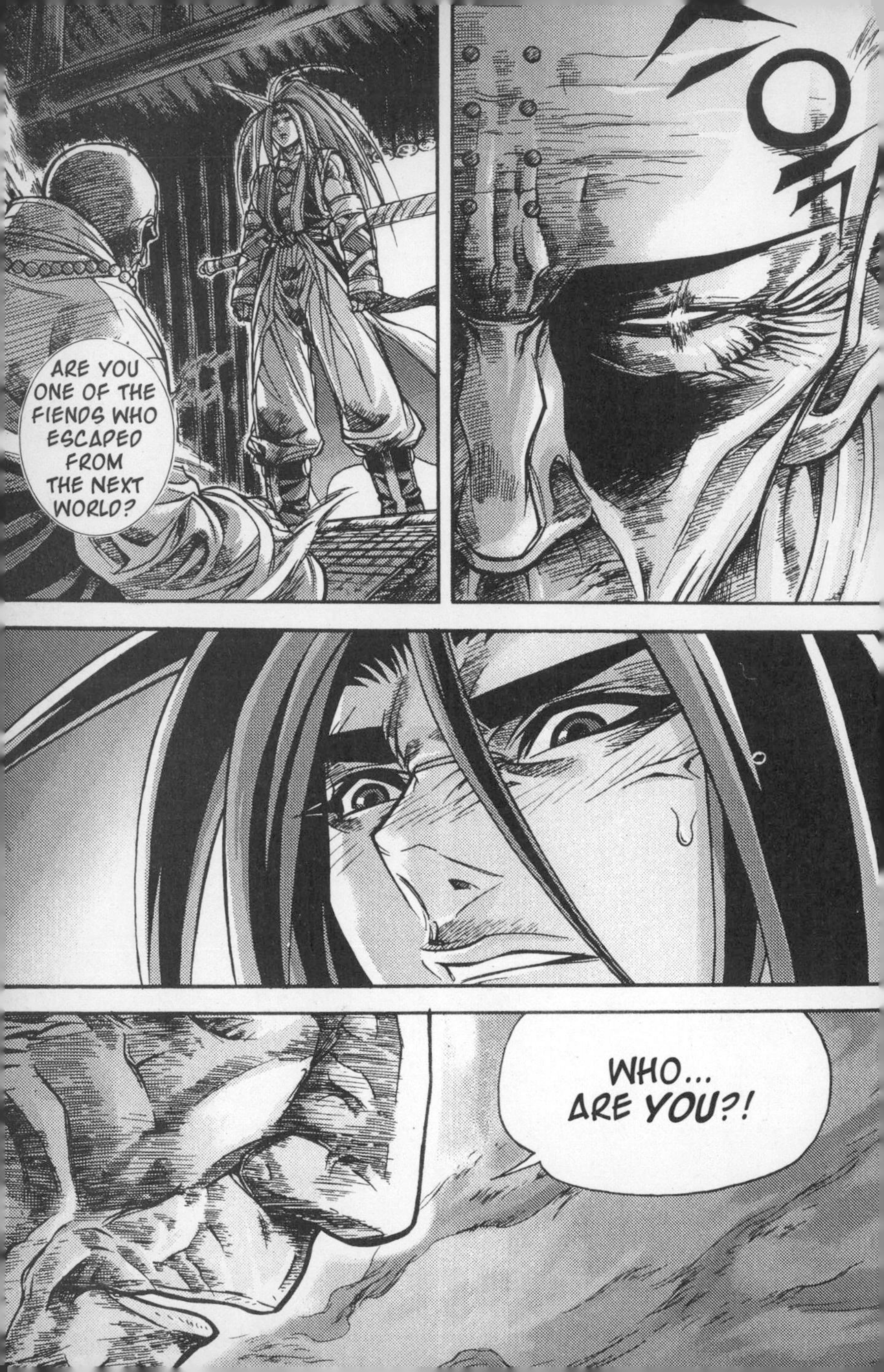
ARE YOU ONE OF THE FIENDS WHO ESCAPED FROM THE NEXT WORLD?
WHO... ARE YOU?!

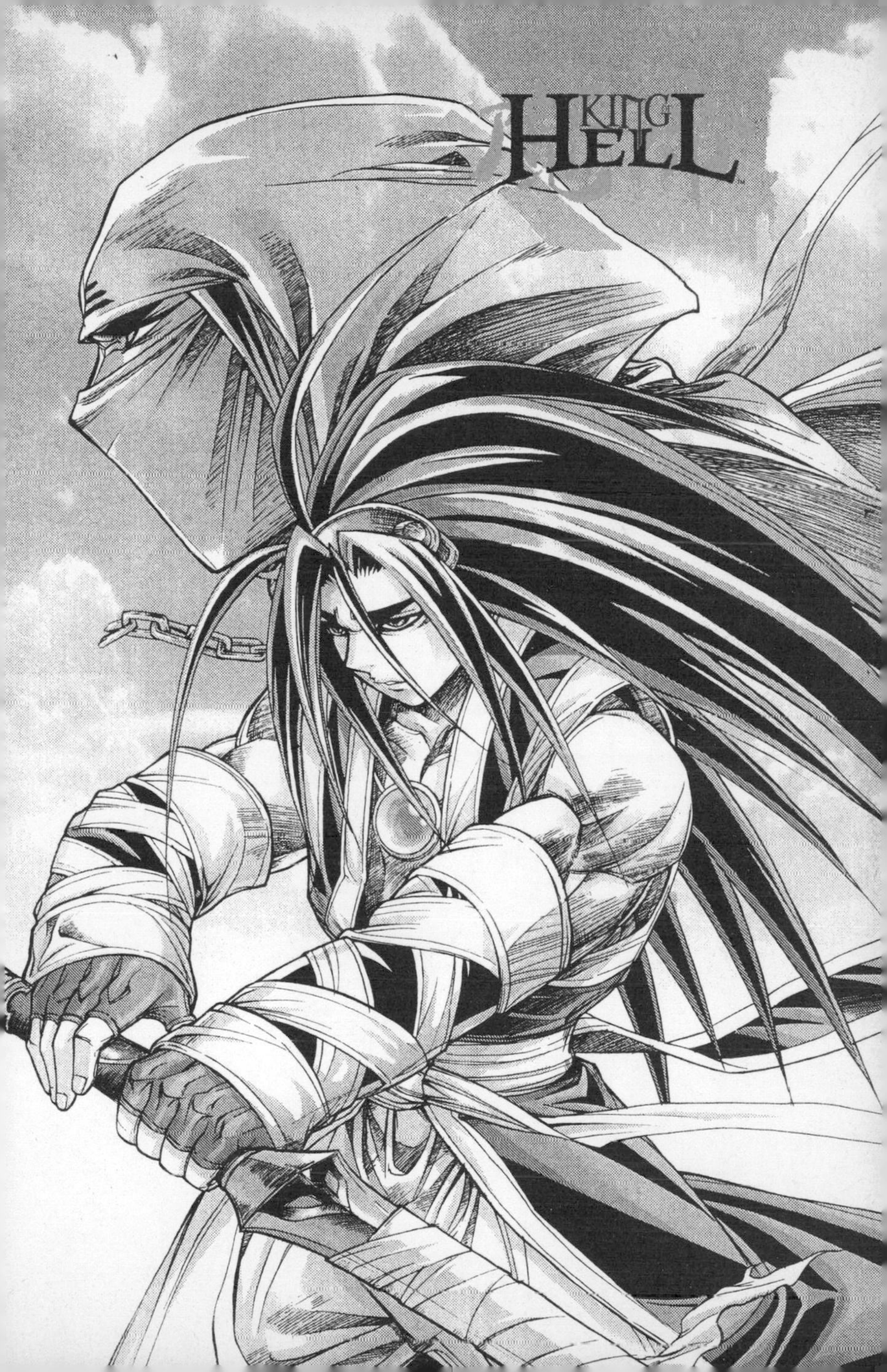
KING HELL

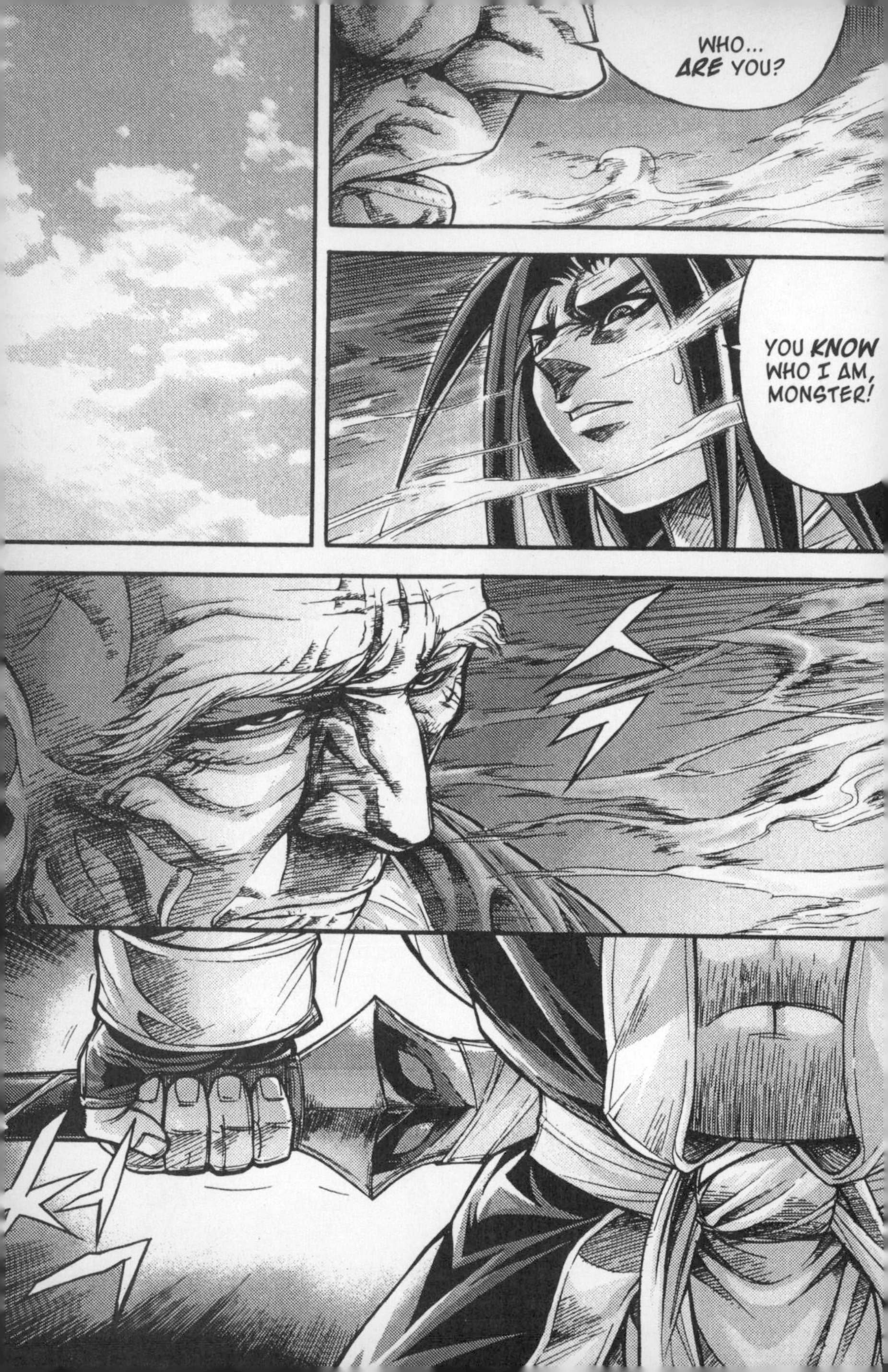
WHO... ARE YOU?
YOU KNOW WHO I AM, MONSTER!

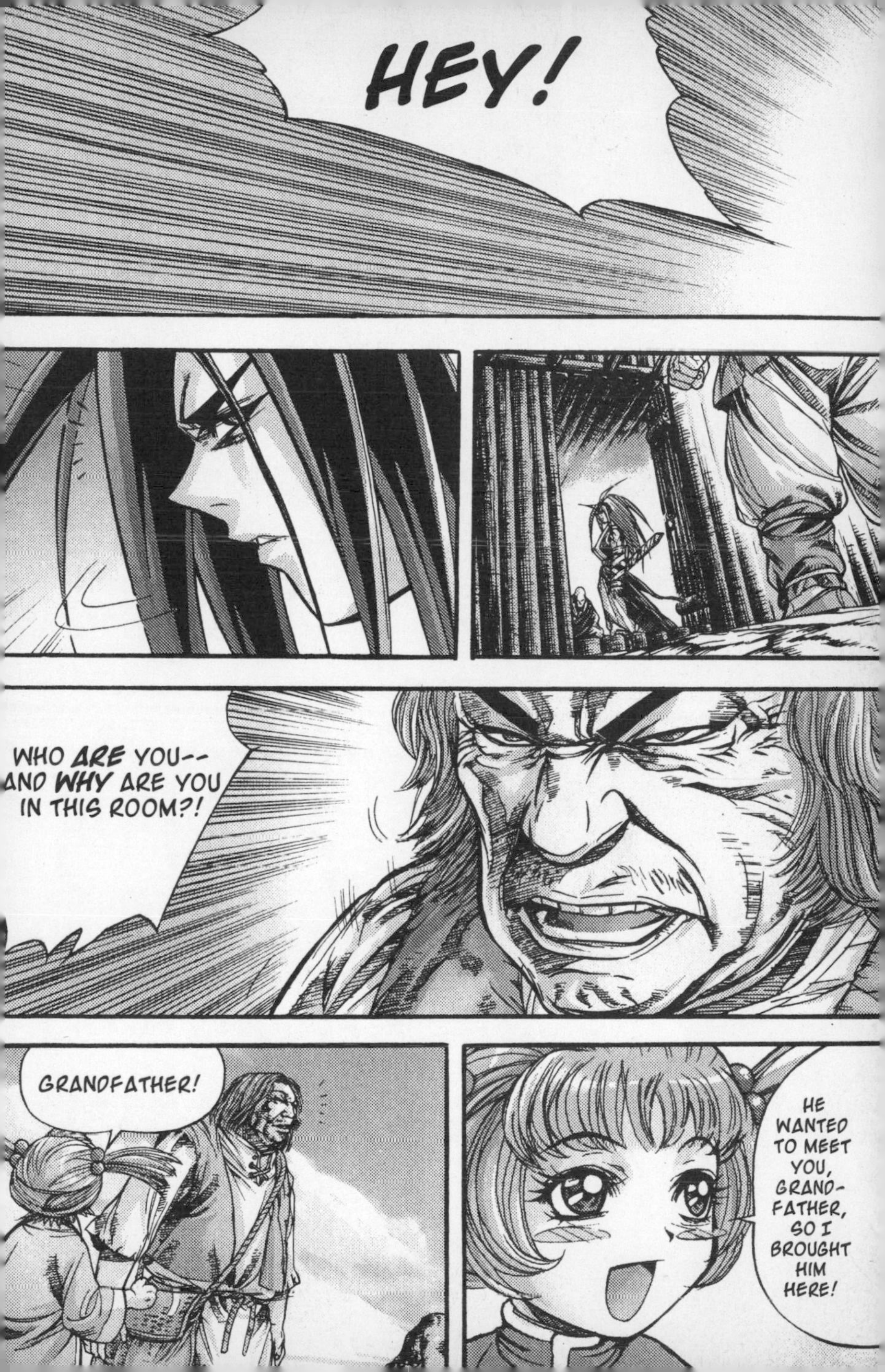
HEY!
WHO ARE YOU-- AND WHY ARE YOU IN THIS ROOM?!
GRANDFATHER!
HE WANTED TO MEET YOU, GRAND-FATHER, SO I BROUGHT HIM HERE!

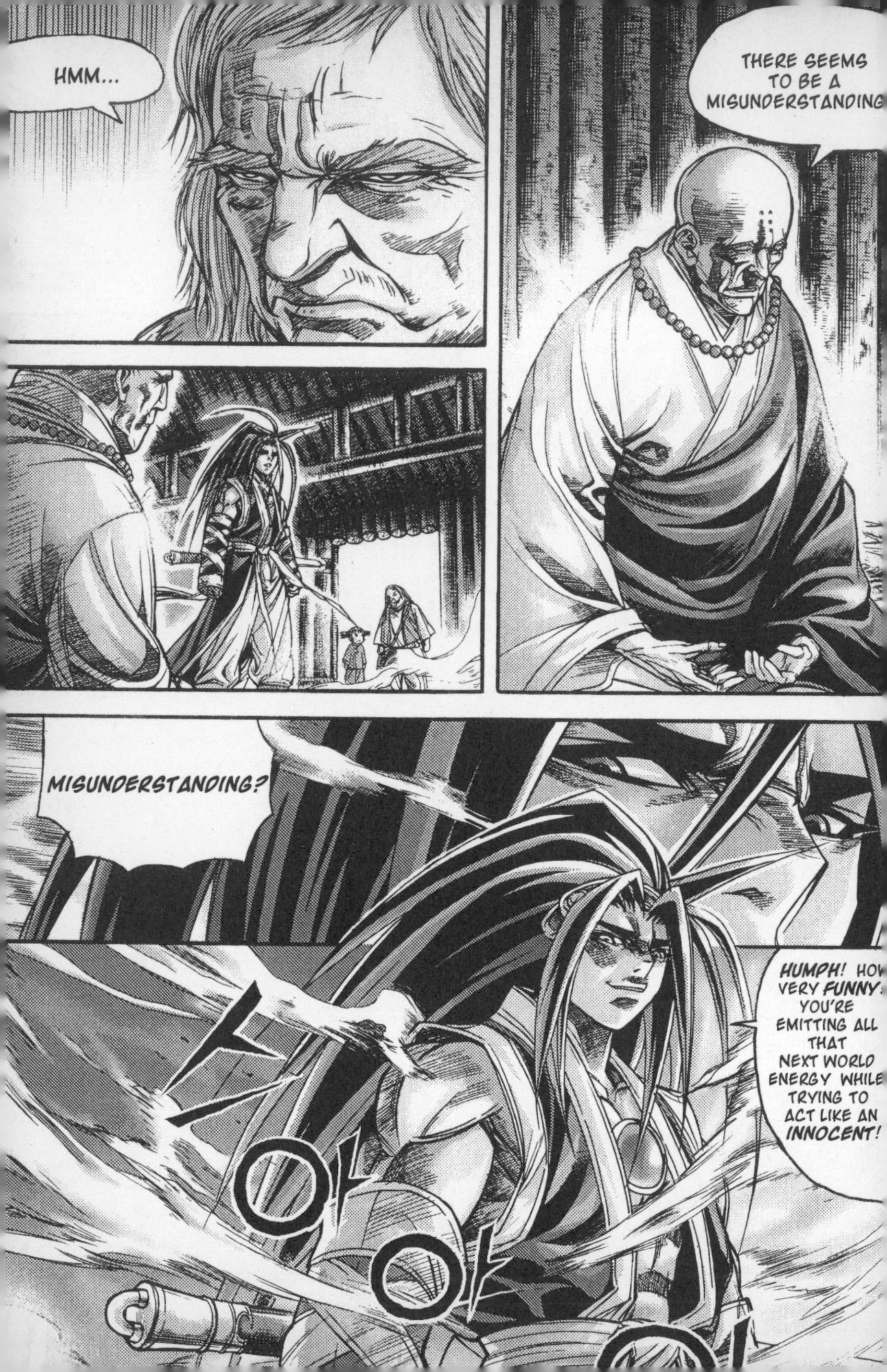
HMM...
THERE SEEMS TO BE A MISUNDERSTANDING
MISUNDERSTANDING?
HUMPH! HOW VERY FUNNY. YOU'RE EMITTING ALL THAT NEXT WORLD ENERGY WHILE TRYING TO ACT LIKE AN INNOCENT!

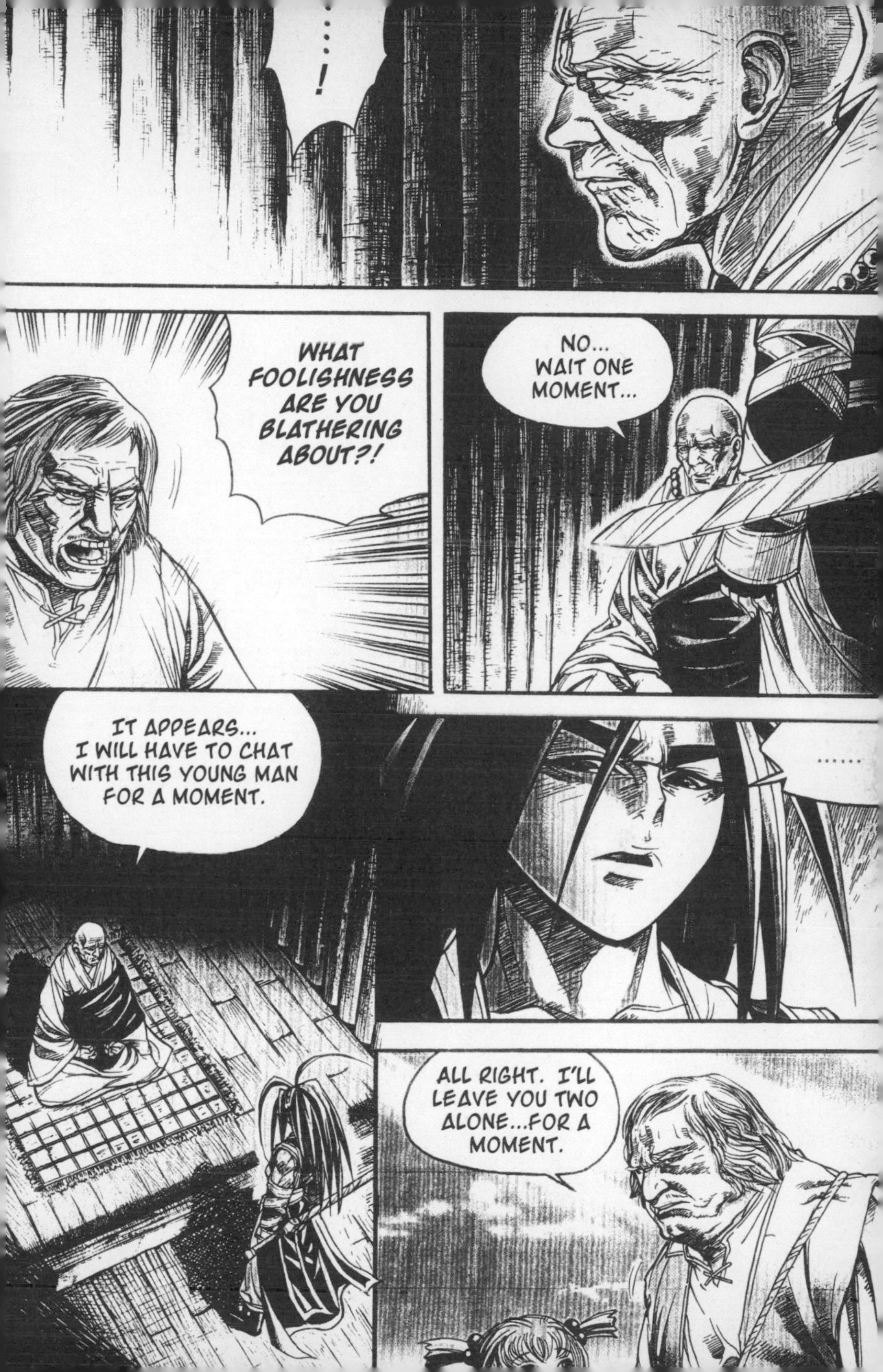
....!
WHAT FOOLISHNESS ARE YOU BLATHERING ABOUT?!
NO... WAIT ONE MOMENT...
IT APPEARS... I WILL HAVE TO CHAT WITH THIS YOUNG MAN FOR A MOMENT.
......
ALL RIGHT. I'LL LEAVE YOU TWO ALONE...FOR A MOMENT.

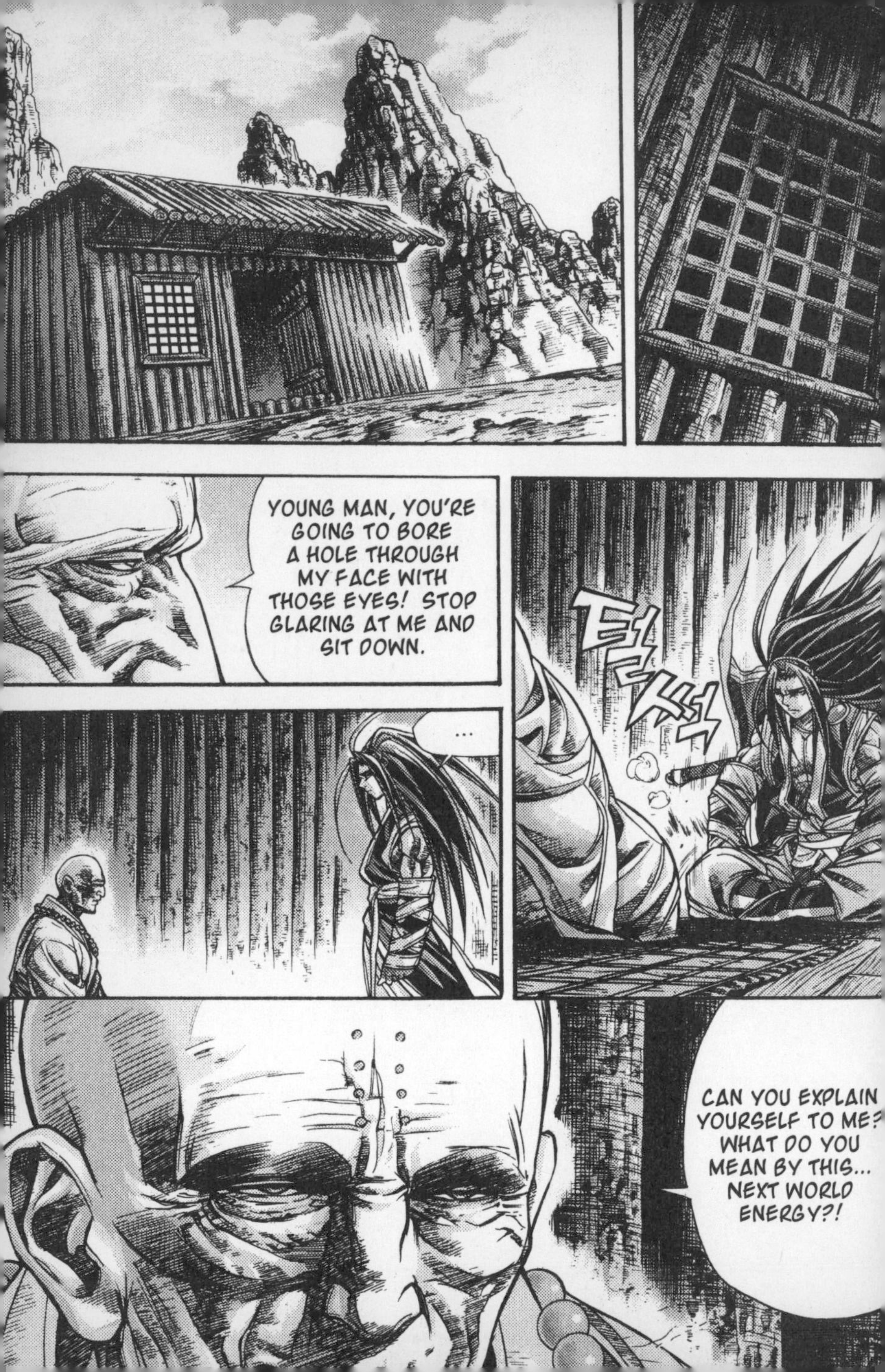
YOUNG MAN, YOU'RE GOING TO BORE A HOLE THROUGH MY FACE WITH THOSE EYES! STOP GLARING AT ME AND SIT DOWN.
...
털썩
CAN YOU EXPLAIN YOURSELF TO ME? WHAT DO YOU MEAN BY THIS... NEXT WORLD ENERGY?!

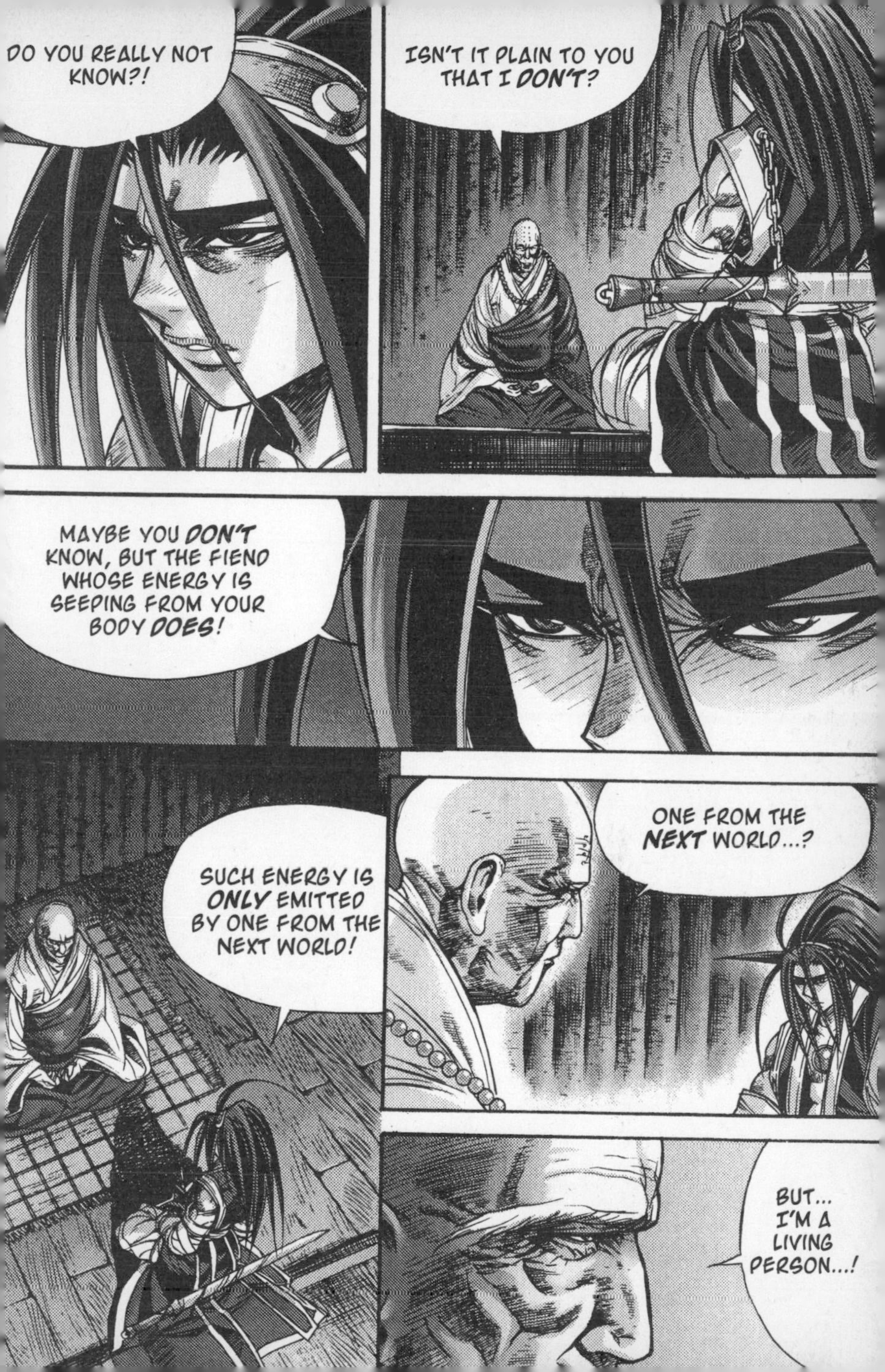
DO YOU REALLY NOT KNOW?!
ISN'T IT PLAIN TO YOU THAT I DON'T?
MAYBE YOU DON'T KNOW, BUT THE FIEND WHOSE ENERGY IS SEEPING FROM YOUR BODY DOES!
SUCH ENERGY IS ONLY EMITTED BY ONE FROM THE NEXT WORLD!
ONE FROM THE NEXT WORLD...?
BUT... I'M A LIVING PERSON...!

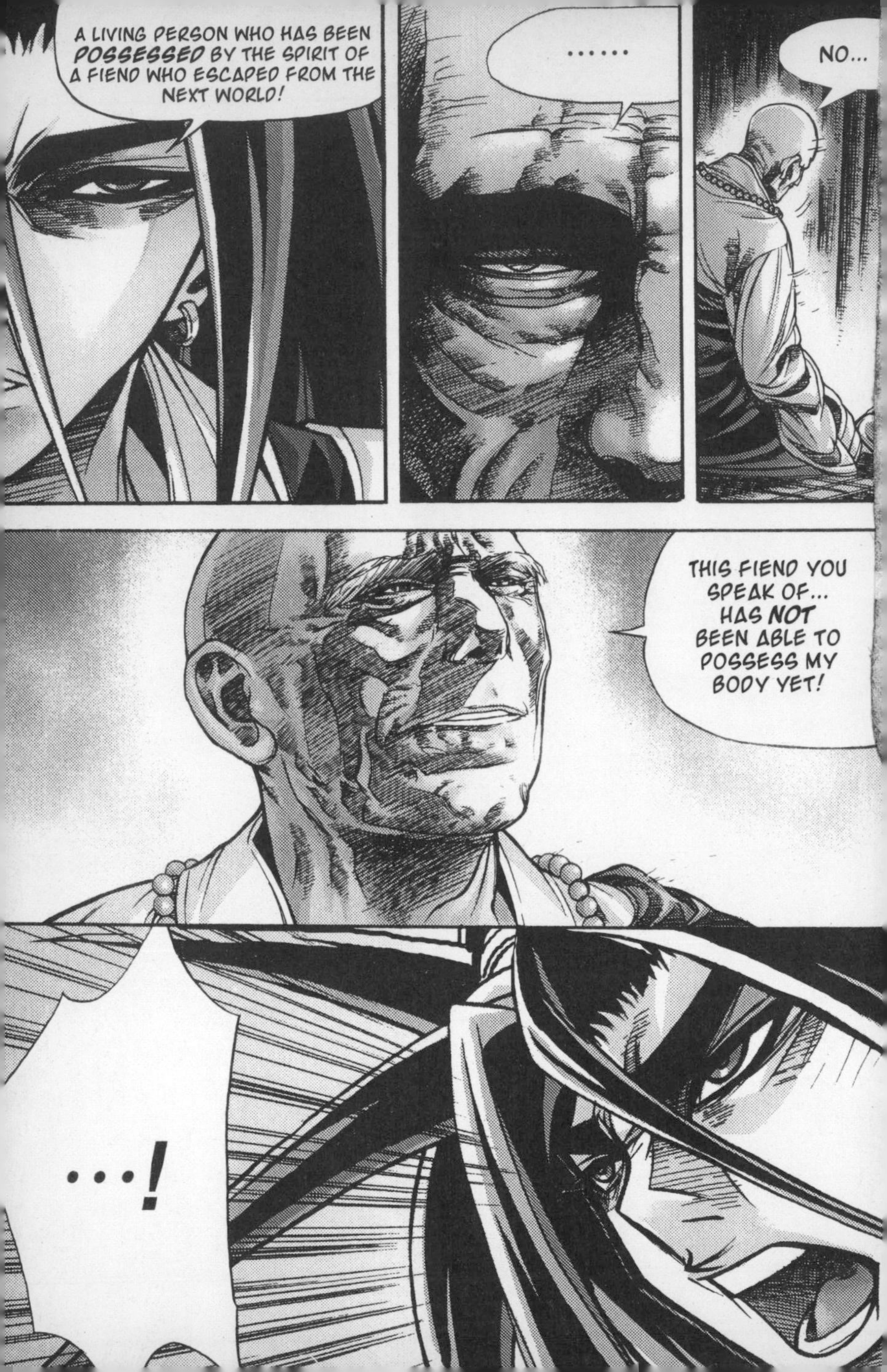
A LIVING PERSON WHO HAS BEEN POSSESSED BY THE SPIRIT OF A FIEND WHO ESCAPED FROM THE NEXT WORLD!
......
NO...
THIS FIEND YOU SPEAK OF... HAS NOT BEEN ABLE TO POSSESS MY BODY YET!
...!

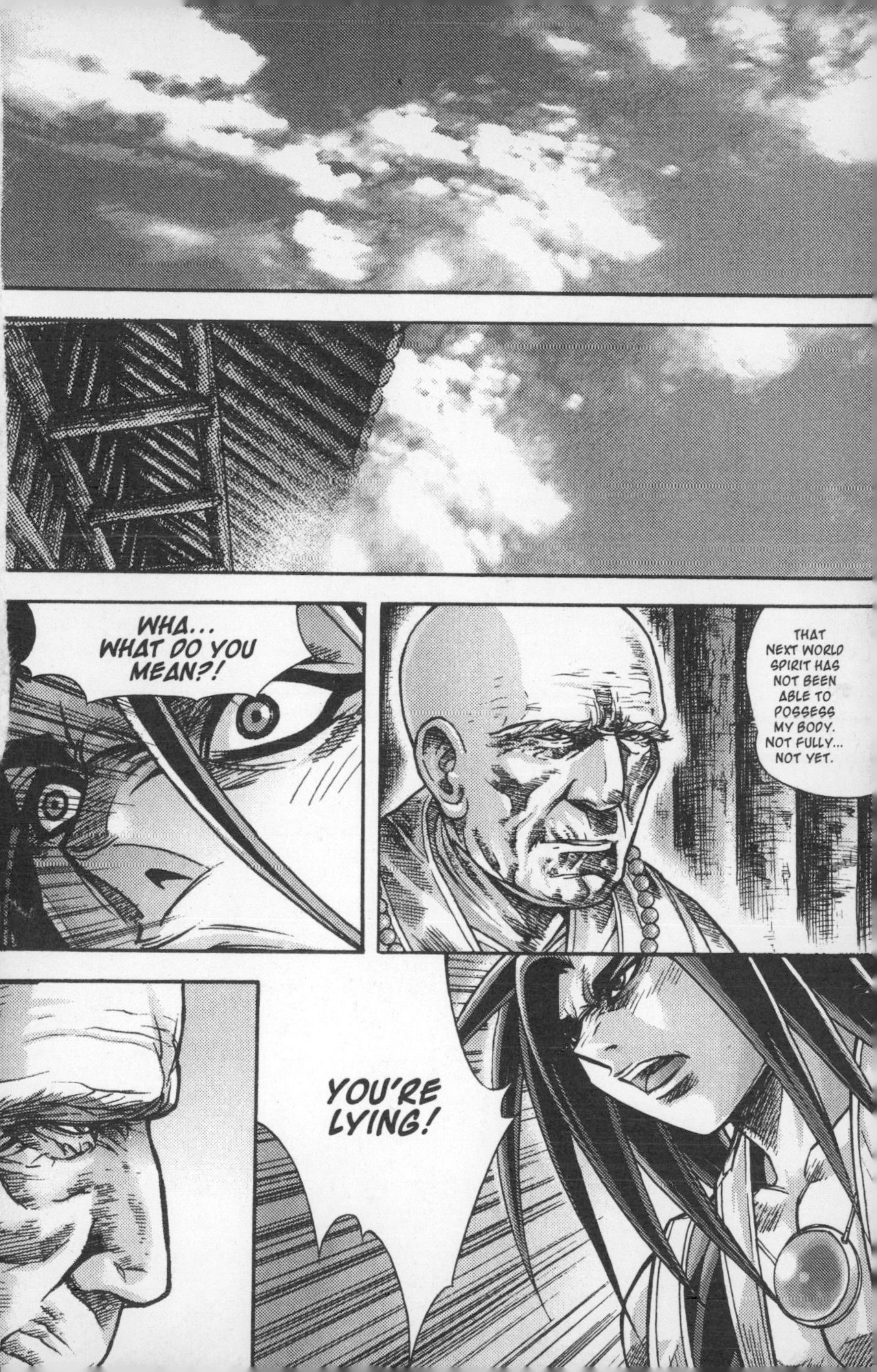
WHA... WHAT DO YOU MEAN?!
THAT NEXT WORLD SPIRIT HAS NOT BEEN ABLE TO POSSESS MY BODY. NOT FULLY... NOT YET.
YOU'RE LYING!

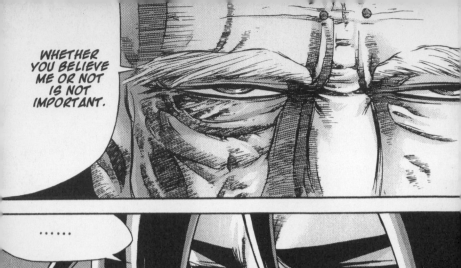

WHETHER YOU BELIEVE ME OR NOT IS NOT IMPORTANT.

......

BUT TELL ME, BOY... HOW DID YOU FIND OUT ABOUT MY CIRCUMSTANCES...

...AND WHO ARE YOU THAT YOU WOULD TRY TO DRIVE THIS SPIRIT FROM ME?!

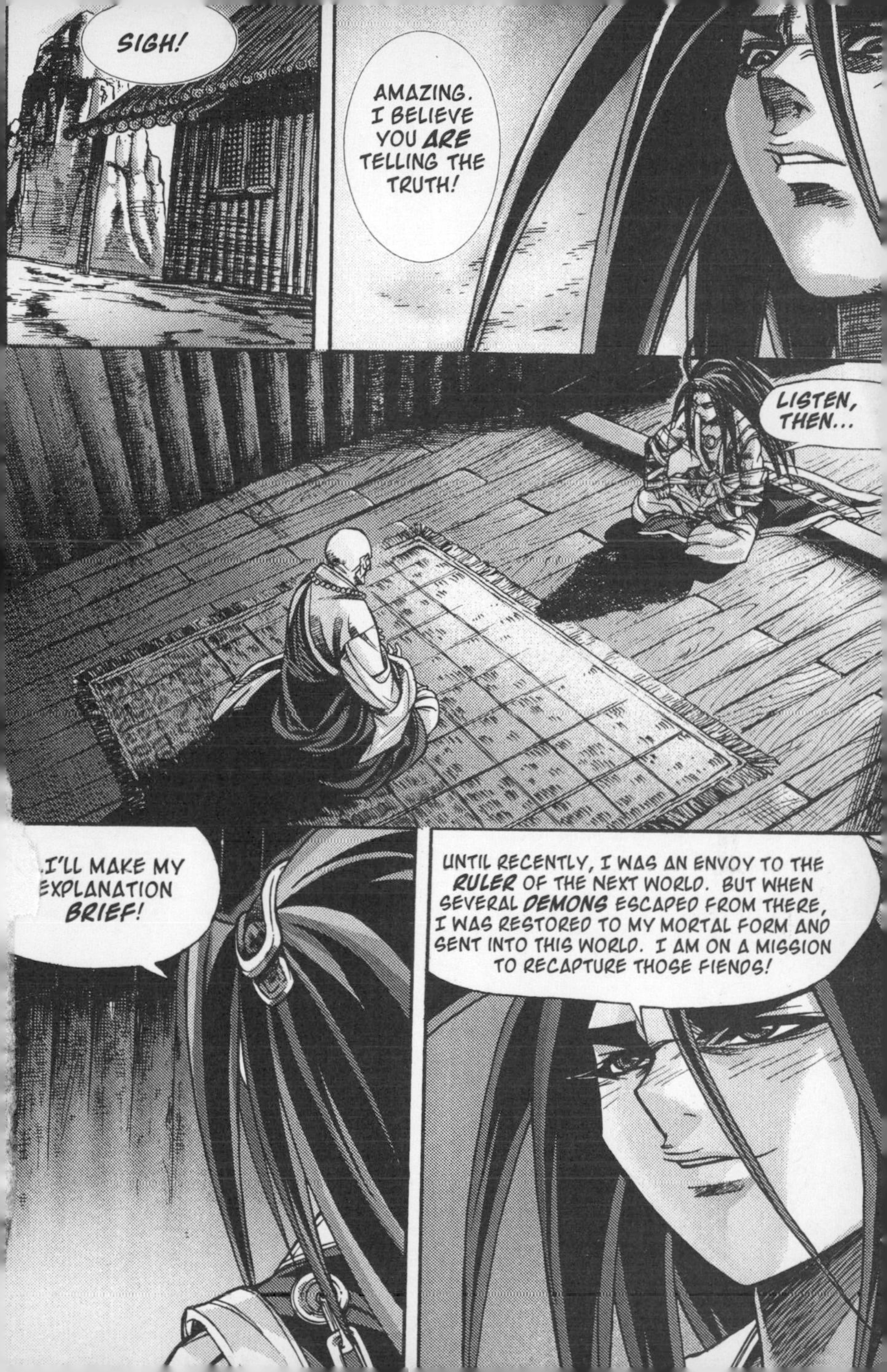
SIGH!
AMAZING. I BELIEVE YOU ARE TELLING THE TRUTH!
LISTEN, THEN...
...I'LL MAKE MY EXPLANATION BRIEF!
UNTIL RECENTLY, I WAS AN ENVOY TO THE RULER OF THE NEXT WORLD. BUT WHEN SEVERAL DEMONS ESCAPED FROM THERE, I WAS RESTORED TO MY MORTAL FORM AND SENT INTO THIS WORLD. I AM ON A MISSION TO RECAPTURE THOSE FIENDS!

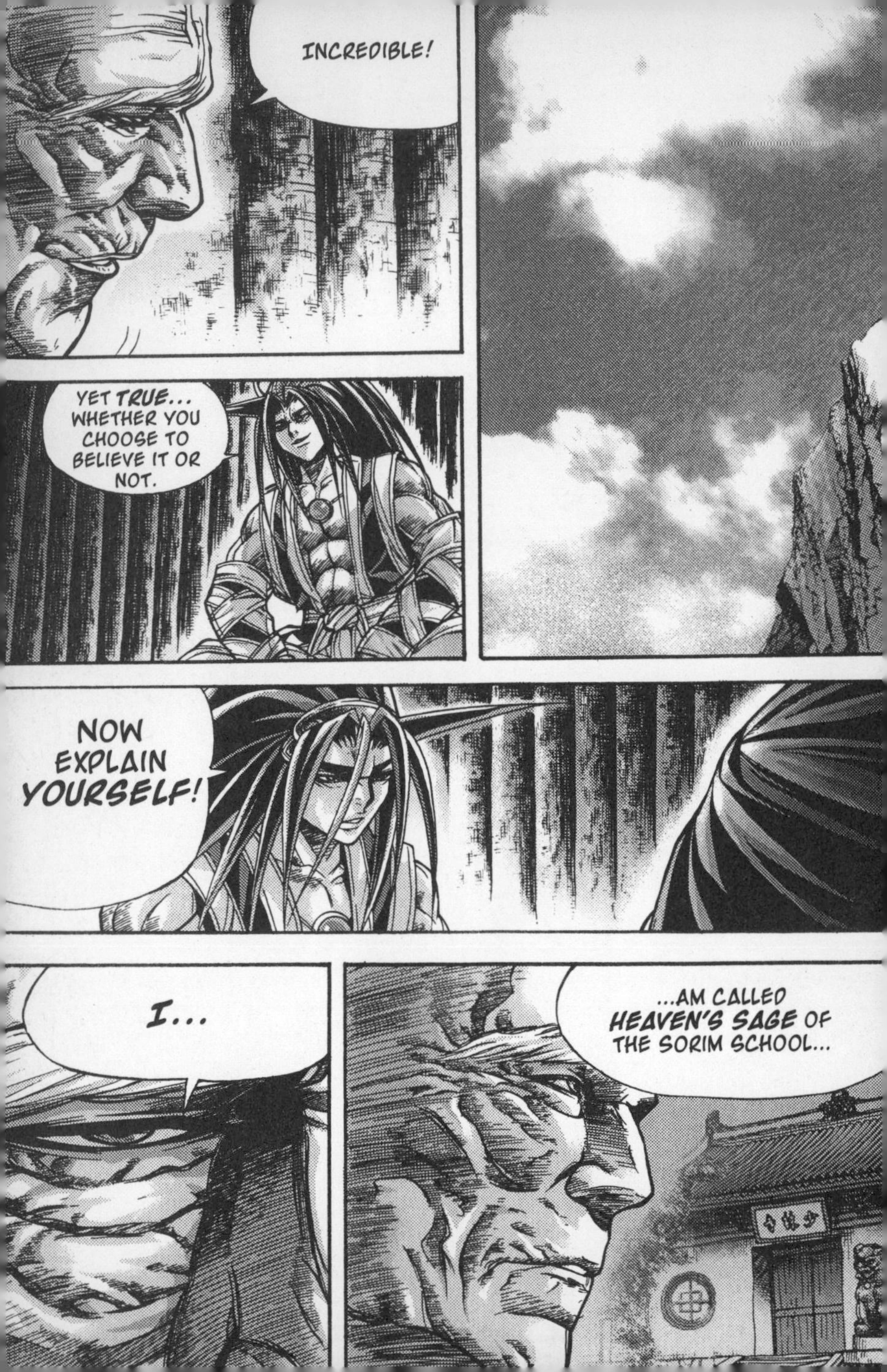
INCREDIBLE!
YET TRUE... WHETHER YOU CHOOSE TO BELIEVE IT OR NOT.
NOW EXPLAIN YOURSELF!
I...
...AM CALLED HEAVEN'S SAGE OF THE SORIM SCHOOL...

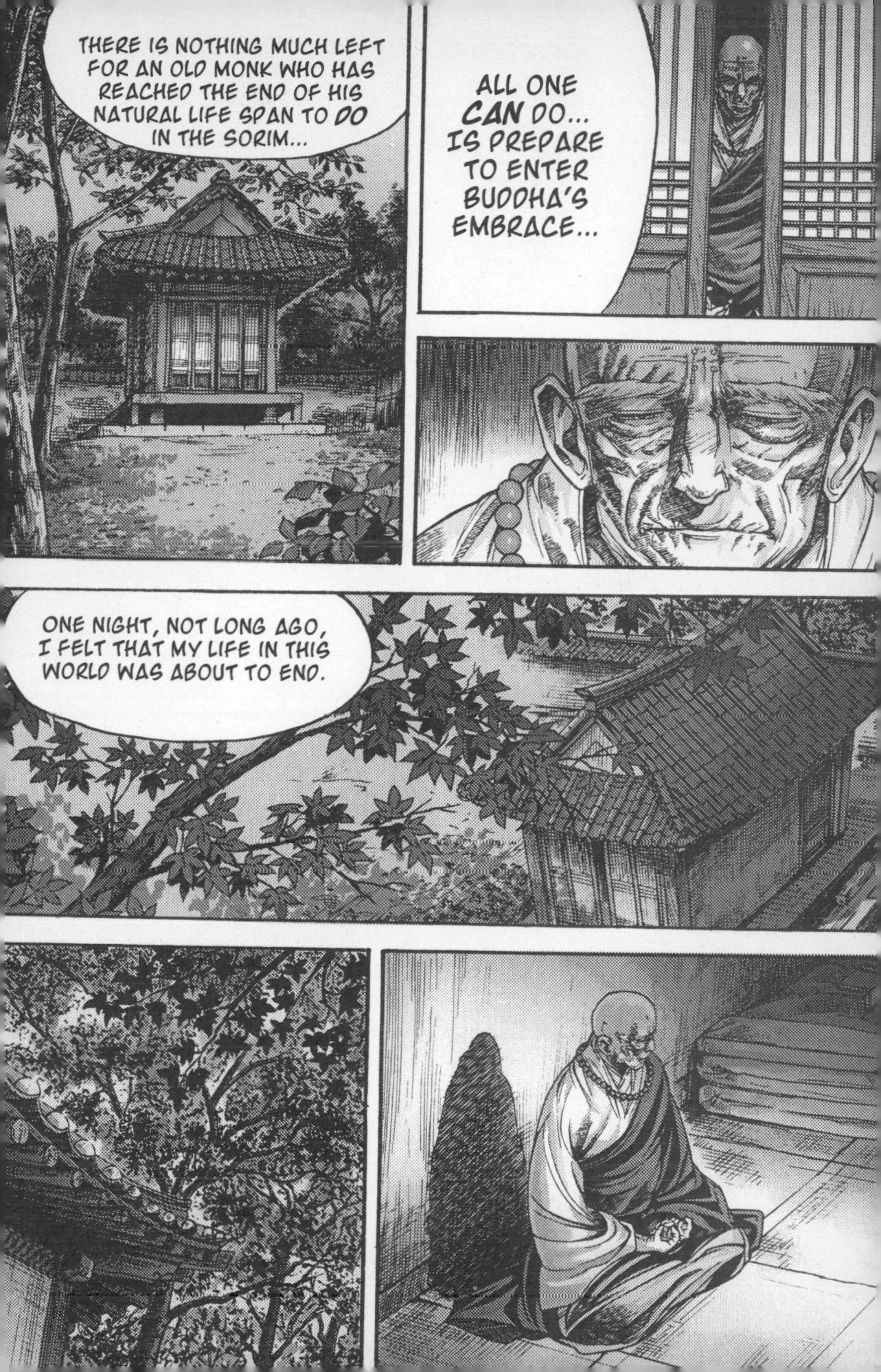
THERE IS NOTHING MUCH LEFT FOR AN OLD MONK WHO HAS REACHED THE END OF HIS NATURAL LIFE SPAN TO *DO* IN THE SORIM...
ALL ONE **CAN** DO... IS PREPARE TO ENTER BUDDHA'S EMBRACE...
ONE NIGHT, NOT LONG AGO, I FELT THAT MY LIFE IN THIS WORLD WAS ABOUT TO END.

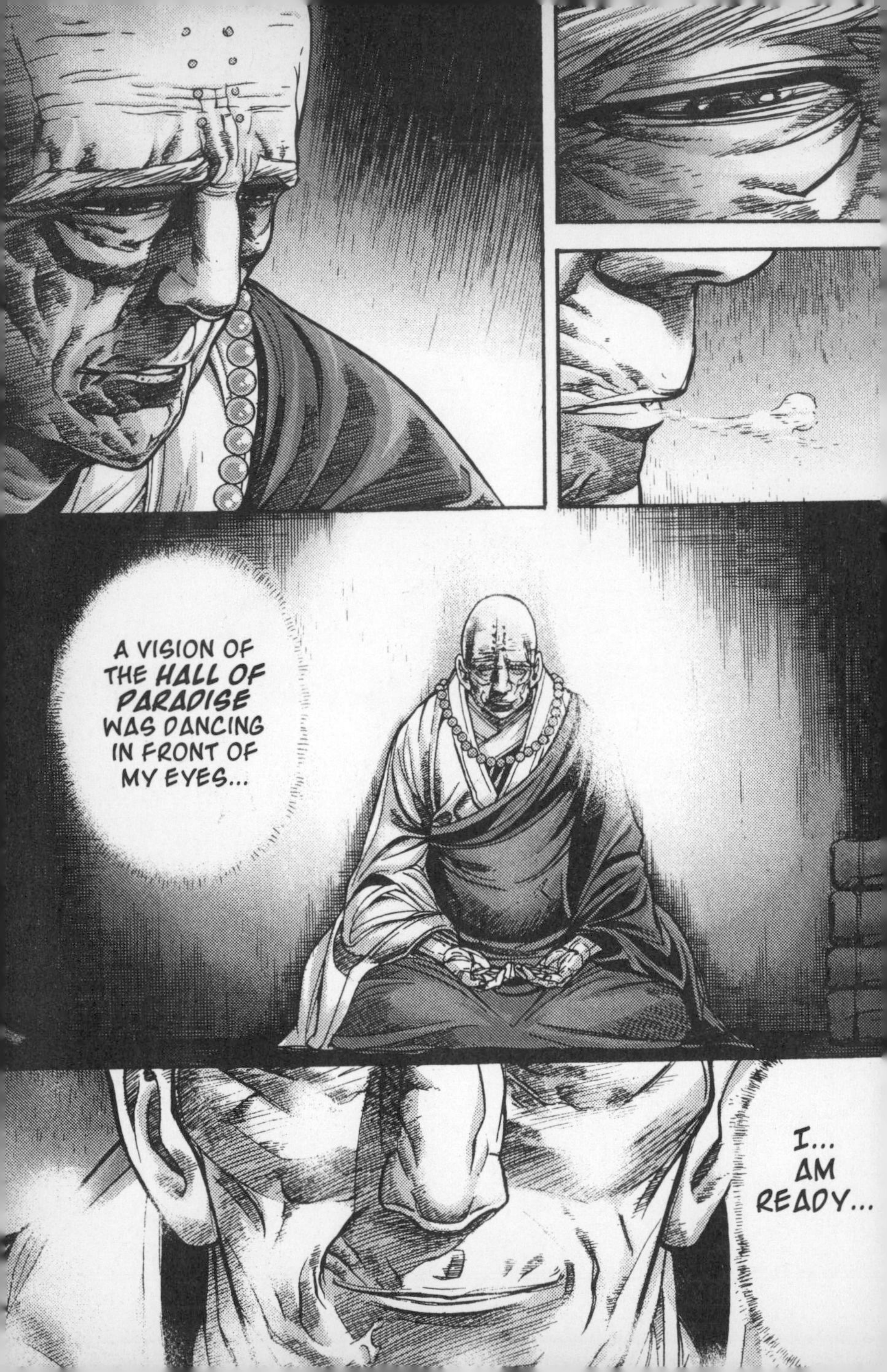
A VISION OF THE HALL OF PARADISE WAS DANCING IN FRONT OF MY EYES...
I... AM READY...

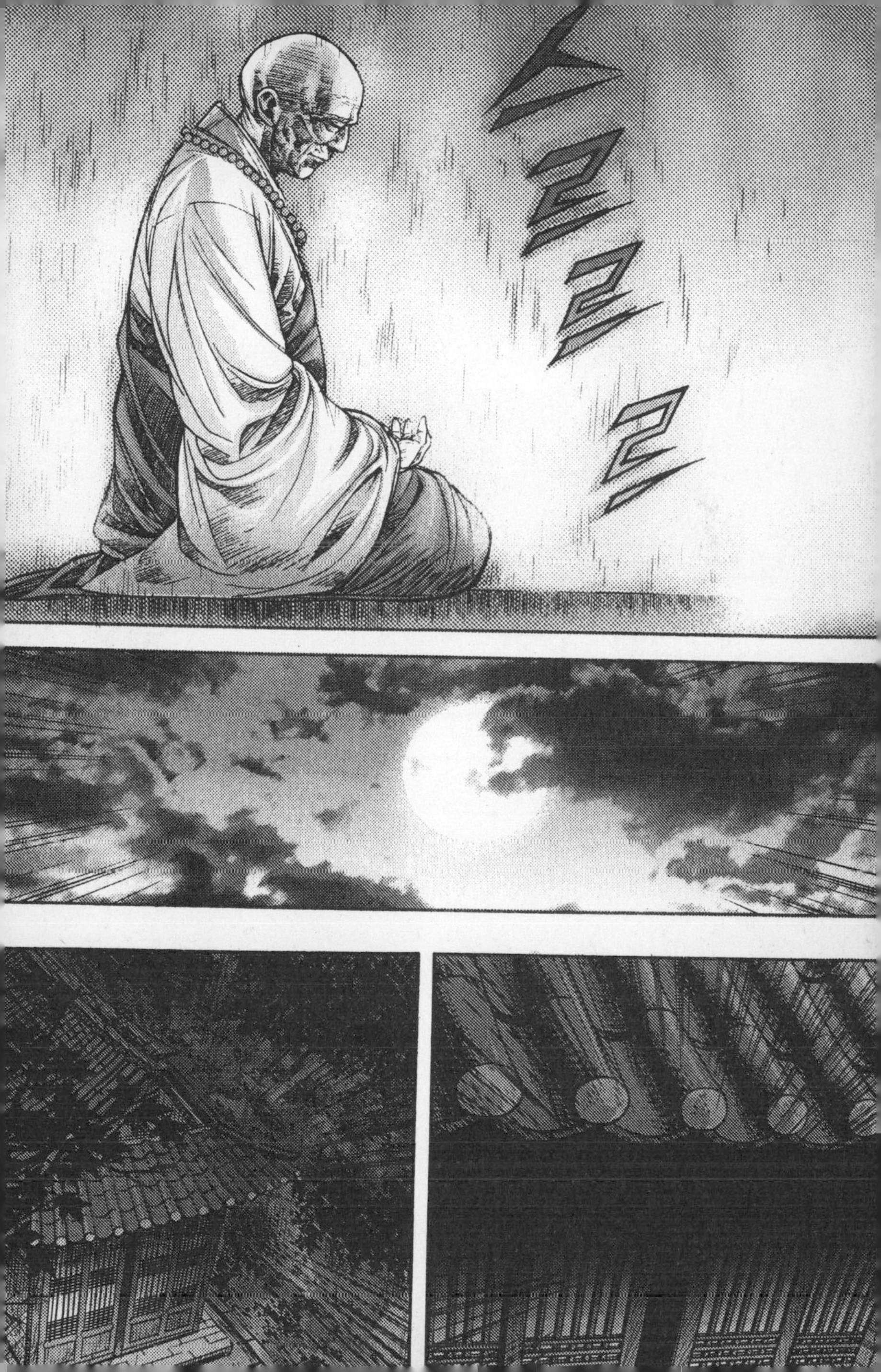

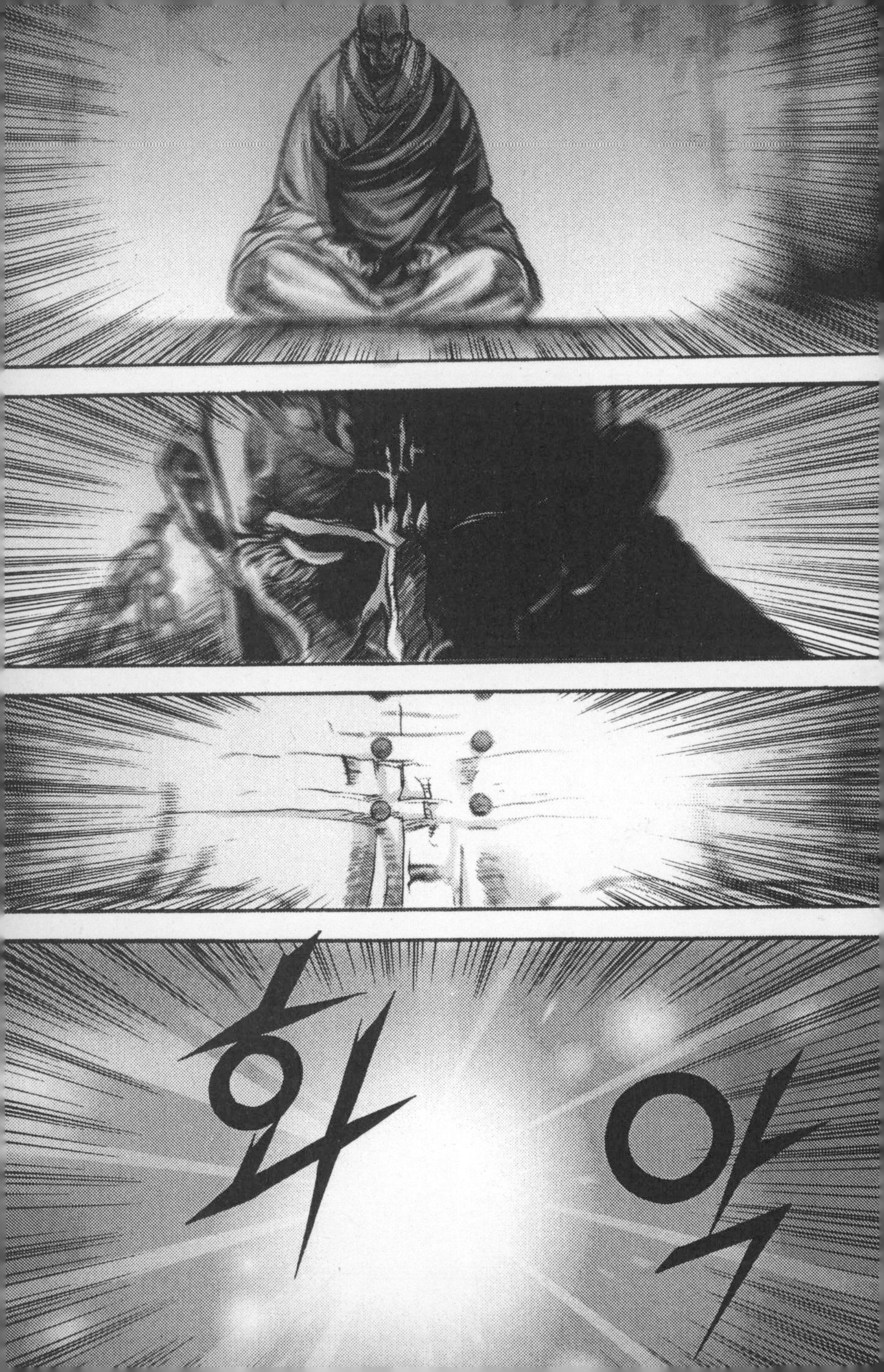
화악

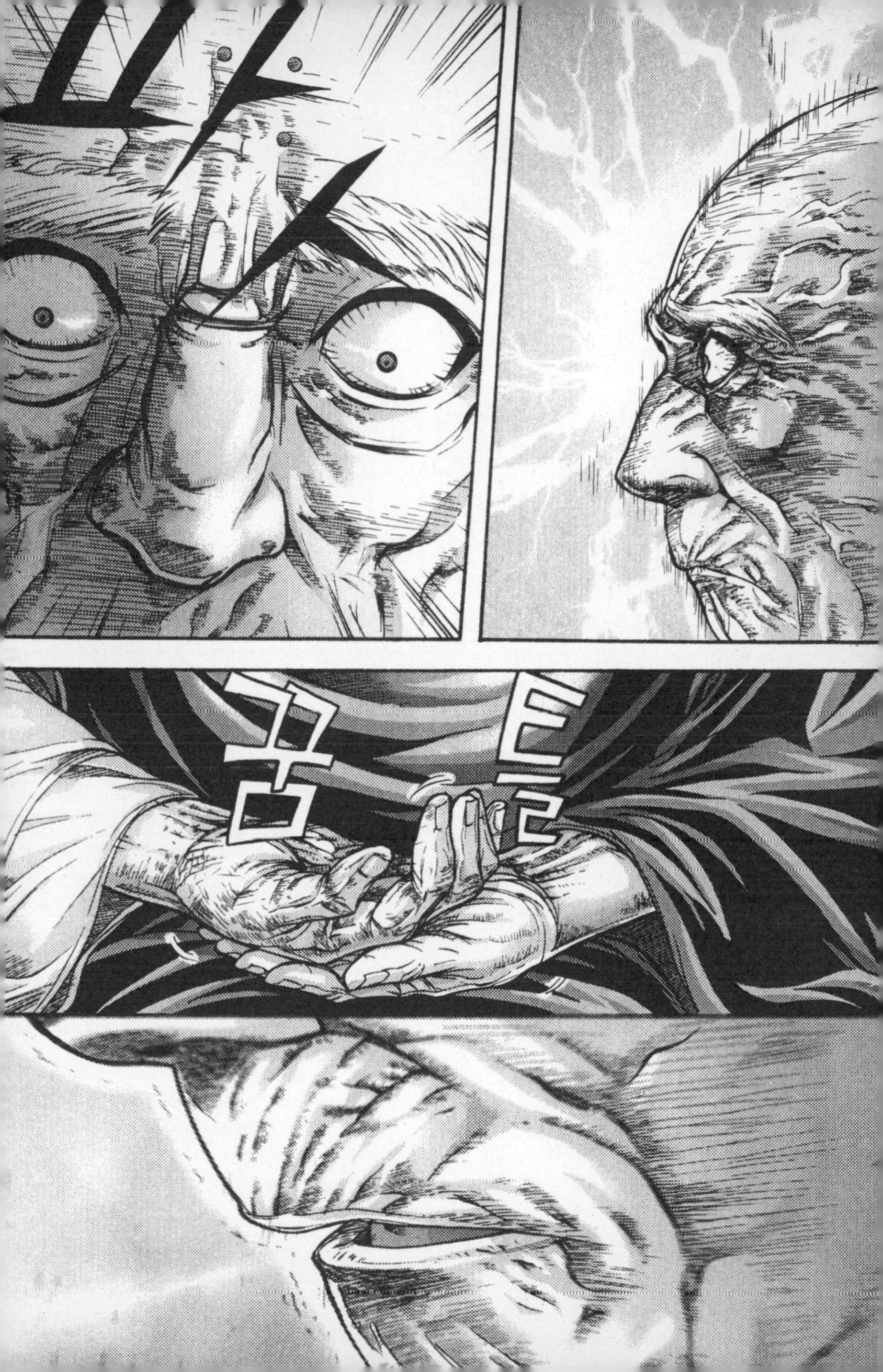
꿈틀

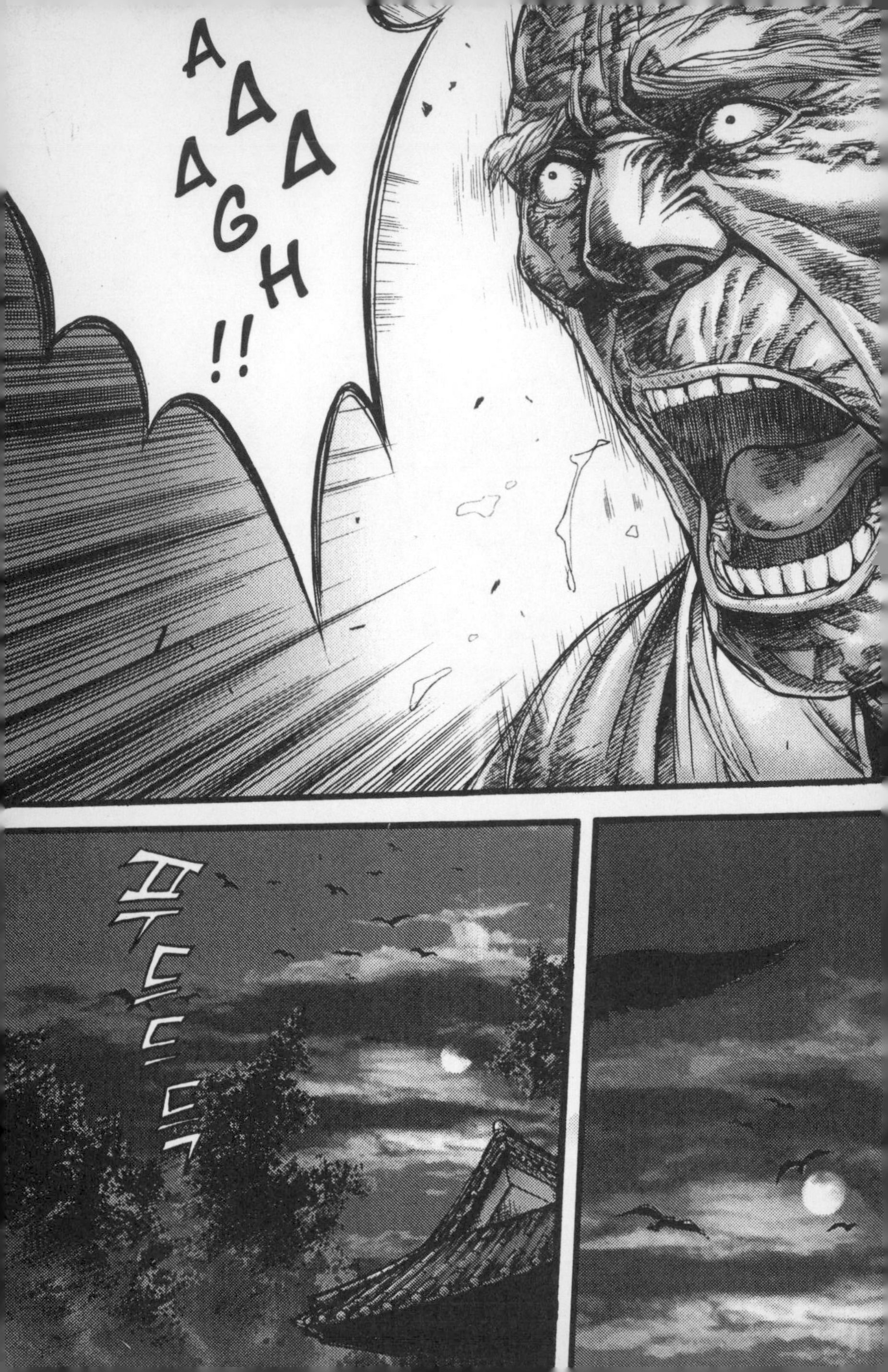
AAAAGH!!

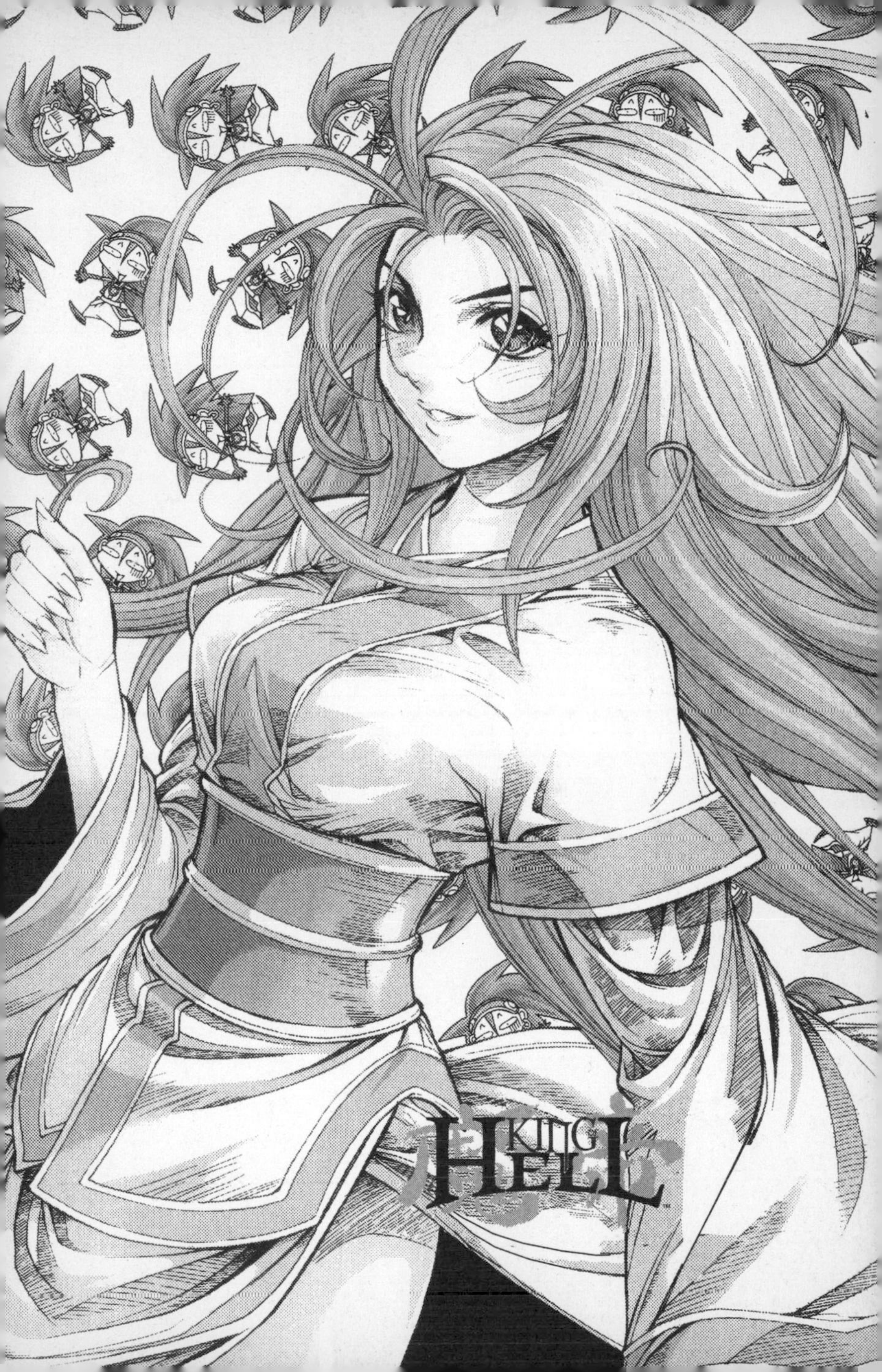
KING HELL

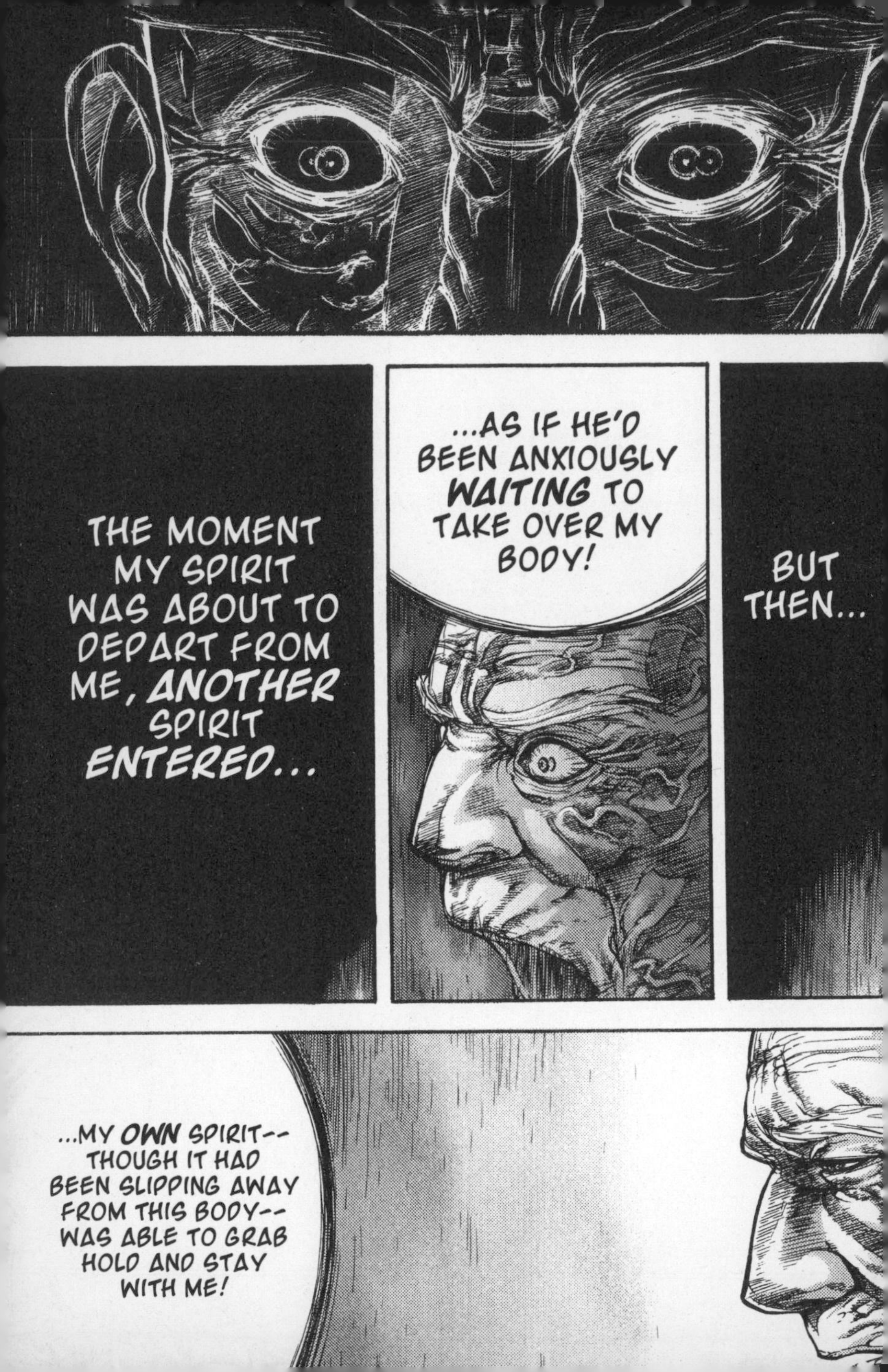
THE MOMENT MY SPIRIT WAS ABOUT TO DEPART FROM ME, **ANOTHER** SPIRIT **ENTERED...**
...AS IF HE'D BEEN ANXIOUSLY **WAITING** TO TAKE OVER MY BODY!
BUT THEN...
...MY **OWN** SPIRIT--THOUGH IT HAD BEEN SLIPPING AWAY FROM THIS BODY--WAS ABLE TO GRAB HOLD AND STAY WITH ME!

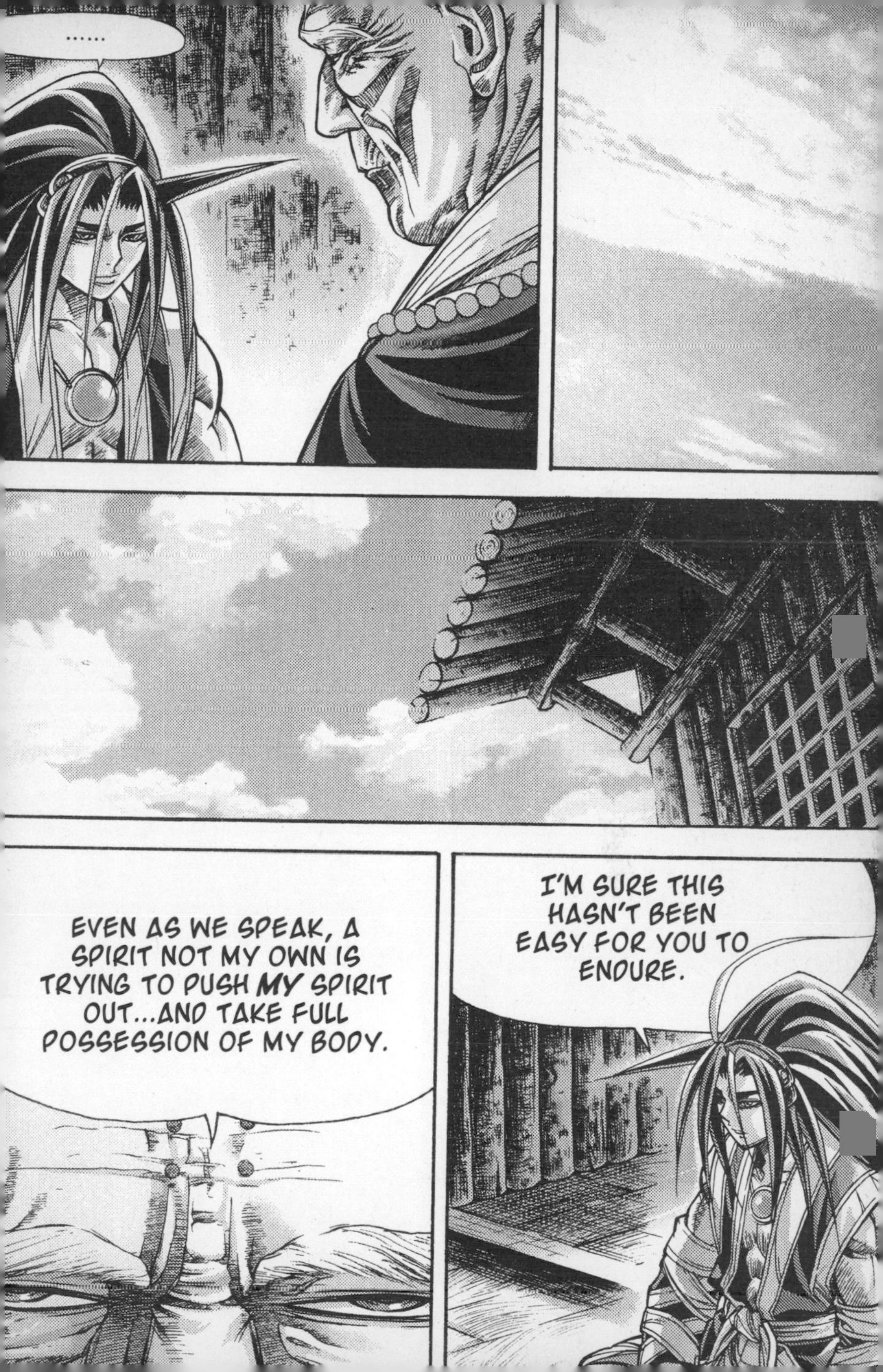
......
EVEN AS WE SPEAK, A SPIRIT NOT MY OWN IS TRYING TO PUSH *MY* SPIRIT OUT...AND TAKE FULL POSSESSION OF MY BODY.
I'M SURE THIS HASN'T BEEN EASY FOR YOU TO ENDURE.

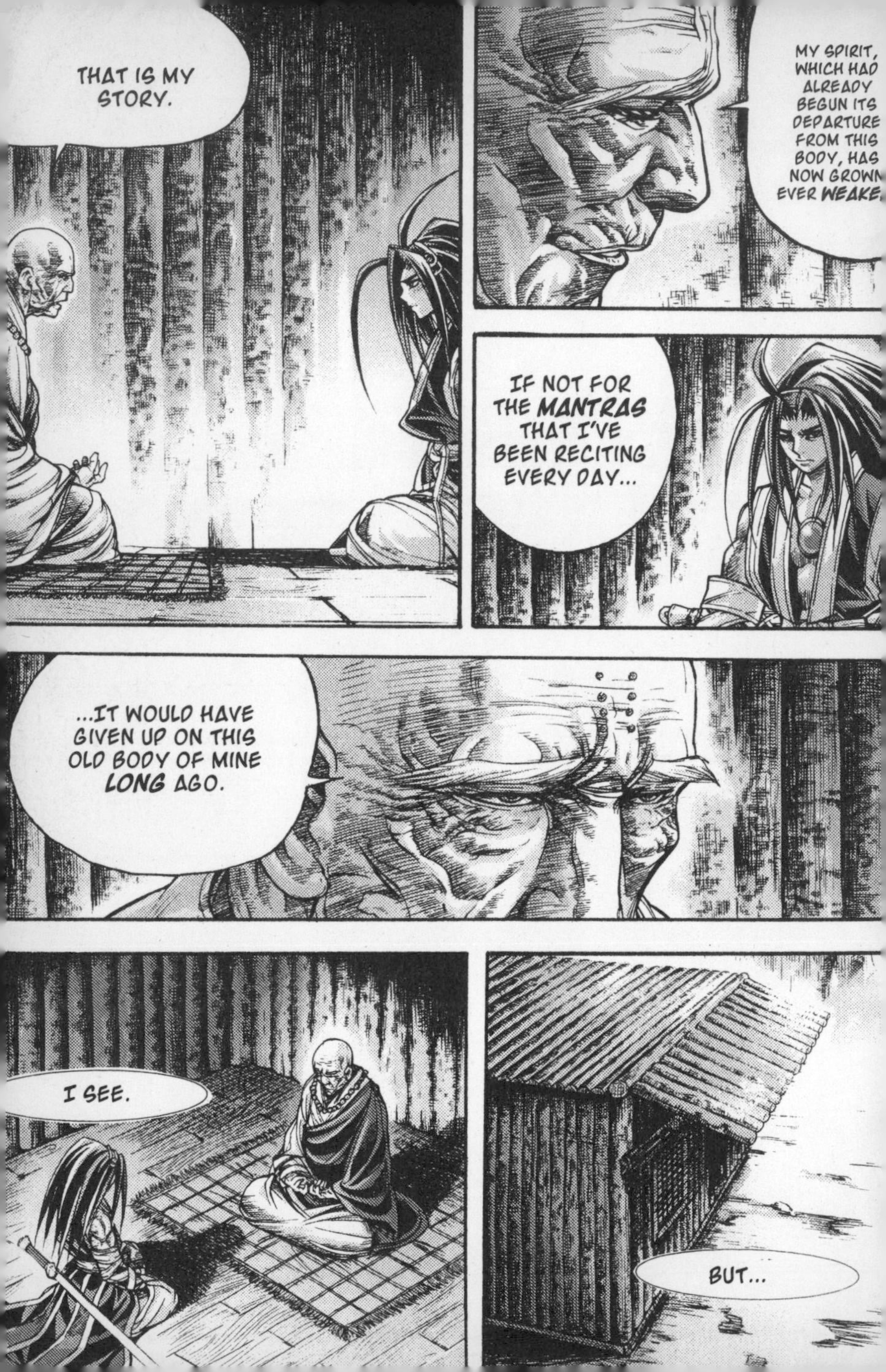

THAT IS MY STORY.
MY SPIRIT, WHICH HAD ALREADY BEGUN ITS DEPARTURE FROM THIS BODY, HAS NOW GROWN EVER WEAKER.
IF NOT FOR THE MANTRAS THAT I'VE BEEN RECITING EVERY DAY...
...IT WOULD HAVE GIVEN UP ON THIS OLD BODY OF MINE LONG AGO.
I SEE.
BUT...

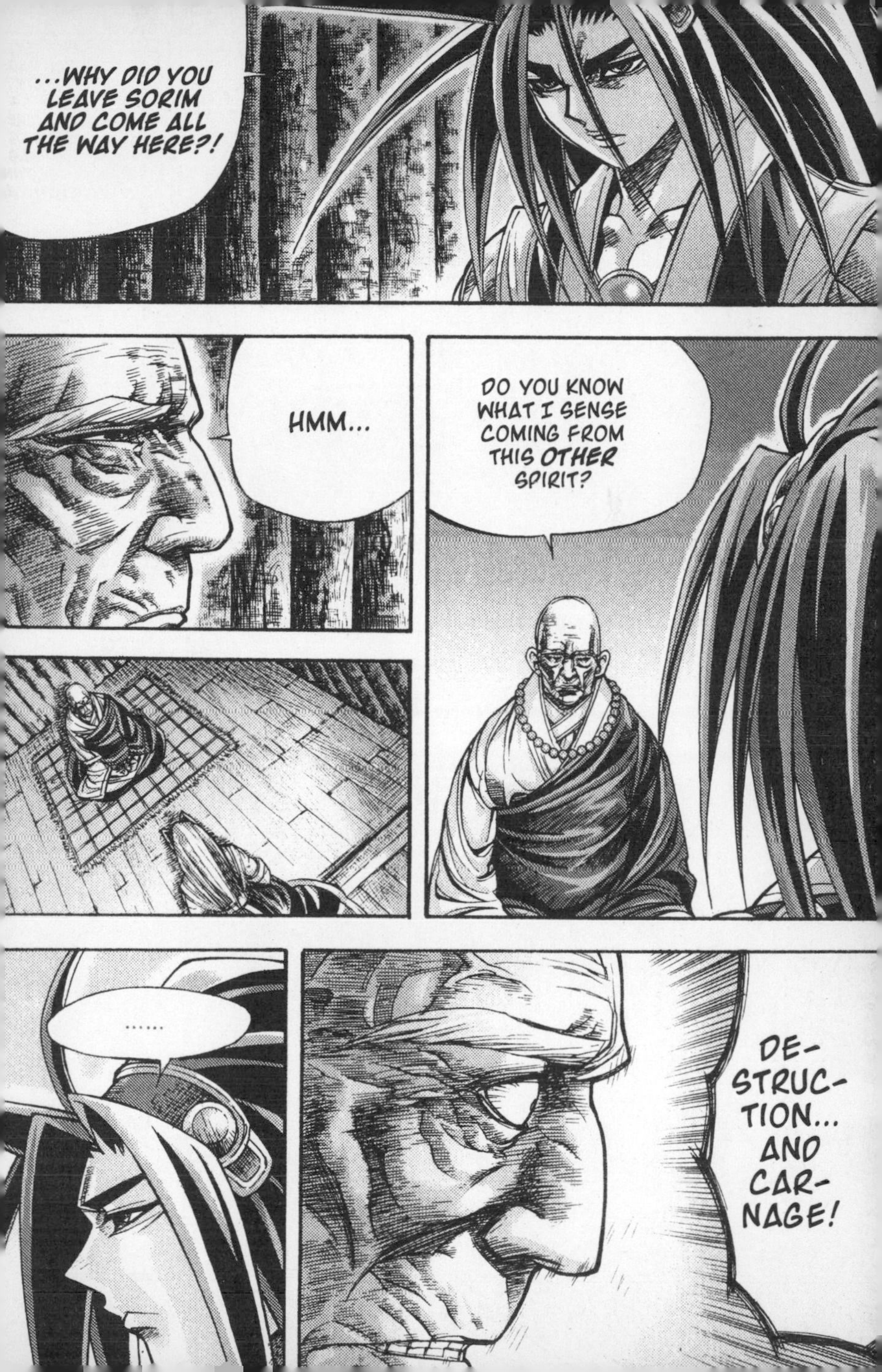
...WHY DID YOU LEAVE SORIM AND COME ALL THE WAY HERE?!
HMM...
DO YOU KNOW WHAT I SENSE COMING FROM THIS *OTHER* SPIRIT?
......
DE-STRUC-TION... AND CAR-NAGE!

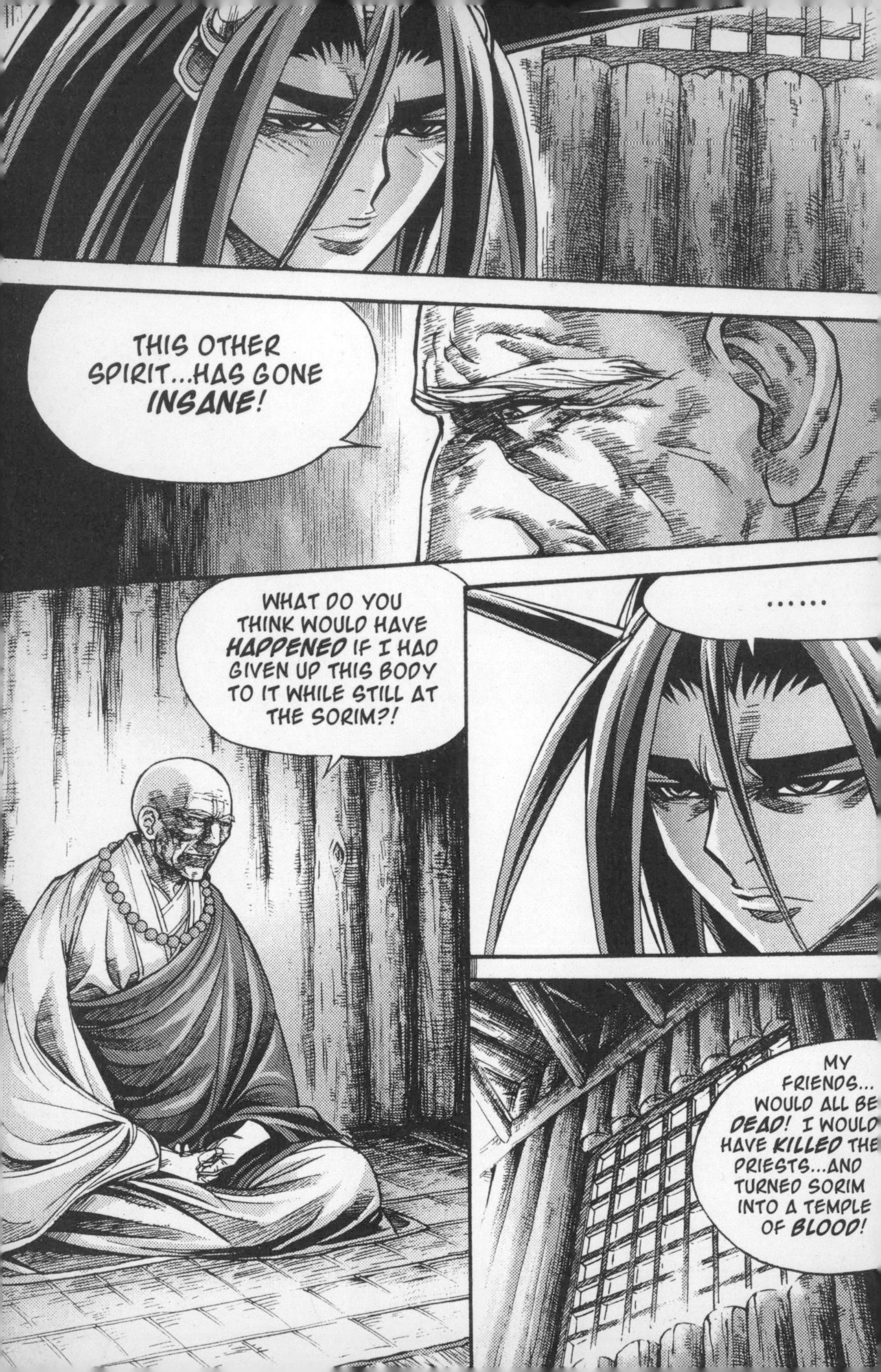
THIS OTHER SPIRIT...HAS GONE *INSANE!*
WHAT DO YOU THINK WOULD HAVE *HAPPENED* IF I HAD GIVEN UP THIS BODY TO IT WHILE STILL AT THE SORIM?!
......
MY FRIENDS... WOULD ALL BE *DEAD!* I WOULD HAVE *KILLED* THE PRIESTS...AND TURNED SORIM INTO A TEMPLE OF *BLOOD!*

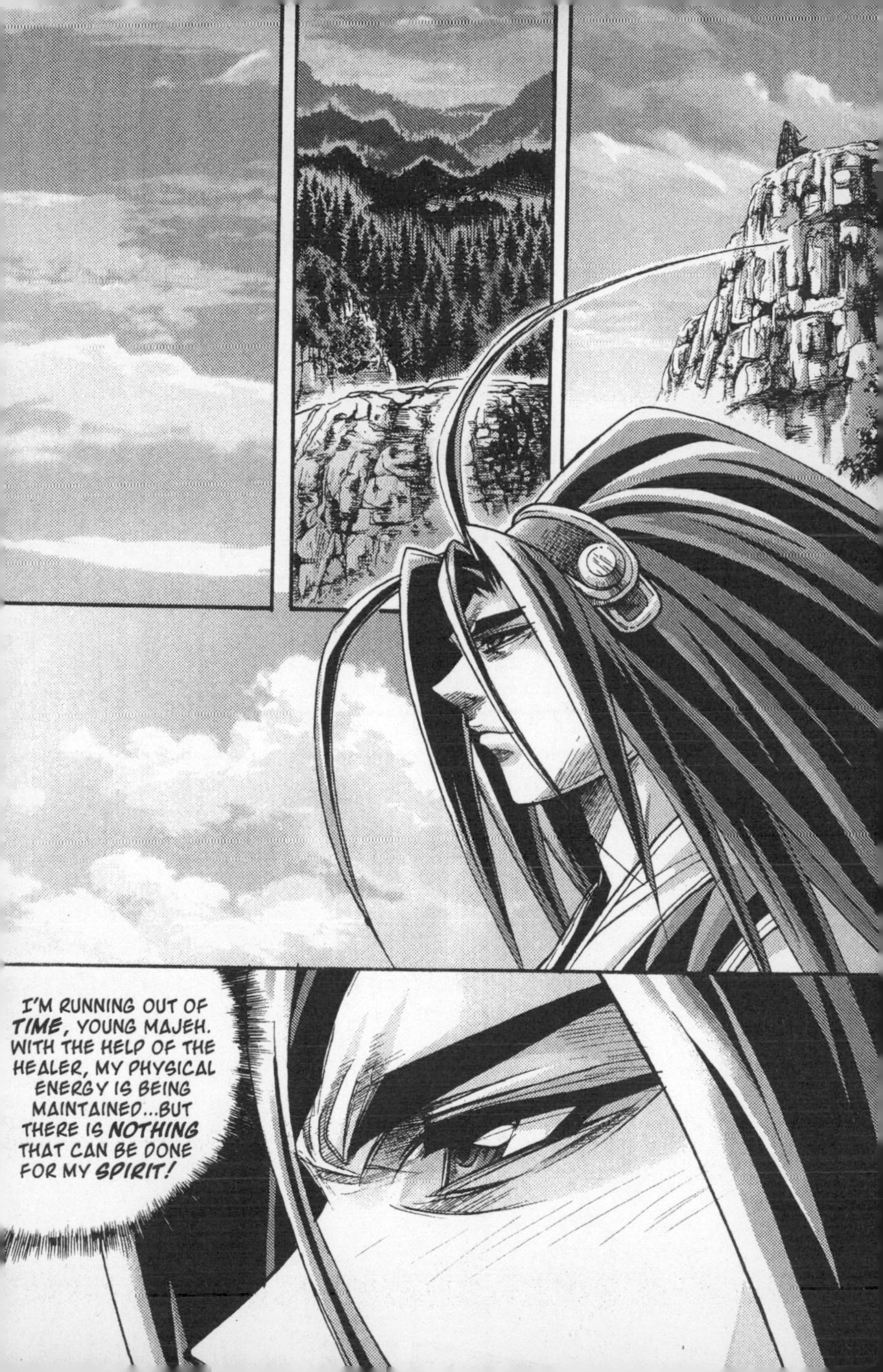
I'M RUNNING OUT OF TIME, YOUNG MAJEH. WITH THE HELP OF THE HEALER, MY PHYSICAL ENERGY IS BEING MAINTAINED...BUT THERE IS NOTHING THAT CAN BE DONE FOR MY SPIRIT!

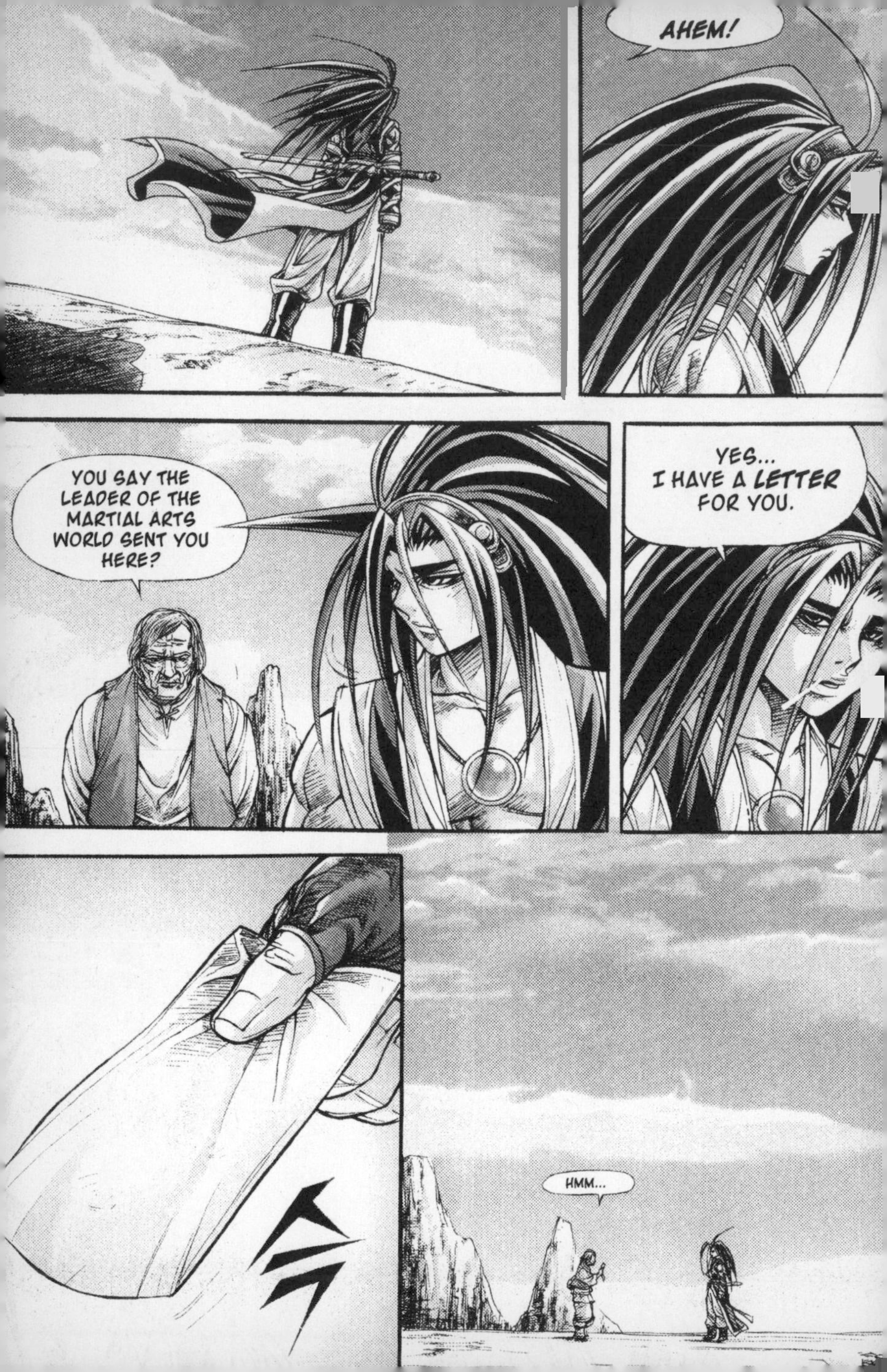
AHEM!
YOU SAY THE LEADER OF THE MARTIAL ARTS WORLD SENT YOU HERE?
YES... I HAVE A LETTER FOR YOU.
HMM...

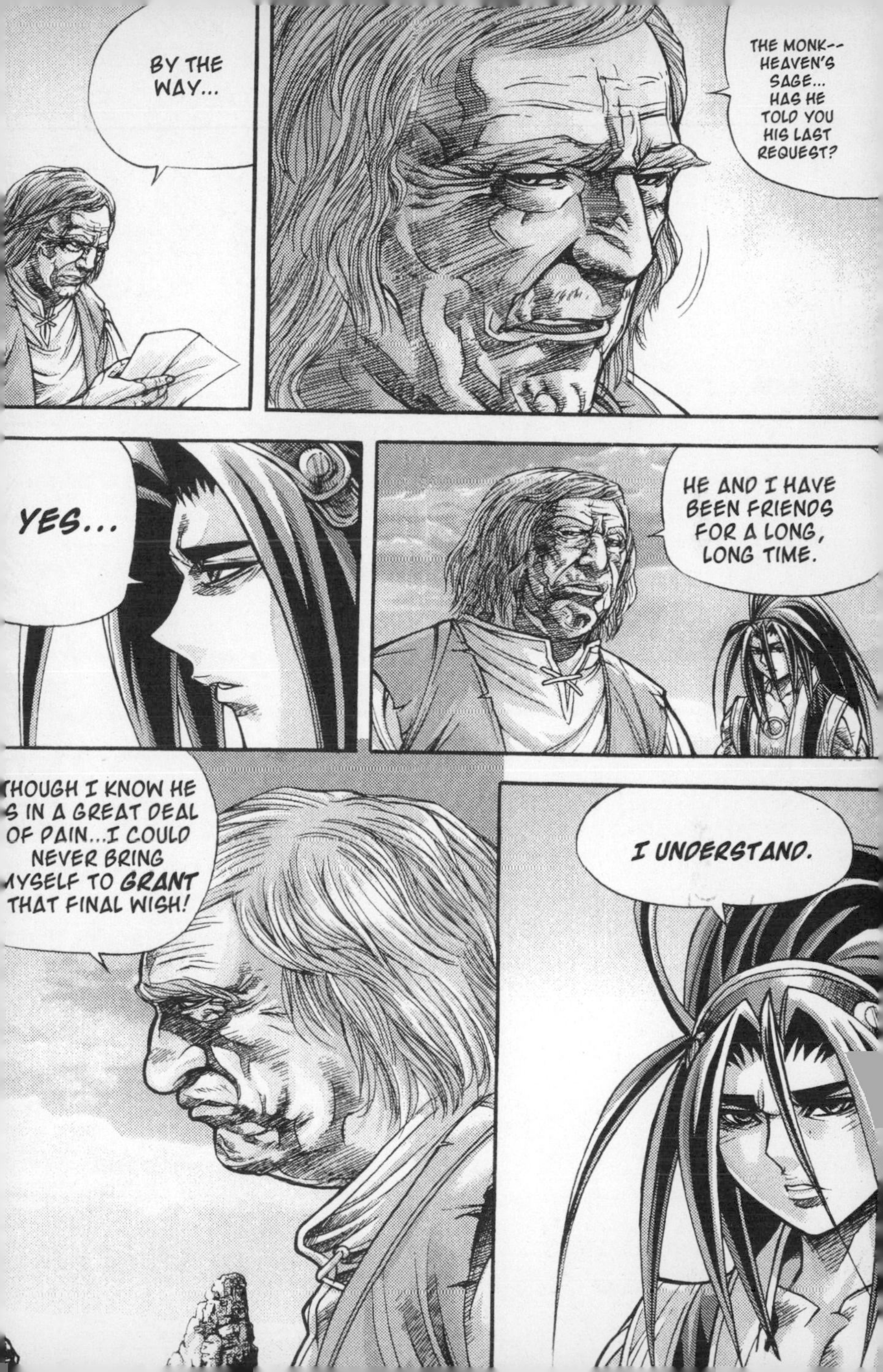
BY THE WAY...
THE MONK--HEAVEN'S SAGE... HAS HE TOLD YOU HIS LAST REQUEST?
YES...
HE AND I HAVE BEEN FRIENDS FOR A LONG, LONG TIME.
THOUGH I KNOW HE S IN A GREAT DEAL OF PAIN...I COULD NEVER BRING MYSELF TO GRANT THAT FINAL WISH!
I UNDERSTAND.

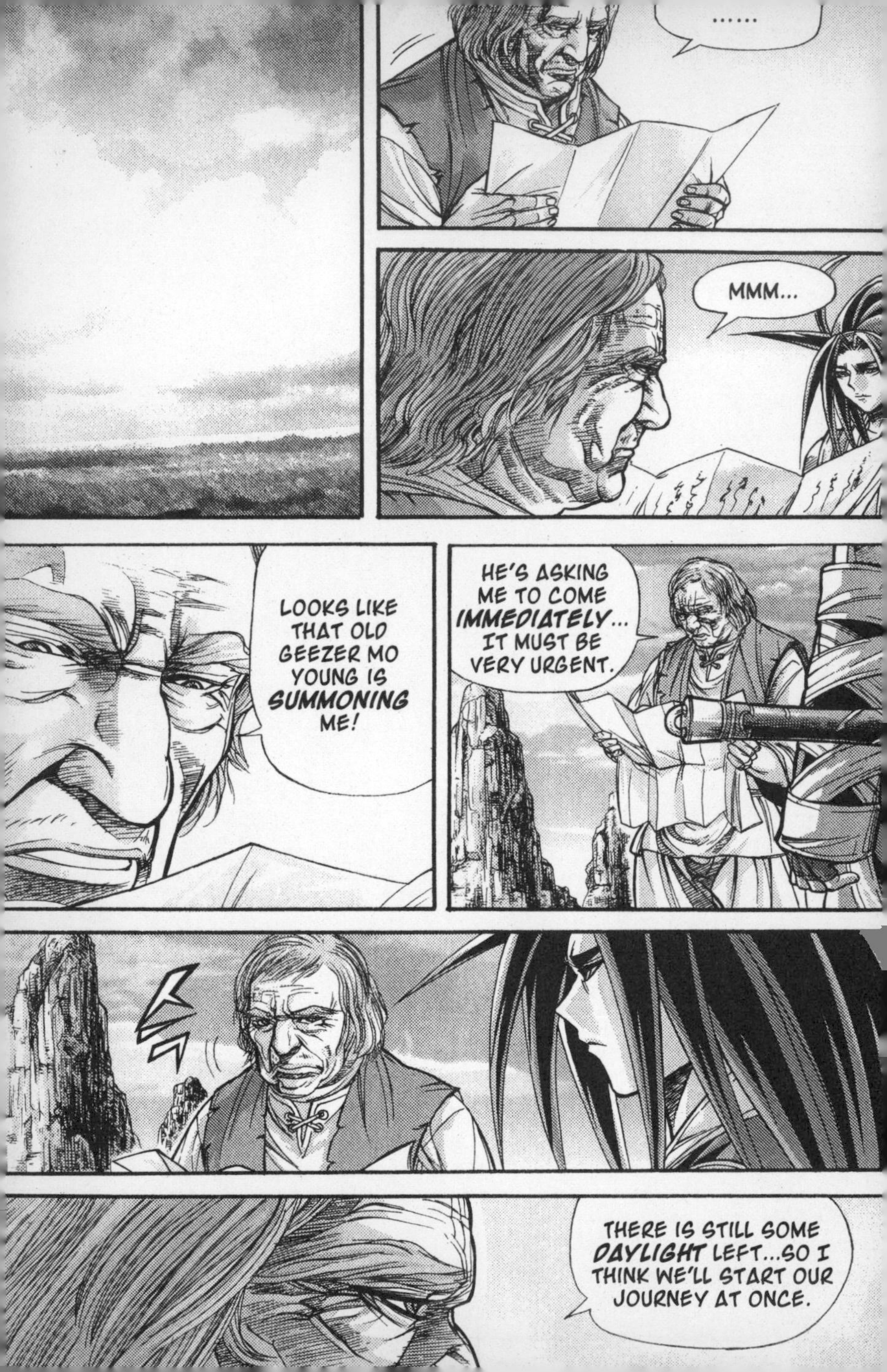
......
MMM...
LOOKS LIKE THAT OLD GEEZER MO YOUNG IS SUMMONING ME!
HE'S ASKING ME TO COME IMMEDIATELY... IT MUST BE VERY URGENT.
THERE IS STILL SOME DAYLIGHT LEFT...SO I THINK WE'LL START OUR JOURNEY AT ONCE.

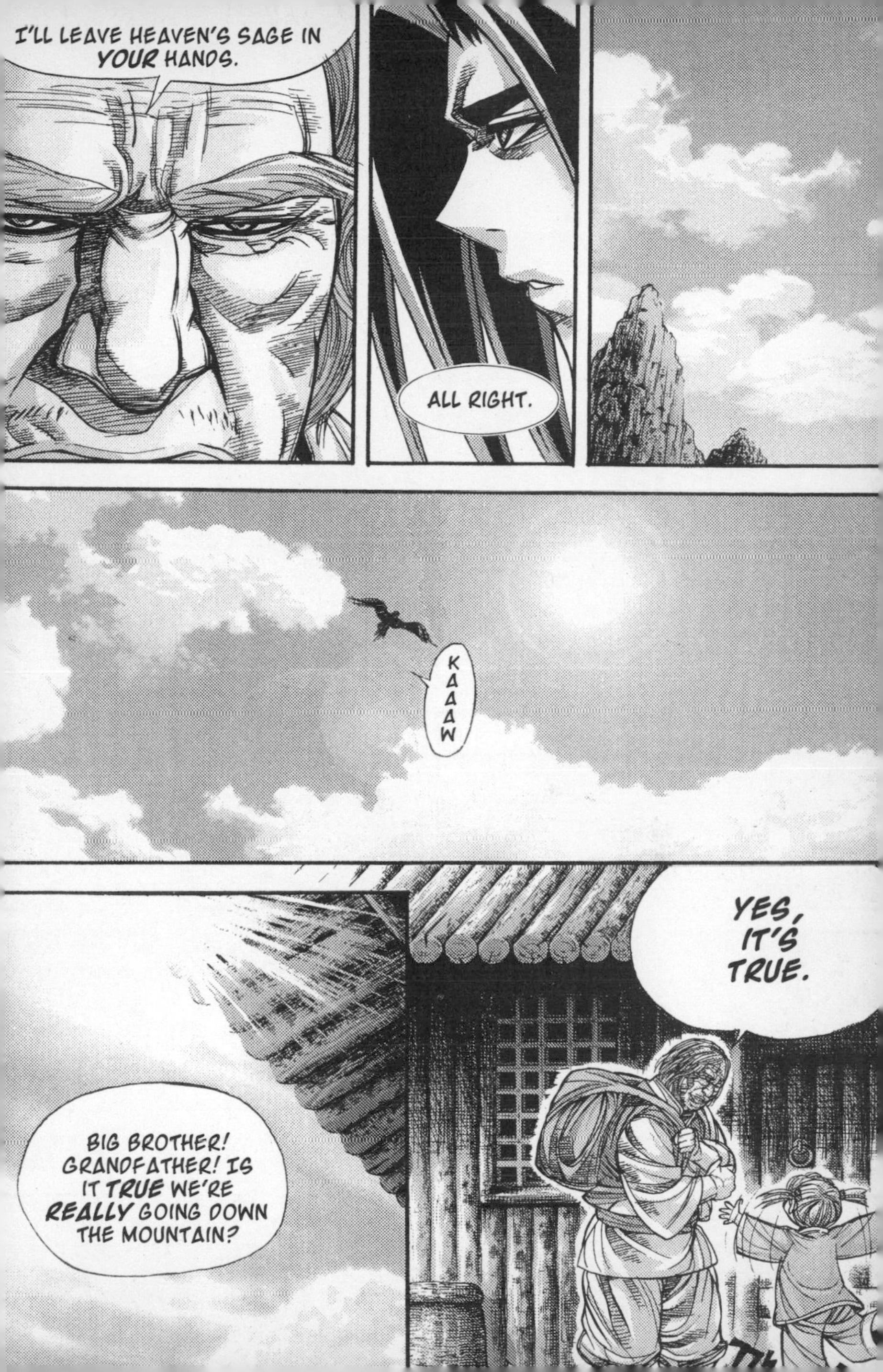
I'LL LEAVE HEAVEN'S SAGE IN *YOUR* HANDS.
ALL RIGHT.
KAAAAW
BIG BROTHER! GRANDFATHER! IS IT *TRUE* WE'RE *REALLY* GOING DOWN THE MOUNTAIN?
YES, IT'S TRUE.

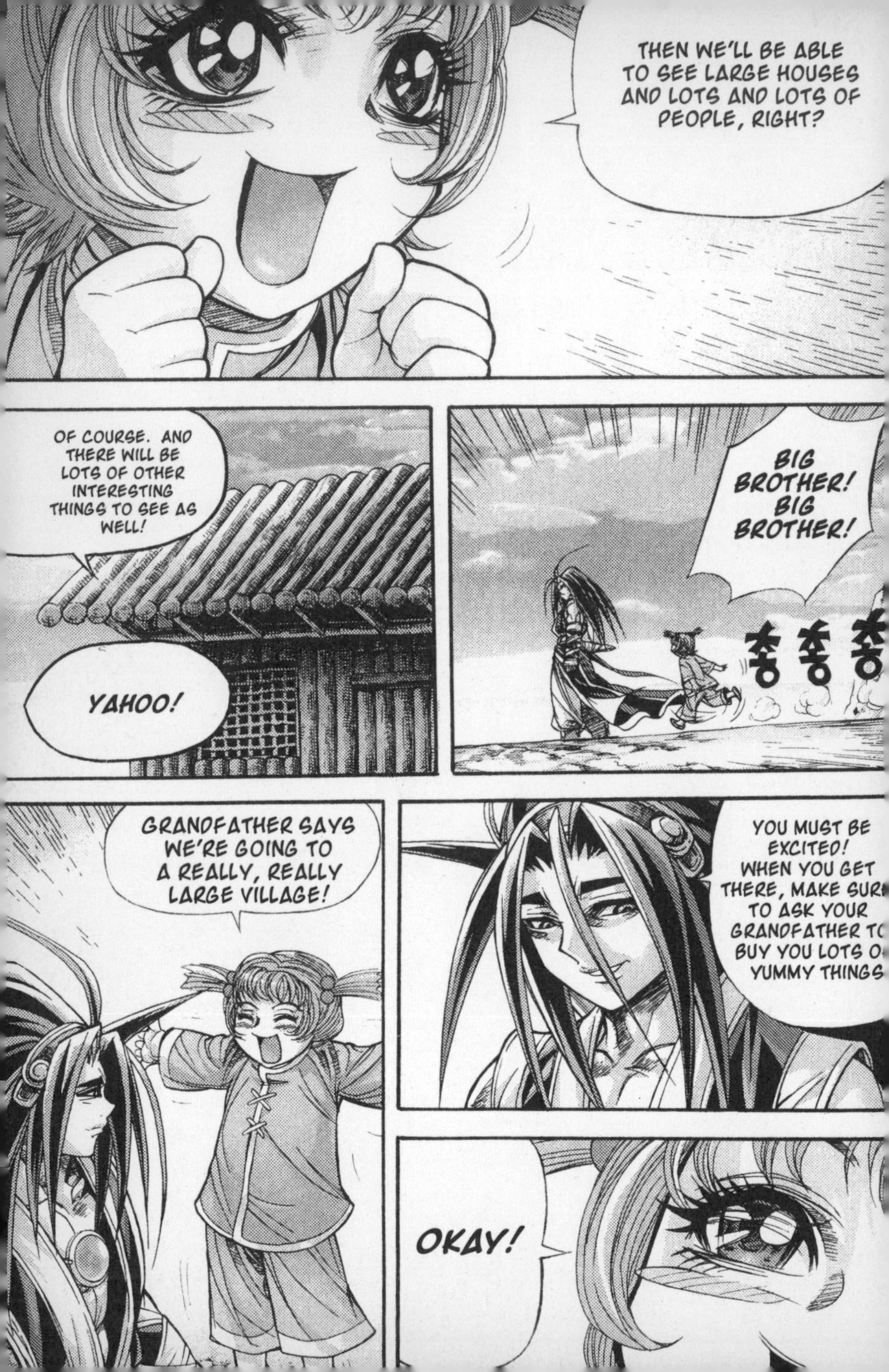
THEN WE'LL BE ABLE TO SEE LARGE HOUSES AND LOTS AND LOTS OF PEOPLE, RIGHT?
OF COURSE. AND THERE WILL BE LOTS OF OTHER INTERESTING THINGS TO SEE AS WELL!
YAHOO!
BIG BROTHER! BIG BROTHER!
총 총 총
GRANDFATHER SAYS WE'RE GOING TO A REALLY, REALLY LARGE VILLAGE!
YOU MUST BE EXCITED! WHEN YOU GET THERE, MAKE SUR TO ASK YOUR GRANDFATHER T BUY YOU LOTS O YUMMY THINGS
OKAY!

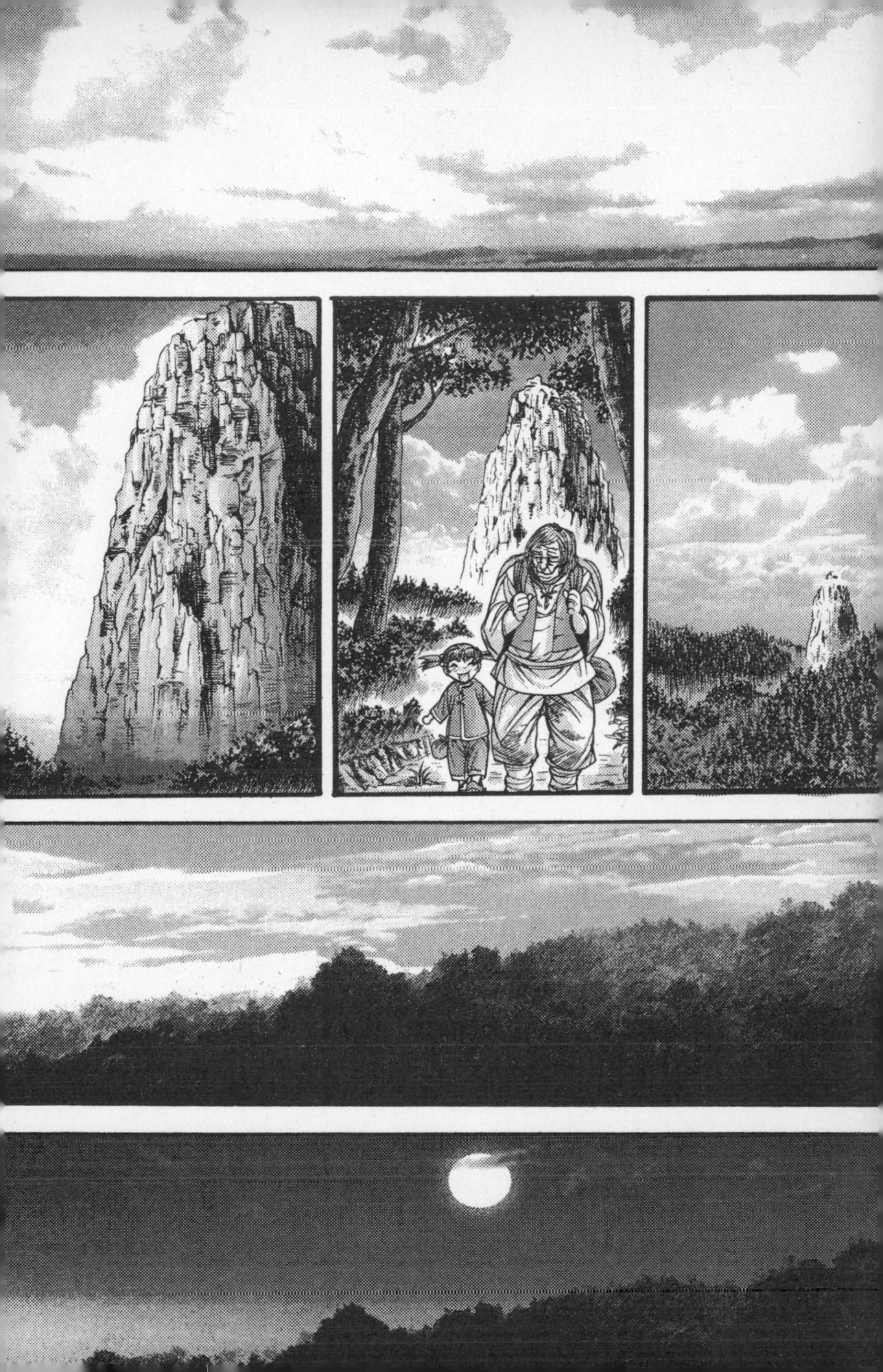

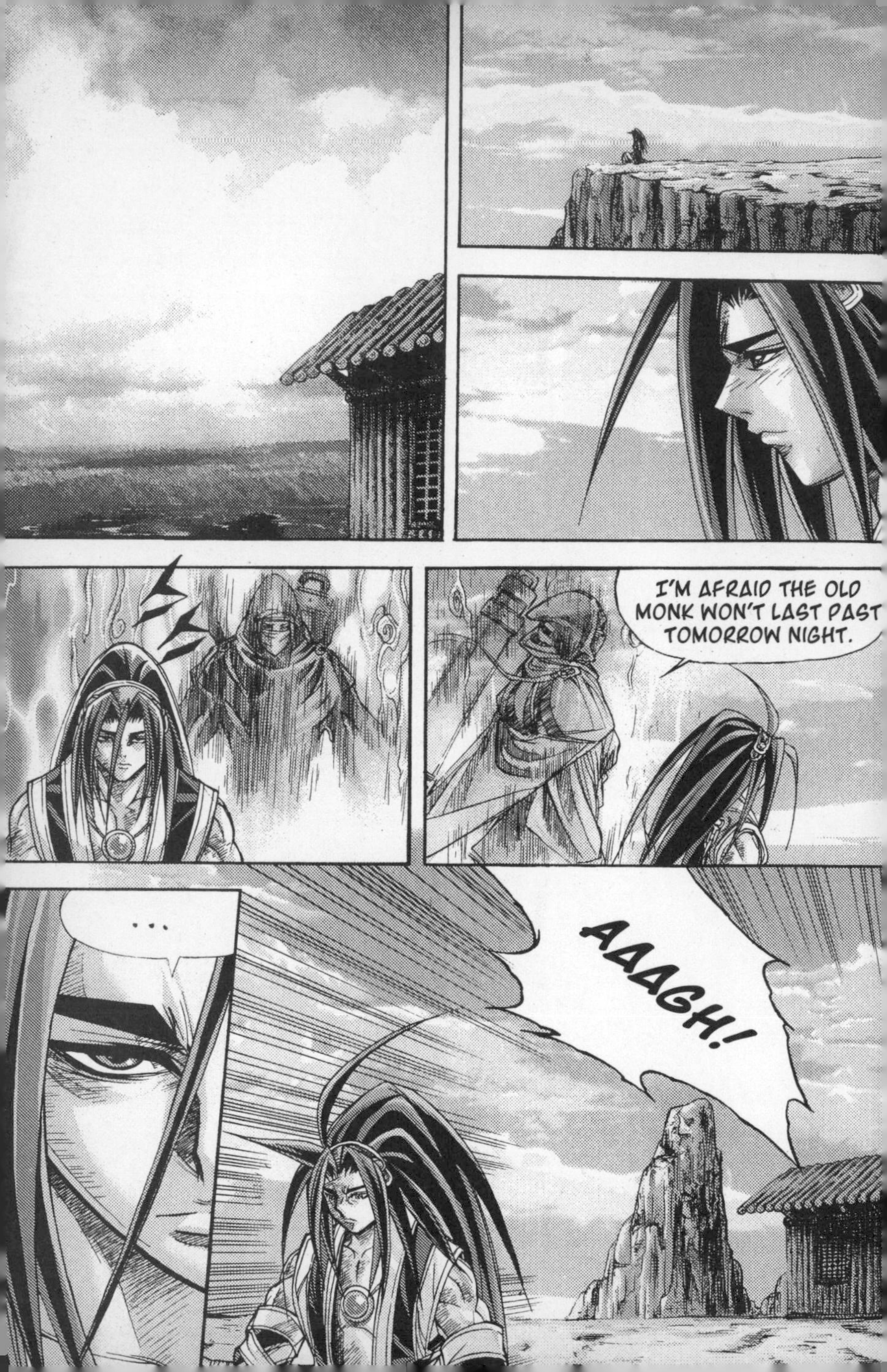
I'M AFRAID THE OLD MONK WON'T LAST PAST TOMORROW NIGHT.
...
AAAGH!

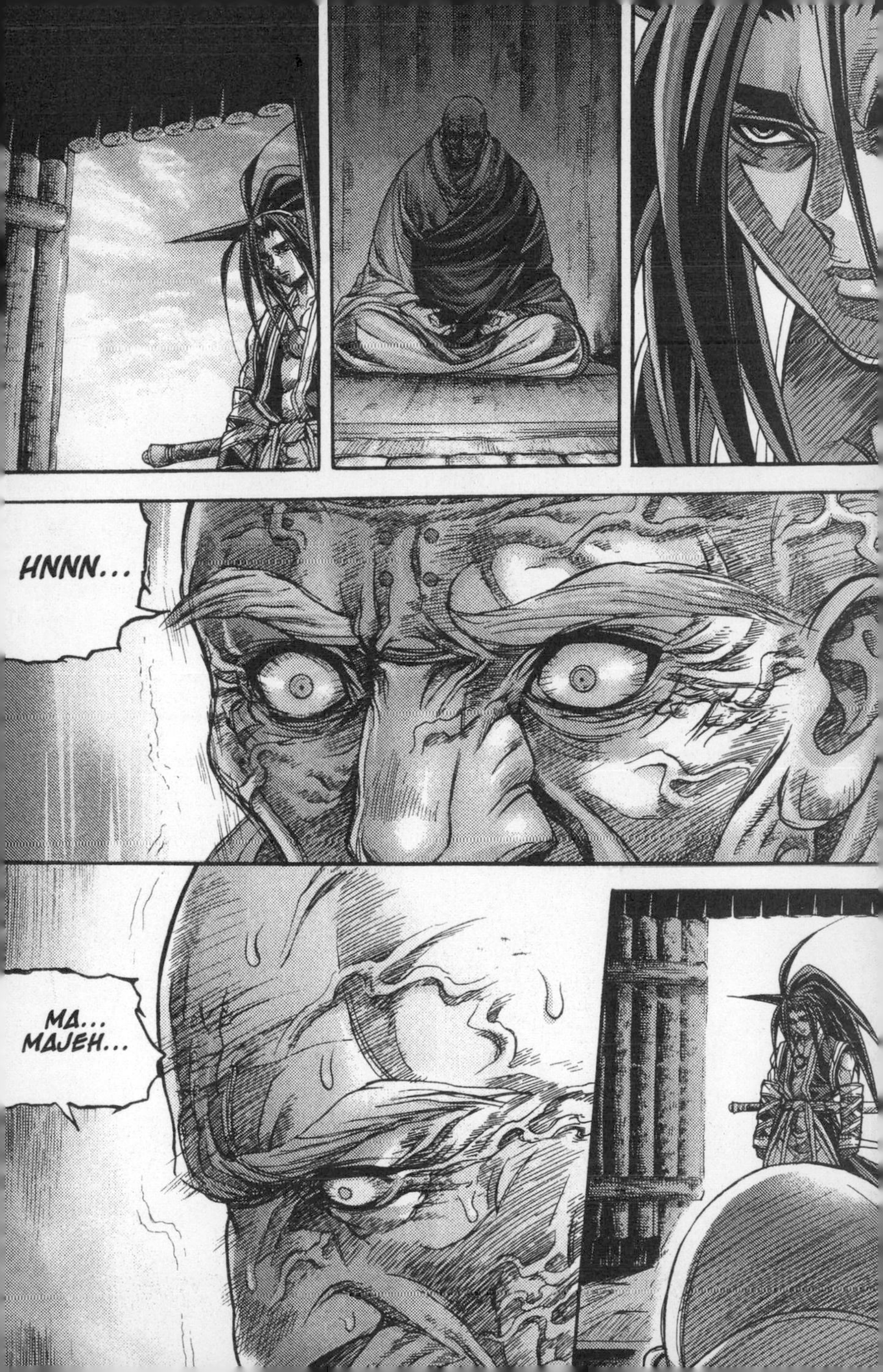
HNNN...
MA... MAJEH...

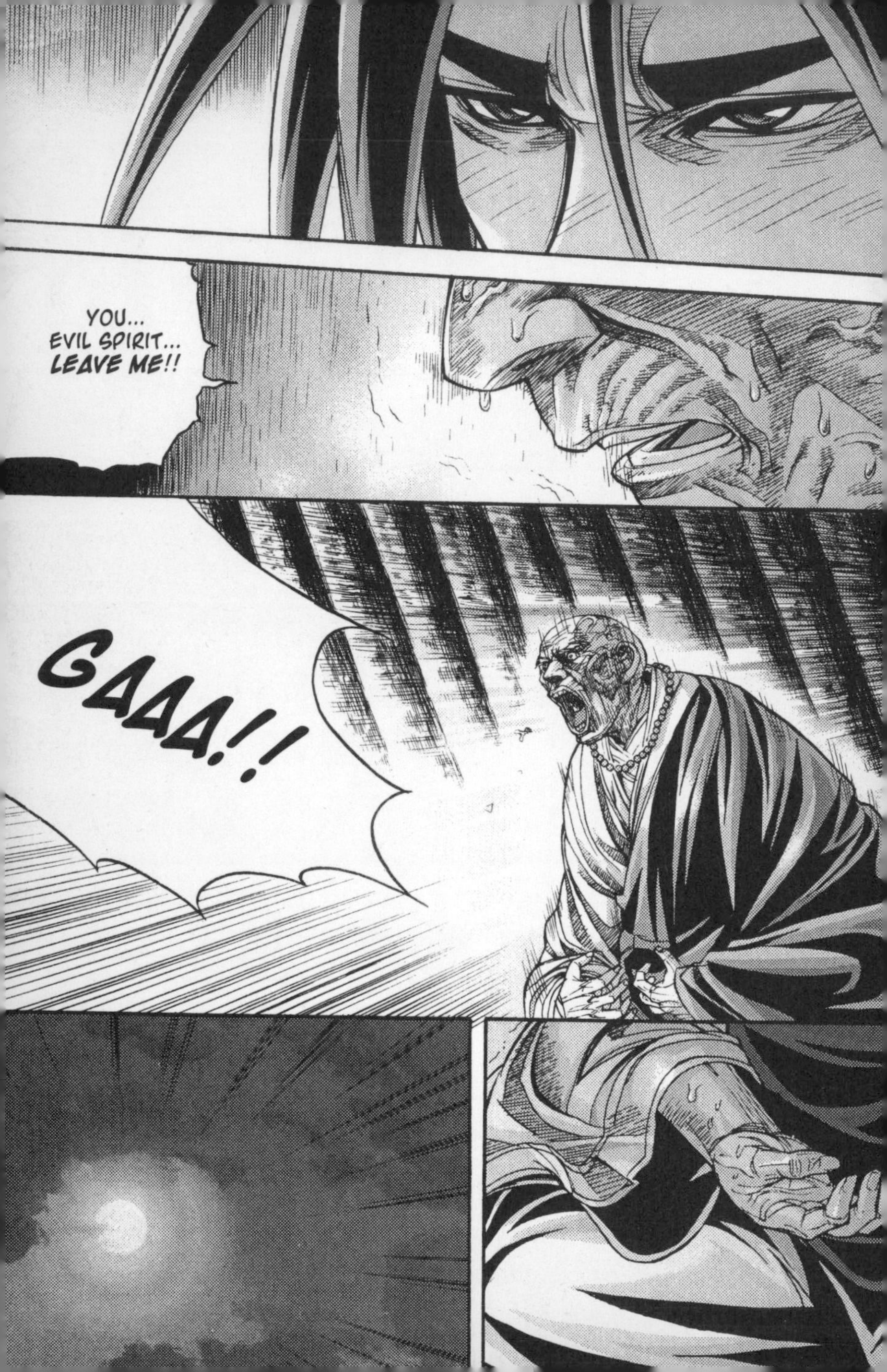
YOU...
EVIL SPIRIT...
LEAVE ME!!
GAAA!!

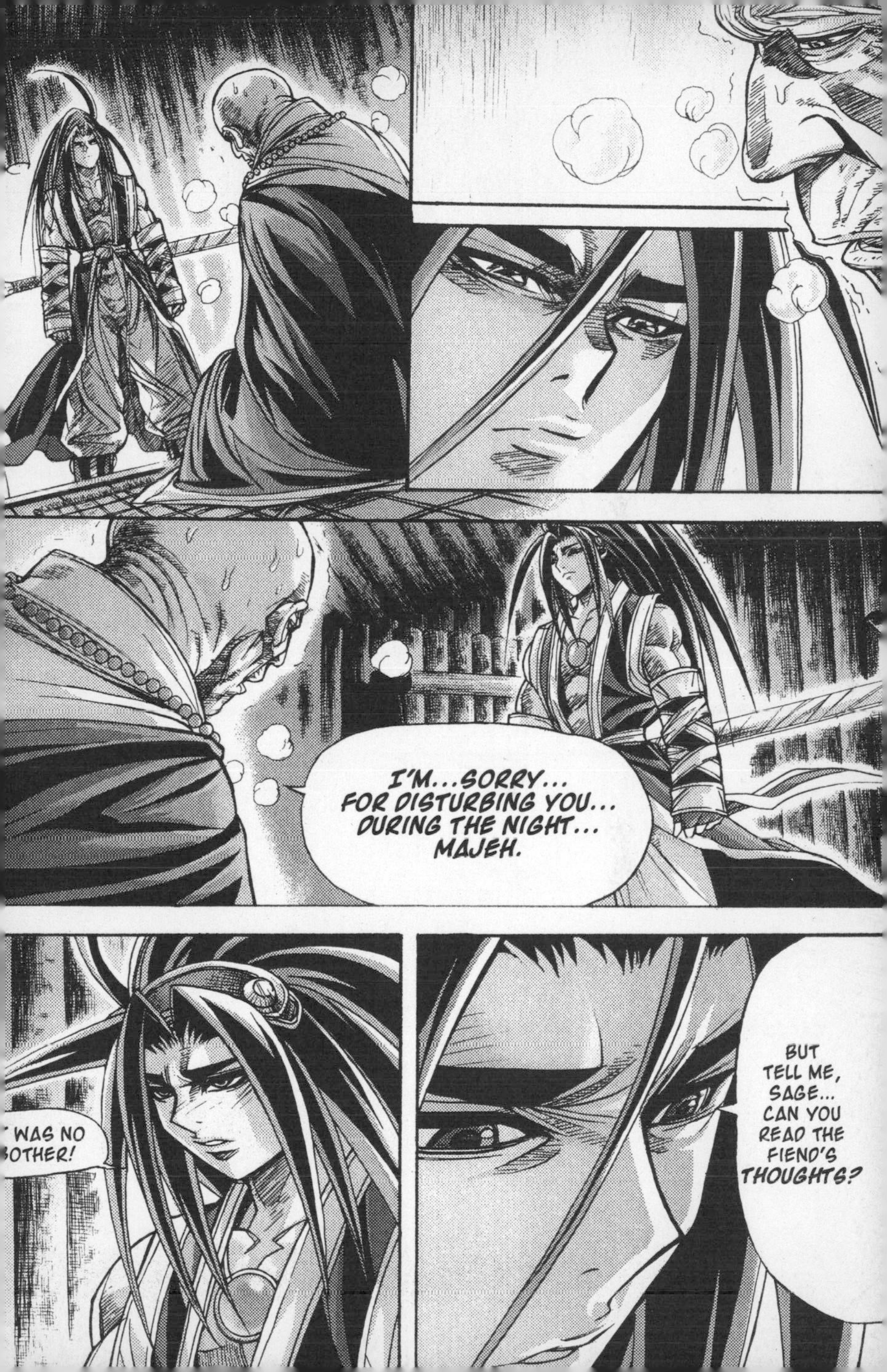
I'M...SORRY... FOR DISTURBING YOU... DURING THE NIGHT... MAJEH.
WAS NO OTHER!
BUT TELL ME, SAGE... CAN YOU READ THE FIEND'S THOUGHTS?

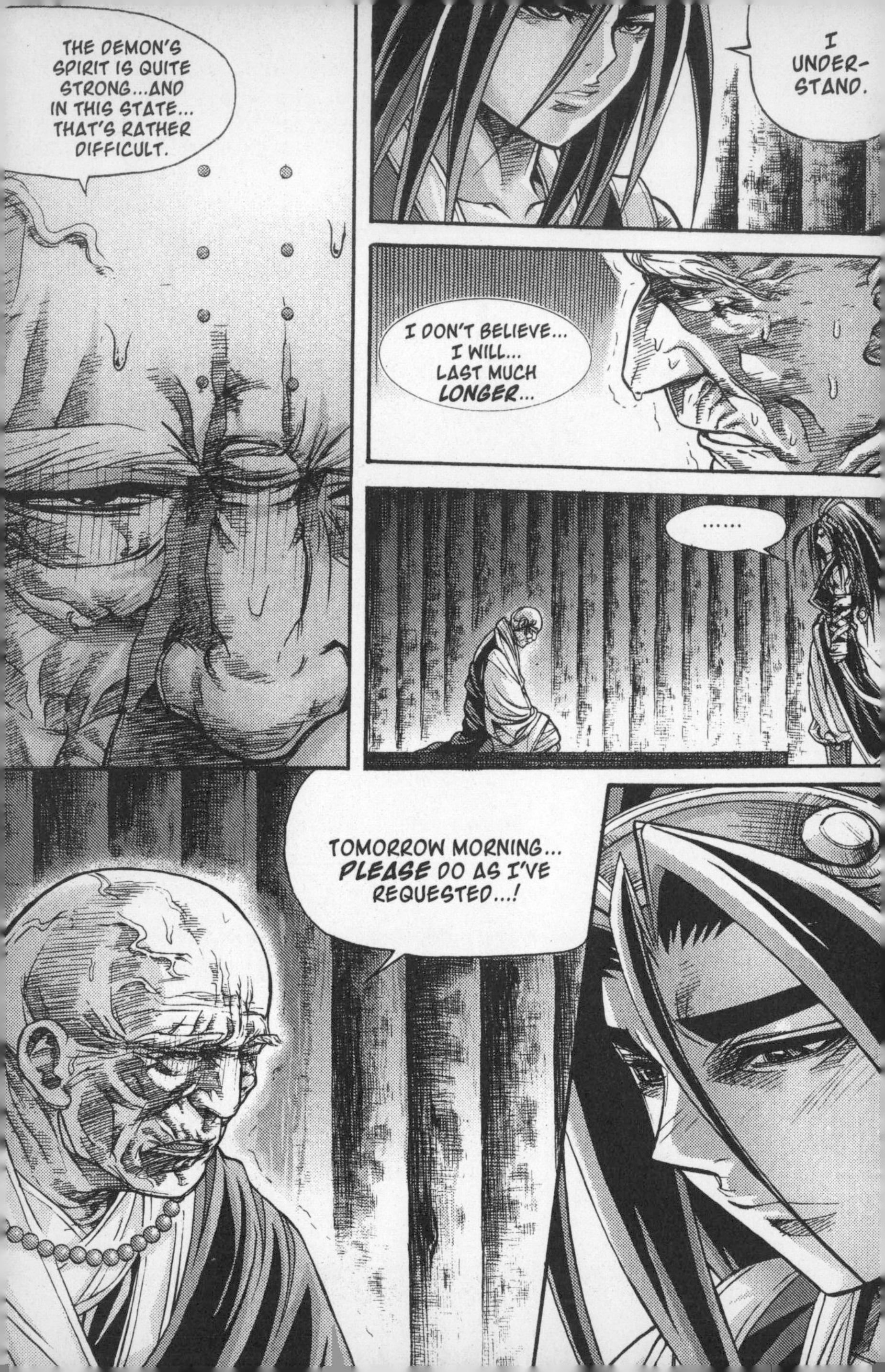
THE DEMON'S SPIRIT IS QUITE STRONG...AND IN THIS STATE... THAT'S RATHER DIFFICULT.
I UNDER-STAND.
I DON'T BELIEVE... I WILL... LAST MUCH LONGER...
......
TOMORROW MORNING... PLEASE DO AS I'VE REQUESTED...!

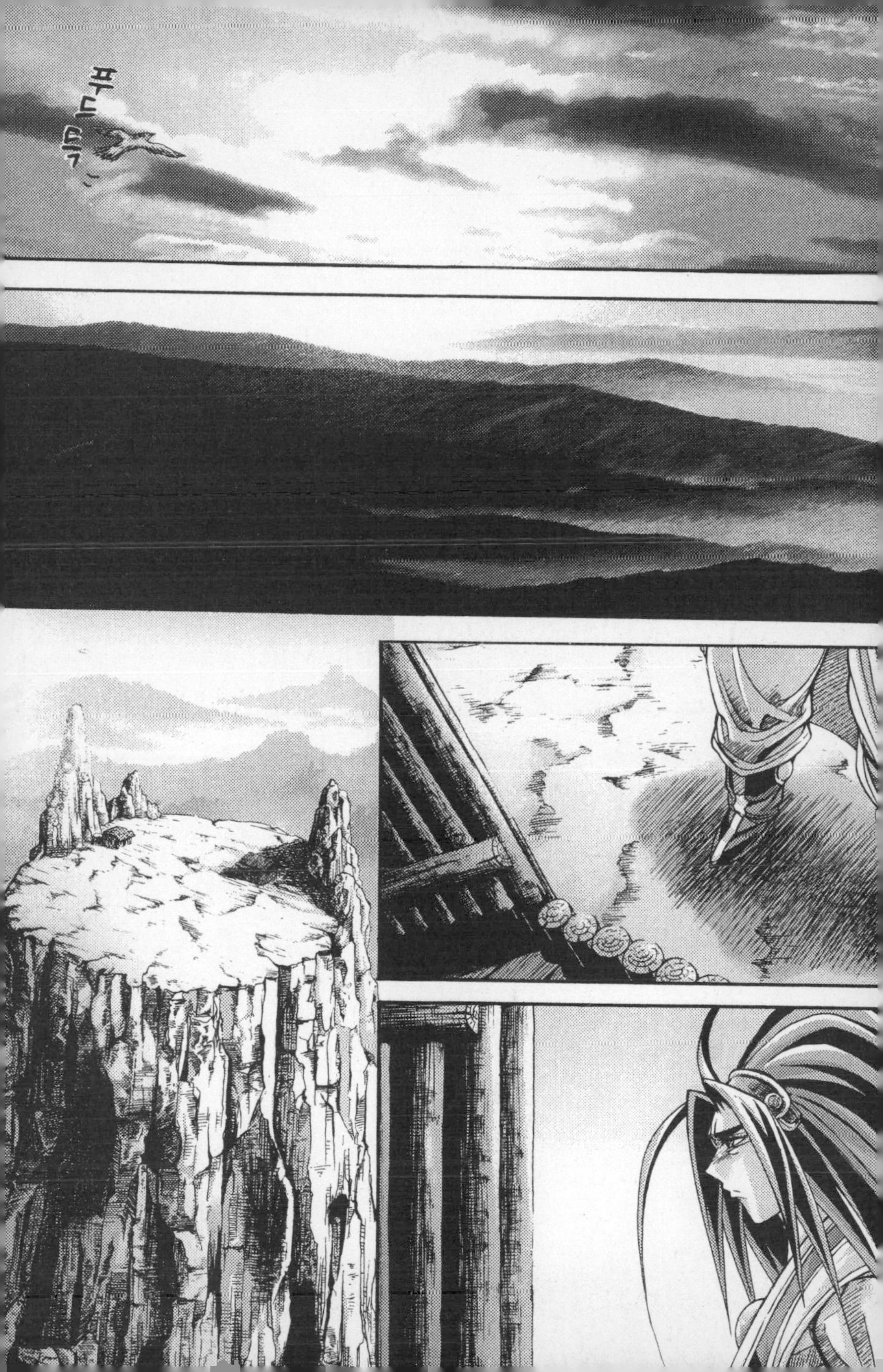
푸드득

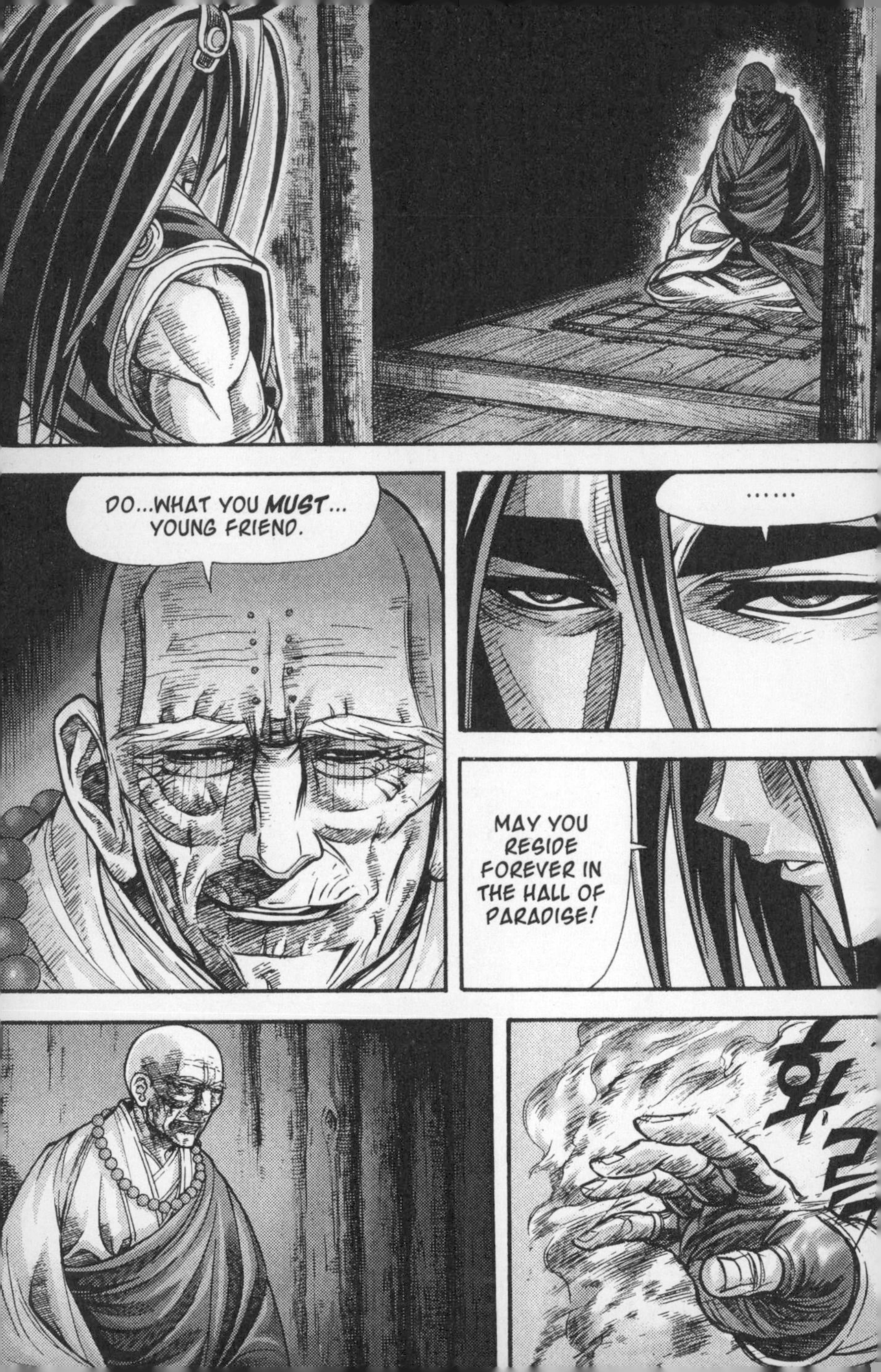
DO...WHAT YOU **MUST**... YOUNG FRIEND.
......
MAY YOU RESIDE FOREVER IN THE HALL OF PARADISE!

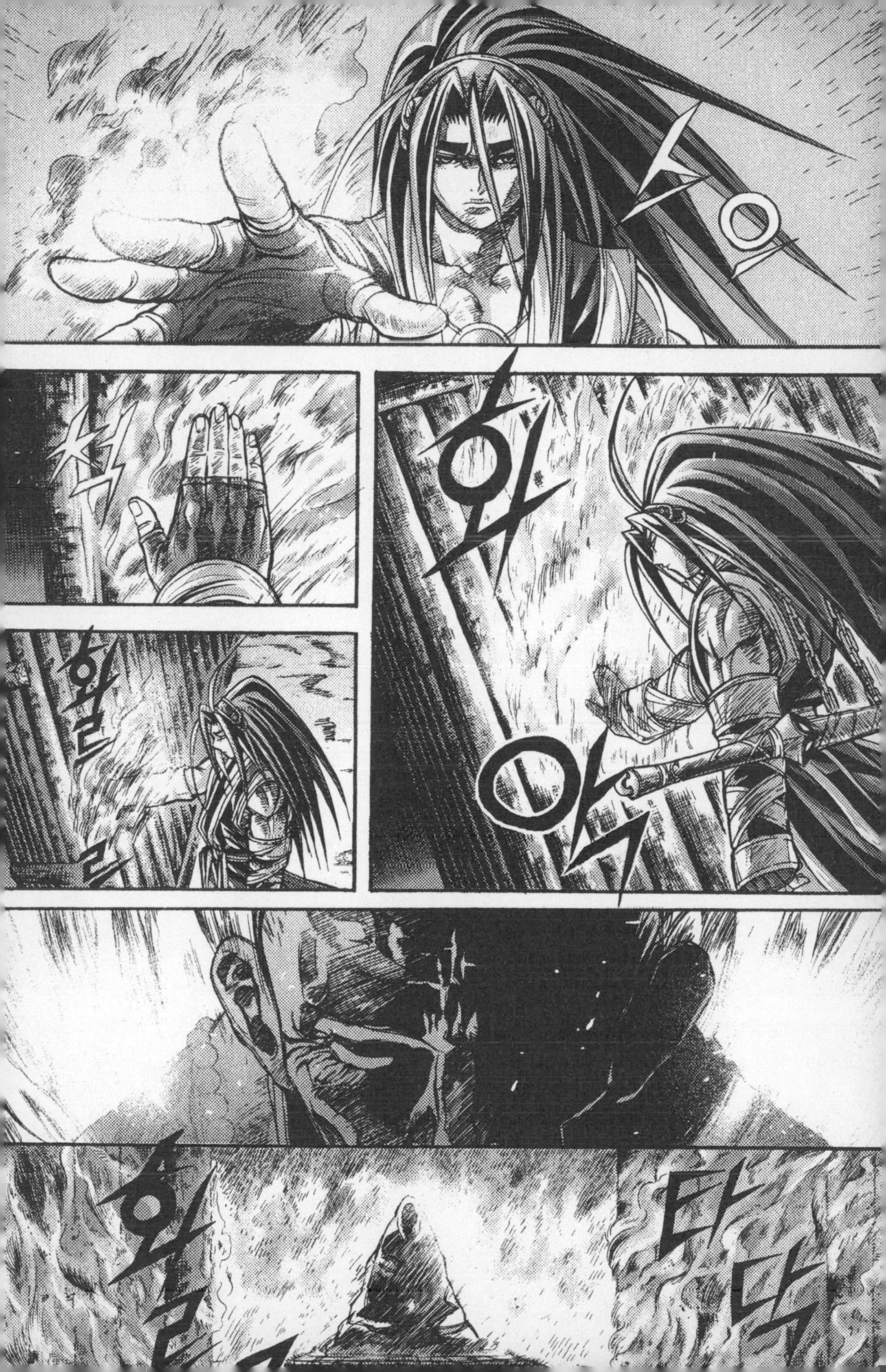

스으
척
화르르
화악
화르르
타닥

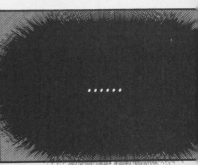

......

WHA...
WHAT ARE YOU
DOING?!

YOU
BASTARD!
STOP THIS
AT ONCE!

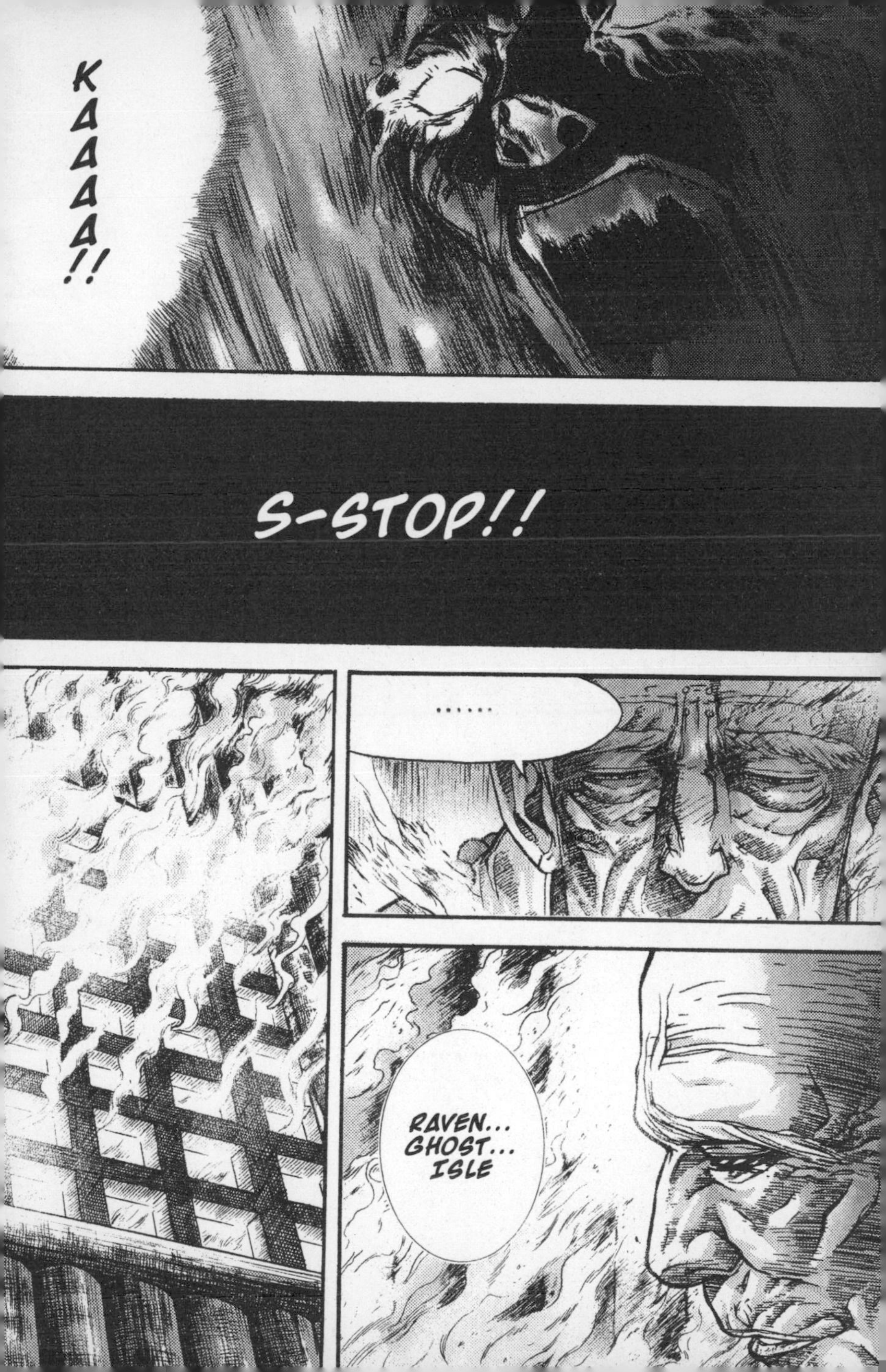
KAAAAA!!
S-STOP!!
......
RAVEN... GHOST... ISLE

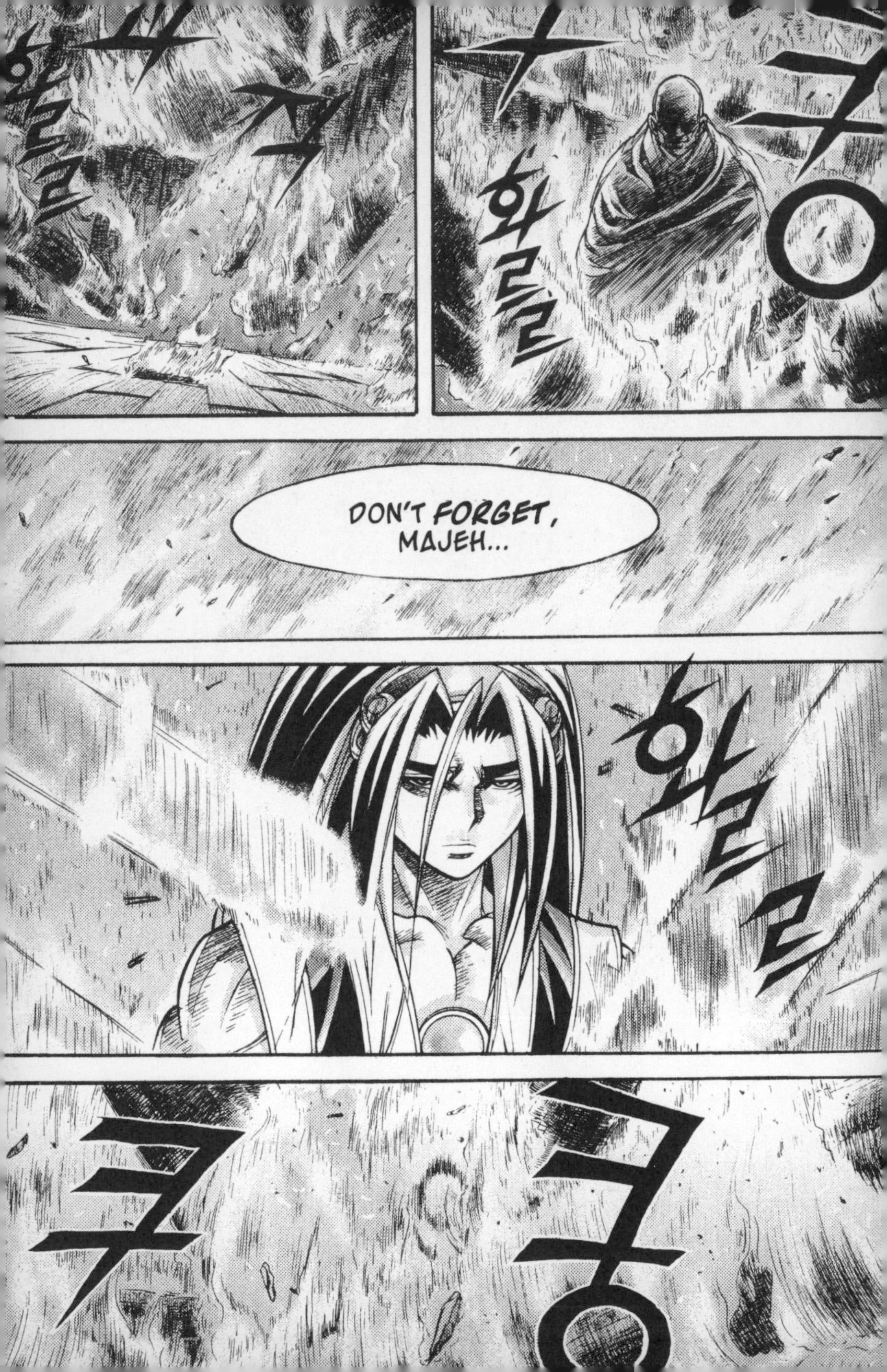

화르르
화르르
DON'T FORGET, MAJEH...
화르르

FINE--BURN *EVERYGHING* DOWN, YOU OLD FOOL!

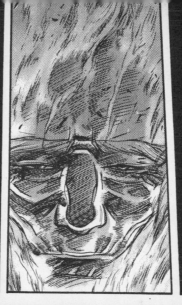

BUT *REMEMBER*-- AS YOUR BODY BURNS...AS YOUR FLESH IS MELTED AWAY...

...*YOUR* SPIRIT WILL LEAVE THIS BODY *FIRST*...

...AND IN THAT INSTANT, *I* WILL *ESCAPE* FROM THIS PIT OF FIRE...AND I WILL COVER THIS ENTIRE WORLD WITH *BLOOD*!

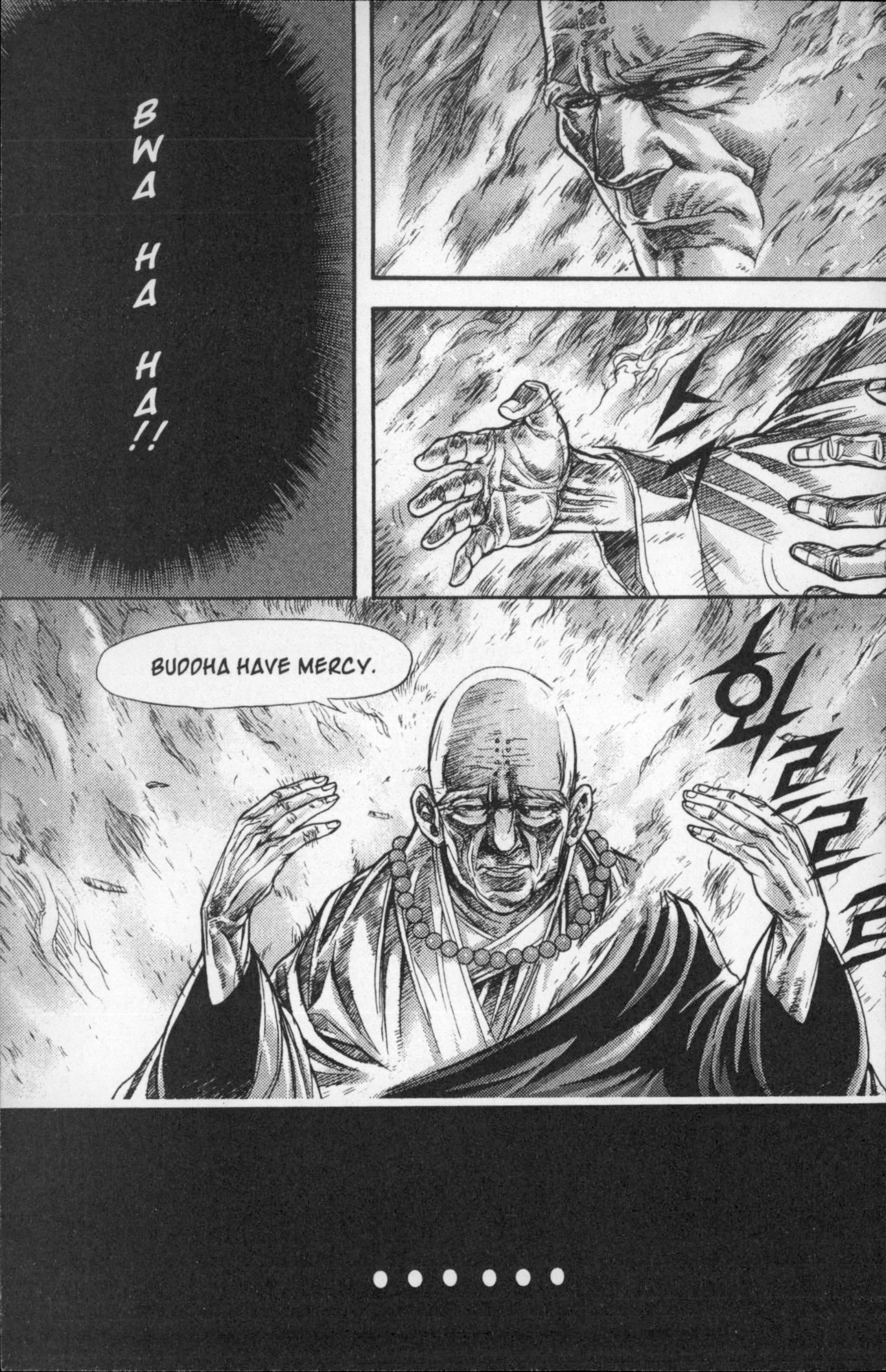
BWA HA HA!!
BUDDHA HAVE MERCY.
......

I INVOKE...
THE POWER OF THE
**SPIRIT DEATH
HAND!**

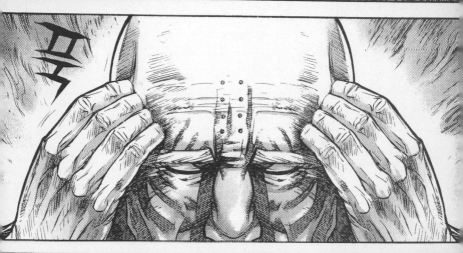

NOOO!!
YOU...
YOU CRAZY
FOOL...!

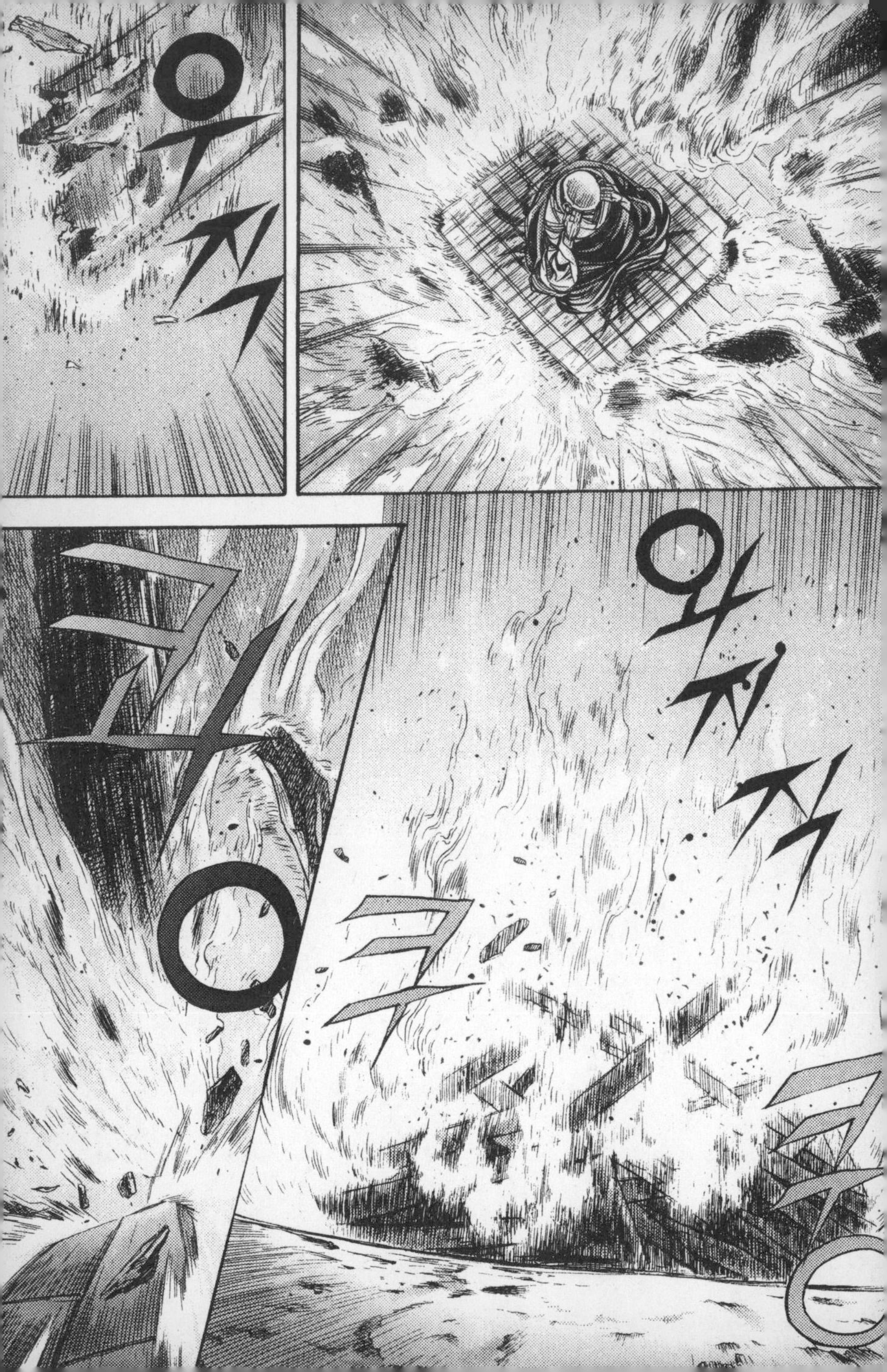

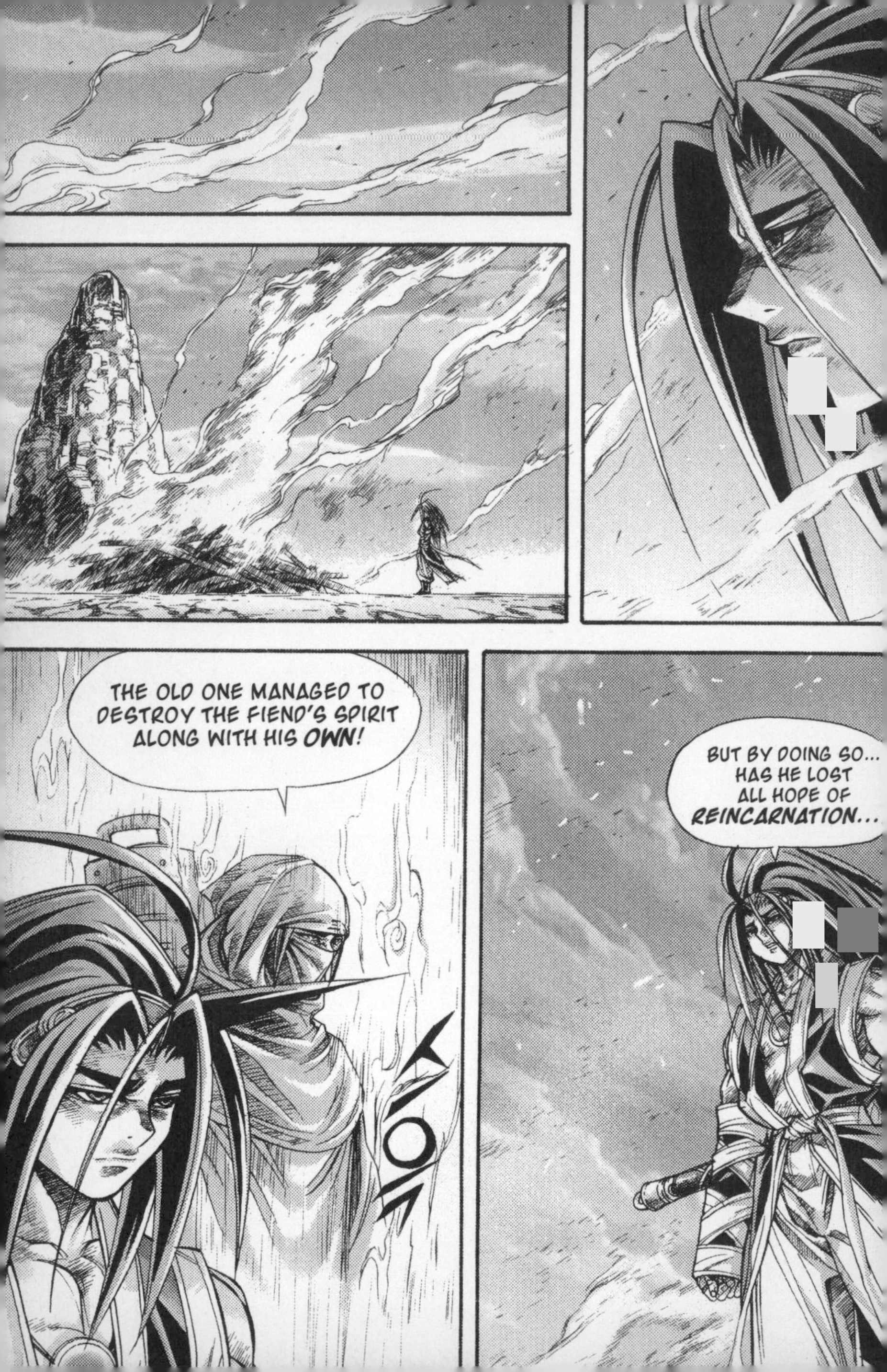
THE OLD ONE MANAGED TO DESTROY THE FIEND'S SPIRIT ALONG WITH HIS *OWN*!
BUT BY DOING SO... HAS HE LOST ALL HOPE OF *REINCARNATION*...

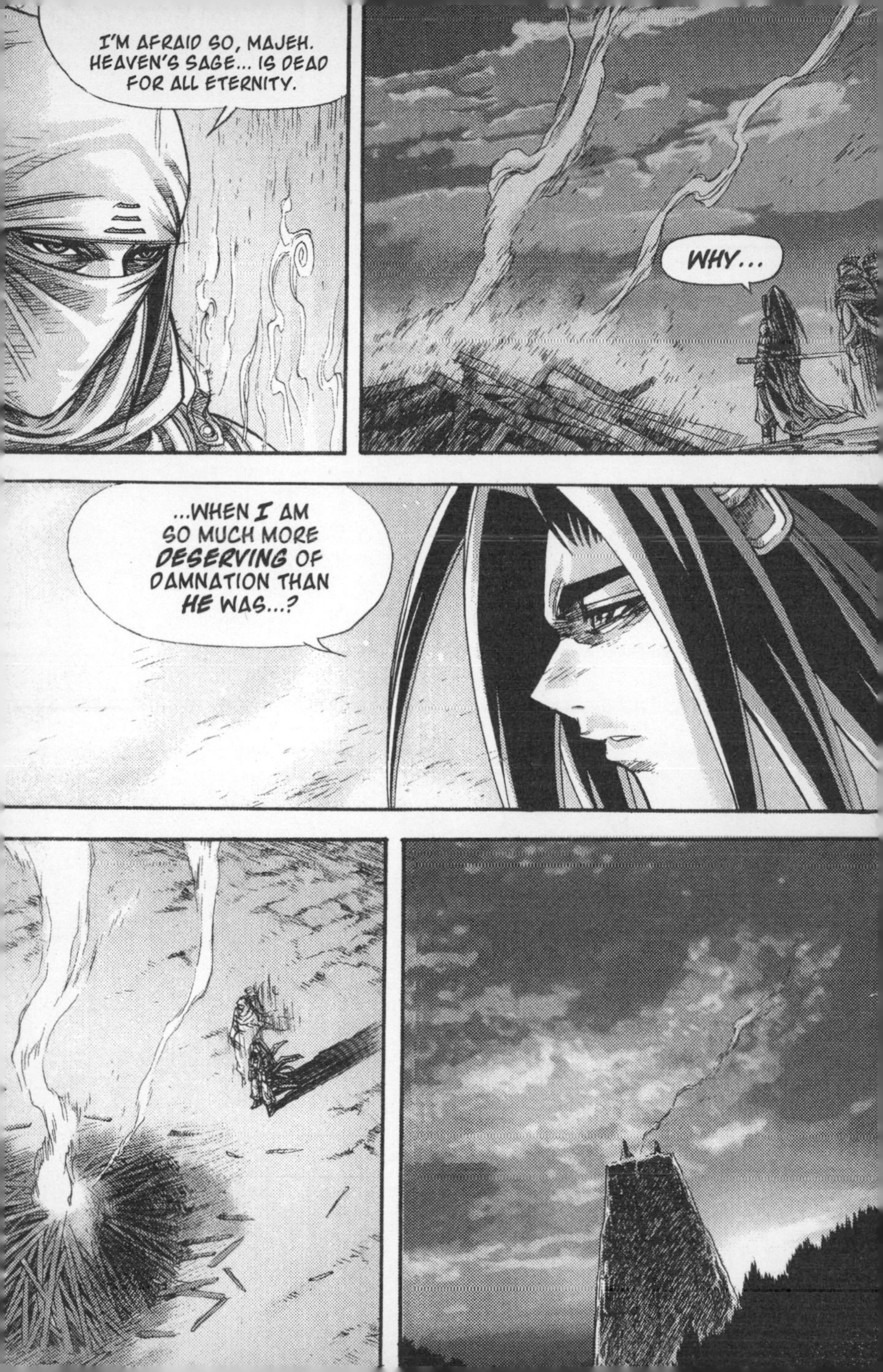
I'M AFRAID SO, MAJEH. HEAVEN'S SAGE... IS DEAD FOR ALL ETERNITY.
WHY...
...WHEN I AM SO MUCH MORE DESERVING OF DAMNATION THAN HE WAS...?

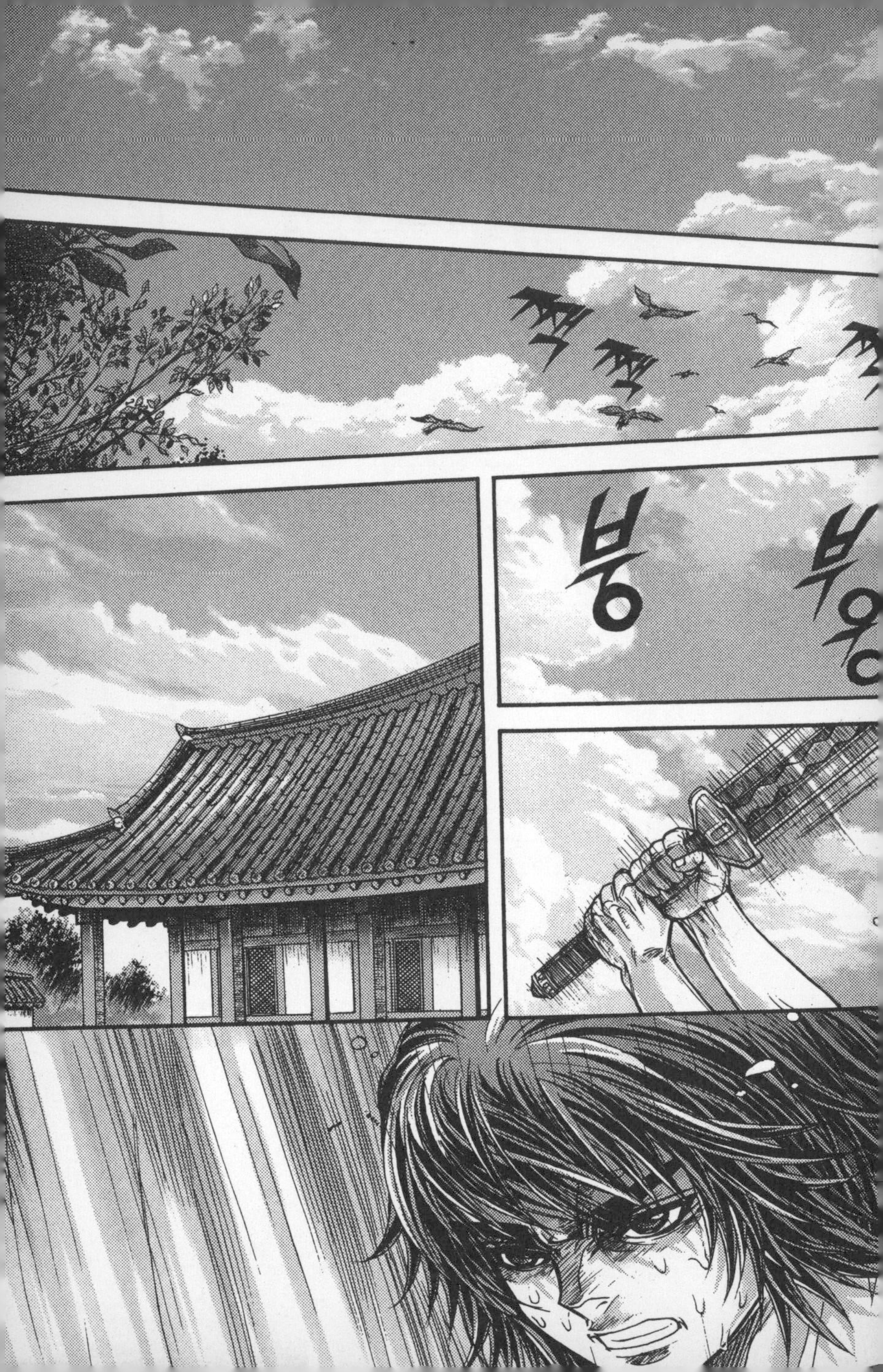

짹
짹
붕
부웅

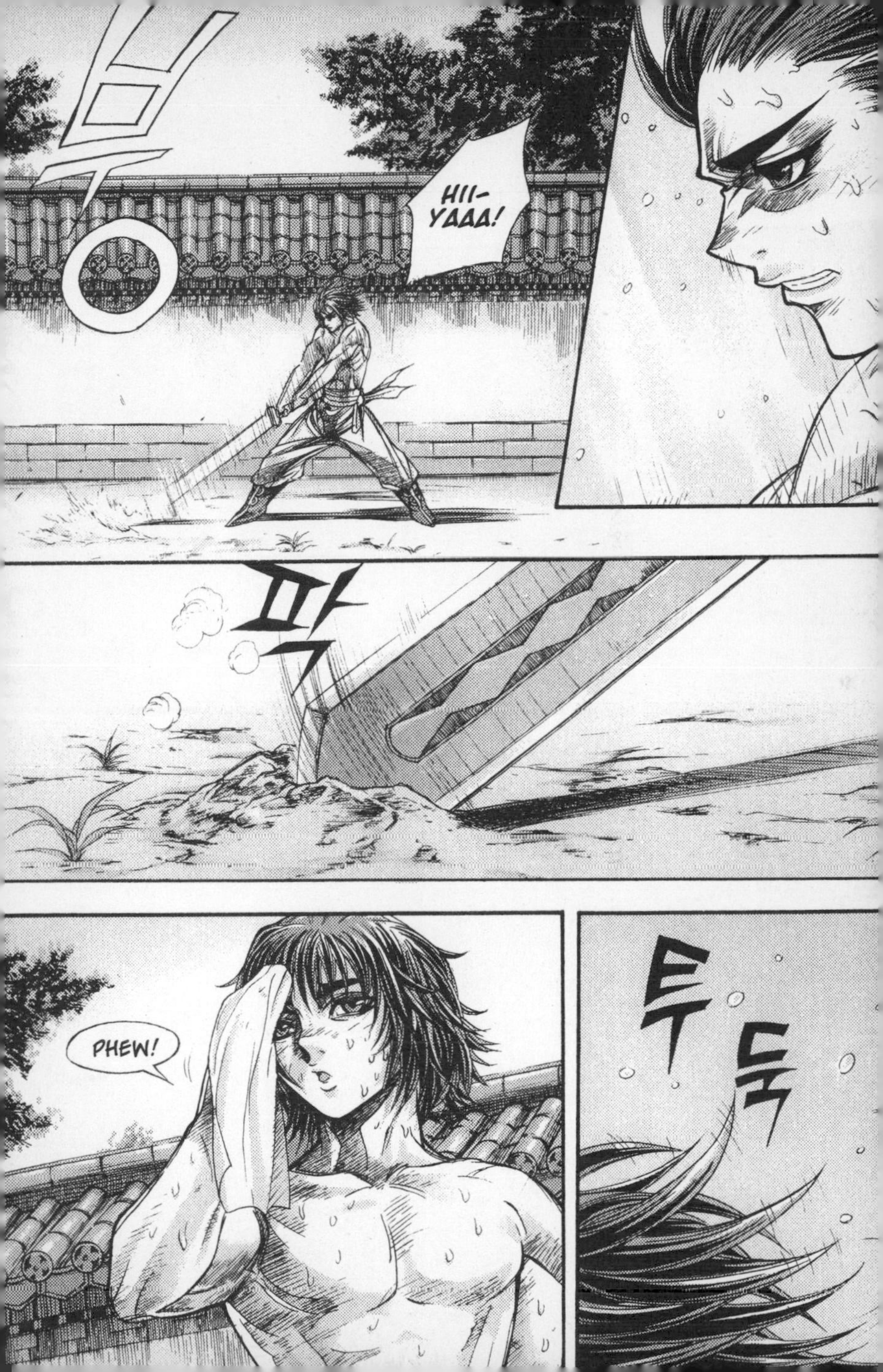
붕
HII-YAAA!
팍
PHEW!
투 둑

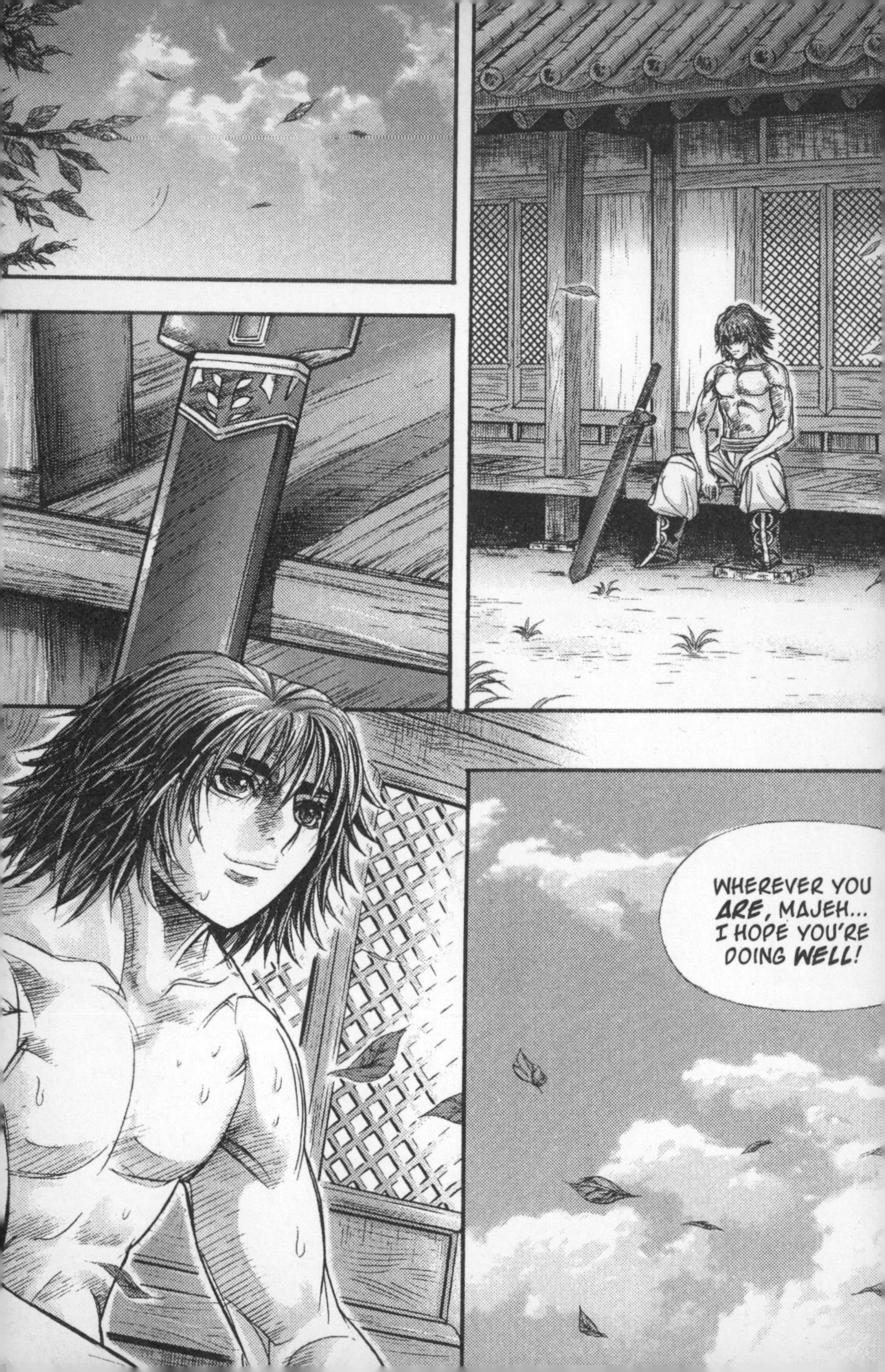
WHEREVER YOU ARE, MAJEH... I HOPE YOU'RE DOING WELL!

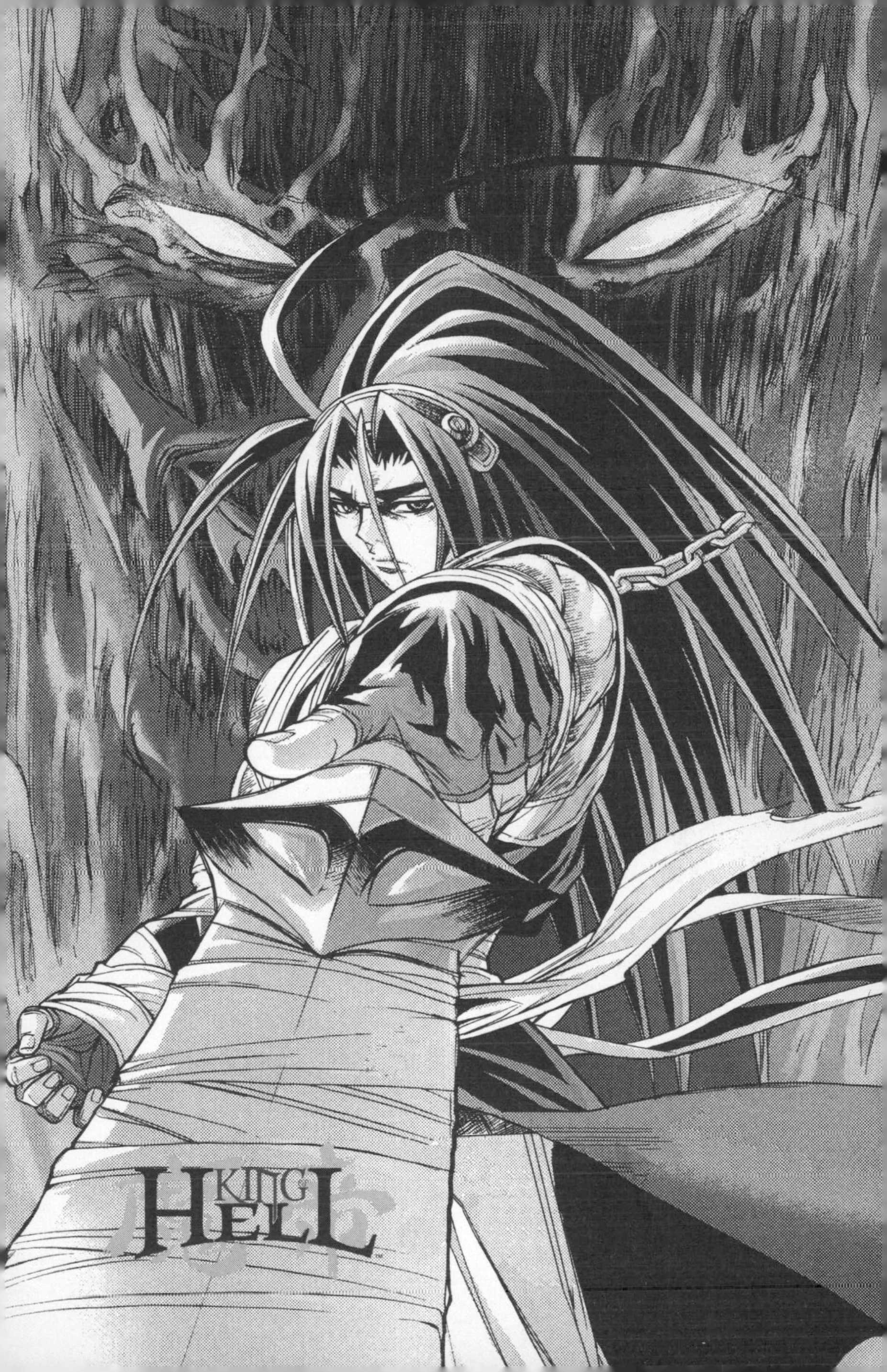
KING
HELL

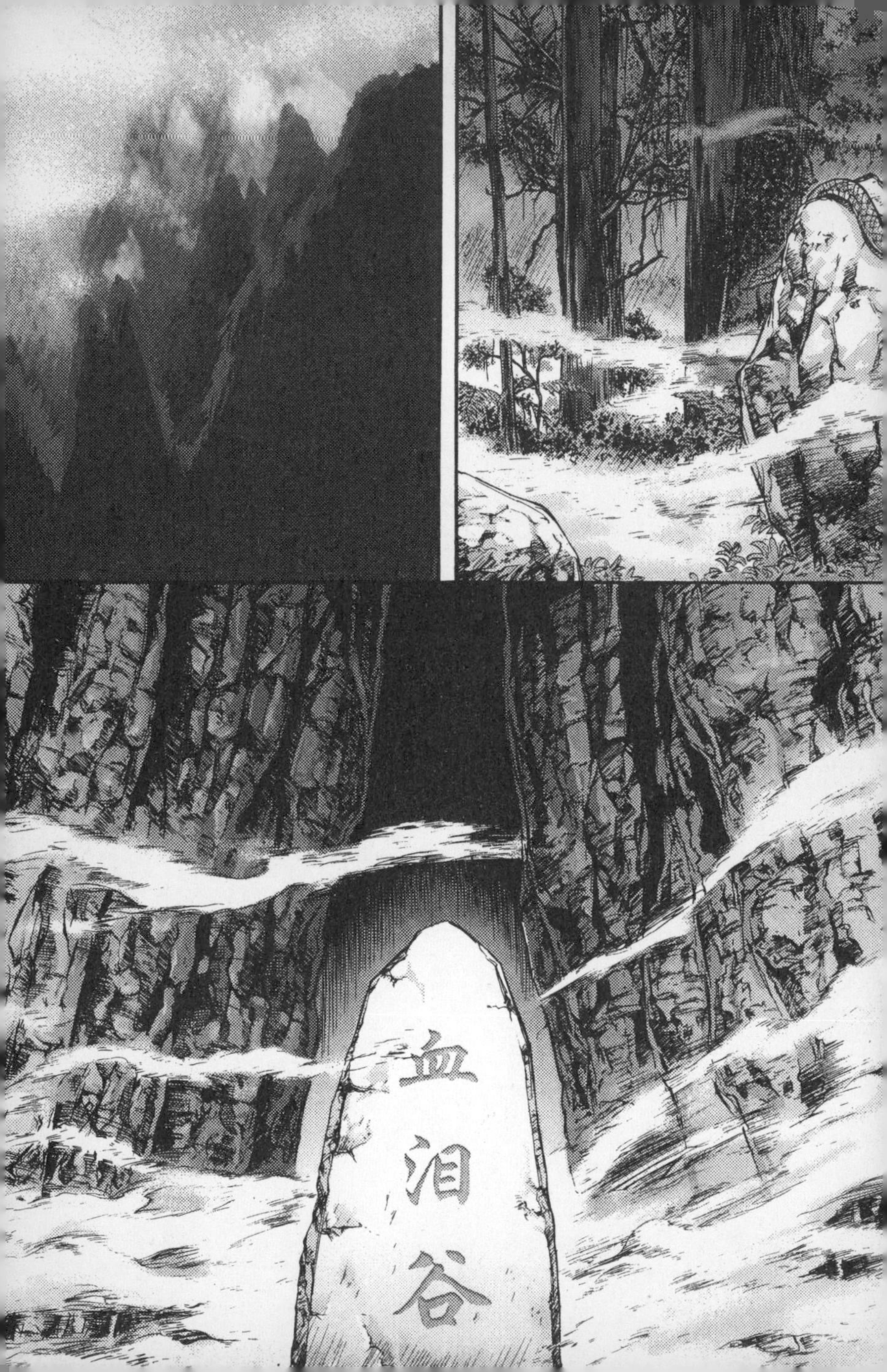
血泪谷

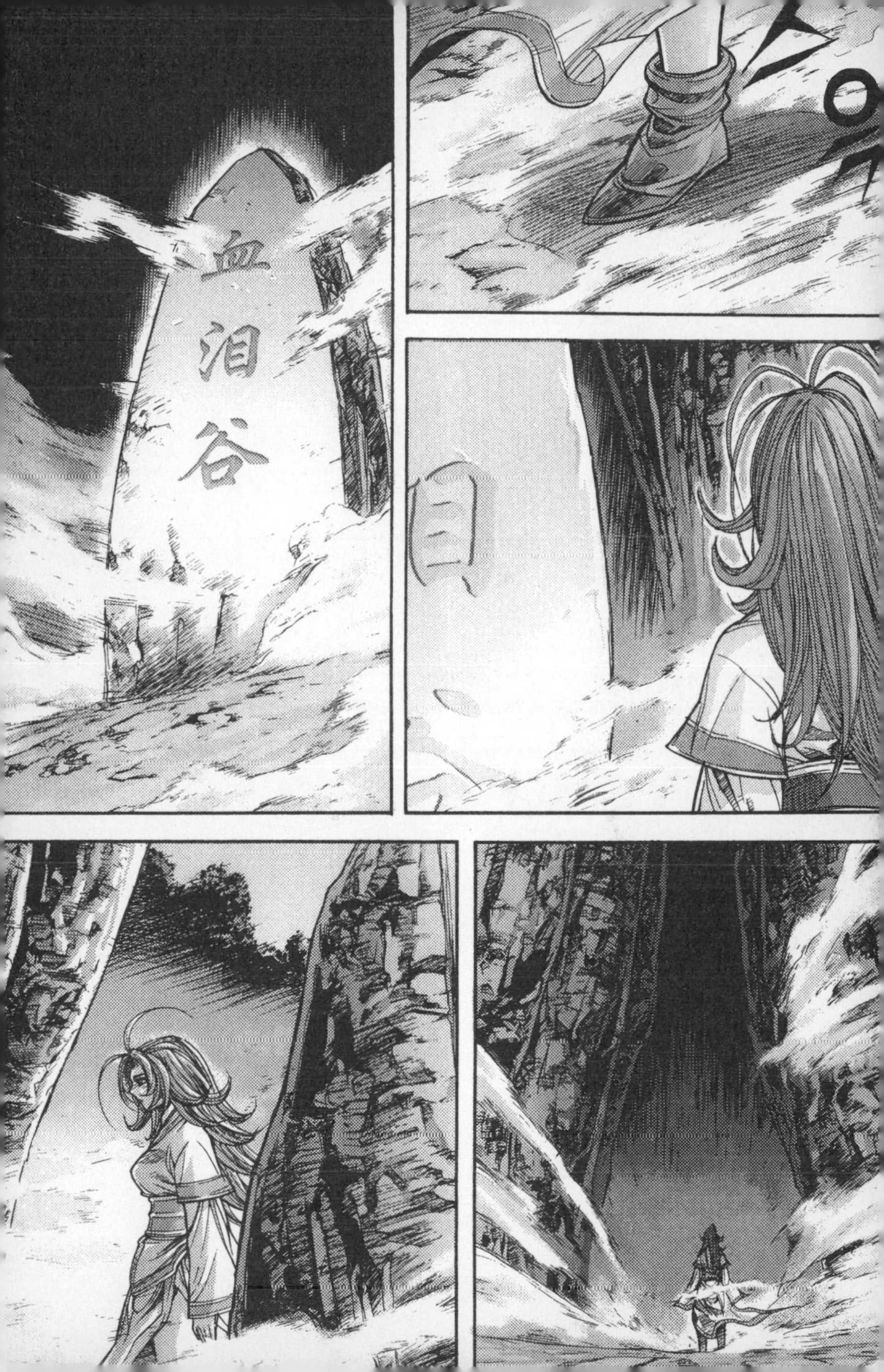
血泪谷

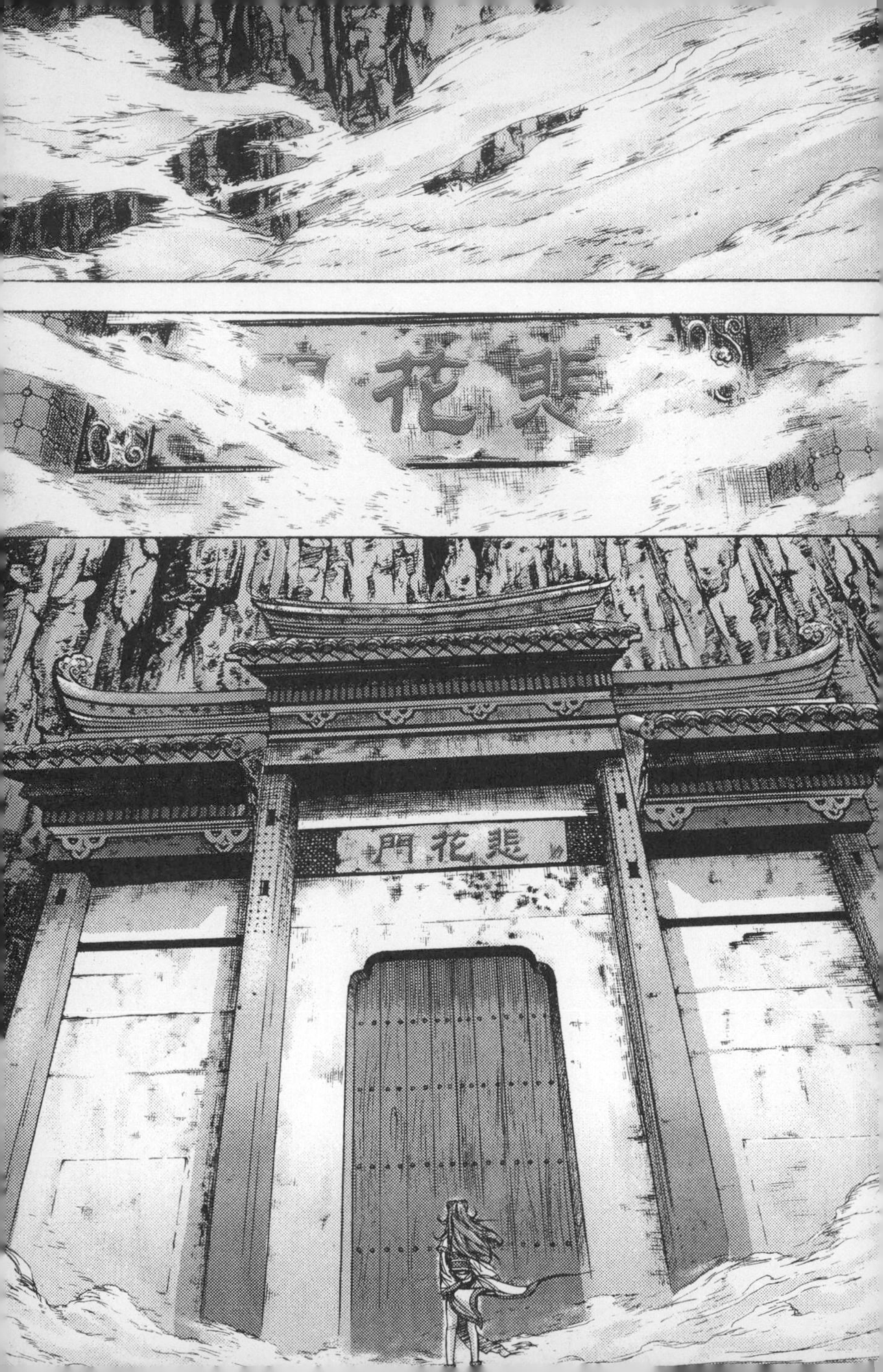
悲花
悲花門

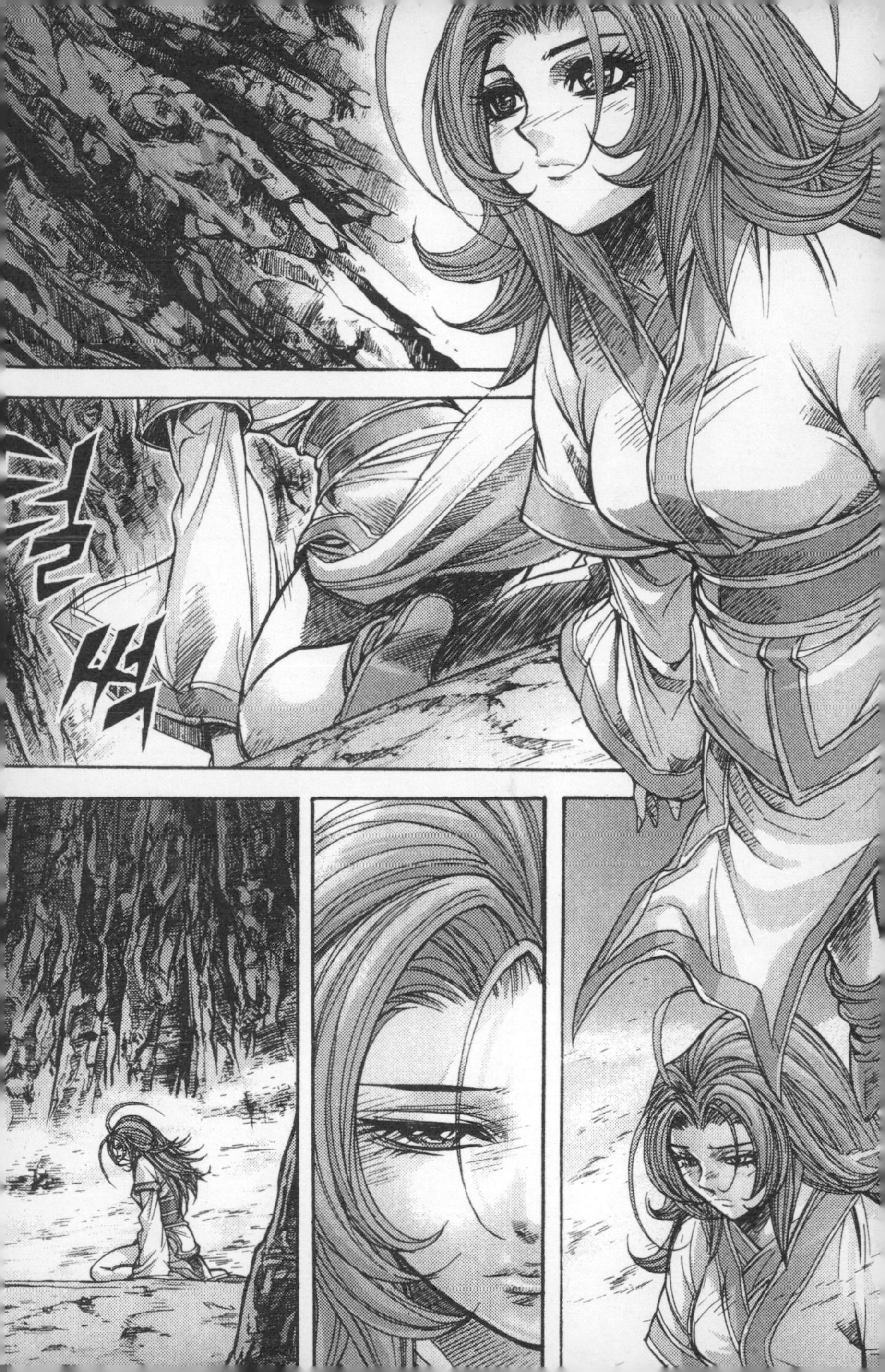

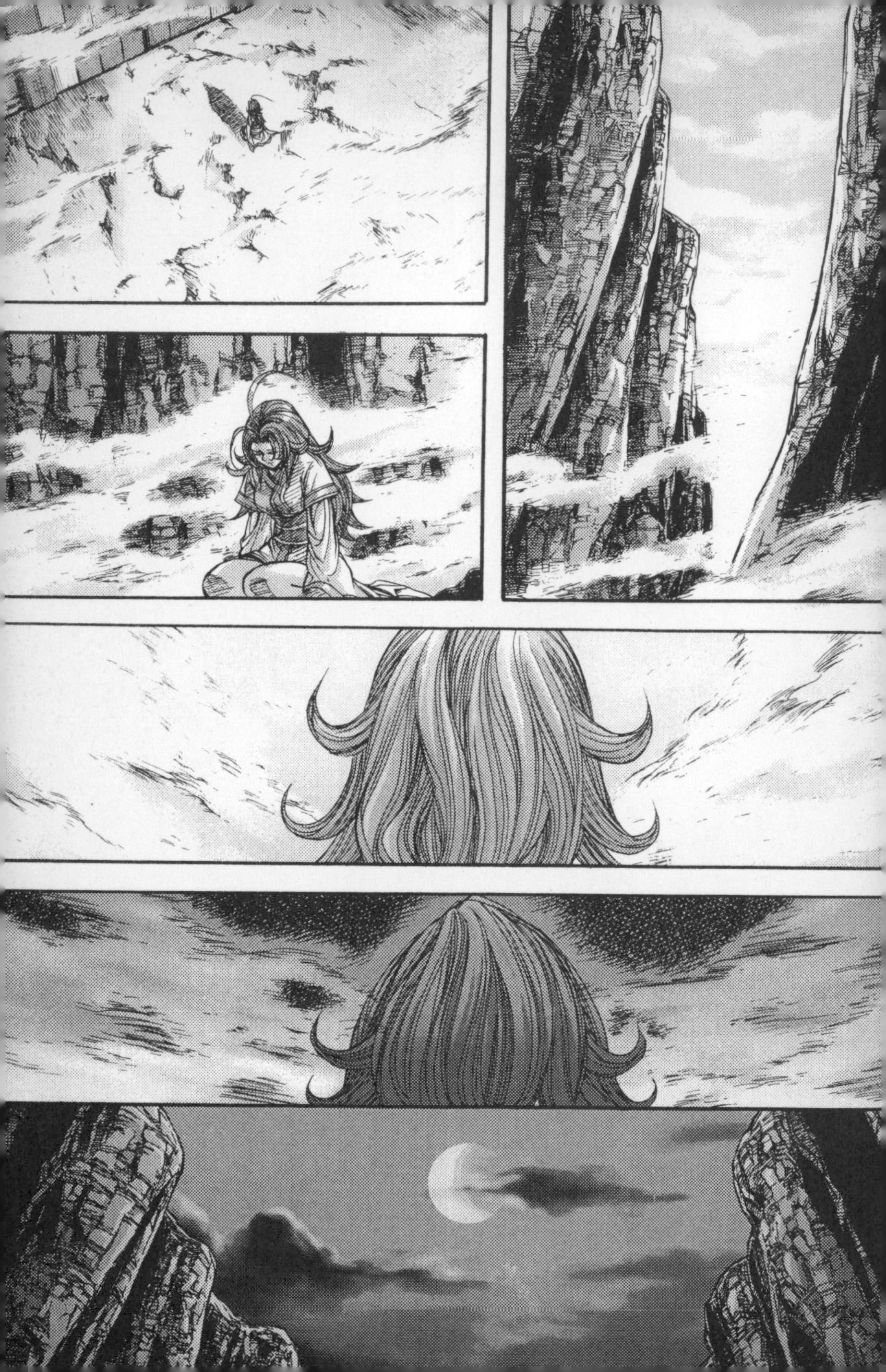

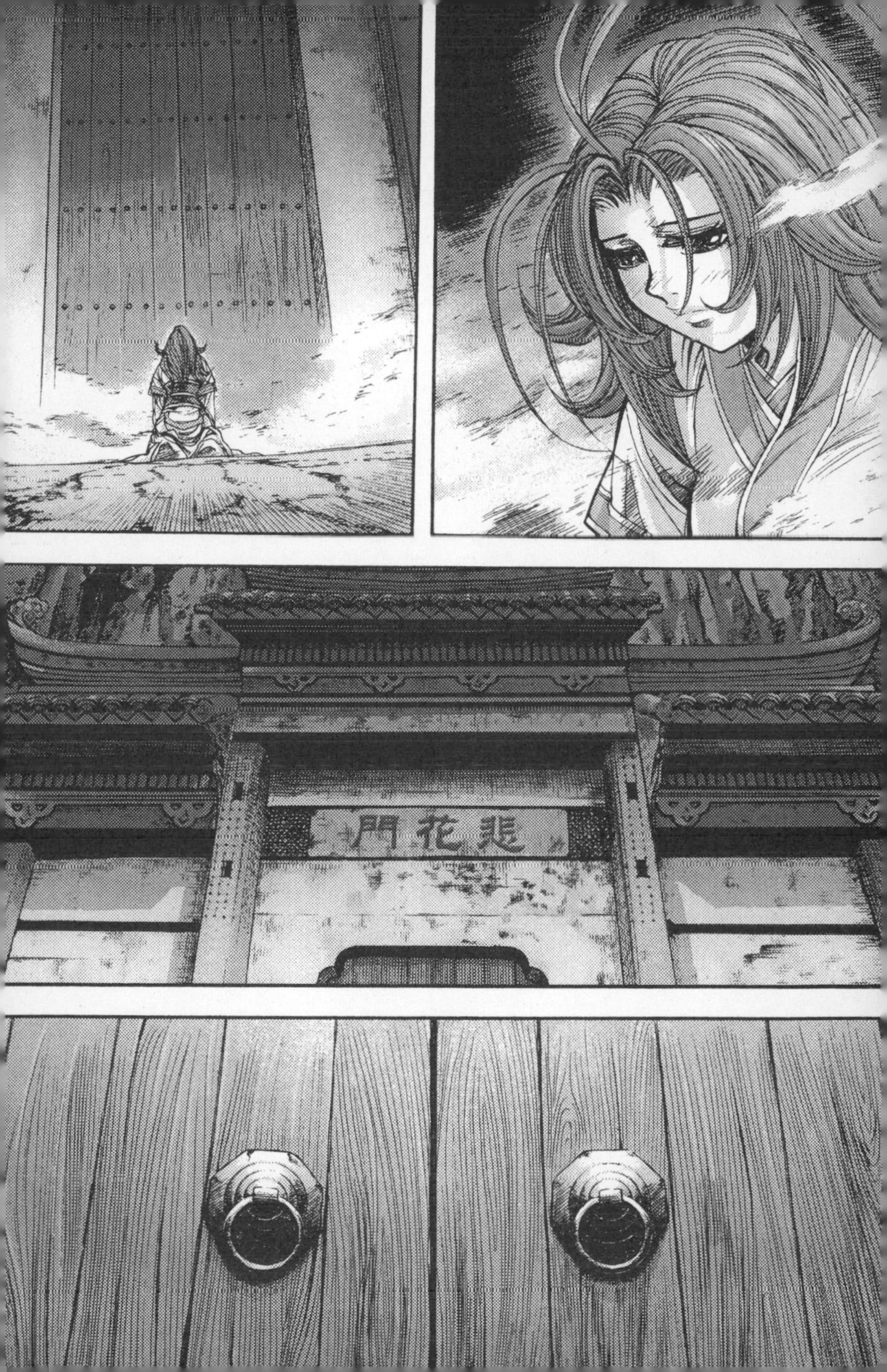
悲花門

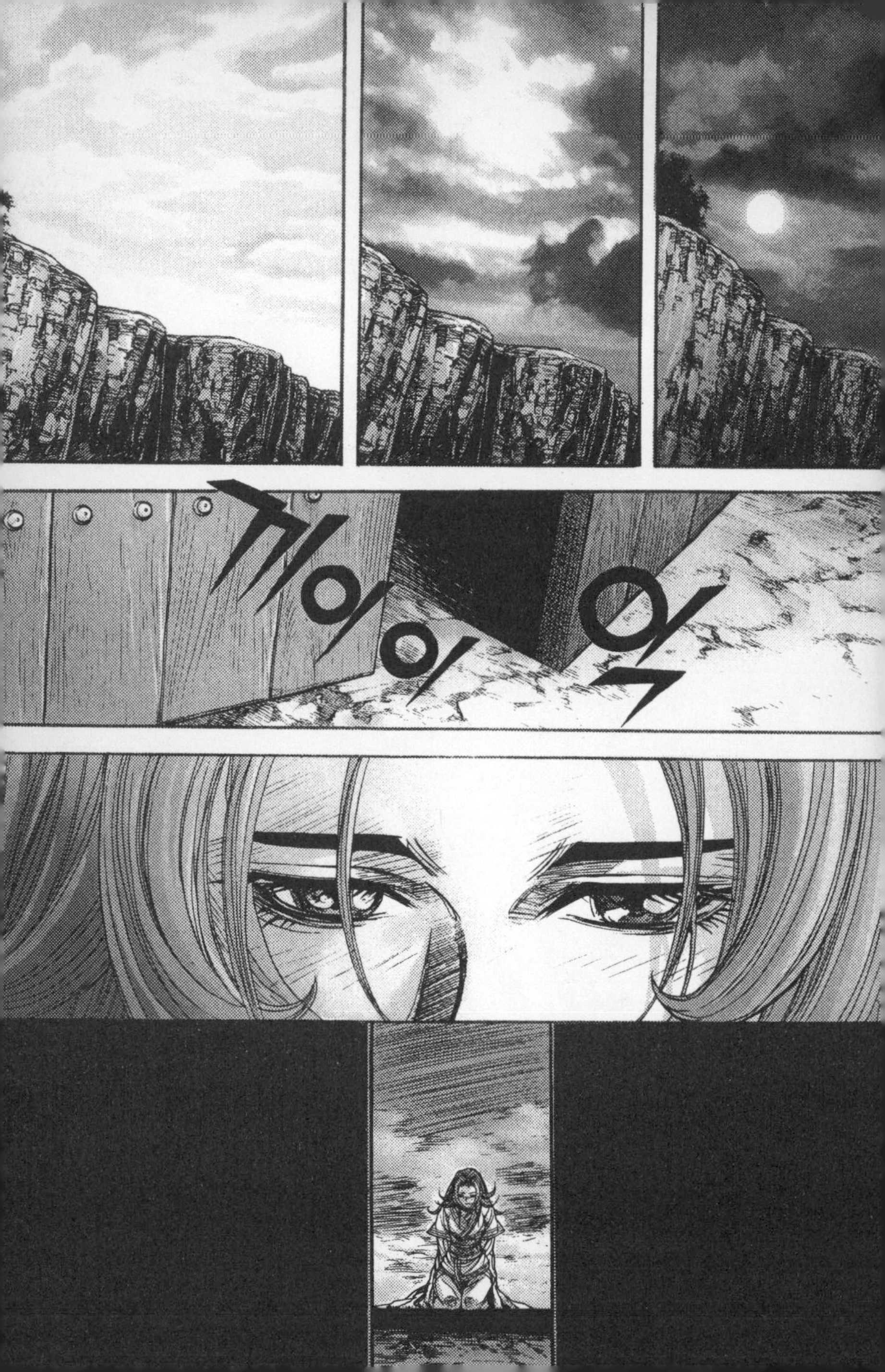
끼이이억

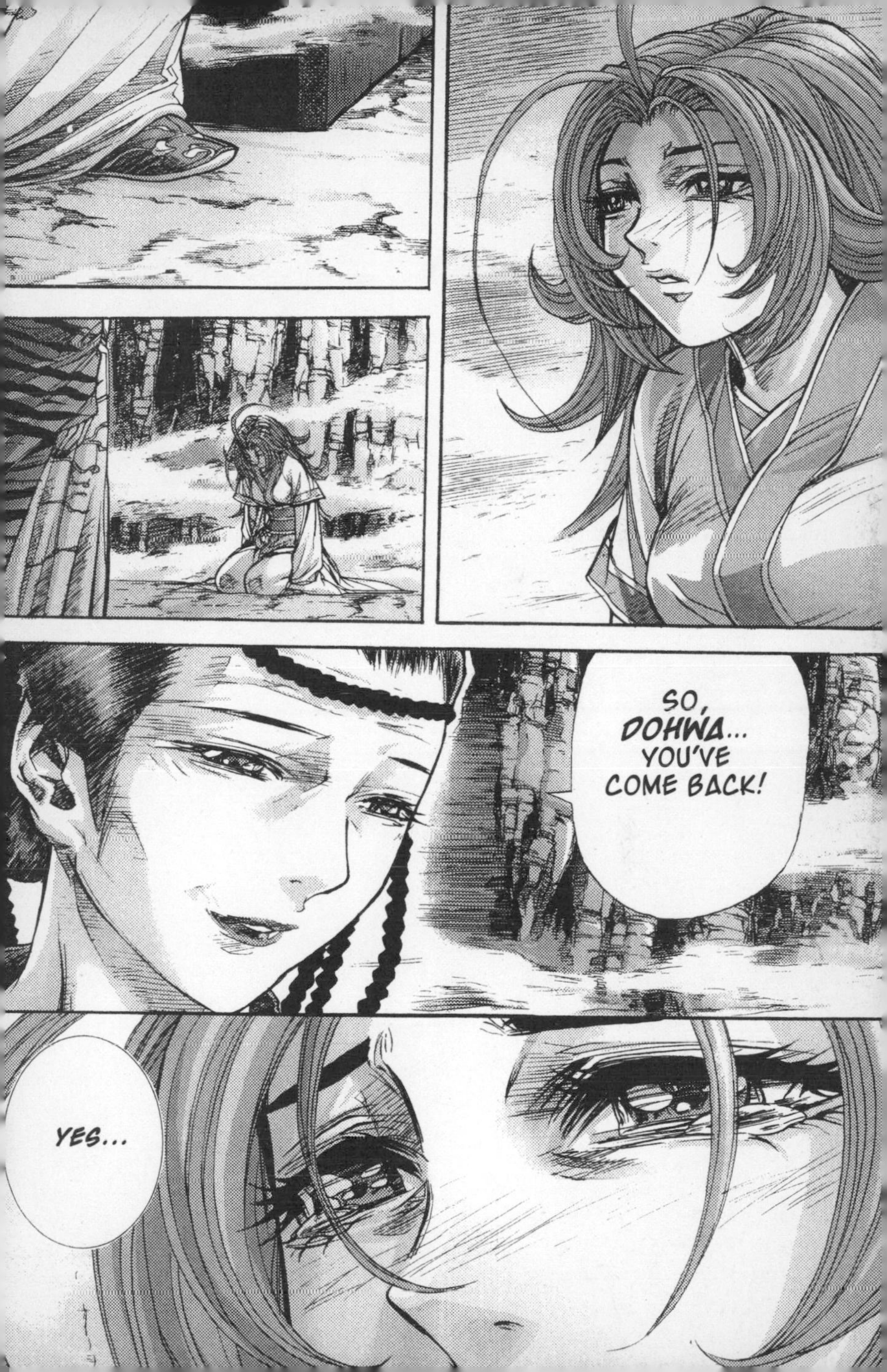
SO, DOHWA... YOU'VE COME BACK!
YES...

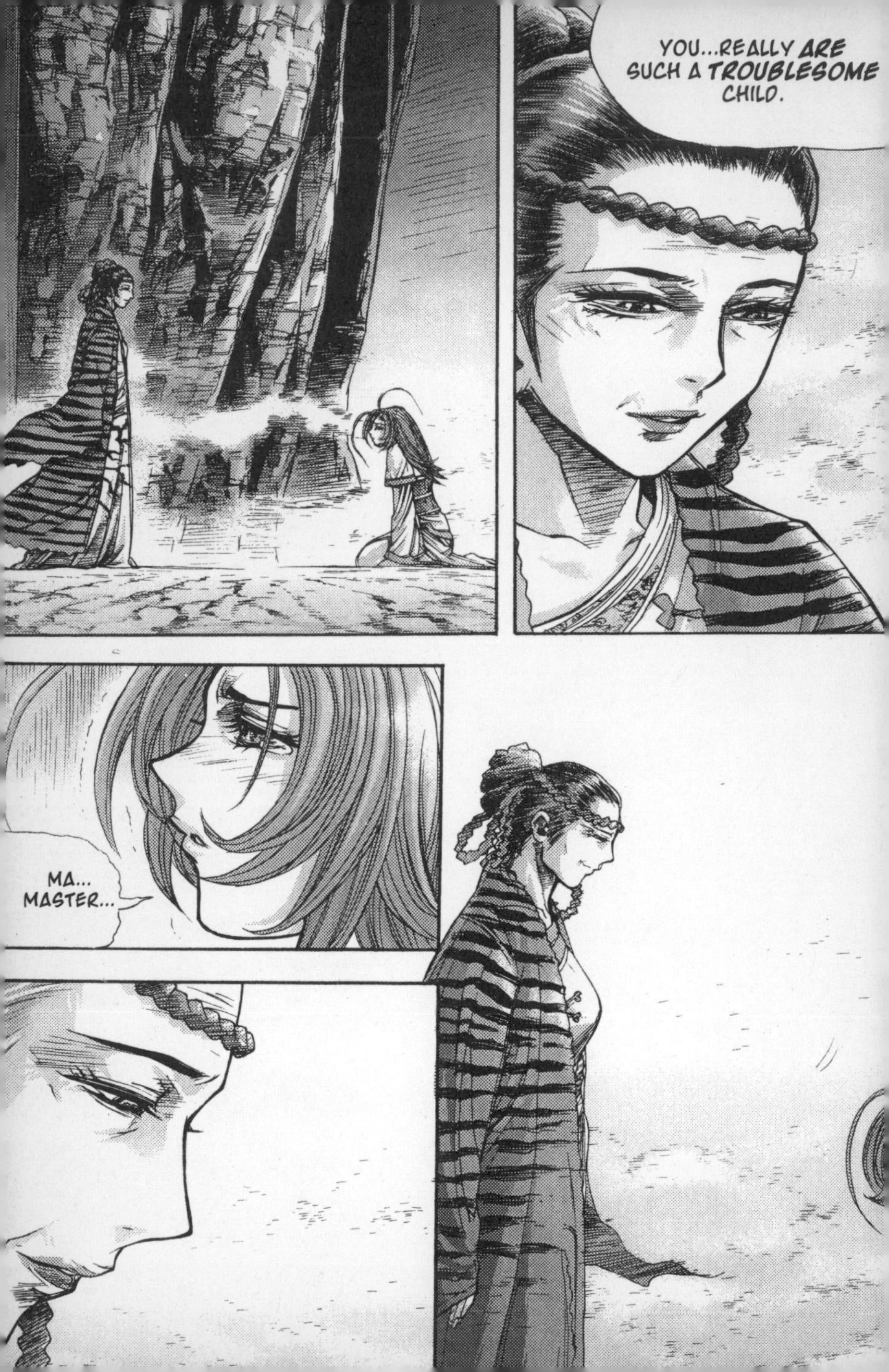
YOU...REALLY ARE SUCH A TROUBLESOME CHILD.
MA... MASTER...

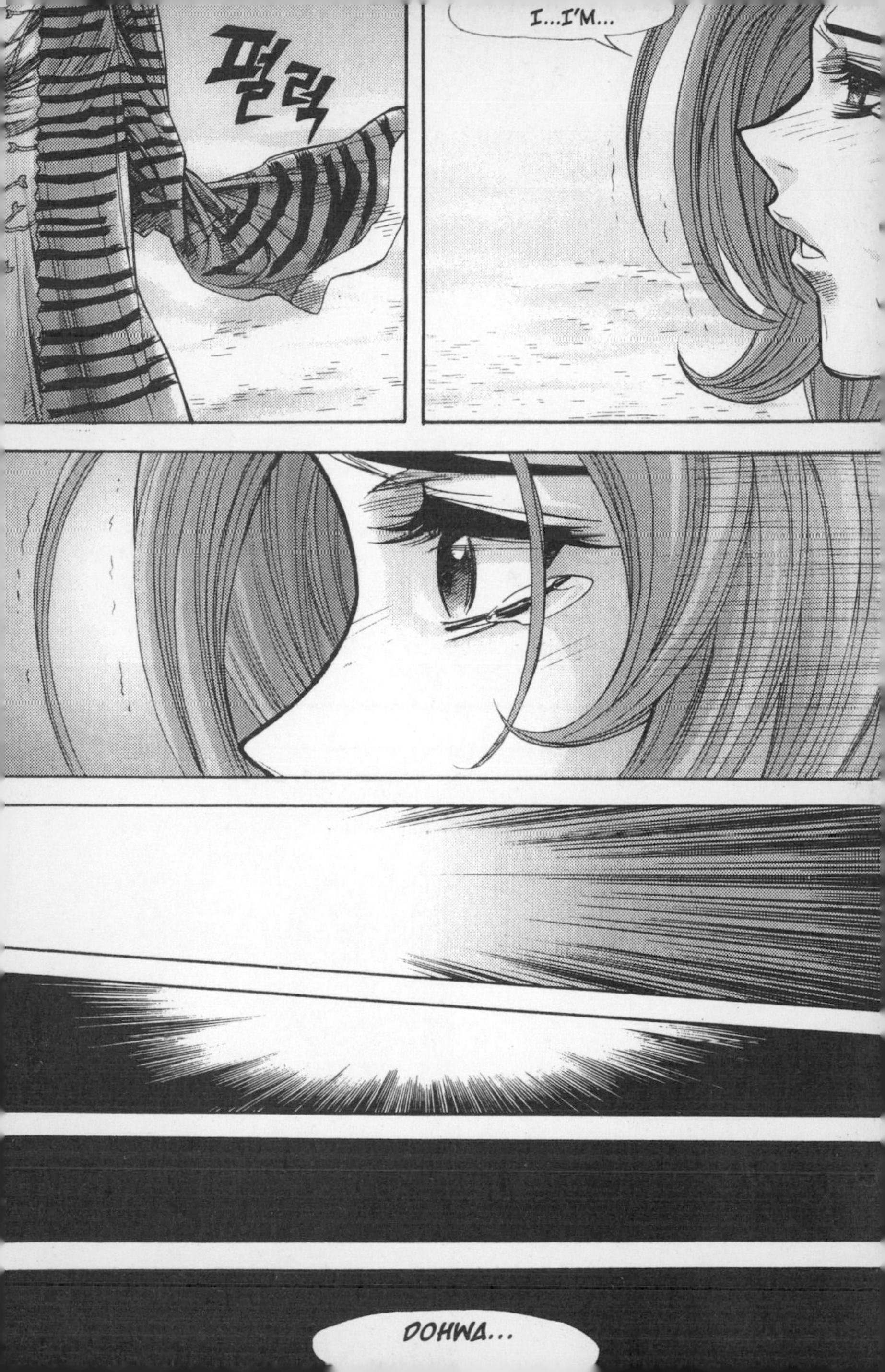

펄럭
I...I'M...
DOHWA...

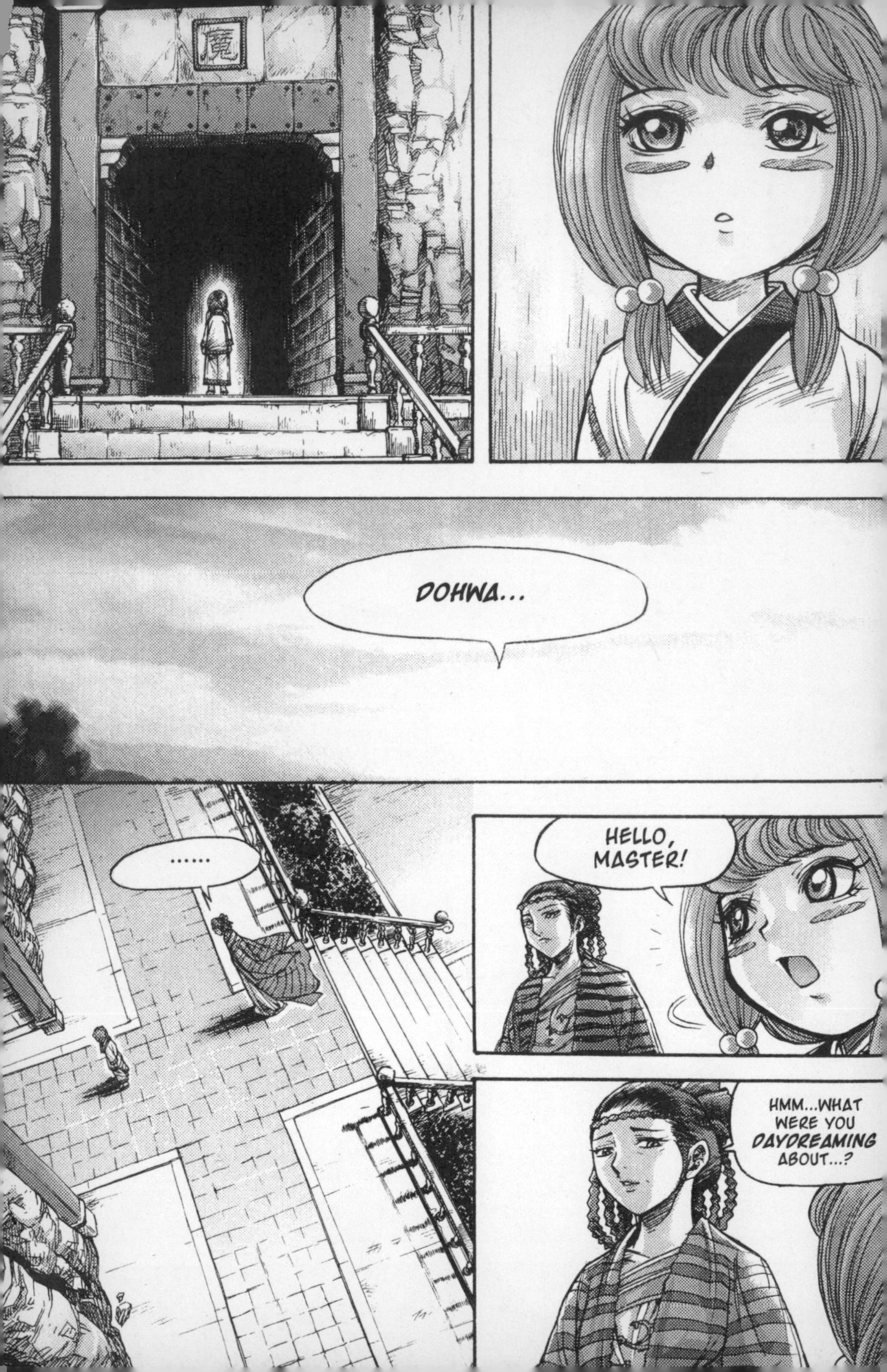
魔
DOHWA...
......
HELLO, MASTER!
HMM...WHAT WERE YOU *DAYDREAMING* ABOUT...?

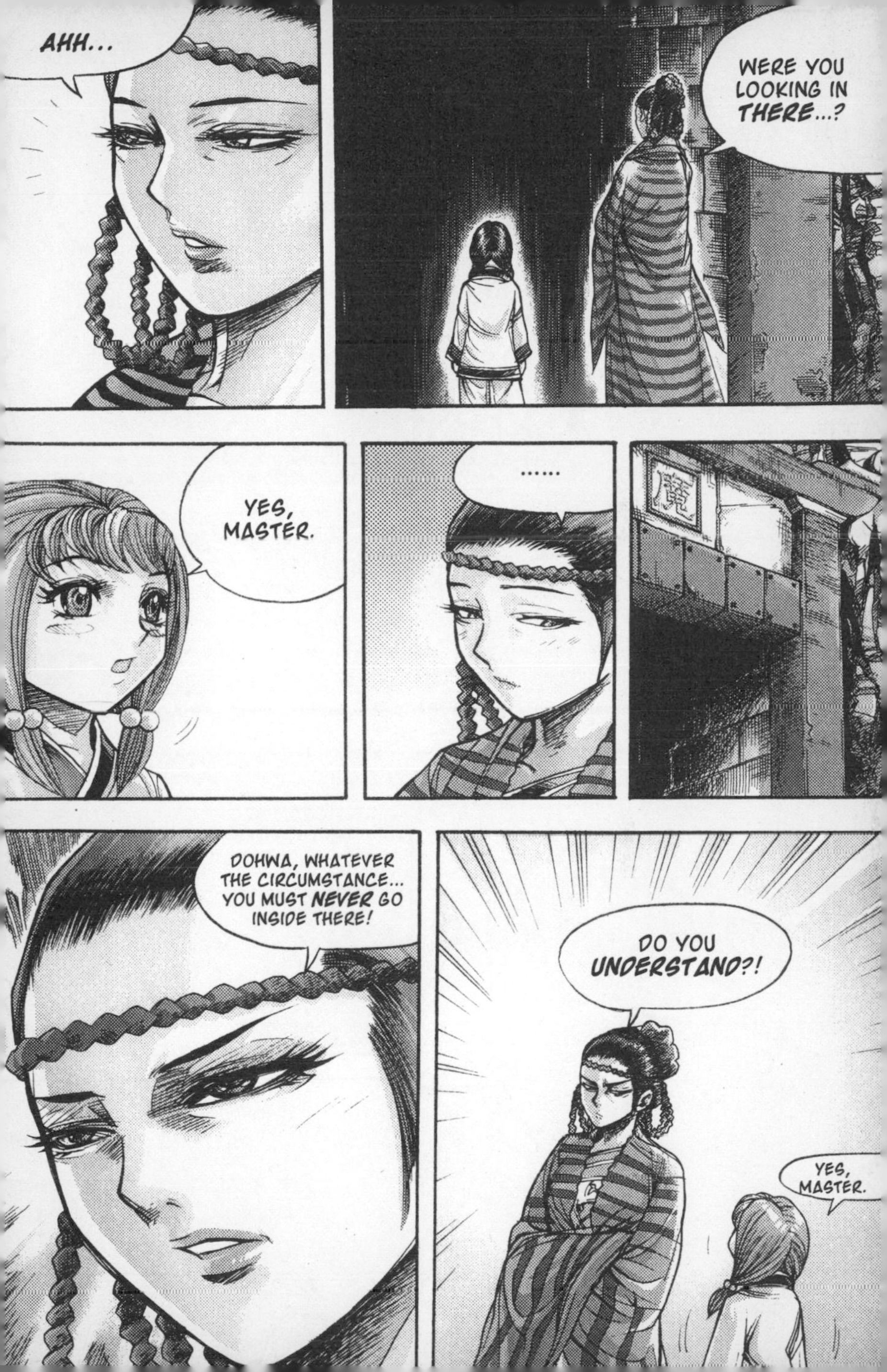
AHH...
WERE YOU LOOKING IN THERE...?
YES, MASTER.
......
DOHWA, WHATEVER THE CIRCUMSTANCE... YOU MUST NEVER GO INSIDE THERE!
DO YOU UNDERSTAND?!
YES, MASTER.

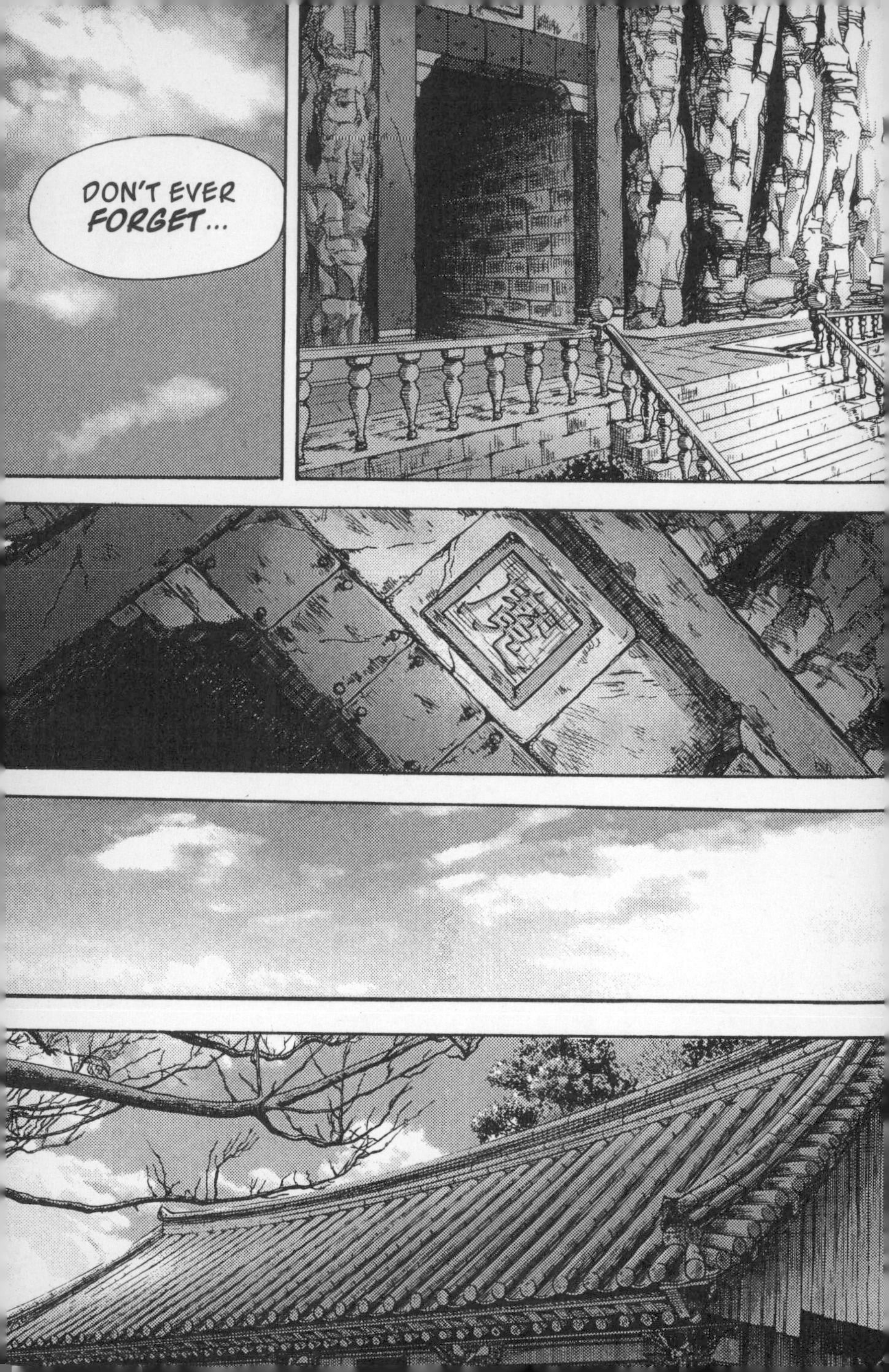
DON'T EVER FORGET...

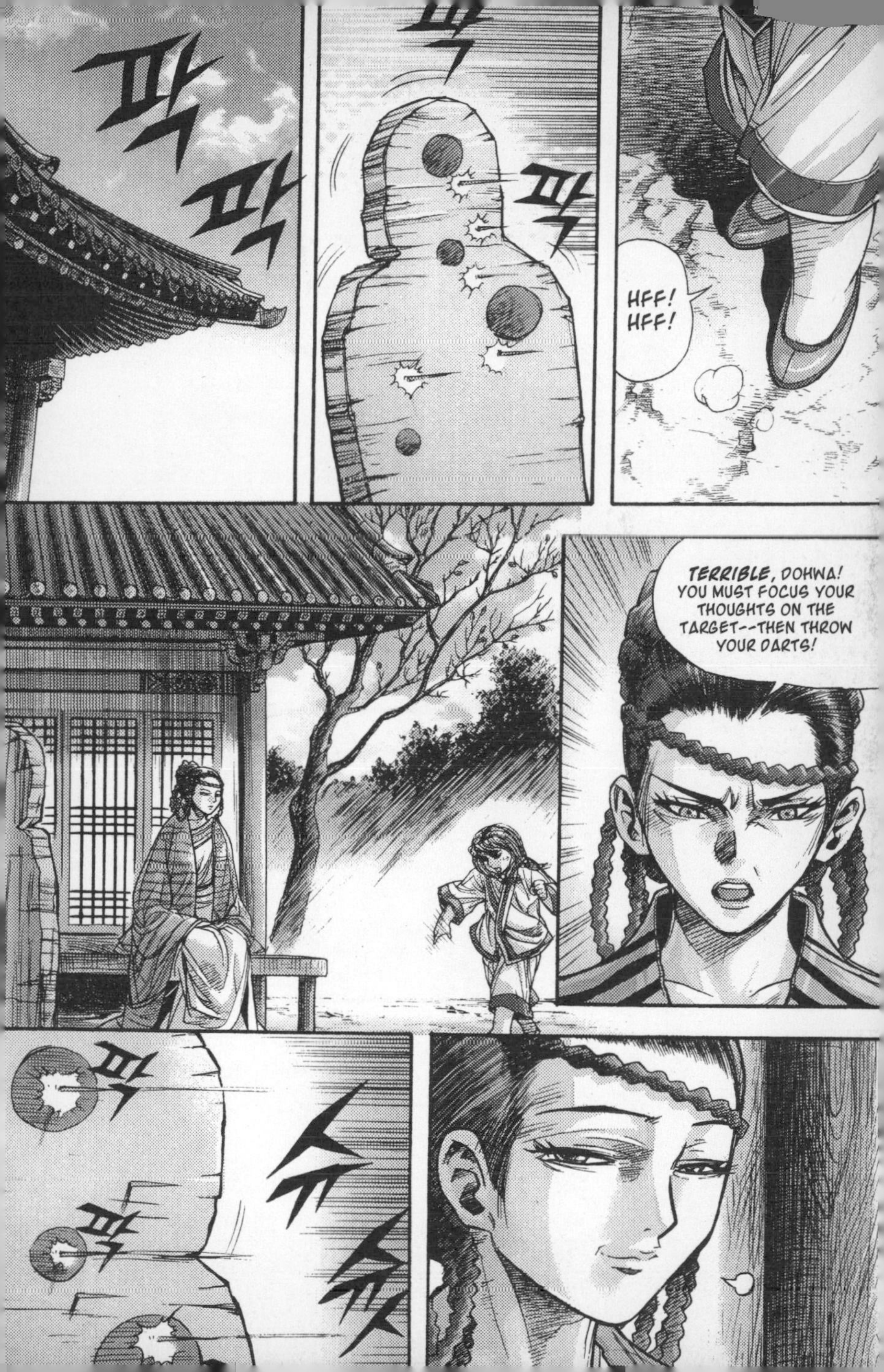
팍
팍
팍
HFF! HFF!
TERRIBLE, DOHWA! YOU MUST FOCUS YOUR THOUGHTS ON THE TARGET--THEN THROW YOUR DARTS!
팍
팍

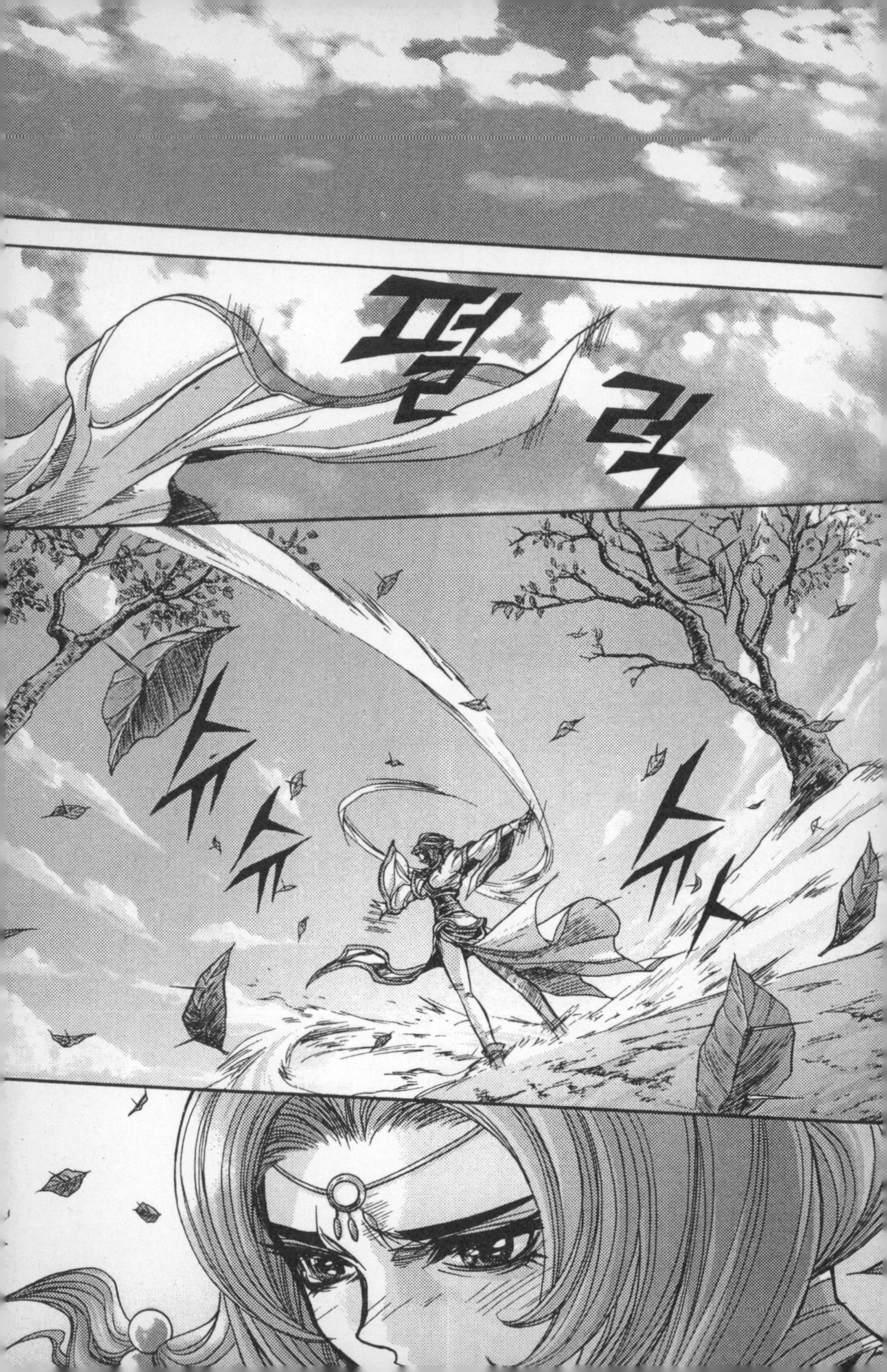
펄럭
슈슈
슈ㅅ

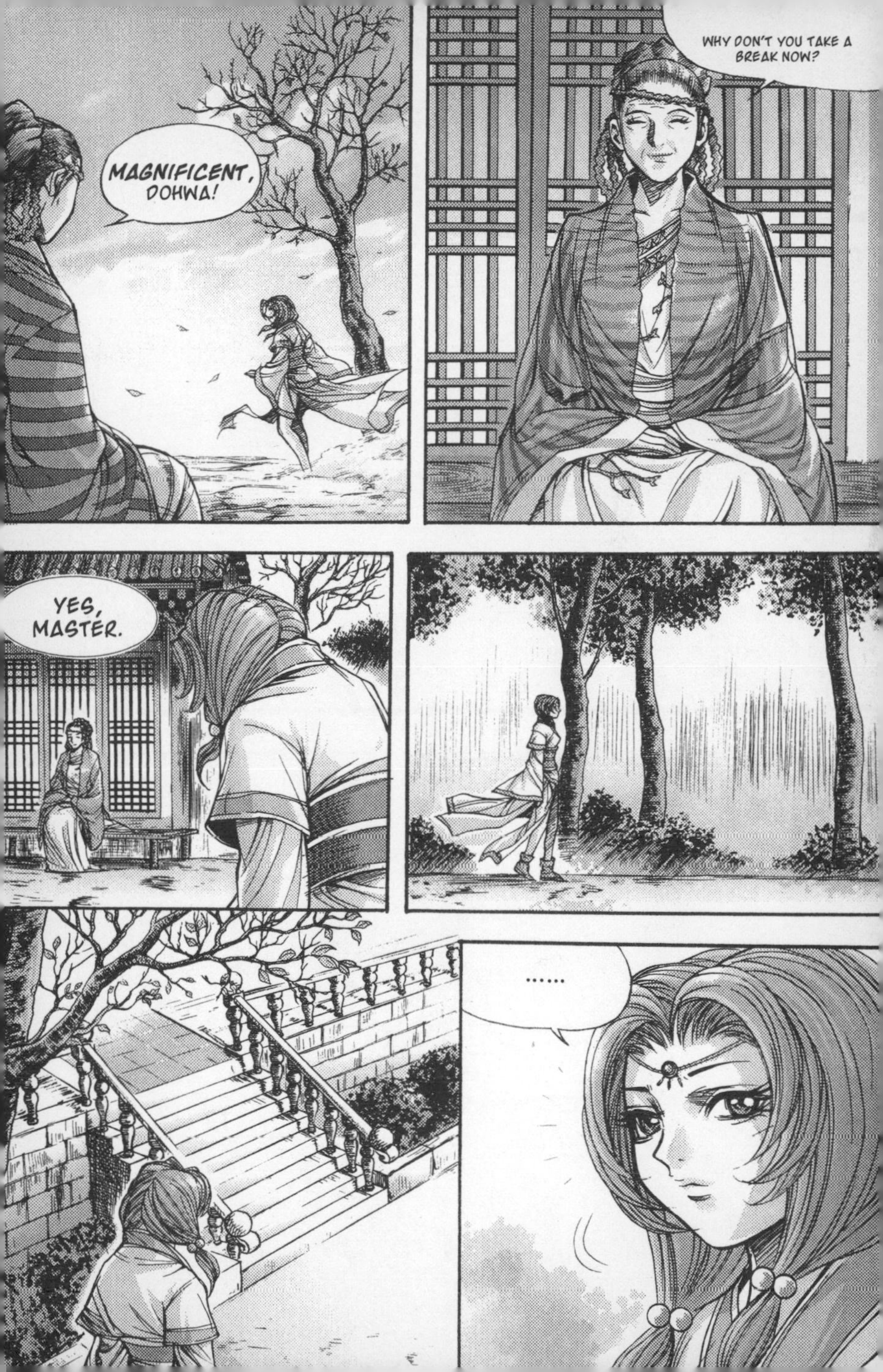
MAGNIFICENT, DOHWA!
WHY DON'T YOU TAKE A BREAK NOW?
YES, MASTER.
......

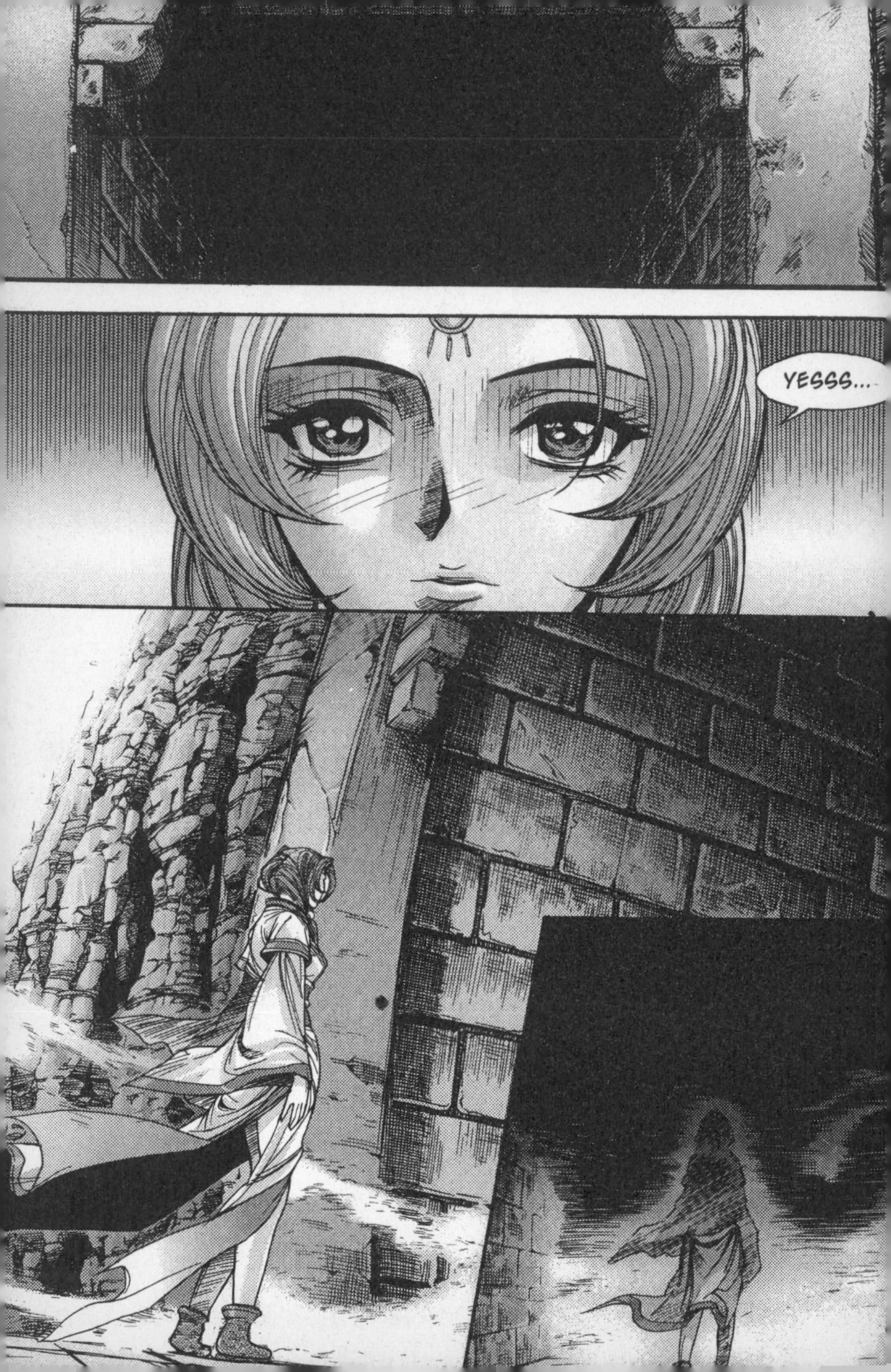
YESSS...

TO BE CONTINUED

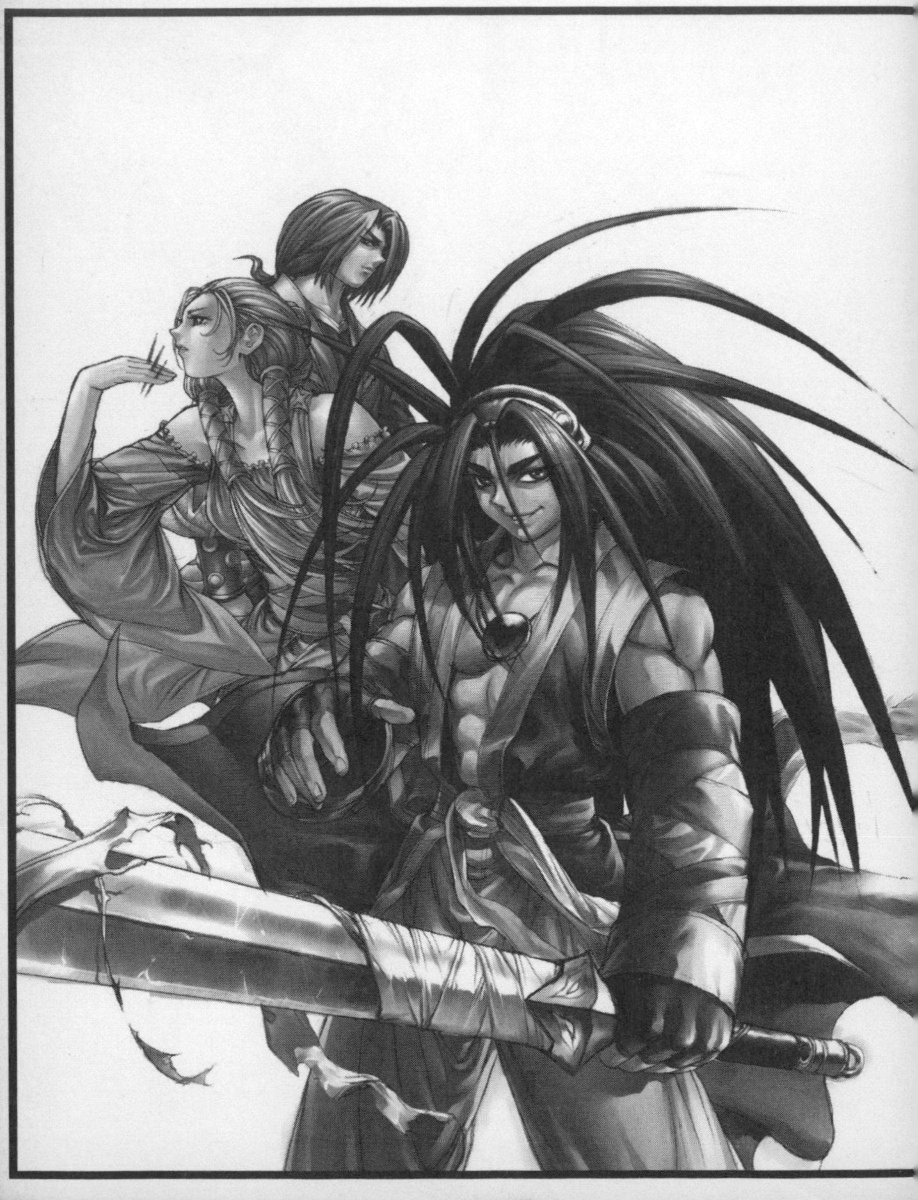

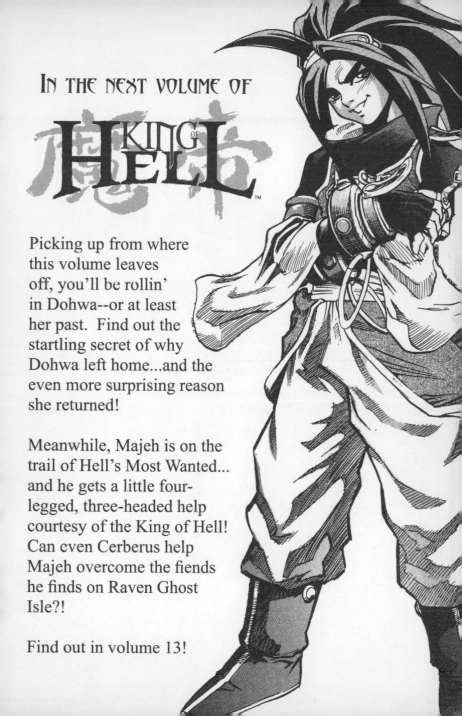

In the next volume of

King of Hell™

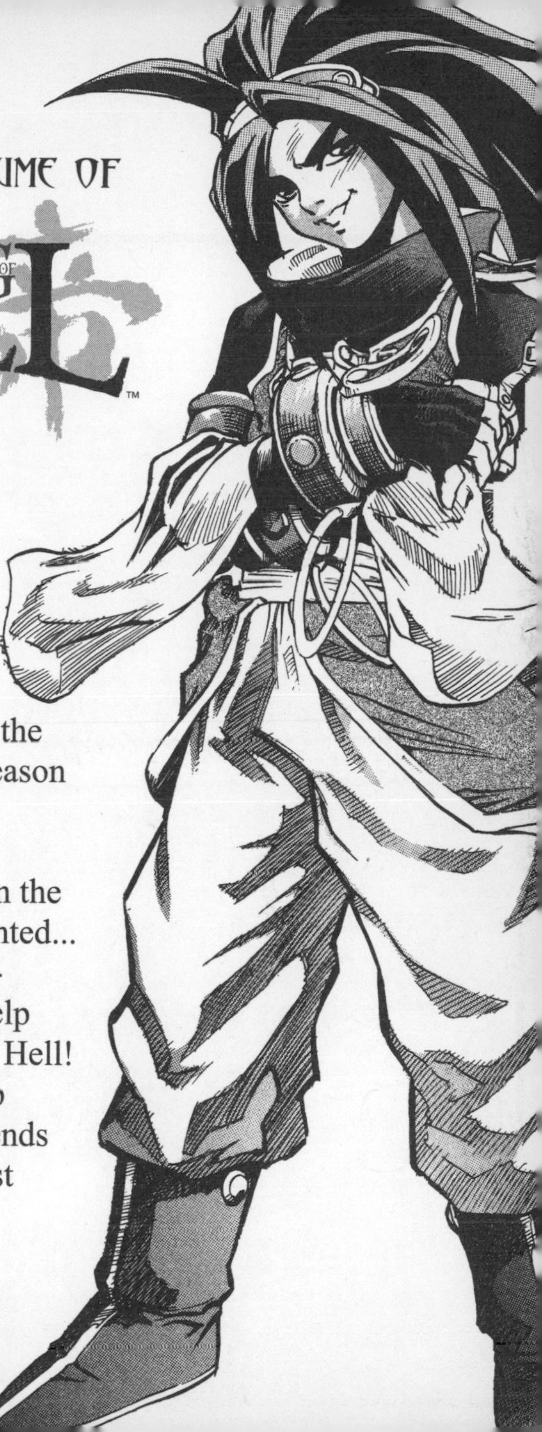

Picking up from where this volume leaves off, you'll be rollin' in Dohwa--or at least her past. Find out the startling secret of why Dohwa left home...and the even more surprising reason she returned!

Meanwhile, Majeh is on the trail of Hell's Most Wanted... and he gets a little four-legged, three-headed help courtesy of the King of Hell! Can even Cerberus help Majeh overcome the fiends he finds on Raven Ghost Isle?!

Find out in volume 13!

LIFE
BY KEIKO SUENOBU

Ordinary high school teenagers...
Except that they're not.

OT
OLDER TEEN
AGE 16+

© Keiko Suenobu

Ayumu struggles with her studies, and the all-important high school entrance exams are approaching. Fortunately, she has help from her best bud Shii-chan, who is at the top of the class. But when the test results come back, the friends are surprised: Ayumu surpasses Shii-chan's scores and gets into the school of her choice—without Shii-chan! Losing her friend is so painful for Ayumu that she starts cutting herself to ease her sorrow. Finally, Ayumu seeks comfort in a new friend, Manami. But will Manami prove to be the friend that Ayumu truly needs? Or will Ayumu continue down a dark path?

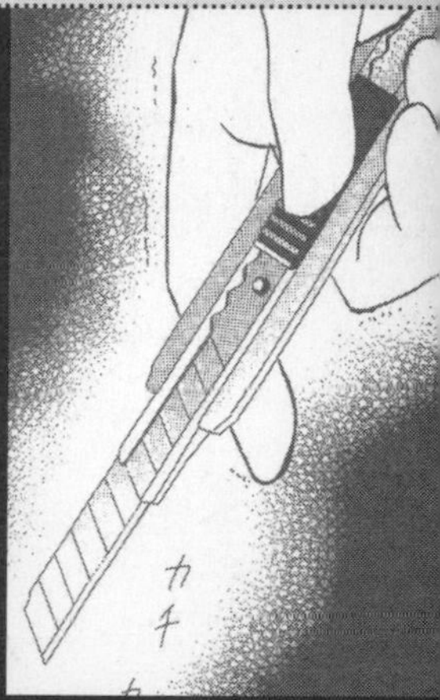
カチ

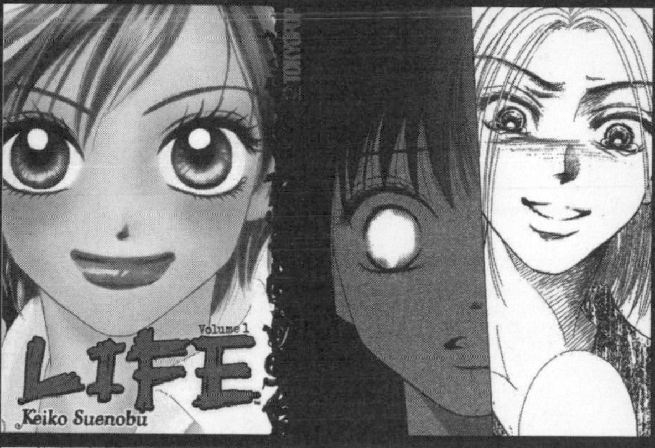
Volume 1
LIFE
Keiko Suenobu

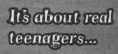

It's about real teenagers...

It's about real high school...

It's about real life.

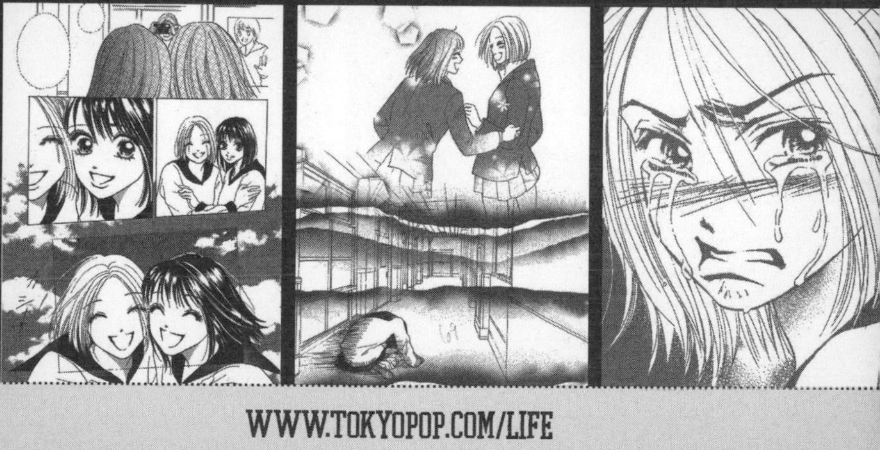

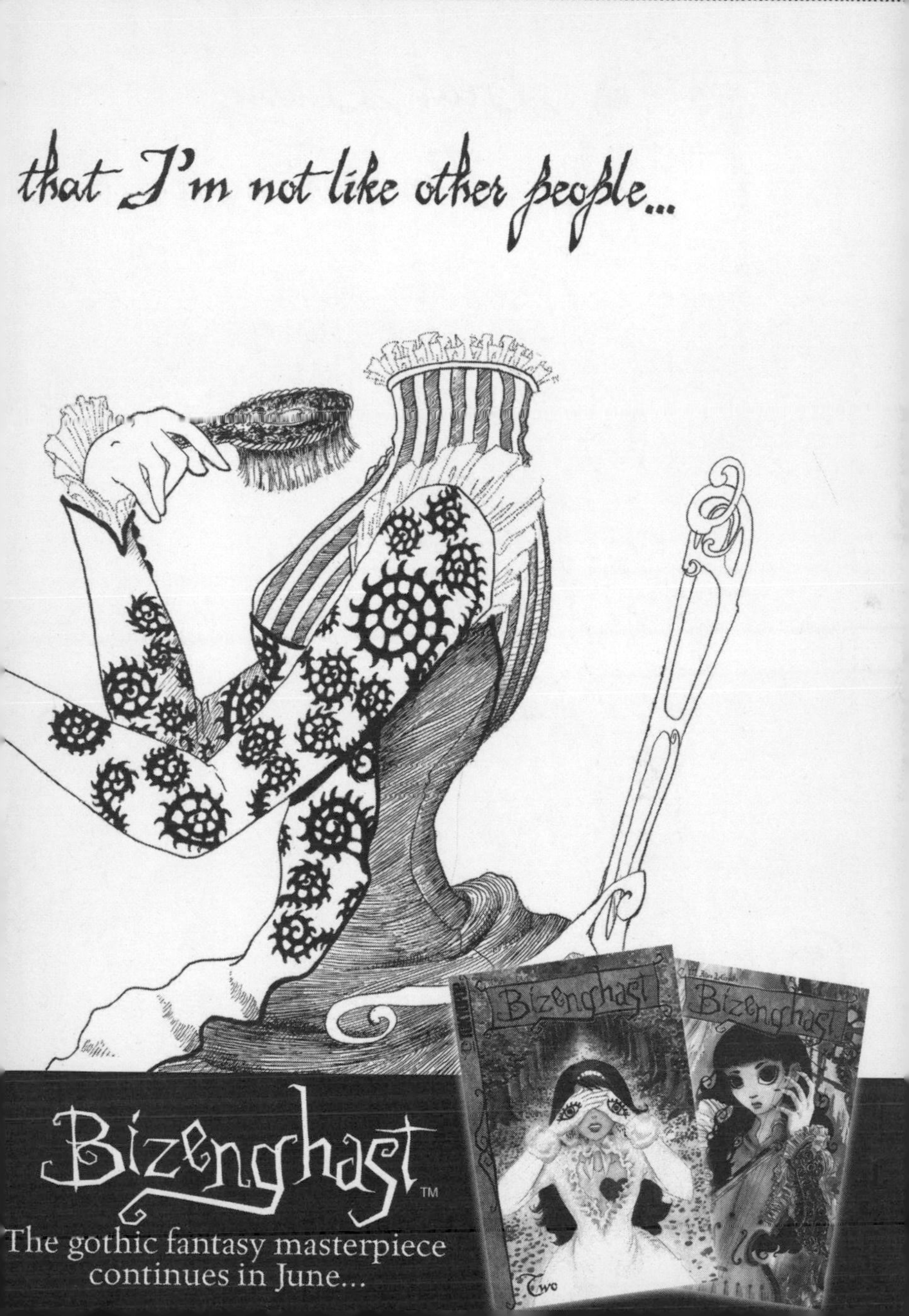
that I'm not like other people...
Bizenghast
Bizenghast
two
Bizenghast™
The gothic fantasy masterpiece
continues in June...

TOKYOPOP SHOP

WWW.TOKYOPOP.COM/SHOP